AF449135

POLITICAL LEADERS AND MILITARY FIGURES OF THE SECOND WORLD WAR

This work is dedicated to my parents,

Roger and Ethel Chambers

Political Leaders and Military Figures of the Second World War

A Bibliography

STEVEN D. CHAMBERS

Dartmouth

Aldershot • Brookfield USA • Singapore • Sydney

Published by
Dartmouth Publishing Company Limited
Gower House
Croft Road
Aldershot
Hants GU11 3HR
England

Dartmouth Publishing Company
Old Post Road
Brookfield
Vermont 05036
USA

British Library Cataloguing in Publication Data
Political leaders and military figures of the Second World
    War : a bibliography
    1. World War, 1939-1945 - Biography - Bibliography
    I. Title
    016.9'4053'0922

Library of Congress Cataloging-in-Publication Data
Chambers, Steven D., 1955-
    Political leaders and military figures of the Second World War : a
bibliography / by Steven D. Chambers.
        p   cm.
    Includes index.
    ISBN 1-85521-646-9
    1. World War, 1939-1945–Biography–Bibliography. 2. Heads of
state–Biography–Bibliography. 3. Military biography-
-Bibliography. 4. Military history, Modern–20th century-
-Bibliography. I. Title.
Z6207.W8C48   1996
[D736]
016.94053'092'2–dc20
[B]   95-47697
                                                          CIP

ISBN 1 85521 646 9

Printed in Great Britain by Galliard (Printers) Ltd, Great Yarmouth

Table of Contents

Foreword

Warfare before or since the Second World War has not reached the level of death and destruction that occurred from 1937 to 1945. The war was truly global in scope. Monumental battles were fought in Asia, North Africa, and Europe as well as on the seas and in the skies. Mobilization of armies, navies, and air forces to fight these battles occurred on an unprecedented scale. The Allies, primarily the United States, the Soviet Union, Great Britain, and China, had armed forces totalling over 34 million personnel. The Axis powers, Germany, Italy, and Japan, had military forces of more than 21 million. The economic cost to wage the war was equally staggering. The United States alone contributed some 288 billion dollars to finance the war effort and it is estimated that the total economic cost exceeded one trillion 600 billion dollars. Even a greater and more terrible toll was the tremendous loss of life that occurred during the course of the war. Completely accurate figures are not available, but it has been estimated that the total deaths of combat personnel and civilians exceeded 53 million. The Soviet Union suffered the most with over 21 million deaths, of which more than 7.7 million were civilian.*

Causes of the war were many and varied. In Europe, the earliest date to the First World War (1914-1918). Battles were fought primarily in Eastern and Western Europe, Africa, and the Middle East. The Allies, notably France, Great Britain, and the United States, emerged victorious over Germany, Austro-Hungary, and Turkey in the fall of 1918 after four brutal years of warfare. The Treaty of Versailles, signed in June 1919 by all major participating nations except the United States, imposed exceedingly harsh reparations upon the defeated nations, especially Germany. The Weimar government struggled to pay the reparations during the 1920s, but when the Great Depression of 1929 collapsed the world economy, Germany's paper currency became virtually worthless, making it nearly impossible to keep up with the debt payments. During this time, a former German Army corporal and his political party gained favour with some segments of the German populace. Adolf Hitler blamed the current Weimar government, the Communists, and the Jewish race for Germany's terrible economic plight and the loss of the war in 1918. When elections were held in late 1932, the Nazi party received more votes than all other parties. Though not gaining a clear majority, Hitler was legally granted the power to form a coalition government by President Paul von Hindenberg.

Hitler quickly established a dictatorship and began to rearm Germany's military in direct violation of the Versailles Treaty. Hitler was not concerned with compliance; he was interested in revitalizing the economy and restoring Germany to its rightful place in Europe. In 1936, he ordered the German Army to reoccupy the Rhineland. This action was also a treaty violation, but the French and British governments, involved with their own staggering economies and not possessing strong political leadership, failed to contest him. Austria was added to the German Reich via a plebiscite in 1937 and the Sudetenland of Czechoslovakia was added in 1938 as a result of the now infamous Munich Agreement, engineered by Hitler and British Prime Minister Neville Chamberlain. The British prime minister was totally naive when it came to negotiating with someone like Hitler. Chamberlain thought he was achieving 'peace for our time', but only gave Hitler another bloodless conquest in his plan to expand Germany's influence and territory and gave new meaning to a word that is still acknowledged as a sign of weakness: appeasement. German troops occupied the remainder of Czechoslovakia in 1939 after the Czech government gave in to continued political pressure by the Nazi government.

In a separate diplomatic and political arrangement, Hitler aligned Germany with Benito Mussolini's fascist Italy in 1936. The partnership was known as the Rome-Berlin Axis. On 22 May 1939, the two nations signed the Pact of Steel, which aligned them militarily. Japan joined the Axis on 27 September 1940 when the three nations signed the Tripartite Pact in Berlin, linking them economically and militarily.

In Asia, Japan embarked on a massive industrialization program to upgrade its economy and armed forces after United States Navy Commodore Matthew Perry opened the eastern nation to western trade in 1853. With its new economic and military power, Japan began to expand its influence in Asia. Wars were fought with China in 1894-95 and with Russia in 1904-05. Victorious, the island nation gained control of Korea and the city of Port Arthur in northern China.

As the Japanese population continued to grow, political and military leaders began to regard China as territory available for expansionist purposes. To establish a reason for aggression, elements of the Japanese Kwangtung Army destroyed a small section of the Japanese-owned railroad in Mukden, Manchuria in 1931 and then blamed the Chinese. The military action that followed the 'Manchurian Incident' gave Japan control of the area and signalled the beginning of serious diplomatic problems with the United States and Great Britain. China attempted to regain the lost territory by appealing to the League of Nations. The League condemned Japan's use of aggression, but was powerless to force the removal of Japanese troops from Manchurian soil. The Japanese, in turn, continued to increase the size of the Kwangtung Army during the 1930s.

The Second World War began in Asia on 7 July 1937 when the Japanese Kwangtung Army invaded China. Despite many battlefield victories, the Japanese did not totally defeat Generalissimo Chiang Kai-shek's Chinese Army and the conflict was stalemated by 1941. In Europe, Nazi Germany invaded Poland on 1 September 1939. France and Great Britain immediately declared war on Germany in accordance with their treaty obligations with Poland. Both nations felt the time had come to confront Hitler militarily. However, Poland was conquered by in a matter of weeks.

After a winter of relative inactivity, German armed forces invaded and defeated Norway, France, and the Low Countries by June 1940. Only Great Britain, and its new prime minister, Winston Churchill, remained to challenge Hitler's control of western Europe. The German dictator expanded the war immensely when he launched his armed forces against the Soviet Union on 22 June 1941. America's entry into the conflict came on 7 December 1941 when Japanese naval planes attacked the U.S. naval base at Pearl Harbor, Hawaii. On 8 December, President Franklin D. Roosevelt asked Congress to declare that a state of war existed between the United States and Japan. Congress passed the war resolution with only one dissenting vote. On 11 December, Germany and Italy declared war on the United States. The war had become global. What began in 1937 would not end until late summer 1945 after two Japanese cities, Hiroshima and Nagasaki, were destroyed by atomic bombs. The war would claim millions of lives, devastate entire continents, and cost nearly two trillion dollars. Results of the war are still felt today. The Soviet Union and the United States became the two most dominant nations on earth and adversaries in world politics during the Cold War and the Atomic Age. Only recently have good relations been re-established, brought about in part by the breakup of the Soviet empire. China, at the conclusion of its civil war in 1949, became communist. Great Britain lost its empire and its influence in world politics. Germany was partitioned after the war and only recently has been reunited after 45 years of division. Japan, virtually destroyed, rebuilt itself and channeled its people's energy into business ventures and is now a powerful force in the global economy.

* Statistics on military personnel, costs, and deaths were obtained from Robert Goralski, *World War II Almanac: 1931-1945. A Political and Military Record*. New York: Putnam, 1981.

It should be noted that revised figures for military and civilian deaths in the Soviet Union now approach fifty million. As Russian and western historians gain access to previously classified material, more accurate figures should be forthcoming.

Preface

The events described in the Foreword were engineered by individuals. These individuals, especially the dictators, wielded huge political, military, and economic power. The purpose of this bibliography is to list English-language works by and about the major political leaders and military figures of the Second World War. The bibliography is intended to aid librarians in answering reference questions concerning what works are available on a particular individual and can serve as an acquisitions tool for works that are still in print. The bibliography should aid graduate and undergraduate students in researching potential historical topics and aid the general reader who desires to read a good biography of a particular individual. The bibliography should also indicate to the political or military historian that certain figures need to have additional or updated works written about their careers. Other major figures, conspicuous by their absence, should indicate that more research and scholarly writing is needed to complete the literature of the Second World War.

Parts I and II cover the political leaders. Each chapter contains a short biographical profile of each leader and recommended readings. Following each profile is a bibliography of works. Parts III and IV list works written by or about the major Allied and Axis military commanders. There is a short biographical profile of each officer with recommended readings, followed by a bibliography of works. Please note that the military rank listed is the highest achieved, even if it occurred after the end of hostilities in September 1945. Part V consists of other noteworthy Allied and Axis figures as well as miscellaneous entries that are relevant to this bibliography, but did not properly fit into any of the first four parts. Part VI consists of an author index.

Works recommended for reading were chosen on their content, scope, importance to the field of Second World War literature, and their use of historical research methods. In many cases, such as the works concerning the major political leaders, only a few were recommended. However, the reader will have a sizeable list to choose from and can make his or her own decision as to what to read. Also, it should be noted that works published prior to 1975 do not mention the existence of "ULTRA" which involved the Allies' ability to secretly read the Axis powers' coded radio transmissions. Allied governments forbad all individuals who had knowledge of "ULTRA" to divulge any information until thirty years after the conclusion of the war. Researchers and readers should take this fact into account when selecting works for review or reading.

Works listed in this bibliography pertain generally to the Second World War historical period. For example, works about President Franklin D. Roosevelt's New Deal administration are not included. However, works concerning his foreign policy before and during the war are included as are biographies published before the war. In a few instances, a work will be listed more than once. An example is *Churchill and Roosevelt: The Complete Correspondence* which is listed in the bibliography of President Franklin D. Roosevelt and that of Prime Minister Winston Churchill. If a work has been published in both hard cover and paperback, only the hard cover edition will be listed in the bibliography. If a work has been published in more than one country, only one publisher will be listed. If a work has been reprinted by the same publisher or a different publisher, only the original edition will be listed unless the work has been revised or updated in some manner. Works for juvenile readers are noted at the end of an entry in this manner: (juvenile). All entries except where noted, should be available through the interlibrary loan system if your local public or academic library does not have them. Inquire at your library about the interlibrary loan system. Doctoral dissertations can be ordered for a fee from University Microfilms Incorporated. The order number is included with each dissertation entry.

The following reference sources were used to check dates, proper spellings, and obtain biographical data not known by the compiler.

Dictionary of American Military Biography, Greenwood Press, Westport, CT.

The Historical Encyclopedia of World War II, Greenwich House, New York.

The Simon and Schuster Encyclopedia of World War II, Simon & Schuster, New York.

Webster's American Military Biographies, G. and C. Merriam Co., Springfield, MA.

The World Almanac Book of World War II, World Almanac, New York.
World War II Almanac, 1931-1945, Putnam, New York.
World War II: America at War, 1941-1945, Random House, New York.

All of these sources are highly recommended and should be found in most large public and academic libraries. Complete bibliographic citations of these works and others are listed in Part V, Chapter 23, "Miscellaneous Entries", under the heading "Reference".

The bibliography was compiled from the following library catalogues and bibliographic sources.

Library of Congress Catalog.
The Ohio State University Library Online Catalog (OSCAR).
OhioLINK Online Catalog.
Columbus, Ohio Metropolitan Library Online Catalog.
American Book Publishing Record, R. R. Bowker, New Providence, NJ.
Books in Print, R. R. Bowker, New Providence, NJ.
British Library General Catalogue of Printed Materials to 1975, K. G. Saur, London.
British Library General Subject Catalogue 1975 to 1985, K. G. Saur, London.
Dissertation Abstracts International, University Microfilms International, Ann Arbor, MI.
Whitaker's Books in Print, J. Whitaker & Sons Ltd., London.

Any mistakes concerning dates, spellings, historical inaccuracies or any bibliographic omissions are the sole responsibility of this compiler.

List of Abbreviations

AL	Alabama
AK	Alaska
AZ	Arizona
AR	Arkansas
CA	California
CO	Colorado
comp.	compiler
CT	Connecticut
DAI	Dissertation Abstracts International
DE	Delaware
DC	District of Columbia
diss.	dissertation
ed.	editor/edition
FL	Florida
GA	Georgia
HI	Hawaii
HMS	His/Her Majesty's Ship
ID	Idaho
IL	Illinois
IN	Indiana
IA	Iowa
KS	Kansas
KY	Kentucky
LA	Louisiana
ME	Maine
MD	Maryland
MA	Massachusetts
MI	Michigan
MN	Minnesota
MS	Mississippi

MO	Missouri
MT	Montana
NE	Nebraska
NV	Nevada
NH	New Hampshire
NJ	New Jersey
NM	New Mexico
NY	New York
NC	North Carolina
ND	North Dakota
n.d.	no date
n.p.	no publisher
OH	Ohio
OK	Oklahoma
OR	Oregon
PA	Pennsylvania
Ph.D.	Doctor of Philosophy
RI	Rhode Island
SC	South Carolina
SD	South Dakota
TN	Tennessee
TX	Texas
UMI	University Microfilms International
US	United States
USS	United States Ship
UT	Utah
VT	Vermont
VA	Virginia
WA	Washington
WV	West Virginia
WI	Wisconsin
WY	Wyoming

PART I

ALLIED POLITICAL LEADERS

1 Prime Minister Sir Winston Spencer Churchill 1874-1965

Great Britain

Winston Churchill assumed the duties of prime minister on 10 May 1940, the same day German military forces invaded France and the Low Countries. Six weeks later France had been defeated, the British Expeditionary Force had been forced to evacuate the European continent at Dunkirk, and Adolf Hitler stood as master of western Europe. Churchill was 65 years old in June 1940. Many men would consider retiring at that age, but Churchill was determined to defeat Hitler regardless of the time and cost it took.

Churchill was born into a wealthy English aristocratic family, but was not content to live a life devoid of adventure. He graduated from Sandhurst and saw military action on several occasions. At times, he was at the battle site only as a newspaper reporter, but still participated in the combat. Entering politics, he was first elected to Parliament in 1900 and steadily advanced as a political force. He was First Lord of the Admiralty at the outbreak of the First World War, but resigned in 1915 after his Dardanelles plan failed. After resigning as First Lord, he served on the Western Front with a British battalion for a short time before being appointed Minister of Munitions by Prime Minister Lloyd George.

Churchill served in Parliament during the 1920s and the 1930s, but did not hold an official cabinet position from 1929 to 1939. In 1939, he was again appointed First Lord of the Admiralty. Despite the fact that he did not hold a cabinet position for most of the 1930s, he constantly made speeches and wrote articles detailing the aggressiveness of Adolf Hitler and urged the British government to rebuild and upgrade its armed forces to respond to any external military threat, namely Nazi Germany. For his efforts he was labelled a warmonger.

Once Churchill was named prime minister, replacing Neville Chamberlain, he devoted all his energies to the monumental task of running the war effort. During the Battle of Britain in the fall of 1940, he visited the bombed ruins of cities to bolster the confidence of the

British populace. While his nation endured the German air onslaught, he worked to obtain much needed materials and armaments from the United States. When Germany invaded the Soviet Union on 22 June 1941, he immediately sought an alliance with Josef Stalin, even though he was at political odds with the Communist dictator.

Churchill met with President Franklin D. Roosevelt at Newfoundland in August 1941. They issued the Atlantic Charter which pledged freedom of governmental choice for all peoples, freedom of trade, and freedom of the seas. In December 1941, shortly after the United States entered the war on the side of the Allies following the attack on Pearl Harbor, Hawaii, Churchill travelled to Washington, D.C. to meet with Roosevelt and his military commanders. In August 1942, he travelled to Moscow to meet with Stalin. Stalin demanded a second front in western Europe, but Churchill told him that the western Allies were not prepared to invade Europe at this time, but that an invasion of North Africa would be undertaken in the late fall.

Following the successful invasion of North Africa, Churchill and Roosevelt met at Casablanca in January 1943 to discuss strategy for 1943. Once again, a western European invasion was ruled out. Instead, Sicily and Italy would be invaded. Churchill always thought that the best way back into Europe was by the southern route. By mid-1943, the loss of North Africa and Sicily caused the Italian Fascist Grand Council to remove Benito Mussolini from power. Italy was invaded on 3 September and the Italian government surrendered shortly, but the German armed forces stationed there resisted and did not surrender until May 1945 after nearly two years of deadly warfare.

The Big Three, Churchill, Roosevelt, and Stalin, met at Tehran in November 1943 to discuss grand strategy for 1944. Churchill and Roosevelt finally agreed upon a western European invasion. The date was tentatively set for May 1944. When they met again at Yalta in February 1945, the war in Europe was nearing its conclusion. France, Belgium, and the Netherlands had been liberated and western Allied armies and Red Army units were poised to deal the death blow to Nazi Germany. At Yalta, Stalin agreed to declare war on Japan within three months after the defeat of Germany. The decision to form the United Nations was reached and it was agreed to divide Germany into zones of occupation after the war ended.

Churchill attended his last war summit at Potsdam in July 1945. Events had changed dramatically since February. Roosevelt had died in April, Germany had surrendered in May after Hitler committed suicide in his chancellory bunker, and, at home, British citizens were preparing to vote. While at the conference, Churchill's Conservative party was dealt a tremendous defeat and the Labour party's Clement Attlee was named the new prime minister. Churchill remained active in politics after the war, regaining the post of prime minster in 1951 and serving until 1955 when he retired. He died on 15 January 1965. Because of his tenacity and determination, Great Britain was able to withstand the blows it received during the early years of the war. Though Britain lost its empire and could not win the war by itself, Churchill was a leading member of the Allied coalition that united to defeat Nazi Germany, Fascist Italy, and Imperial Japan.

After the war, Churchill wrote a six-volume history of the Second World War, published between 1948 and 1953. All are recommended for reading. The titles are: *The Gathering Storm*, *Their Finest Hour*, *The Grand Alliance*, *The Hinge of Fate*, *Closing the Ring*, and *Triumph and Tragedy*. Churchill was awarded the Nobel prize in Literature in 1953 for his effort. An abridgement of the six-volume set, *Memoirs of the Second World War*, was published in 1959. Numerous volumes of his speeches to the British people and to Parliament have been published. The two sets of mention are *War Speeches*, a three-volume set compiled by Charles Eade, and an eight-volume set, *Winston S. Churchill: His Complete Speeches, 1897-1963*, compiled and edited by Robert Rhodes James. A condensed version, *Churchill Speaks: Winston Spencer Churchill in Peace and War, 1897-1963* has also been published. Many of his words are still remembered after the passage of many years. Upon being named prime minister, he said, "I have nothing to offer but blood, toil, tears, and sweat." With France nearing defeat and the British Expeditionary Force having just evacuated the continent at Dunkirk, he stated on 4 June 1940 on the BBC, "We shall fight on the beaches, we shall fight on the landing-grounds, we shall fight in the fields and in the streets, we shall fight in the hills; we shall never surrender..."

Though many authors have chronicled Winston Churchill's life, none have gone into such in-depth study as has his son, Randolph S. Churchill, and Martin Gilbert. Randolph wrote the first two volumes in the 1960s and Gilbert recently finished the eighth and final volume in 1988. The eight volumes, according to the *New York Time Book Review*, total over 9.2 million words. Only those truly interested in Churchill will take the time to read all eight volumes, but for those who do, they will find it worthwhile. All the volumes are entitled *Winston S. Churchill* and each has a subtitle. A one-volume abridgement entitled *Churchill: A Life* is recommended for those who do not wish to read the eight volume set.

Other recommendations for reading are Piers Brendon's *Winston*

Churchill, Lewis Broad's two-volume set, *Winston Churchill*, Alistair Cooke's *General Eisenhower on the Military Churchill*, Ronald Lewin's *Churchill as Warlord*, Ted Morgan's *Churchill: Young Man in A Hurry 1874-1915*, William Manchester's *The Last Lion, Winston Spencer Churchill, Visions of Glory, 1874-1932* and *The Last Lion, Winston Spencer Churchill, Alone, 1932-1940*, Robert Payne's *The Great Man*, and Henry Pelling's *Winston Churchill*. These works and others are listed in the bibliography that follows.

Bibliography

Addison, Paul. *Churchill on the Home Front, 1900-1955*. London: Pimlico, 1992.

Agrafiotis, Chris J., comp. *Was Churchill Right in Greece?* Manchester, NH: Granite State Press, 1945.

Albjerg, Victor L. *Winston Churchill*. New York: Twayne Publishers, 1973.

American Heritage. *Churchill, The Life Triumphant: The Historical Record of Ninety Years*. New York: American Heritage Publishing Co., 1965.

Arthur, George. *Concerning Winston Spencer Churchill*. New York: H. C. Kinsey & Co., 1941.

Ashley, Maurice. *Churchill as Historian*. New York: Charles Schribner's Sons, 1969.

Baciu, Nicolas. *Sell-Out to Stalin: The Tragic Errors of Churchill and Roosevelt. The Untold Story*. New York: Vantage Press, 1984.

Bailey, Eva. *Churchill*. Hove: Wayland, 1981.

Bardens, Dennis. *Churchill in Parliament*. South Brunswick, NJ: A. S. Barnes, 1967.

Barker, Elisabeth. *Churchill and Eden at War*. London: Macmillan, 1978.

Bellamy, Frank. *High Command: The Stories of Sir Winston Churchill and General Montgomery*. Dragon's Dream. Distributed by Quick Fox, 1981.

Ben-Moshe, Tuvia. *Churchill, Strategy and History*. Boulder, CO: Lynne Rienner Publishers, 1992.

Berlin, Isaiah. *Mr. Churchill in 1940*. Boston: Houghton Mifflin, 1964.

Bibescu, Martha. *Sir Winston Churchill: Master of Courage*. Translated from the French by Vladimir Kean. New York: John Day, 1959.

Birkenhead, Frederick Winston Furneaux Smith. *Churchill: 1874-1922*. Edited by John Colville. London: Harrap, 1978.

Black, Edgar. *Sir Winston Churchill: The Compelling Life Story of One of the Towering Figures of the 20th Century*. Derby, CT: Monarch Books, 1961.

Blake, Robert and William Roger Louis, eds. *Churchill*. New York: Oxford University Press, 1992.

______. *Winston Churchill as Historian*. Austin: College of Liberal Arts, Harry Ransom Humanities Research Center, University of Texas at Austin, 1990.

Bloncourt, Pauline. *An Old and A Young Leader: Winston Churchill and John Kennedy*. London: Faber, 1970.

Bocca, Geoffrey. *Adventurous Life of Winston Churchill*. New York: Messner, 1958.

Bonham-Carter, Violet. *Winston Churchill: An Intimate Portrait*. New York: Harcourt, Brace & World, 1965.

Booth, Arthur H. *The True Story of Sir Winston Churchill*. Chicago: Children's Press, 1964. (juvenile)

Bradley, John. *Churchill and the British*. New York: Gloucester Press, 1990. (juvenile)

Brendon, Piers. *Winston Churchill: A Biography*. New York: Harper & Row, 1984.

Briquebec, John. *Winston Churchill*. London: Hart-Davis, 1972.

British Broadcasting Corporation. *A Selection from the Broadcasts Given in Memory of Winston Churchill, K.G., O.M., C.H., in the Sound and Television Services of the British Broadcasting Corporation, 24 to 30 January, 1965*. London, n.p., 1965.

Broad, Lewis. *The War That Churchill Waged*. London: Hutchinson, 1960.

______. *Winston Churchill: A Biography*. 2 volumes. New York: Hawthorn Books, 1958.

______. *Winston Churchill: Architect of Victory and Peace*. Rev. and further extended. London: Hutchinson, 1956.

______. *Winston Churchill: Man of War*. London: Hutchinson & Co. Ltd., 1940.

Bruce, George. *Churchill: A Life in Pictures. A Memorial Edition*. New York: Dell Publishing Co., 1965.

Buchan, William. *Winston Churchill*. London: Pilot Press, Ltd., 1940.

Butler, William Vivian. *Winston Churchill: Never Surrender*. London: Hodder & Stoughton, 1980. (juvenile)

Callahan, Raymond. *Churchill: Retreat from Empire*. Wilmington, DE: Scholarly Resources, 1984.

Cawthorne, Graham. *The Churchill Legend, An Anthology*. London: Cleaver-Hume Press, 1965.

Charmley, John. *Churchill: The End of Glory*. London: Hodder & Stoughton, 1993.

______. *Churchill's Grand Alliance: The Anglo-American Special Relationship, 1940-57*. New York: Harcourt Brace & Co., 1995.

Churchill, Randolph S. *Winston S. Churchill. Volume I. Youth, 1874-1900*. Boston: Houghton Mifflin, 1966.

______. *Companion to Volume I*. (In two parts). Boston: Houghton Mifflin, 1967.

______. *Winston S. Churchill. Volume II. Young Statesman, 1900-1914*. Boston: Houghton Mifflin, 1967.

______. *Companion to Volume II*. (In three parts). Boston: Houghton Mifflin, 1969.

______ and Helmut Gernsheim, eds. *Churchill: His Life in Photographs*. New York: Rinehart, 1955.

Churchill, Sarah. *A Thread in the Tapestry*. New York: Dodd, Mead, 1967.

Churchill, Winston, Sir. *Addresses Delivered in the Year Nineteen Hundred and Forty to the People of Great Britain, of France, and to the Members of English House of Commons, by the Prime Minister, Winston Churchill*. San Francisco: Ransohoffs, 1940.

______ and Franklin D. Roosevelt. *Addresses of Franklin D. Roosevelt and Winston Churchill*. Washington: U.S. Government Printing Office, 1942.

______. *Amid These Storms: Thoughts and Adventures*. New York: Scribner's Sons, 1932.

______. *Arms and the Covenant: Speeches*. London: G. G. Harrap, 1938.

______. *Blood, Sweat, and Tears*. Speeches made between May 1938 and November 1940. New York: Putnam, 1941.

______. *Blood, Toil, Tears and Sweat: The Speeches of Winston Churchill*. David Cannadine, ed. Boston: Houghton Mifflin, 1989.

______. *Broadcast Addresses to the People of Great Britain, Italy, Poland, Russia, and the United States by the Prime Minister of the British Empire, Winston Churchill, 1940-1941*. San Francisco: Ransohoffs, 1941.

______ and Franklin D. Roosevelt. *Churchill and Roosevelt: The Complete Correspondence*. 3 volumes. Edited with commentary by Warren F. Kimball. Princeton, NJ: Princeton University Press, 1984.

______. *A Churchill Anthology*. F. W. Heath, ed. London: Odhams Press, 1962.

______. *Churchill Reader: The Wit and Wisdom of Sir Winston Churchill, Constructed from His Own Sayings and Writings*. Boston: Houghton Mifflin, 1954.

_____. *Churchill Speaks: Winston Spencer Churchill in Peace and War. Collected Speeches, 1897-1963*. Edited by Robert Rhodes James. Condensed version. New York: Chelsea House, 1980.

_____. *The Churchill War Papers: At the Admiralty, September, 1939 - May, 1940*. Compiled by Martin Gilbert. New York: W. W. Norton, 1993.

_____. *The Churchill Wit*. Edited by Bill Adler. New York: Coward-McCann, 1965.

_____. *Closing the Ring. The Second World War. Volume V*. Boston: Houghton Mifflin, 1951.

_____. *The Collected Essays of Sir Winston Churchill*. 4 volumes. Michael Wolff, general editor. London: Library of Imperial History, 1976.

_____. *The Collected Works of Sir Winston Churchill*. 34 volumes. London: Library of Imperial History, 1973-1975.

_____. *The Dawn of Liberation: War Speeches by the Right Hon. Winston S. Churchill*. Complied by Charles Eade. Boston: Little, Brown, 1945.

_____. *The End of the Beginning: War Speeches*. Compiled by Charles Eade. London: Cassell, 1943.

_____. *Foreign Policy*. London: The Times Publishing Company Ltd., 1944.

_____. *The Gathering Storm. The Second World War. Volume I*. Boston: Houghton Mifflin, 1948.

_____. *The Grand Alliance. The Second World War. Volume III*. Boston: Houghton Mifflin, 1950.

_____. *Great Contempories*. Chicago: University of Chicago Press, 1973. Originally published in 1937.

_____. *Great Destiny: Sixty Years of the Memorable Events in the Life of the Man of the Century Recounted in His Own Incomparable Words*. Edited by F. W. Heath. New York: Putnam, 1965.

_____. *Great War Speeches*. London: Corgi Books. Published by Transworld Publishers, 1965.

_____. *The Hinge of Fate. The Second World War. Volume IV*. Boston: Houghton Mifflin, 1950.

_____. *If I Lived My Life Again*. Compiled and edited by Jack Fishman. London: W. H. Allen, 1974.

_____. *Immortal Jester: A Treasury of the Great Good Humor of Sir Winston Churchill, 1874-1965*. Compiled by Leslie Frewin. London: Frewin, 1973.

______. *Irrepressible Churchill: A Treasury of Winston Churchill's Wit.* Selected and compiled by Kay Halle. Cleveland, OH: World Publishing Co., 1966.

______. *Maxims and Reflections.* Selected by Colin Coote and Denzel Batcheler. Boston: Houghton Mifflin, 1949.

______. *Memoirs of the Second World War.* An abridgement of the six volumes of *The Second World War.* Abridgement by Denis Kelly. Boston: Houghton Mifflin, 1959.

______. *Memories and Adventures.* New York: Weidenfeld & Nicolson, 1989.

______ and Franklin D. Roosevelt. *The Messages Between Franklin D. Roosevelt and Winston S. Churchill, 1939-1945 and Related Materials in the Franklin D. Roosevelt Library.* 6 reels of 35mm film. National Historical Publications Commission, 1973.

______. *My Early Life: A Roving Commission.* New York: Scribner, 1930.

______. *Never Give In. The Challenging Words of Winston Churchill.* Selected by Dorothy Price and Dean Walley. Kansas City: Hallmark Editions, 1967.

______. *Onwards to Victory: War Speeches... 1943.* Compiled by Charles Eade. Boston: Little, Brown & Company, 1944.

______. *The Roar of the Lion.* London: A. Wingate Ltd., 1969.

______ and Franklin D. Roosevelt. *Roosevelt and Churchill: Their Secret Wartime Correspondence.* Edited by Francis L. Loewenheim, and others. New York: Da Capo Press, 1990.

______. *The Sayings of Winston Churchill.* Edited by J. L. Lane. London: Duckworth, 1992.

______. *The Second World War.* 6 volumes. Boston: Houghton Mifflin. See *The Gathering Storm*, 1948. *Their Finest Hour*, 1949. *The Grand Alliance*, 1950. *The Hinge of Fate*, 1950. *Closing the Ring*, 1951. *Triumph and Tragedy*, 1953.

______. *The Sinews of Peace, Post-War Speeches.* Edited by Randolph S. Churchill. Boston: Houghton Mifflin, 1949.

______. *Sir Winston Churchill, K.G., P.C., O.M., C.H., M.P.: Selections from His Writings and Speeches.* 2nd ed. Guy Boas, ed. London: Macmillan, 1966.

______. *Step by Step, 1936-1939.* New York: G. Putnam's Sons, 1939.

______. *Their Finest Hour. The Second World War. Volume II.* Boston: Houghton Mifflin, 1949.

______. *Third Secret Speech.* Chicago: Time Inc., 1946.

______. *Thoughts and Adventures.* London: L. Cooper, 1990.

______. *Triumph and Tragedy. The Second World War. Volume VI.* Boston: Houghton Mifflin, 1953.

______. *The Unrelenting Struggle: War Speeches.* Compiled by Charles Eade. Boston: Little, Brown, 1942.

______. *Victory: War Speeches.* Complied by Charles Eade. Speeches made between January and August 1945. Boston: Little, Brown, 1946.

______. *War Speeches.* 3 volumes. Compiled by Charles Eade. Boston: Houghton Mifflin, 1953.

______. *While England Slept: A Survey of World Affairs, 1932-1938.* New York: Putnam, 1938.

______. *Winston Churchill on America and Britain: A Selection of His Thoughts on Anglo-American Relations.* Collected and edited with an introduction by Kay Halle. New York: Walker, 1970.

______. *Winston Churchill's Secret Session Speeches.* Compiled, and with introductory notes, by Charles Eade. New York: Simon & Schuster, 1946.

______. *Winston S. Churchill: His Complete Speeches, 1897-1963.* 8 volumes. Edited by Robert Rhodes James. New York: Chelsea House Publishers, 1974.

______. *Winston S. Churchill, War Correspondent, 1895-1900.* Edited by Fredrick Woods. London: Brassey's 1992.

______. *The Wisdom of Winston Churchill: Being A Selection of Aphorisms, Reflections, Precepts, Maxims, Epigrams, Paradoxes, and Opinions from His Parliamentary and Public Speeches, 1900-1955.* London: Allen & Unwin, 1956.

______. *The Wit and Wisdom of Winston Churchill: A Treasury of More Than 1000 Quotations and Anecdotes.* Compiled by James C. Humes. New York: HarperCollins, 1994.

______. *The Wit of Sir Winston.* Compiled by Adam Sykes and Iain Sproat. London: L. Frewin, 1965.

Churchill Memorial and Library. *The Winston Churchill Memorial and Library.* Fulton, MO., n.p., 1970.

Clark, Ronald William. *Sir Winston Churchill.* New York: Roy Publishers, 1962. (juvenile)

Cohen, Michael J. *Churchill and the Jews.* London: F. Cass, 1985.

Colville, John. *Winston Churchill and His Inner Circle.* New York: Wyndham Books, 1981.

Connell, John. *Winston Churchill.* London: Longmans, Green & Co., 1956.

Cooke, Alistair. *General Eisenhower on the Military Churchill: A Conversation.* Edited by James Nelson. New York: Norton, 1970.

Coolidge, Olivia. *Winston Churchill and the Story of Two World Wars*. Boston: Houghton Mifflin, 1960. (juvenile)

Cosgrave, Patrick. *Churchill at War*. London: Collins, 1974.

Costello, John. *Days of Infamy: MacArthur, Roosevelt, Churchill. The Shocking Truth Revealed*. New York: Pocket Books, 1994.

Country Beautiful eds. *A Man of Destiny: Winston S. Churchill*. Waukesha, WI: Country Beautiful Foundation, 1965.

Cowles, Virginia. *Winston Churchill: The Era and the Man*. New York: Harper, 1953.

Cummins, Howard W. *Mao, Hsiao, Churchill, and Montgomery: Personal Values and Decision Making*. Beverly Hills, CA: Sage Publications, 1974.

Davenport, John and Charles J. V. Murphy. *The Lives of Winston Churchill*. New York: C. Scribner's Sons, 1945.

Davis, Richard Harding. *Young Winston Churchill, Soldier of Fortune*. New York: C. Scribner's Sons, 1941.

Day, David. *Menzies and Churchill at War: A Controversial New Account of the 1941 Struggle for Power*. New York: Paragon House, 1988.

De Mendelssohn, Peter. *The Age of Churchill*. New York: Alfred A. Knopf, 1961.

Dilks, David. *Sir Winston Churchill*. London: Hamish Hamilton, 1965.

Dolan, Ellen M. *Churchill*. St. Louis: Webster Division, McGraw-Hill, 1968. (juvenile)

Driemen, J. E. (John Evans). *Winston Churchill: An Unbreakable Spirit*. Minneapolis: Dillon Press, 1990. (juvenile)

Dupuy, Trevor Nevitt. *The Military Life of Winston Churchill of Britain*. New York: F. Watts, 1970. (juvenile)

Eade, Charles, ed. *Churchill: By His Contemporaries*. New York: Simon & Schuster, 1954.

Eden, Guy. *Portrait of Churchill*. London: Hutchinson & Co., 1945.

Edmonds, Robin. *The Big Three: Churchill, Roosevelt and Stalin in Peace and War*. New York: Norton, 1990.

Eggleston, George T. *Roosevelt, Churchill and the World War II Opposition: A Revisionist Autobiography*. Old Greenwich, CT: Devin-Adair, 1979.

Ehrman, John. *Lloyd George and Churchill as War Ministers*. London: n.p, n.d.

Emmert, Kirk Rettig. "*Winston Churchill on Empire*." Ph.D. diss., University of Chicago, 1972. (microform) (Not available from UMI)

Engstrom, J. Eric. *The Medallic Portraits of Sir Winston Churchill*. London: Spink, 1972.

Eppler, Elizabeth E., comp. *Churchill, the Jews, and Zionism: A Bibliography and Catalogue Prepared on the Occasion of Jewish Book Week 1974.* London: World Jewish Congress British Section, 1974.

Epstein, Sam and Beryl Epstein. *Winston Churchill: Lion of Britain.* Champaign, IL: Garrard Publishing Co., 1971. (juvenile)

Farmer, Bernard J. *Bibliography of the Works of Sir Winston S. Churchill.* London, n.p., 1958.

Farrell, Alan. *Winston Churchill.* New York: Putnam, 1964. (juvenile)

Feis, Herbert. *Churchill, Roosevelt, Stalin: The War They Waged and the Peace They Sought.* 2nd edition. Princeton, NJ: Princeton University Press, 1967.

Ferrier, Neil, ed. *Churchill, Man of the Century: A Pictorial Biography.* Garden City, NY: Doubleday, 1965.

Finlayson, Iain. *Winston Churchill.* London: H. Hamilton, 1980. (juvenile)

Fishman, Jack. *My Darling Clementine: The Story of Lady Churchill.* New York: D. McKay Co., 1963.

Fowler, Michael. *Winston S. Churchill, Philosopher and Statesman.* Lanham, MD: University Press of America, 1985.

Gardner, Brian. *Churchill in Power, As Seen by His Contemporaries.* Boston: Houghton Mifflin, 1970.

Gilbert, Martin. *Churchill.* Garden City, NY: Doubleday, 1980.

______. *Churchill: A Life.* New York: Holt, 1991.

______. *Churchill: A Photographic Portrait.* Boston: Houghton Mifflin, 1974.

______. *Churchill's Political Philosophy.* Oxford: Published for the British Academy by the Oxford University Press, 1981.

______. *In Search of Churchill: A Historian's Journey.* New York: Wiley & Sons, 1994.

______ and others. *Proceedings of the International Churchill Society, 1987.* Contoocook, NH: Churchill Literacy Foundation, 1989.

______. *Winston Churchill.* London: Oxford University Press, 1966.

______, comp. *Winston Churchill.* New York: Grossman Publishers, 1969.

______. *Winston S. Churchill: The Challenge of War, 1914-1916. Volume III.* Boston: Houghton Mifflin, 1971.

______. *Companion to Volume III.* (In two parts). Boston: Houghton Mifflin, 1973.

______. *Winston S. Churchill: Finest Hour, 1939-1941. Volume VI.* Boston: Houghton Mifflin, 1983.

______. *Winston S. Churchill: Never Despair, 1945-1965. Volume VIII.* Boston: Houghton Mifflin, 1988.

______. *Winston S. Churchill: Prophet of Truth, 1929-1939. Volume V.* Boston: Houghton Mifflin, 1977.

______. *Companion to Volume V. The Exchequer Years, 1923-1929.* Boston: Houghton Mifflin, 1981.

______. *Companion to Volume V. The Wilderness Years, 1929-1935.* Boston: Houghton Mifflin, 1982.

______. *Companion to Volume V. The Coming of War, 1936-1939.* Boston: Houghton Mifflin, 1983.

______. *Winston S. Churchill: Road to Victory, 1941-1945. Volume VII.* Boston: Houghton Mifflin, 1986.

______. *Winston S. Churchill, 1917-1922. Volume IV.* Boston: Houghton Mifflin, 1975.

______. *Companion to Volume IV.* (In three parts). Boston: Houghton Mifflin, 1977.

Gollin, A. M. (Alfred M.) *From Omdurman to V.E. Day: The Life Span of Sir Winston Churchill.* London: Blond Educational, 1964.

Graebner, Walter. *My Dear Mr. Churchill.* Boston: Houghton Mifflin, 1965.

Grant, R. G. *Winston Churchill: An Illustrated Biography.* New York: Gallery, 1989.

Graubard, Stephen Richards. *Burke, Disraeli and Churchill: The Politics of Perseverance.* Cambridge, MA: Harvard University Press, 1961.

Green, David Bronte. *Sir Winston Churchill at Blenheim Palace: An Anthology.* Oxford: Alden, 1959.

Greene, Jay Elihu. *Four Complete Biographies.* New York: Globe Book Co., 1962. (Winston Churchill is the subject of one of the biographies.)

Gretton, Peter. *Winston Churchill and the Royal Navy.* New York: Coward McCann, 1968.

Guedalla, Philip. *Mr. Churchill.* New York: Reynal & Hitchcock, 1942.

Harbutt, Fraser J. *The Iron Curtain: Churchill, America, and the Origins of the Cold War, 1945-46.* New York: Oxford University Press, 1986.

Harrity, Richard and Ralph G. Martin. *Man of the Century: Churchill.* Des Moines, IA: Meredith Press, 1962.

Harvard University. *The Ceremonies in Honor of the Right Honorable Winston Spencer Churchill; Being the Proceedings of An Academic Meeting Held in Sanders Theater and of an Assemblage in the Harvard Yard of the Military and Naval Forces of the United States in Training at the University.* Cambridge, September 6th, 1943.

Harvey-Watt, G. S. *Most of My Life.* London: Springwood Books, 1980.

Havas, Laslo. *The Long Jump. (Or the 1943 Plot to Assassinate Churchill, Roosevelt and Stalin)*. Translated by Kathleen Szasz. London: Spearman, 1967.

Hawthorne, Hildegarde. *Long Adventure: The Story of Winston Churchill*. New York: D. A. Appleton-Century Co., 1942.

Herbert, F. John. *The Collected Poems of Sir Winston Churchill*. College Park, MD: Sun & Moon Press, 1981.

Higgins, Trumbull. *Winston Churchill and the Second Front, 1940-1943*. New York: Oxford University Press, 1957.

Hilditch, Neville, comp. *In Praise of Churchill, An Anthology in His Honour*. London: F. Muller Ltd., 1946.

Holley, Darrell. *Churchill's Literary Allusions: An Index to the Education of A Soldier, Statesman, and Litterateur*. Jefferson, NC: McFarland, 1987.

Hough, Richard. *Former Naval Person: Churchill and the War at Sea*. London: Weidenfeld & Nicolson, 1985.

______. *The Greatest Crusade: Roosevelt, Churchill, and the Naval Wars*. New York: Morrow, 1986.

______. *Winston and Clementine: The Triumphs and Tragedies of the Churchills*. New York: Bantam Books, 1991.

Howells, Roy. *Churchill's Last Years*. New York: David McKay Co., 1966.

Hughes, Emrys. *Winston Churchill, British Bulldog: His Career in War and Peace*. New York: Exposition Press, 1955.

Humes, James C. *Churchill: Speaker of the Century*. New York: Stein & Day, 1980.

______. *The Sir Winston Methods: The Five Secrets of Speaking the Language of Leadership*. New York: Quill/William Morrow, 1993.

Ingram, Bruce Stirling. *An Eightieth Year Tribute to Winston Churchill*. London: The Illustrated London News, 1954.

Irving, David. *Churchill's War: The Struggle for Power*. Bullsbrook, W.A., Australia: Veritas Publishing Co., 1987.

Italia, Bob. *Winston Churchill*. Minneapolis, MN: Abdo & Daughters, 1990. (juvenile)

Jablonsky, David. *Churchill & Hitler: Essays on the Political-Military Direction of Total War*. Portland, OR: International Specialized Book Services, 1994.

______. *Churchill, The Great Game and Total War*. Portland, OR: Frank Cass, 1991.

______. *Churchill: The Making of A Grand Strategist*. Carlisle Barracks, PA: Strategic Studies Institute, U.S. Army War College, 1990.

Jaffa, Harry V., ed. *Statesmanship: Essays in Honor of Sir Winston Spencer Churchill*. Durham, NC: Carolina Academic Press, 1981.

James, Robert Rhodes. *Churchill: A Study in Failure, 1900-1939*. New York: World Publishing Co., 1970.

Jeffreys, Kevin. *The Churchill Coalition and Wartime Politics, 1940-1945*. Manchester: Manchester University Press, 1991.

Johnson, Ann Donegan. *The Value of Leadership: The Story of Winston Churchill*. San Diego: Value Communications, 1987. (juvenile)

Jones, Madeline. *Churchill*. London: Batsford, 1980. (juvenile)

Keegan, John, ed. *Churchill's Generals*. New York: Grove Weidenfeld, 1991.

Keller, Mollie. *Winston Churchill*. New York: F. Watts, 1984. (juvenile)

Kersaudy, Francois. *Churchill and De Gaulle*. New York: Antheneum, 1981.

Kilzer, Louis C. *Churchill's Deception: The Dark Secret That Destroyed Nazi Germany*. New York: Simon & Schuster, 1994.

Kraus, Rene. *Winston Churchill: A Biography*. New York: Literary Guild of America, 1941.

______. *Winston Churchill in the Mirror: His Life in Pictures and Story*. New York: E. P. Dutton & Co., 1944.

Lamb, Richard. *Churchill as War Leader*. New York: Carroll & Graf, 1993.

Lambakis, Steven James. *Winston Churchill, Architect of Peace: A Study of Statesmanship and the Cold War*. Westport, CT: Greenwood Press, 1993.

Langworth, Richard M., ed. *Proceedings of the International Churchill Societies, 1988-1989*. Contoocook, NH: Churchill Literacy Foundation, 1990.

Lash, Joseph. *Roosevelt and Churchill, 1939-1941: The Partnership That Saved the West*. New York: Norton, 1976.

Lawlor, Sheila. *Churchill and the Politics of War, 1940-1941*. Cambridge, NY: Cambridge University Press, 1994.

Le Vien, Jack and John Lord. *Winston Churchill: The Valiant Years*. New York: Avon Books, 1962.

Lee, J. M. (John Michael). *The Churchill Coalition, 1940-1945*. London: Batsford, 1980.

Leutze, James Richard. *"If Britain Should Fall: Roosevelt and Churchill and British-American Naval Relations, 1938-1940."* Ph.D. diss., Duke University, 1970. (DAI, 31:10, 5325A, UMI Order # 7110390)

Lewin, Ronald. *Churchill as Warlord*. New York: Stein & Day, 1973.

Life eds. *The Unforgettable Winston Churchill: Giant of the Century*. New York: Time Inc., 1965.

Lockhart, John Gilbert. *Winston Churchill*. London: G. Duckworth, 1951.

Longford, Elizabeth. *Winston Churchill: A Pictorial Life Story*. Chicago: McNally, 1974.

Lukacs, John. *The Duel. 10 May - 31 July 1940: The Eighty-Day Struggle Between Churchill and Hitler*. New York: Ticknor & Fields, 1991. Distributed by Houghton Mifflin.

Lynch, Mary Anne. *"Winston Churchill and the Post War Social Reconstruction Plans of His Wartime Administration, 1940-1945."* Ph.D. diss., University of Notre Dame, 1977. (DAI, 38:2, 960A, UMI Order # 7717583)

MacNalty, Arthur Salusbury. *The Three Churchills*. London: Essential Books, 1949.

Malkus, Alida. *The Story of Winston Churchill*. New York: Grosset & Dunlap, 1957. (juvenile)

Manchester, William. *The Last Lion, Winston Spencer Churchill: Alone, 1932-1940*. Boston: Little, Brown, 1988.

______. *The Last Lion, Winston Spencer Churchill: Visions of Glory, 1874-1932*. Boston: Little, Brown, 1983.

Manning, Paul and Milton Bronner. *Mr. England: The Life Story of Winston Churchill*. Philadelphia: John C. Winston Co., 1942.

Marchant, James. *Winston Spencer Churchill: Servant of Crown and Commonwealth. A Tribute by Various Hands to Him on His Eightieth Birthday*. London: Cassell, 1954.

Marder, Arthur. *Winston is Back: Churchill at the Admiralty, 1939-1940*. London: Longman, 1972.

Marsh, John. *The Young Winston Churchill*. New York: Scholastic Book Services, 1955.

Martin, David. *The Web of Disinformation: Churchill's Yugoslav Blunder*. San Diego: Harcourt Brace Jovanovich, 1990.

Martin, Hugh. *Battle: The Life Story of the Rt. Hon. Winston S. Churchill*. London: Sampson Low, Marston & Co. Ltd., 1932.

Martin, John. *Downing Street: The War Years*. London: Bloomsbury, 1991.

Mason, David. *Churchill*. New York: Ballantine Books, 1972.

Matthews, Rupert O. *Winston Churchill*. New York: Bookwright Press, 1988. (juvenile)

Mayer, Frank A. *"The Opposition Years: Winston S. Churchill and the Conservative Party, 1945-1951."* Ph.D. diss., University of Southern California, 1987. (Not available from UMI)

_____. *The Opposition Years: Winston S. Churchill and the Conservative Party, 1945-1951*. New York: P. Lang, 1992.

McGowan, Norman. *My Years with Churchill*. New York: British Book Centre, 1958.

Mearns, Martha. *Churchill*. Adapted from the French. London: Nelson, 1966. (juvenile)

Miers, Earl S. *The Story of Winston Churchill*. New York: Grosset & Dunlap, 1965. (juvenile)

Miller, H. Tatlock and Loudon Sainthill, eds. *Churchill: The Walk with Destiny*. New York: Macmillan, 1959.

Miller, Marvin. *Churchill, A Man of Destiny, 1874-1965*. Los Angeles: Marvin Miller, 1965.

Miner, Steven Merritt. *Between Churchill and Stalin: The Soviet Union, Great Britain, and the Origins of the Grand Alliance*. Chapel Hill, NC: University of North Carolina Press, 1988.

Moir, Phyllis. *I Was Winston Churchill's Private Secretary*. New York: W. Funk, Inc., 1941.

Moore, R. J. (Robin James). *Churchill, Cripps, and India, 1939-1945*. New York: Oxford University Press, 1979.

Moorehead, Alan. *Churchill: A Pictorial Biography*. New York: Viking, 1960.

_____. *Winston Churchill in Trial and Triumph*. Boston: Houghton Mifflin, 1955.

Moran, Charles McMoran Wilson. *Churchill: The Struggle for Survival, 1940-1965*. Taken from the diaries of Lord Moran. Boston: Houghton Mifflin, 1966.

Morgan, Ted. *Churchill: Young Man in a Hurry, 1874-1915*. New York: Simon & Schuster, 1982.

Morin, Relman. *Churchill: Portrait of Greatness*. Englewood Cliffs, NJ: Prentice-Hall, 1965.

Morton, H. C. (Henry Canova). *Atlantic Meeting: An Account of Mr. Churchill's Voyage on H.M.S. Prince of Wales, in August, 1941 and the Conference with President Roosevelt Which Resulted in the Atlantic Charter*. New York: Dodd, Mead, Co., 1943.

Murray, Edmund. *I Was Churchill's Bodyguard*. London: W. H. Allen, 1987.

Nadeau, Remi A. *Stalin, Churchill and Roosevelt Divide Europe*. New York: Praeger, 1990.

Nave, Eric and James Rusbridger. *Betrayal at Pearl Harbor: How Churchill Lured Roosevelt Into World War II*. New York: Summit Books, 1991.

Neilson, Francis. *Churchill and Yalta*. New York: Revisionist Press, 1981.

______. *Churchill Legend*. Appleton, WI: C. C. Nelson, 1954.

______. *Churchill's War Memoirs*. New York: Revisionist Press, 1981.

Nel, Elizabeth. *Mr. Churchill's Secretary*. New York: Coward-McCann, 1958.

New York Times eds. *Churchill*. New York: Bantam Books, 1965.

Newfield, Dalton. *Young Winston: 1874-1898. A Biography Using Stamps*. Hopkinton, NH: International Churchill Society, 1990.

Norris, Albert George Samuel. *A Very Great Soul: A Biographical Character Study of the Rt. Hon. Sir Winston S. Churchill, K.G., P.C., O.M., C.H., M.P.* Edinburgh: International Pub. Co., 1957.

Northcote, H. (Hugo) Stafford. *Winston Churchill: Man of Destiny*. London: Newnes, 1965.

Nott, Stanley. *The Young Churchill: A Biography*. New York: Coward-McCann Inc., 1941.

Observer, The. *Churchill by His Contemporaries*. London: Hodder & Stoughton, 1965.

O'Neill, Herbert Charles. *Men of Destiny: Being Studies of the Four Who Rode the War and Made This Precarious Landfall*. London: Phoenix House, 1953.

Pawle, Gerald. *The War and Colonel Warden. Based on the Recollections of C. R. Thompson, Personal Assistant to the Prime Minister, 1940-1945*. New York: Knopf, 1963.

Payne, Robert. *The Great Man: A Portrait of Winston Churchill*. New York: Coward, McCann & Geoghegan, 1974.

Pearson, John. *The Private Lives of Winston Churchill*. New York: Simon & Schuster, 1991.

Pedraza, Howard. *Winston Churchill, Enoch Powell, and the Nation*. London: Cleveland Press, 1986.

Pelling, Henry. *Winston Churchill*. 2nd ed. Houndmills, Basingstoke, Hampshire: Macmillan, 1989.

Pilpel, Robert H. *Churchill in America, 1895-1961: An Affectionate Portrait*. London: New English Library, 1977.

Pitt, Barrie. *Churchill and the Generals*. New York: Bantam Books, 1981.

Quantrill, John R. *Churchill and Wavell: A Study in Political/Military Relationships*. Carlisle Barracks, PA: U.S. Army War College, 1990.

Rabinowicz, Oscar K. *Winston Churchill on Jewish Problems: A Half-Century Survey*. London: Published for the World Jewish Congress, British Section by Lincolns-Praeger, 1956.

Ray, John Philip. *Lloyd George and Churchill*. London: Heinemann Educational, 1970. (juvenile)

Reade, John Collingwood. *Man of Valour: Winston Spencer Churchill: A Critical Appreciation*. Toronto: Canadian Association Broadcasters, 1941.

Readers Digest eds. *Man of the Century: A Churchill Cavalcade*. Boston: Little, Brown, 1965.

Reid, Percy G. *Churchill, Townsman of Westerham*. Folkestone (Kent): Regency International Publications, 1969.

Reynolds, Ernest Edwin. *Four Modern Statesmen: Winston S. Churchill, Franklin D. Roosevelt, Joseph Stalin, Chiang Kai-shek*. New York: Oxford University Press, 1944.

Reynolds, Quentin James. *Winston Churchill*. New York: Random House, 1963. (juvenile)

Richards, Kenneth G. *Sir Winston Churchill*. Chicago: Children's Press, 1968. (juvenile)

Richardson, Stewart, ed. *The Secret History of World War II: The Ultra-Secret Wartime Letters and Cables of Roosevelt, Stalin and Churchill*. New York: Richardson & Steirman, 1986.

Rintala, Marvin. *Lloyd George and Churchill: How Friendship Changed Politics*. Lanham, MD: Madison Books, 1994.

Robbins, Keith. *Churchill*. New York: Longman, 1992.

Roberts, Andrew. *Eminent Churchillians*. New York: Simon & Schuster, 1995.

Roberts, Brian. *Churchills in Africa*. New York: Taplinger, 1971.

Roberts, C. E. Bechhofer (Carl Eric Bechhofer). *Winston Churchill, Being an Account of the Life of the Right Hon. Winston Leonard Spencer Churchill, P.C., C.H., T.D., M.P. ...* New York: R. M. McBride & Co., 1928.

Rodgers, Judith. *Winston Churchill*. New York: Chelsa House Publishers, 1986. (juvenile)

Rose, Norman. *Churchill: Unruly Giant*. New York: Free Press, 1995.

Roskill, Stephen Wentworth. *Churchill and the Generals*. New York: Morrow, 1978.

Russell, Douglas. *The Orders, Decorations and Medals of Sir Winston Churchill*. Contoocook, NH: Churchill Literacy Foundation, 1990.

Sainsbury, Keith L. *Churchill and Roosevelt at War: The War They Fought and the Peace They Hoped to Make*. New York: New York University Press, 1994.

______. *The Turning Point: Roosevelt, Stalin, Churchill, and Chiang Kai-shek, 1943. The Moscow, Cairo, and Tehran Conferences*. Oxford: Oxford University Press, 1985.

Schoenfeld, Maxwell P. *Sir Winston Churchill: His Life and Times*. Malabar, FL: R. E. Krieger Pub. Co., 1986.

______. *The War Ministry of Winston Churchill*. Ames, IA: Iowa State University Press, 1972.

Schwedes, Jeffrey Taylor. "*Winston Churchill's War Aims in Europe, 1940-1945*." Ph.D. diss., University of Minnesota, 1977. (DAI, 39:1, 412A, UMI Order # 7809743)

Scott, A. Maccallum. *Winston Churchill in Peace and War*. London: G. Newnes, 1916.

______. *Winston Spencer Churchill*. London: Methuen, 1905.

Sencourt, Robert (pseud.) *Winston Churchill*. London: Faber & Faber, 1940. First published in 1911.

Shogun, Robert. *Hard Bargain. How FDR Twisted Churchill's Arm, Evaded the Law, and Changed the Role of the American Presidency*. New York: Scribner, 1995.

Silverman, Al, ed. *Churchill: A Memorial Album. His Finest Hours in Words, in Pictures*. New York: Macfadden-Bartell, 1965.

Smith, Arthur L., Jr. *Churchill's German Army: Wartime Strategy and Cold War Politics, 1943-1947*. Beverly Hills, CA: Sage Publications, 1977.

Smith, Charles Roger. "*Winston Churchill and the Challenge of Totalitarianism: Statesmanship and the Challenge of Modern Tyranny*." Ph.D. diss., The Catholic University of America, 1983. (DAI, 43:10, 3409A, UMI Order # DA8304644)

Smith, Norman David. *Winston Churchill*. New York: Roy Publishers, 1964.

Soames, Mary. *Clementine Churchill: The Biography of A Marriage*. Boston: Houghton Mifflin, 1979.

______. *A Family Album: A Personal Selection from Four Generations of Churchills*. Boston: Houghton Mifflin, 1982.

______. *Winston Churchill: His Life As A Painter. A Memoir by His Daughter*. London: Collins, 1990.

Sparrow, Gerald. *Churchill, Man of the Century, 1874-1965*. London: Odhams Books, 1965.

Stansky, Peter, comp. *Churchill: A Profile*. New York: Hill & Wang, 1973.

Stevens, Lawrence. *Winston Churchill: Mini-Play and Activities*. Stockton, CA: Stevens & Shea Publishers, 1981. (juvenile)

Stewart, Herbert Leslie. *Winged Words: Sir Winston Churchill As Writer and Speaker*. New York: Bouregy & Curl, 1954.

Taylor, A. J. P. (Alan John Percivale), and others. *Churchill Revised: A Critical Assessment*. New York: Dial Press, 1969.

Taylor, Robert Lewis. *The Amazing Mister Churchill*. New York: McGraw-Hill, 1962.

______. *Winston Churchill: An Informal Study of Greatness*. Garden City, NY: Doubleday, 1952.

Thomas, David A. *Churchill: A Member for Woodford*. Ilford, Essex, England: F. Cass, 1994.

Thompson, Carlos. *The Assassination of Winston Churchill*. Gerrards Cross: Smythe, 1969.

Thompson, Kenneth W. *Foreign Policy and Arms Control: Churchill's Legacy*. Lanham, MD: University Press of America, 1990.

______. *Winston Churchill's World View: Statesmanship and Power*. Baton Rouge, LA: Louisiana State University Press, 1983.

Thompson, R. W. (Reginald William). *Churchill and Morton: The Quest for Insight in the Correspondence of Major Sir Desmond Morton and the Author*. London: Hodder & Stoughton, 1976.

______. *Generalissimo Churchill*. New York: Scribner, 1973.

______. *Winston Churchill: The Yankee Marlborough*. Garden City, NY: Doubleday, 1963.

Thompson, W. H. (Walter Henry). *Assignment: Churchill*. New York: Farrar, Straus & Young, 1955. (juvenile)

______. *I Was Churchill's Shadow*. London: C. Johnson, 1951.

______. *Sixty Minutes with Winston Churchill*. London: C. Johnson, 1953.

Thomson, George Malcolm. *Vote of Censure*. London: Secker & Warburg, 1968.

Thomson, Malcolm. *The Life and Times of Winston Churchill*. London: Odhams Press Ltd., 1945.

Thorton-Kemsley, Colin. *Through Winds and Tides*. Montrose: Standard Press, 1974.

Tickell, Jerrard. *Ascalon: The Story of Sir Winston Churchill's Wartime Flights from 1943 to 1945. Based on the Records of Group Captain John Mitchell*. London: Hodder & Stoughton, 1964.

Times, London (Newspaper). *The Churchill Years, 1874-1965*. New York: Viking Press, 1965.

Titus, Warren Irving. *Winston Churchill*. New York: Twayne Publishers, 1963.

Towers, Frederick, comp. *Sir Winston Churchill: A Memorial*. London: Macdonald, 1965.

Trory, Ernie. *Churchill and the Bomb: A Study in Pragmatism*. Hove, Sussex: Crabtree Press, 1984.

Trukhanovsky, V. G. (Vladimir Grigorevich). *Winston Churchill*. Translated from the Russian by Kenneth Russell, and others. Moscow: Progress Publishers, 1978.

Tucker, Ben. *Winston Churchill, 1874-1955: His Life in Pictures*. London: Allman, 1955.

United States. Congress. (89th, 1st session, 1965). *Memorial Addresses in the Congress of the United States and Tributes in Eulogy of Sir Winston Churchill, Soldier, Statesman, Author, Orator, Leader*. Washington: U.S. Government Printing Office, 1965.

Urquhart, Fred. *W. S. C.: A Cartoon Biography*. London: Cassell, 1955.

Venkataramani, M. S. and B. K. Shrivastava. *Roosevelt, Gandhi, Churchill: America and the Last Phase of India's Freedom Struggle*. New Dehli: Radiant Publishers, 1983.

Waszak, Leon J. *"Agreement in Principle: The Wartime Partnership of General Wladyslaw Sikorski and Winston Churchill, and the Course of Anglo-Polish Relations, 1939-1943*." Ph.D. diss., University of Southern California, 1988. (Not available from UMI)

Watney, John. *The Churchills: Portrait of A Great Family*. New York: Gordon & Cremonesi, 1977.

Webb, John Edward. *Churchill: Savior or Wrecker?* Sydney: n.p., 1962.

Webb, Robert N. *Winston Churchill: Man of the Century*. New York: Franklin Watts, 1968. (juvenile)

Weidhorn, Manfred. *Churchill's Rhetoric and Political Discourse*. Lanham, MD: University Press of America, 1987.

______. *A Harmony of Interests: Explorations in the Mind of Sir Winston Churchill*. Rutherford, NJ: Farleigh Dickinson University Press, 1992.

______. *Sir Winston Churchill*. Boston: Twayne Publishers, 1979.

______. *Sword and Pen: A Survey of the Writings of Sir Winston Churchill*. Albuquerque, NM: University of New Mexico Press, 1974.

Wheeler-Bennett, John, ed. *Action This Day: Working with Churchill*. Memoirs by Lord Normanbrook [and others]. New York: St. Martin's Press, 1968.

Wibberley, Leonard. *The Life of Winston Churchill*. New York: Ariel Books, 1965.

Williams, Brian. *Winston Churchill*. New York: Marshall Cavendish, 1988. (juvenile)

Williams, Geoffrey and Charles Roetter. *The Wit of Winston Churchill*. London: M. Parrish, 1955.

Wilson, Theodore. *The First Summit: Roosevelt and Churchill at Placentia Bay*. Rev. ed. Lawrence, KS: University of Kansas Press, 1991.

Wolff, Michael. *Winston Churchill*. London: Heron Books, 1970.

Woods, Frederick. *Artillery of Words: The Writings of Sir Winston Churchill*. London: L. Cooper, 1992.

_____, ed. *A Bibliography of the Works of Sir Winston Churchill*. 2nd rev. ed. Godalming, England: St. Paul's Bibliographies, 1979.

Wrinch, Pamela N. *The Military Strategy of Winston Churchill*. Boston: Department of Government, Boston University, 1961.

Young, Kenneth. *Churchill and Beaverbrook: A Study in Friendship and Politics*. London: Eyre & Spottiswoode, 1966.

2   Premier Josef Stalin
1879-1953

Soviet Union

Josef Stalin was absolute dictator of the Soviet Union from 1929 to 1953. During his reign, he transformed a backward, primarily agricultural society into a modern industrialized state. This modernization occurred at the expense of his people. Millions died who opposed his changes. Even his closest associates were not safe as he periodically liquidated any perceived opposition to retain total control.

Stalin was born in Georgia, a part of southwest Russia. As a student, he read the literature of Karl Marx and Vladimir Lenin. In 1898, he joined a secret Marxist group and organized protests against poor working conditions of factory workers. In 1901, he joined Lenin's Social Democratic Labour Party. From 1903 to 1917, Stalin was arrested numerous times and exiled to Siberia twice. During these years he gained more influence in the party. He was twice editor of Pravda, the party newspaper, was named to the Central Committee, and began using the name of Stalin, which meant man of steel.

When the Czar abdicated in 1917 due to political unrest and Russia's military defeat by Germany, Lenin immediately formed an armed resistance against the provincial government. The revolt was successful and the Bolsheviks assumed control of the government. Later, Stalin greatly enhanced his role in the revolution and the civil war that followed, ordering historians to re-write the history books and credit him with being Lenin's principal assistant and advisor.

In 1922, Stalin was named Secretary General of the Central Committee and was one of the five members of the newly formed Politburo. These positions made him the most powerful man in Russia. Belatedly, Lenin recognized this fact, but was too ill to oppose him. Lenin died before he could remove Stalin from office.

Between 1924 and 1928, Stalin consolidated his power and by 1929, emerged as absolute dictator of the Soviet Union. In 1928, he started the first five-year plan for economic development. Stalin wanted to industrialize on a massive scale and collectivize the agricultural lands.

Peasants who opposed the collectivization program were arrested and either shot or sent to concentration camps in Siberia. Estimates are that millions died in the late 1920s and early 1930s due to resistance to Stalin's programmes or from starvation.

All during his life, Stalin believed that various factions in the government and the military were plotting to overthrow him. From time to time, to stop this supposed plotting, he purged the party hierarchy to keep absolute control and to remind the ones not purged that it was always possible that they could be next if they stepped out of line. The first major purge came in 1935. Many party members were executed, as were numerous top-ranking officers in the Red Army. As a result, when war came with Germany six years later, the Red Army was vastly undertrained and unprepared. The next purge came after the Second World War in 1949-50. Reports were he was planning a third purge when he died in 1953.

Stalin and Adolf Hitler, at opposite ends of the political spectrum, astounded other governments when they signed a non-aggression pact in August 1939. The real purpose was to divide Poland and give the Soviet Union control of Estonia, Latvia, and Lithuania. Stalin believed that by securing these states and eastern Poland, the area would serve as a buffer zone against Nazi Germany until the Red Army was prepared to defend the Soviet Union. However, Hitler did not allow Stalin enough time to complete the re-organization of the Red Army. German armed forces invaded the Soviet Union on 22 June 1941.

During the Second World War, Stalin aligned the Soviet Union with Great Britain and the United States. He, British Prime Minister Winston Churchill, and American President Franklin D. Roosevelt became the Big Three. Though Stalin was diametrically opposed to the political philosophies of Churchill and Roosevelt, and they to his, the three leaders worked together, though not always harmoniously, to defeat Nazi Germany. Stalin remained suspicious of the western Allies' motives during the war. He believed they were deliberately attempting to weaken the Soviet Union by their failure to open a second front in western Europe.

The Big Three met at Tehran in 1943 and at Yalta in 1945 to discuss war aims. A final conference was held at Potsdam, a suburb of Berlin, in July 1945. By then, Harry S. Truman had replaced Roosevelt as president and Churchill was informed during the talks that he had lost the summer election to Clement Attlee. Still, the Allied leaders managed to agree on the partition of Germany and Stalin kept his promise to invade Japanese-held Manchuria once the fighting in Europe ended. The invasion gave the Soviet Union control of northern Korea and allowed

Stalin to give Mao Tse-tung's Communist forces direct aid against Chiang Kai-shek's Nationalist forces.   He also set up Communist governments in Eastern Europe, thus extending his political influence westward and providing a buffer zone against the west as the Cold War began.

There are many excellent works on the life and career of Josef Stalin. A few recommendations are Robert Conquest's *The Great Terror* and *Stalin*, Alex De Jonge's *Stalin and the Shaping of the Soviet Union*, Isaac Deutscher's *Stalin*, John Erickson's *Stalin's War with Germany*, Ian Grey's *Stalin*, Ronald Hingley's *Joseph Stalin*, Walter Lacqueur's *Stalin*, Roy Medvedev's *Let History Judge*, Boris Souvarine's *Stalin*, Leon Trotsky's *Stalin*, Robert Tucker's *Stalin as Revolutionary, 1879-1929*, Adam Ulam's *Stalin*, and Dmitri Volkogonov's *Stalin*.   Also recommended are Josef Stalin's *The Great Patriotic War of the Soviet Union* and *Stalin's Correspondence with Churchill, Attlee, Roosevelt, and Truman, 1941-1945*, Seweryn Bialer's *Stalin and His Generals*, Albert Seaton's *Stalin as Military Commander and* Harold Shukman's *Stalin's Generals*.   These works and others are listed in the bibliography that follows.

Bibliography

Adams, Arthur E. *Stalin and His Times*. New York: Holt, Rinehart & Winston, 1972.

Ali, Tariq, ed. *The Stalinist Legacy: Its Impact on Twentieth-Century World Politics*. New York: Penguin Books, 1984.

Antonov-Ovseyeneko, Anton. *The Time of Stalin: Portrait of A Tyranny*. New York: Harper & Row, 1981.

Archer, Jules. *Man of Steel: Joseph Stalin*. New York: J. Messner, 1965. (juvenile)

Armstrong, Hamilton Fish. *Tito and Goliath*. New York: Macmillan, 1951.

Avtorkhanov, Abdurakhman. *The Reign of Stalin*. Translated from the French by L. J. Smith. London: Bodley Head, 1953.

Baciu, Nicolas. *Sell-Out to Stalin: The Tragic Errors of Churchill and Roosevelt. The Untold Story*. New York: Vantage Press, 1984.

Backer, George. *The Deadly Parallel: Stalin and Ivan the Terrible*. New York: Random House, 1950.

Banac, Ivo. *With Stalin Against Tito: Conformist Splits in Yugoslav Communism*. Ithaca, NY: Cornell University Press, 1988.

Barbusse, Henri. *Stalin: A New World Seen Through One Man*. Translated by Vyvyan Holland. New York: Macmillan Company, 1935.

Basseches, Nikolaus. *Stalin*. Translated from the German by E. W. Dickes. New York: Dutton, 1952.

Bazhanov, Boris. *Bazhanov and the Damnation of Stalin*. Translation and commentary by David W. Doyle. Athens, OH: Ohio University Press, 1990.

Berezhkov, V. M. *At Stalin's Side: His Interpreter's Memoirs from the October Revolution to the Fall of the Dictator's Empire*. Secaucus, NJ: Carol Publishing Group, 1994.

Bialer, Seweryn, comp. *Stalin and His Generals: Soviet Military Memoirs of World War II*. New York: Pegasus, 1969.

Blank, Stephen. *The Sorcerer as Apprentice: Stalin As Commissar of Nationalities, 1917-1924*. Westport, CT: Greenwood Press, 1993.

Blassingame, Wyatt. *Joseph Stalin and Communist Russia*. Champaign, IL: Garrard Publishing Co., 1971. (juvenile)

Bloomberg, Marty and Buckley Barry Barrett. *Stalin: An Annotated Guide to Books in English*. San Bernardino, CA: Borgo Press, 1993.

Boffa, Giuseppe. *The Stalin Phenomenon*. Translated by Nicholas Fersen. Ithaca: Cornell University Press, 1992.

Bortoli, Georges. *The Death of Stalin*. Translated by Raymond Rosenthal. New York: Praeger, 1975.

Brackman, Roman Sorin. *"Anti-Semitism of Joseph Stalin."* Ph.D. diss., New York University, 1980. (DAI, 41:6, 2727A, UMI Order # 8027869)

Bullock, Alan. *Hitler and Stalin: Parallel Lives*. Toronto: McClelland & Stewart, 1991.

Calkins, Janet. *Joseph Stalin*. New York: F. Watts, 1990. (juvenile)

Cameron, Kenneth Neill. *Stalin, Man of Contradiction*. Toronto: NC Press, 1987.

Campeanu, Pavel. *The Origins of Stalinism: From Leninist Revolution to Stalinist Society*. Translated by Michael Vale. Armonk, NY: M.E. Sharpe, 1986.

Carmichael, Joel. *Stalin's Masterpiece: The Show Trials and Purges of the Thirties, The Consolidation of the Bolshevik Dictatorship*. New York: St. Martin's Press, 1976.

Carrere d'Encausse, Helene. *Stalin, Order Through Terror*. Translated by Valence Ionescu. London: Longman, 1981.

Chapman, Derek. *Stalin: Man of Steel*. White Plains, NY: Longman Publishing Group, 1988.

Cole, David M. *Josef Stalin, Man of Steel*. New York: Rich & Cowan, 1942.

Conquest, Robert. *The Great Terror: A Reassessment*. New York: Oxford University Press, 1990.

______. *The Great Terror: Stalin's Purge of the Thirties*. Rev. ed. New York: Macmillan, 1973.

______. *Stalin: Breaker of Nations*. New York: Viking, 1991.

Contract, Alexander. *The Back Room: My Life with Khruschev and Stalin*. New York: Vantage Press Inc., 1991.

Dallin, Alexander and Bertrand M. Patenaude, eds. *Stalin and Stalinism*. New York: Garland, 1992.

Daniels, Robert V. *Trotsky, Stalin, and Socialism*. Boulder: Westview Press, 1991.

Davis, Jerome. *Behind Soviet Power: Stalin and the Russians*. West Haven, CT: The Readers' Press Inc., 1949.

De Jonge, Alex. *Stalin and the Shaping of the Soviet Union*. New York: Morrow, 1986.

Delbars, Yves. *The Real Stalin*. Translated from the French by Bernard Miall. London: Allen & Unwin, 1953.

Deutscher, Isaac. *Russia After Stalin*. Indianapolis, IN: Bobbs-Merrill, 1968.

______. *Stalin: A Political Biography*. 2nd ed. New York: Oxford University Press, 1967.

Djilas, Milovan. *Conversations with Stalin*. Translated from the Serbo-Croat by Michael B. Petrovich. London: Hart-Davis, 1962.

Duranty, Walter. *Stalin and Co., the Politburo, the Men Who Run Russia*. New York: W. Sloan Associates, 1949.

Edmonds, Robin. *The Big Three: Churchill, Roosevelt and Stalin in Peace and War*. New York: Norton, 1990.

Elleinstein, Jean. *The Stalin Phenomenon*. English translation by Peter Latham. London: Lawrence & Wishart, 1976.

Erickson, John. *The Road to Berlin: Continuing the History of Stalin's War with Germany*. Boulder, CO: Westview Press, 1983.

______. *Stalin's War With Germany*. New York: Harper & Row, 1975.

Essad-Bey. *Stalin, the Career of a Fanatic*. Translated from the German by Huntley Paterson. New York: Viking Press, 1932.

Feis, Herbert. *Churchill, Roosevelt, Stalin: The War They Waged and the Peace They Sought*. 2nd ed. Princeton, NJ: Princeton University Press, 1967.

Feldman, A. Bronson. *Stalin: Red Lord of Russia, 1879-1953*. Philadelphia: Mercury Books, 1962.

Fischer, Louis. *Gandhi and Stalin: Two Signs at the World's Crossroads*. New York: Harper, 1947.

______. *The Life and Death of Stalin*. New York: Harper, 1952.

Fishman, Jack and J. Bernard Hutton. *The Private Life of Josef Stalin*. London: W. H. Allen, 1962.

Gibson, Michael. *Russia Under Stalin*. New York: G. P. Putnam's Sons, 1972.

Gill, Graeme J. *The Origins of the Stalinist Political System*. New York: Cambridge University Press, 1990.

______. *Stalinism*. Atlantic Highlands, NJ: Humanities Press International, 1990.

Graham, Stephen. *Stalin: An Impartial Study of the Life and Work of Joseph Stalin*. London: Hutchinson, 1939.

Grey, Ian. *Stalin, Man of History*. Garden City, NY: Doubleday, 1979.

Havas, Laslo. *The Long Jump. (Or the 1943 Plot to Assassinate Churchill, Roosevelt and Stalin)*. Translated by Kathleen Szasz. London: Spearman, 1967.

Hayes, David and F. H. Gregory. *Joseph Stalin*. Hove: Wayland, 1977.

Heizer, James Lee. "*The Cult of Stalin, 1929-1939*." Ph.D. diss., University of Kentucky, 1977. (DAI, 39:6, 3759A, UMI Order # 7824398)

Hershman, D. Jablow and Julian Lieb. *A Brotherhood of Tyrants: Manic Depression and Absolute Power*. Amhurst, NY: Prometheus Books, 1994.

Hingley, Ronald. *Joseph Stalin: Man and Legend*. New York: McGraw-Hill, 1974.

Hochschild, Adams. *The Unquiet Ghost: Russians Remember Stalin*. New York: Viking, 1994.

Hoobler, Dorothy and Thomas Hoobler. *Joseph Stalin*. New York: Chelsea House, 1985. (juvenile)

Hoxha, Enver. *With Stalin: Memoirs*. Tirana: 8 Nentori Publishing House, 1979.

Hutton, Joseph Bernard. *Stalin: The Miraculous Georgian*. London: N. Spearman, 1961.

Hyde, H. Montgomery. *Stalin: The History of a Dictator*. New York: Farrar, Straus & Giroux, 1971.

Institut Marksizma-Leninizma. *Joseph Stalin, A Political Biography*. New York: International Publishers, 1949.

Italia, Bob. *The Story of Joseph Stalin*. Edina, MN: Abdo & Daughter, 1990. (juvenile)

Jacobs, William Jay. *Stalin*. Beverly Hills, CA: Benzinger, 1976.

Kahle, Hans. *Stalin the Soldier*. London: The Russia Today Society, 1945.

Kalinin, M. I. (Mikhail Ivanovich). *Stalin: Sixty Years*. Moscow: Foreign Languages Pub. House, 1939.

Kallen, Stuart A. *The Stalin Era: 1925-1953*. Edited by Rosemary Wallner. Edina, MN: Abdo & Daughters, 1992. (juvenile)

Khrushchev, Nikita. *Anatomy of Terror: Khrushchev's Revelations about Stalin's Regime*. Washington, DC: Public Affairs Press, 1956.

Killingray, David. *Stalin*. London: Harrap, 1976.

King-Hall, Stephen. *Three Dictators: Mussolini, Hitler, and Stalin*. London: Faber & Faber, 1964. (juvenile)

Kolarz, Walter. *Stalin and Eternal Russia*. London: L. Drummond, 1944.

Kosiba, Harold John. "*Stalin's Great Game: Anglo-Soviet Relations in the Near East, 1939-1943*." Ph.D. diss., Indiana University, 1991. (DAI, 52:9, 3398A, UMI Order # DA9205948)

Krotkov, Yuri. *The Red Monarch: Scenes from the Life of Stalin*. Translated from the Russian by Tanya E. Mairs. Edited by Carol Houck Smith. New York: Norton, 1979.

Laqueur, Walter. *Stalin: The Glasnost Revelations*. New York: Scribners, 1990.

Latsis, O. R. (Otto Rudol'fovich). *The Turning Point*. Moscow: Novosti, 1990.

Leonhard, Wolfgang. *Betrayal: The Hitler-Stalin Pact of 1939*. New York: St. Martin's Press, 1983.

Levine, Issac Don. *Stalin*. New York: Cosmopolitan Book Corporation, 1931.

______. *Stalin's Great Secret*. New York: Coward-McCann, 1956.

Lewis, Jonathan and Phillip Whitehead. *Stalin: A Time for Judgement*. London: Methuen, 1990.

Liversidge, Douglas. *Joseph Stalin*. London: Franklin Watts Ltd., 1969. (juvenile)

Ludwig, Emil. *Stalin*. New York: G. P. Putnam's Sons, 1942.

______. *Three Portraits: Hitler, Mussolini, Stalin*. New York: Alliance Book Corporation, Longmans, Green & Co., 1940.

Lyons, Eugene. *Stalin, Czar of all the Russias*. Philadelphia: J. B. Lippincott Co., 1940.

Marples, David R. *Stalinism in Ukraine in the 1940s*. New York: St. Martin's Press, 1992.

Marrin, Albert. *Stalin*. New York: Viking Kestel, 1988. (juvenile)

______. *Stalin: Russia's Man of Steel*. New York: Puffin Books, 1993. (juvenile)

Marsh, Rosalind J. *Images of Dictatorship: Portraits of Stalin in Literature*. London: Routledge, 1989.

Matlock, Jack F., Jr. and Fred C. Holling, Jr. *An Index to the Collected Works of J. V. Stalin*. Washington, DC: External Research Staff, Office of Intelligence Research, Department of State, 1955.

McCabe, Joseph. *The Life of Joseph Stalin: The Rebel and the Statesman*. Girard, KS: Haldeman-Julius Publications, 1944.

McCagg, William O., Jr. *Stalin Embattled, 1943-1948*. Detroit: Wayne State University Press, 1978.

McCauley, Martin. *Stalin and Stalinism*. Harlow, Essex, England: Longman, 1983.

______. *The Stalin File*. London: Batsford, 1979.

McNeal, Robert H. *The Bolshevik Tradition: Lenin, Stalin, Khrushchev*. Rev. 3rd printing. Englewood Cliffs, NJ: Prentice-Hall, 1966.

______. *Stalin: Man and Ruler*. Basingstoke, England: Macmillan in association with St. Anthony's College, Oxford, 1988.

______, comp. *Stalin's Works: An Annotated Bibliography*. Stanford, CA: Hoover Institution on War, Revolution, and Peace, 1967.

McSherry, James E. *Stalin, Hitler, and Europe*. Cleveland, OH: World Publishing Co., 1968.

Medvedev, Roy. *Let History Judge: The Origins and Consequences of Stalinism*. Rev. ed. Edited and translated by George Shriver. New York: Columbia University Press, 1989.

______. *On Stalin and Stalinism*. Translated by Ellen de Kadt. New York: Oxford University Press, 1979.

Merridale, Catherine. *Moscow Politics and the Rise of Stalin: The Communist Party in the Capital, 1925-32*. New York: St. Martin's Press, 1990.

Miner, Steven Merritt. *Between Churchill and Stalin: The Soviet Union, Great Britain, and the Origins of the Cold War*. Chapel Hill, NC: University of North Carolina Press, 1988.

______. *"Stalin's 'Minimum Aims': The USSR, Great Britain and the Soviet Union's Frontiers, 1940-1942."* Ph.D. diss., Indiana University, 1987. (DAI, 48:5, 1293A, UMI Order # 8717786)

Molotov, M., and others. *Stalin*. New York: Workers Library Publishers, 1940.

Monitor, pseud. *The Death of Stalin: An Investigation by Monitor*. London: Wingate, 1958.

Murphy, J. T. *Stalin, 1879-1944*. London: John Lane, 1945.

Nadeau, Remi A. *Stalin, Churchill and Roosevelt Divide Europe*. New York: Praeger, 1990.

Nichol, Jim. *Stalin's Crimes Against the Non-Russian Nations: The 1987-1990 Revelations and Debate*. Pittsburgh: University of Pittsburgh, Center for Russian and East European Studies, 1991.

Nisbet, Robert A. *Roosevelt and Stalin: The Failed Courtship*. Washington, DC: Regnery Gateway, 1988.

Nomad, Max. *Apostles of Revolution*. Boston: Little, Brown & Co., 1939.

Nove, Alec, ed. *The Stalin Phenomenon*. New York: St. Martin's Press, 1992.

______. *Stalinism and After: The Road to Gorbachev*. Boston: Unwin Hyman, 1989.

O'Neill, Herbert Charles. *Men of Destiny: Being Studies of the Four Who Rode the War and Made This Precarious Landfall*. London: Phoenix House, 1953.

Orlov, Alexander. *The Secret History of Stalin's Crimes*. New York: Random House, 1953.

Otfinoski, Steven. *Joseph Stalin: Russia's Last Czar*. Brookfield, CT: Millbrook Press, 1993. (juvenile)

Owen, Frank. *The Three Dictators: Mussolini, Stalin, Hitler*. London: G. Allen & Unwin Ltd., 1940.

Paley, Alan L. *Stalin: The Iron Fisted Dictator of Russia*. Charlottesville, NY: SamHar Press, 1971.

Payne, Robert. *The Rise and Fall of Stalin*. New York: Simon and Schuster, 1965.

Perlmutter, Amos. *FDR & Stalin: A Not So Grand Alliance, 1943-1945*. Columbia, MO: University of Missouri Press, 1993.

Pomper, Philip. *Lenin, Trotsky, and Stalin: The Intelligentsia and the Power*. New York: Columbia University Press, 1990.

Proskurin, Alexander, comp. *The Stalin Phenomenon*. New Delhi: Sterling Publishers, 1989

Rancour-Leferriere, Daniel. *The Mind of Stalin: A Psychoanalytic Study*. Ann Arbor, MI: Ardis, 1988.

Randall, Francis B. *Stalin's Russia: An Historical Reconsideration*. New York: Free Press, 1965.

Rapoport, Louis. *Stalin's War Against the Jews: The Doctors' Plot and the Soviet Solution*. New York: The Free Press, 1990.

Read, Anthony and David Fisher. *The Deadly Embrace: Hitler, Stalin, and the Nazi-Soviet Pact, 1939-1941*. New York: Norton, 1988.

Resis, Albert. *Stalin, the Politburo, and the Onset of the Cold War, 1941-1946*. Pittsburgh: University of Pittsburgh, Center for Russian and East European Studies, 1988.

Reynolds, Ernest Edwin. *Four Modern Statesmen: Winston S. Churchill, Franklin D. Roosevelt, Joseph Stalin, Chiang Kai-shek*. New York: Oxford University Press, 1944.

Richardson, Rosamond. *Stalin's Shadow: Inside the Family of One of the World's Greatest Tyrants*. New York; St. Martin's Press, 1994.

Richardson, Stewart, ed. *The Secret History of World War II: The Ultra-Secret Wartime Letters and Cables of Roosevelt, Stalin, and Churchill*. New York: Richardson & Steirman, 1986.

Rigby, T. H. (Thomas Henry). *Stalin*. Englewood Cliffs, NJ: Prentice-Hall, 1966.

______, ed. *The Stalin Dictatorship: Khruschev's "Secret Speech" and Other Documents*. London: Methuen, 1968.

Rirdans, E. *Uncle Joe*. London: Produced for E. Ridans by Wardland Ltd., 1952.

Roberts, Elizabeth Mauchline. *Stalin: Man of Steel*. New York: Roy Publishers, 1968.

Roberts, Geoffrey. *The Unholy Alliance: Stalin's Pact with Hitler*. London: Tauris, 1989.

Romano-Petrova, N. *Stalin's Doctor, Stalin's Nurse: A Memoir*. Translated from the Russian by Michelle Petroff. Princeton, NJ: Kingston Press, 1984.

Rosenfeldt, Niels Erik. *Stalin's Special Departments: A Comparative Analysis of Key Sources*. Translated from the Danish. Copenhagen: University of Copenhagen, Institute of Slavonic and East European Studies, 1989. Distribution by C. A. Rutzels Forlag.

Ross, Stewart. *The USSR Under Stalin*. New York: Bookwright Press, 1991. (juvenile)

Rothnie, Niall. *Stalin and Russia, 1924-1953*. Basingstoke: Macmillan, 1991.

Sainsbury, Keith. *The Turning Point: Roosevelt, Stalin, Churchill, and Chiang Kai-shek, 1943, The Moscow, Cairo, and Tehran Conferences*. Oxford: Oxford University Press, 1985.

Scherger, George L. *Men of the Hour: Mussolini, Gandhi, Stalin, Hitler*. Chicago: Popular Interest Series Publishing Co., 1933.

Seaton, Albert. *Stalin as Military Commander*. New York: Praeger, 1976.

Shantz, Marshall. *Stalin, the Great Purge, and Russian History: A New Look at the "New Class"*. Pittsburgh: Russian and East European Studies Program, University of Pittsburgh, 1984.

Shimotomai, Nobuo. *Moscow Under Stalin's Rule, 1931-34*. New York: St. Martin's Press, 1991.

Shukman, Harold, ed. *Stalin's Generals*. New York: Grove Press, 1993.

Shulman, Marshall Darrow. *Stalin's Foreign Policy Reappraised*. Cambridge: Harvard University Press, 1963.

Slusser, Robert M. *Stalin in October: The Man Who Missed the Revolution*. Baltimore: Johns Hopkins University Press, 1987.

Smith, Edward Ellis. *The Young Stalin: The Early Years of An Elusive Revolutionary*. New York: Farrar, Straus & Giroux, 1967.

Souvarine, Boris. *Stalin: A Critical Survey of Bolshevism*. New York: Alliance Book Corporation, 1939.

Stalin, Josef. *Essential Stalin: Major Theoretical Writings, 1905-1952*. Edited with an introduction by Bruce Franklin. Garden City, NY: Anchor Books, 1972.

______. *The Great Patriotic War of the Soviet Union*. New York: International Publishers, 1945.

______. *Selected Writings*. Westport, CT: Greenwood Press, 1970.

______. *Stalin's Correspondence with Churchill, Attlee, Roosevelt and Truman, 1941-1945*. New York: Dutton, 1958.

______. *Stalin's Kampf: Joseph Stalin's Credo, Written by Himself*. Edited by M. R. Werner. New York: Howell, Soskin & Co., 1940.

______. *War of National Liberation*. 2 volumes. New York: International Publishers, 1942-43.

______. *Works, 1901-1934*. 13 volumes. Moscow: Foreign Languages Pub. House, 1953.

______. *Works, 1934-[1952]*. 3 volumes. Edited by Robert H. McNeal. Stanford, CA: Hoover Institution on War, Revolution, and Peace, 1967.

Svanidze, Budu. *My Uncle, Joseph Stalin*. Translated by Waverley Root. New York: Putnam, 1953.

Taubman, William. *Stalin's American Policy: From Entent to Detente to Cold War*. New York: Norton, 1982.

Tolstoy, Nikolai. *Stalin's Secret War Against Russia*. New York: Holt, Rinehart & Winston, 1981.

Topitsch, Ernst. *Stalin's War: A Radical New Theory of the Origins of the Second World War*. Translated from the German by A. and B. E. Taylor. New York: St. Martin's Press, 1987.

Tremain, Rose. *Stalin*. New York: Ballantine Books, 1975.

Trotsky, Leon. *The Real Situation in Russia*. Translated by Max Eastman. New York: Harcourt, Brace, 1928.

______. *Stalin: An Appraisal of the Man and His Influence*. Translated from the Russian by Charles Malamuth. New York: Harper & Brothers, 1941. Reprinted from books and pamphlets by Leon Trotsky.

_____. *The Stalin School of Falsification*. Translated by John G. Wright. Annotated by Max Schachtman. 3rd ed. New York: Pathfinder Press, 1972.

Tucker, Robert C. *The Soviet Political Mind: Stalinism and Post-Stalin Change*. Rev. ed. New York: Norton, 1971.

_____. *Stalin as Revolutionary, 1879-1929: A Study in History and Personality*. New York: Norton, 1973.

_____. *Stalin in Power: The Revolution from Above, 1928-1941*. New York: Norton, 1990.

_____, ed. *Stalinism: Essays in Historical Interpretation*. New York: Norton, 1977.

_____. *Stalin's Revolution from Above: An Interpretive History*. New York: W. W. Norton & Co. Inc., 1990.

Ulam, Adam B. *Stalin: The Man and His Era*. New York: Viking Press, 1973.

Urban, George, ed. *Stalinism: Its Impact on Russia and the World*. New York: St. Martin's Press, 1982.

Vaksberg, Arkady. *Stalin Against the Jews*. Translated by Antonia W. Bouis. New York: Knopf, 1994.

Volkogonov, D. A. (Dmitri Antonovich). *Stalin: Triumph and Tragedy*. London: Grove Weidenfeld, 1991.

Voroshilov, Kliment Efremovich. *A Commander of Genius of the Great Patriotic War*. Moscow: Foreign Languages Publishing House, 1950.

Vucinich, Wayne S., ed. *At the Brink of War and Peace: The Tito-Stalin Split in A Historic Perspective*. New York: East European Quarterly, 1982.

Warth, Robert D. *Joseph Stalin*. New York: Twayne Publishers, 1969.

Watson, Emile Emdon. *Meditations of Joseph Vissarionovich Djagashvili, Alias Joseph Stalin*. Washington, DC: The American Corporation, 1952.

Whitelaw, Nancy. *Joseph Stalin: From Peasant to Premier*. New York: Dillon Press, 1992. (juvenile)

Wolfe, Bertram David. *Three Who Made A Revolution: A Biographical History*. 4th rev. ed. New York: Dial Press, 1964.

Wolman, Benjamin B., ed. *Psychoanalytic Interpretation of History*. New York: Basic Books, 1971.

Wood, Alan. *Stalin and Stalinism*. New York: Routledge, 1990.

Yindrich, Jan Holman. *Tito vs Stalin: The Battle of the Marshals*. London: Benn, 1950.

3   President Franklin Delano Roosevelt 1882-1945

United States of America

Franklin D. Roosevelt, a Democrat, was first elected president in 1932. He was re-elected in 1936 and again in 1940. On 7 December 1941, the United States naval base at Pearl Harbor, Hawaii was attacked by planes of the Japanese Imperial Navy. Roosevelt asked Congress on 8 December to declare that a state of war existed between the United States and Japan. Congress quickly complied with only one dissenting vote. On 11 December, Germany and Italy declared war on the United States. During the next three years and four months, Roosevelt devoted his full energies to directing the war effort against the Axis powers. He was re-elected to a fourth term in 1944, serving longer than any other president. However, by 1945, he was a sick man. Photographs in early 1945 showed him to be gaunt and drawn. Roosevelt did not survive to see the successful conclusion of the war, dying of a cerebral hemorrhage on 12 April 1945. Germany surrendered less than a month later and Japan followed in September.

During his terms as president, Roosevelt had his admirers and his detractors. There did not seem to be any neutral ground when it came to opinions about him. He was born into a wealthy New York family in 1882, graduated from Harvard in 1903, then entered the Columbia University Law School and passed the bar examination in 1907. However, he had little interest in legal practice and soon entered the field of politics of which he had an instant affinity. After serving two years as a New York state senator, he campaigned strongly for Woodrow Wilson's presidential bid in 1912. When Wilson was elected, he appointed Roosevelt Assistant Secretary of the Navy, a post that FDR enjoyed immensely given his love of boats, ships, and naval history. When the United States entered the First World War in 1917, Roosevelt remained as assistant secretary even though he requested to resign so he could join the Navy. His superiors felt that he was too valuable to lose. During the war, he worked on numerous military projects and visited the battlefields in 1918 as a representative of the government. Because of his hard work, his political influence grew and he made many valuable contacts both in his own government and foreign governments as well.

A political setback occurred in 1920 when he was the Democratic Party's vice-presidential candidate, running with Ohio Governor James M. Cox. They were defeated by the Republican ticket of Warren G. Harding and Calvin Coolidge. The Democrats' main platform was America's entry into the League of Nations, but most Americans wanted nothing to do with the troubles of other countries after experiencing the horrors of warfare during the recently ended conflict in Europe.

Roosevelt was stricken by polio in 1921 and for the rest of his life could not walk without the aid of leg braces or the help of attendants. The extent of his disability moved his family and friends to urge him to retire, but he refused to abandon his political career. To aid his physical therapy, he purchased the Warm Springs, Georgia complex and used it as a rehabilitation center for himself and other polio victims who could not afford the cost of medical treatments. Roosevelt's constant exercise and swimming programmes made him strong despite his disability. While in office, both as governor of New York and as president, very few people knew the extent of his disability.

In 1928, Roosevelt ran for the governorship of New York and in a close race, defeated his opponent. He was re-elected in 1930 by a huge margin, establishing a power base. In 1932, he ran for the presidency and secured the Democratic nomination. By then, the nation was in the depths of the Great Depression. Roosevelt, running on the New Deal platform, defeated incumbent President Herbert Hoover in a landslide victory.

From 1933 to 1941, Roosevelt's chief duty was the attempt to reduce America's massive unemployment and somehow end the Great Depression. Numerous laws were passed and the government became more involved with the everyday lives of the American people. At the same time, Roosevelt was concerned with foreign policy. He viewed the rise of Adolf Hitler in Germany and Japanese expansion in the Far East as serious threats to world peace and security. He had many battles with Congress concerning the various neutrality acts it passed in response to the growing threat of war. He was able to persuade Congress to pass the Neutrality Act of 1939 which gave aid to any nation fighting the Axis powers. The Lend-Lease Act, which aided Great Britain, was passed in 1941, as was the first peace time draft. In August, Roosevelt met with Prime Minister Winston Churchill on board a naval ship off the coast of Newfoundland. They issued the Atlantic Charter which pledged freedom of governmental choice for all peoples, freedom of trade, and freedom of the seas. Many American isolationists saw these manoeuvres as part of Roosevelt's plan to involve the country in a war that was not an American concern.

Despite Roosevelt's attempts to prepare his nation for war, America was still not ready for the magnitude of the task when the Japanese Imperial Navy struck Pearl Harbor on 7 December 1941. Roosevelt, though, attacked the situation with all his energy. He, Winston Churchill, and Soviet Premier Josef Stalin became the Big Three. A grand strategy was formulated with the number one priority being the defeat of Germany and Italy. At the same time, Japan would be contained from spreading its empire to India and Australia. Once Germany and Italy were defeated, Japan would be conquered. As the war progressed, more and more emphasis was placed on the Pacific campaign and Japan surrendered only a few months after Germany.

During the war, Roosevelt met twice with Churchill and Stalin to discuss war aims. They met at Tehran in 1943 and at Yalta in 1945. By the time of Yalta, Roosevelt was a sick man. He would live only two more months, dying at Warm Springs, Georgia, on 12 April 1945.

The sheer enormity of the Second World War with all its cost and loss of life did not deter Roosevelt from formulating a winning strategy. His efforts resulted in the total mobilization of the nation's economy to a war footing and astounded the Axis powers with its ability to mass produce ships, tanks, and planes. Roosevelt also gave the go-ahead to develop the atomic bomb, thus bringing about the surrender of Japan without an invasion of the home islands. Military experts have estimated that the planned invasion of Japan would have resulted in hundreds of thousands of Allied casualties.

Roosevelt was president when only strong leadership would guide the United States to victory. His leadership re-assured the nation's people at a time they needed it the most and made them realize that they could complete the task before them. This leadership made Franklin D. Roosevelt one of America's greatest presidents.

There are many excellent works on the life and career of Franklin D. Roosevelt. A few recommendations are Joseph Alsop's *FDR, 1882-1945*, Jim Bishop's *FDR's Last Year, April 1944 - April 1945*, James Burns' two-volume set, *Roosevelt: The Lion and the Fox* and *Roosevelt: Soldier of Freedom*, Frank Freidel's four-volume set *Franklin D. Roosevelt* (covering the years 1882 - 1933) and *Franklin D. Roosevelt: Rendezvous with Destiny*, Waldo Heinrich's *Threshold of War*, Eric Larrabee's *Commander-in-Chief*, Warren F. Kimball's *The Juggler*, Joseph Lash's *Eleanor and Franklin* (winner of the 1972 Pulitzer prize for biography), Nathan Miller's *FDR*, Ted Morgan's *FDR, A Biography*, Basil Rauch's *Roosevelt*, Arthur Schlesinger's three-volume set, *The Age of Roosevelt*, Robert Sherwood's *Roosevelt and Hopkins* (winner of the 1949 Pulitzer prize for biography), and Geoffrey's Ward's *Before the Trumpet* and *A First Class Temperament*. Also recommended are Roosevelt's *Public Papers* and any of the volumes that contain his wartime speeches. These works and others are listed in the bibliography that follows.

Bibliography

Abbott, Philip. *The Exemplary Presidency: Franklin D. Roosevelt and the American Political Tradition*. Amherst: University of Massachusetts Press, 1990.

Aga Rossi, Elena. *Origins of the Bipolar World: Roosevelt's Policy Towards Europe and the Soviet Union: A Reevaluation*. Berkeley, CA: Center for German and European Studies, University of California at Berkeley, 1993.

Aglion, Raoul. *Roosevelt and De Gaulle: Allies in Conflict. A Personal Memoir*. New York: The Free Press, 1988.

Alington, Argentine Francis. *Franklin Roosevelt*. London: SCM Press, 1950.

Allen, Dan Charles. "*Franklin D. Roosevelt and the Development of an American Occupation Policy in Europe.*" Ph.D. diss., The Ohio State University, 1976. (DAI, 37:2, 1167A, UMI Order # 7617957)

Alsop, Joseph. *FDR, 1882-1945: A Centenary Remembrance*. New York: Viking Press, 1982.

Asbell, Bernard. *When F.D.R. Died*. New York: Holt, Rinehart & Winston, 1961.

Baciu, Nicholas. *Sell-Out to Stalin: The Tragic Errors of Churchill and Roosevelt. The Untold Story*. New York: Vantage Press, 1984.

Bailey, Thomas A. and Paul B. Ryan. *Hitler vs Roosevelt: The Undeclared Naval War*. New York: The Free Press, 1979.

Baker, Leonard. *Roosevelt and Pearl Harbor*. New York: Macmillan, 1970.

Barnes, Harry Elmer, ed. *Perpetual War for Perpetual Peace: A Critical Examination of the Foreign Policy of Franklin Delano Roosevelt and Its Aftermath*. New York: Greenwood Press, 1969.

_____. *Was Roosevelt Pushed Into War?* Brooklyn, NY: Revisionist Press, 1971.

Barron, Gloria J. *Leadership in Crisis: FDR and the Path to Intervention*. Port Washington, New York: Kennikat Press, 1973.

_____. *"A Study in Presidential Leadership: Franklin D. Roosevelt in the Prewar Years, 1939-1941."* Ph.D. diss., Tufts University, 1971. (DAI, 33:6, 2848A, UMI Order # 7230257)

Bartlett, Bruce R. *Cover-up: The Politics of Pearl Harbor, 1941-1946.* New Rochelle, NY: Arlington House, 1978.

Baur, Brian C. *Franklin D. Roosevelt and the Stamps of the United States, 1933-1945.* Sidney, OH: Linn's Stamp News, 1993.

Beard, Charles A. *President Roosevelt and the Coming of the War, 1941: A Study in Appearances and Realities.* New Haven, CT: Yale University Press, 1948.

Bellush, Bernard. *"Apprenticeship for the Presidency: Franklin D. Roosevelt As Governor of New York."* Ph.D. diss., Columbia University, 1951. (DAI, 11:3, 647, UMI Order # 2521)

Ben-Zvi, Abraham. *The Illusion of Deterrence: The Roosevelt Presidency and the Origins of the Pacific War.* Boulder, CO: Westview Press, 1987.

Benedict, Blaine David. *"Roosevelt and Poland, 1943-1945: Decision-Making As A Choice Among Value-Goals."* Ph.D. diss., University of Pennsylvania, 1977. (DAI, 38:3, 1634A, UMI Order # 7719825)

Bennett, Edward M. *"Franklin D. Roosevelt and Russian-American Relations, 1933-1939."* Ph.D. diss., University of Illinois, 1961. (DAI, 22:10, 3625A, UMI Order # 62561)

_____. *Franklin D. Roosevelt and the Search for Security: American and Soviet Relations, 1933-1939.* Wilmington, DE: Scholarly Resources, 1985.

_____. *Franklin D. Roosevelt and the Search for Victory: American-Soviet Relations, 1939-1945.* Wilmington, DE: SR Books, 1990.

Beschloss, Michael R. *Kennedy and Roosevelt: The Uneasy Alliance.* New York: Norton, 1980.

Bestor, Arthur, and others. *Three Presidents and Their Books. The Reading of: Jefferson, Lincoln, and Roosevelt.* Urbana, IL: University of Illinois Press, 1955.

Bishop, Donald G. *The Roosevelt-Litvinov Agreements: The American View.* Syracuse, NY: Syracuse University Press, 1965.

Bishop, Jim. *FDR's Last Year, April 1944-April 1945.* New York: W. Morrow, 1974.

Blassingame, Wyatt. *Franklin D. Roosevelt, Four Times President.* Champaign, IL: Garrard Pub. Co., 1966. (juvenile)

Brandeis, Erich. *Franklin D. Roosevelt, the Man.* New York: American Offset Corporation, 1936.

Brockway, Fenner. *Will Roosevelt Succeed? A Study of Fascist Tendencies in America.* London: G. Routledge & Sons, 1934.

Brogan, D. W. (Denis William). *The Era of Franklin D. Roosevelt: A Chronicle of the New Deal and Global War*. New Haven: Yale University Press, 1950.

Burke, Robert Louis. "*Franklin D. Roosevelt and the Far East, 1913-1941*." Ph.D. diss., Michigan State University, 1969. (DAI, 30:11, 4905A, UMI Order # 709505)

Burns, James McGregor. *Roosevelt: Soldier of Freedom*. New York: Harcourt, Brace & Jovanovich, 1970.

______. *Roosevelt: The Lion and the Fox*. New York: Harcourt, 1956.

Busch, Noel F. *What Manner of Man?* New York: Harper & Brothers, 1944.

Butler, William Vivian. *Franklin D. Roosevelt: Nothing to Fear But Fear*. London: Hodder & Stoughton, 1982.

Butterfield, Roger. *F.D.R.* New York: Harper and Row, 1963.

Cameron, Turner Christian, Jr. "*The Political Philosophy of Franklin Delano Roosevelt*." Ph.D. diss., Princeton University, 1940. (DAI, 12:3, 326, UMI Order # 2926)

Carlson, Earland Irving. "*Franklin D. Roosevelt's Fight for the Presidential Nomination, 1928-1932*." Ph.D. diss., University of Illinois, 1955. (DAI, 16:2, 323, UMI Order # 15190)

Carter, Maud Elise. *Franklin Roosevelt*. Edited by E. M. Atwood. London: Longmans, 1960.

Cashman, Sean Dennis. *America, Roosevelt, and World War II*. New York: New York University Press, 1989.

Cavanah, Frances. *Triumphant Adventure: The Story of Franklin Delano Roosevelt*. Chicago: Rand McNally, 1964.

Coady, Joseph William. "*Franklin D. Roosevelt's Early Washington Years, (1913-1920)*." Ph.D. diss., St. John's University, 1968. (DAI, 30:3, 1103A, UMI Order # 6914068)

Cole, Wayne S. *Determinism and American Foreign Relations During the Franklin D. Roosevelt Era*. Lanham, MD: University Press of America, 1995.

______. *Roosevelt and the Isolationists, 1932-1945*. Lincoln, NE: University of Nebraska Press, 1983.

Collier, Peter with David Horowitz. *The Roosevelts: An American Saga*. New York: Simon & Schuster, 1994.

Cook, Fred J. *Franklin D. Roosevelt: Valiant Leader*. New York: Putnam, 1968. (juvenile)

Costello, John. *Days of Infamy: MacArthur, Roosevelt, Churchill; The Shocking Truth Revealed*. New York: Pocket Books, 1994.

Crane, Milton, ed. *The Roosevelt Era*. New York: Boni & Gaer, 1947.

Crocker, George N. *Roosevelt's Road to Russia*. Chicago: H. Regnery, 1959.

Cross, Robin. *Roosevelt and the Americans at War*. New York: Gloucester Press, 1990. (juvenile)

Dall, Curtis B. *FDR: My Exploited Father-in-Law*. Tulsa, OK: Christian Crusade Publications, 1967.

Dallak, Robert. *Franklin D. Roosevelt and American Foreign Policy, 1932-1945*. New York: Oxford University Press, 1979.

______, comp. *The Roosevelt Diplomacy and World War II*. New York: Holt, Rinehart & Winston, 1970.

Daniels, Jonathan. *White House Witness, 1942-1945*. Garden City, NY: Doubleday, 1975.

Davis, Kenneth S. *FDR: Into the Storm, 1937-1940: A History*. New York: Random House, 1993.

______. *FDR: The Beckoning of Destiny, 1882-1928*. New York: G. P. Putnam's Sons, 1971.

______. *FDR, The New Deal Years, 1933-1937*. New York: Random House, 1986.

______. *FDR, The New York Years, 1928-1933*. New York: Random House, 1985.

______. *Invincible Summer: An Intimate Portrait of the Roosevelts. Based on the Recollections of Marion Dickerman*. New York: Atheneum, 1974.

De Cola, Thomas Guido. "*Roosevelt and Mussolini: The Critical Years, 1938-1941*." Ph.D. diss., Kent State University, 1967. (DAI, 28:11, 4568A, UMI Order # 686205)

Delano, Daniel W., Jr. *Franklin Roosevelt and the Delano Influence*. Pittsburgh: J.S. Nudi Publications, 1946.

Devaney, John. *Franklin Delano Roosevelt, President*. New York: Walker & Co., 1987.

Divine, Robert A. *Roosevelt and World War II*. Baltimore: Johns Hopkins Press, 1969.

Dows, Olin. *Franklin Roosevelt at Hyde Park*. New York: American Artists Group, 1949.

Dwan, John Edmund II. "*Franklin D. Roosevelt and the Revolution in the Strategy of National Security: Foreign Policy and Military Planning Before Pearl Harbor (Hawaii)*." Ph.D. diss., Yale University, 1954. (DAI, 44:3, 859A, UMI Order # DA8313251)

Edmonds, Robin. *The Big Three: Churchill, Roosevelt and Stalin in Peace and War*. New York: Norton, 1990.

Eggleston, George T. *Roosevelt, Churchill and the World War II Opposition: A Revisionist Autobiography*. Old Greenwich, CT: Devin-Adair, 1979.

Einaudi, Mario. *The Roosevelt Revolution*. New York: Harcourt Brace, 1959.

Epstein, Sam and Beryl Epstein. *The Picture Life of Franklin Delano Roosevelt*. New York: F. Watts, 1968.

Eyre, James Kline. *The Roosevelt-MacArthur Conflict*. 2nd ed. Chambersburg, PA: Printed for AMG Publications by the Craft Press, 1965.

Ezickson, Aaron Jacob. *Roosevelt Album: The Highlights in the Life and Work of the 32nd President of the United States, Franklin Delano Roosevelt*. New York: Knickerbocker Publishing Company, 1945.

Faber, Doris. *Franklin Delano Roosevelt*. New York: Abelard-Schuman, 1974. (juvenile)

Farley, James Aloysius. *Jim Farley's Story: The Roosevelt Years*. New York: Whittlesley House, 1948.

Farnham, Barbara Rearden. "*Value Conflict in Political Decision-Making: Franklin D. Roosevelt and the Munich Crisis, 1938*." Ph.D. diss., Columbia University, 1991. (DAI, 52:11, 4081A, UMI Order # DA9209818)

Farr, Finis. *FDR*. New Rochelle, NY: Arlington House, 1972.

Fay, Bernard. *Roosevelt and His America*. Translated from the French by Winifred Ray. Boston: Little, Brown & Co., 1933.

Fehrenbach, T. R. *F.D.R.'s Undeclared War, 1939-1941*. New York: David McKay Co., 1967.

Feinberg, Barbara Silberdick. *Franklin D. Roosevelt: Gallant President*. New York: Lothrop, Lee & Shepard Books, 1981. (juvenile)

Feingold, Henry L. *The Politics of Rescue: The Roosevelt Administration and the Holocaust, 1938-1945*. New Brunswick, NJ: Rutgers University Press, 1970.

Feis, Herbert. *Churchill, Roosevelt, Stalin: The War They Waged and the Peace They Sought*. 2nd ed. Princeton, NJ: Princeton University Press, 1967.

Ferdon, Nona Stinson. "*Franklin D. Roosevelt: A Psychological Interpretation of His Childhood and Youth*." Ph.D. diss., University of Hawaii, 1971. (DAI, 32:6, 3202A, UMI Order # 72291

Fish, Hamilton. *FDR: The Other Side of the Coin. How We Were Tricked Into World War II*. New York: Vantage Press, 1976.

______. *Tragic Deception: FDR and America's Involvement in World War II*. Old Greenwich, CT: Devin-Adair, 1983.

Flynn, George Q. *Roosevelt and Romanism: Catholics and American Diplomacy, 1937-1945*. Westport, CT: Greenwood Press, 1976.

Flynn, John Thomas. *Country Squire in the White House*. New York: Doubleday, Doran & Co., 1940.

______. *The Roosevelt Myth*. Rev. ed. New York: Devin-Adair Co., 1956.

Frank, Catherine M. "*Franklin D. Roosevelt and His Conference Advisors: The Determination of the Influence of Certain Men and Institutions on Franklin D. Roosevelt from August 1941 to April 1945, Particularly in Making Certain Conference Decisions and Agreements*." Ph.D. diss., Fordham University, 1955. (Not available from UMI)

Freedman, Russell. *Franklin Delano Roosevelt*. New York: Clarion Books, 1990. (juvenile)

Freidel, Frank Burt. *Franklin D. Roosevelt*. 4 volumes. Boston: Little Brown, 1952-1956 and 1974.

______. *Franklin D. Roosevelt: A Rendezvous with Destiny*. Boston: Little, Brown, 1990.

Gallagher, Hugh Gregory. *FDR's Splendid Deception*. New York: Dodd, Mead & Co., 1985.

Geddes, Donald Porter, ed. *Franklin Delano Roosevelt: A Memorial*. New York: Pocket Books, 1945.

Gelman, Irwin F. *Roosevelt and Batista: Good Neighbor Diplomacy in Cuba, 1933-1945*. Albuquerque, NM: University of New Mexico Press, 1973.

Gerberding, William P. "*Franklin D. Roosevelt's Conception of the Soviet Union in World Politics*." Ph.D. diss., The University of Chicago, 1959. (Not available from UMI)

Giangreco, D. M. *Roosevelt, de Gaulle, and the Posts: Franco-American War Relations Viewed Through Their Effects on the French Postal System, 1942-1944*. Bonita, CA: Joseph V. Bush Inc., 1986.

Gies, Joseph. *Franklin D. Roosevelt: Portrait of a President*. Garden City, NY: Doubleday, 1971.

Goldberg, Richard Thayer. *The Making of Franklin D. Roosevelt: Triumph over Disability*. Cambridge, MA: Abt Books, 1981.

Goodwin, Doris Kearns. *No Ordinary Time: Franklin and Eleanor Roosevelt. The Home Front in World War II*. New York: Simon & Schuster, 1994.

Gordenker, Leon, and others. *FDR's Place in Past and Present: An Evaluation Forty Years After His Death. Lectures*. Middelburg Netherlands: Roosevelt Study Center, 1986.

Gould, Jean. *A Good Fight: The Story of FDR's Conquest of Polio*. New York: Dodd, Mead, 1960.

Graebner, Norman A. *Roosevelt and the Search for a European Policy, 1937-1939: An Inaugural Lecture Delivered Before the University of Oxford on 21 May 1979*. New York: Oxford University Press, 1980.

Graham, Otis L. Jr., and Meghan Robinson Wander. *Franklin D. Roosevelt: His Life and Times, An Encyclopedic View*. Boston: G. K. Hall, 1985.

Greenblatt, Miriam. *Franklin D. Roosevelt: 32nd President of The United States*. Ada, OK: Garrett Educational, 1989. (juvenile)

Greer, Thomas H. *What Roosevelt Thought: The Social and Political Ideas of Franklin D. Roosevelt*. East Lansing, MI: Michigan State University Press, 1958.

Guerrant, Edward U. *Herbert Hoover, Franklin Roosevelt: Comparisons and Contrasts*. Cleveland: H. Allen, 1960.

Gunther, John. *Roosevelt in Retrospect: A Profile in History*. New York: Harper, 1950.

Gurney, Gene and Clare Gurney. *FDR and Hyde Park*. New York: Watts, 1970.

Hacker, Jeffrey H. *Franklin D. Roosevelt*. New York: F. Watts, 1983. (juvenile)

Halasz, Nicholas. *Roosevelt Through Foreign Eyes*. Princeton, NJ: Van Nostrand, 1961.

Halter, Ernest J. *Collecting First Editions of Franklin Roosevelt: Contributions to an FDR Bibliography*. Chicago: Privately published for subscribers, 1949.

Harper, John Lamberton. *American Visions of Europe: Franklin D. Roosevelt, George F. Kennan, and Dean G. Acheson*. New York: Cambridge University Press, 1994.

Harrelson, Elmer Harvey. *"Roosevelt and the United States Army, 1937-1940: A Study in Challenge-Response."* Ph.D. diss., University of New Mexico, 1971. (DAI, 32:7, 3920A, UMI Order # 723992)

Harrity, Richard and Ralph G. Martin. *The Human Side of F.D.R.* New York: Duell, Sloan & Pearce, 1960.

Hassett, William D. *Off the Record with F.D.R., 1942-1945*. New Brunswick, NJ: Rutgers University Press, 1958.

Hatch, Alden. *Citizen of the World, Franklin D. Roosevelt: An Informal Biography*. London: Skeffington, 1948.

Havas, Laslo. *The Long Jump. (Or the 1943 Plot to Assassinate Churchill, Roosevelt and Stalin)*. Translated by Kathleen Szasz. London: Spearman, 1967.

Heardon, Patrick J. *Roosevelt Confronts Hitler: America's Entry into World War II*. De Kalb, IL: Northern Illinois University Press, 1987.

Heinrichs, Waldo H. *Threshold of War: Franklin D. Roosevelt and American Entry Into World War II*. New York: Oxford University Press, 1988.

Herder, John Hart. "*A Human Relations Study of Roosevelt and Mussolini: A Comparative Study of the Principles and Practices of Democratic Conference Leadership as Represented by Franklin Roosevelt and of Autocratic Conference Leadership as Represented by Benito Mussolini.*" Ph.D. diss., New York University, 1954. (DAI, 14:10, 1830, UMI Order # 9312)

Herzstein, Robert Erwin. *Roosevelt and Hitler: Prelude to War*. New York: Paragon House, 1989.

Hickok, Lorena A. *The Story of Franklin D. Roosevelt*. New York: Grosset & Dunlap, 1956. (juvenile)

Hiebert, Roselyn and Ray Eldon Hiebert. *Franklin Delano Roosevelt: President for the People*. New York: F. Watts, 1968.

High, Stanley. *Roosevelt-And Then?* New York: Harper & Brothers, 1937.

Hill, C. P. (Charles Peter). *Franklin Roosevelt*. London: Oxford University Press, 1966.

Hoggan, David L. *President Roosevelt and the Origins of the 1939 War*. Brooklyn, NY: Revisionist Press, 1983.

Hough, Richard. *The Greatest Crusade: Roosevelt, Churchill, and the Naval Wars*. New York: Morrow, 1986.

Hughes, T. W. *Forty Years of Roosevelt*. Detroit: The Author, 1944.

Hurstfield, Julian G. *America and the French Nation, 1939-1945*. Chapel Hill, NC: University of North Carolina Press, 1986.

Israel, Fred L. *Franklin Delano Roosevelt*. New York: Chelsea House, 1985. (juvenile)

Italia, Bob. *The Story of Franklin D. Roosevelt*. Edina, MN: Abdo & Daughters, 1990. (juvenile)

Izek, Hersch. "*Roosevelt and the Polish Question, 1941-1945.*" Ph.D. diss., University of Minnesota, 1980. (DAI, 41:5, 2252A, UMI Order # 8025458)

Jahns, Robert L. *Franklin Roosevelt and General Hap Arnold: The Statesman and the Strategist Build an Air Force*. Carlisle Barracks, PA: U.S. Army War College, 1990.

Johnson, Gerald W. *Franklin D. Roosevelt: Portrait of A Great Man*. New York: Morrow, 1967.

_____. *Roosevelt: Dictator or Democrat?* New York: Harper & Brothers Publishers, 1941.

Josephson, Emanuel Mann. *The Strange Death of Franklin D. Roosevelt: History of the Roosevelt-Delano Dynasty, America's Royal Family.* New York: Chedney Press, 1948.

Kanawada, Leo V., Jr. *Franklin D. Roosevelt's Diplomacy and American Catholics, Italians, and Jews.* Ann Arbor, MI: UMI Research Press, 1982.

Kelly, Regina Z. *Franklin Delano Roosevelt.* Chicago: Follett Publishers, 1966. (juvenile)

Kent, Tyler. *Roosevelt Legacy and the Kent Case.* Brooklyn, NY: Revisionist Press, 1983.

Kimball, Warren F., ed. *Franklin D. Roosevelt and the World Crisis, 1937-1945.* Lexington, MA: D. C. Heath, 1973.

______. *The Juggler: Franklin Roosevelt as Wartime Statesman.* Princeton, NJ: Princeton University Press, 1991.

Kingdon, Frank. *"That Man" in the White House: You and Your President.* New York: Arco Publishing Co., 1944.

Kinnaird, Clark, ed. *The Real F.D.R.: An Intimate Closeup in Pictures and Anecdotes with a Factual Record of His Life and Works.* New York: Citadel Press, 1945.

Kinsella, William E., Jr. *Leadership in Isolation: FDR and the Origins of the Second World War.* Boston: G. K. Hall, 1978.

Kleeman, Rita Halle. *Young Franklin Roosevelt.* New York: Messner, 1946.

Kleiman, Max, ed. *Franklin Delano Roosevelt: The Tribute of the Synagogue.* New York: Bloch Publishing Co., 1946.

Knowles, Archibald Campbell. *A Rendezvous with Destiny.* Philadelphia: David McKay Co., 1946.

Koenig, Louis William. *The Presidency and the Crisis: Powers of the Office from the Invasion of Poland to Pearl Harbor.* New York: Morningside Heights, King's Crown Press, 1944.

Kyvig, David E. *FDR's America.* Saint Charles, MO: Forum Press, 1976.

Langston, Thomas. *Ideologies and Presidents: From the New Deal to the Reagan Revolution.* Baltimore: Johns Hopkins University Press, 1992.

Larrabee, Eric. *Commander-in-Chief: Franklin Delano Roosevelt, His Lieutenants, and Their War.* New York: Simon & Schuster, 1987.

Larsen, Rebecca. *Franklin D. Roosevelt: Man of Destiny.* New York: Franklin Watts, 1991. (juvenile)

Lash, Joseph P. *Eleanor and Franklin: The Story of Their Relationship Based on Eleanor Roosevelt's Private Papers.* New York: Norton, 1971.

______. *Roosevelt and Churchill, 1939-1941: The Partnership That Saved the West*. New York: Norton, 1976.

Lasky, Joseph. *Our President, Franklin Delano Roosevelt: A Biography*. New York: Walters & Mahon, 1933.

Lebeau, John Joseph. "*Civilian Military-Political Leadership in Wartime: Roosevelt, the Military, and the Second Front Decisions*." Ph.D. diss., University of Massachusetts, 1978. (DAI, 39:1, 446A, UMI Order # 7810730)

Lester, DeeGee. *Roosevelt Research: Collections from the Study of Theodore, Franklin, and Eleanor*. Westport, CT: Greenwood Press, 1992.

Leuchtenburg, William E., ed. *Franklin D. Roosevelt: A Profile*. New York: Harper & Row, 1963.

______. *In the Shadow of FDR: From Harry Truman to Bill Clinton*. 2nd ed., rev. and newly updated. Ithaca, NY: Cornell University Press, 1993.

Leutze, James Richard. "*If Britain Should Fall: Roosevelt and Churchill and British-American Naval Relations, 1938-1940*." Ph.D. diss., Duke University, 1970. (DAI, 31:10, 5325A, UMI Order # 7110390)

Lewis, John Menzies. "*Franklin Roosevelt and United States Strategy in World War II*." Ph.D. diss., Cornell University, 1979. (DAI, 39:11, 6940A, UMI Order # 7910853)

Lindley, Christopher. "*Franklin D. Roosevelt and the Politics of Isolationism, 1932-1936*." Ph.D. diss., Cornell University, 1963. (DAI, 24:9, 3712, UMI Order # 643683)

Lindley, Ernest K. *Franklin D. Roosevelt: A Career in Progressive Democracy*. New York: Blue Ribbon Books, 1934.

Link, Arthur S. and William B. Catton. *The Age of Franklin D. Roosevelt, 1921-1945*. 4th ed. New York: Knopf, 1973. Distributed by Random House.

Lippman, Theo, Jr. *The Squire of Warm Springs: F.D.R. in Georgia, 1924-1945*. Chicago: Playboy Press, 1977. Trade distribution by Simon & Schuster.

Looker, Earle. *This Man Roosevelt*. New York: Brewer, Warren & Putnam, 1932.

Lorant, Stefan. *FDR: A Pictorial Biography*. New York: Simon & Schuster, 1950.

Lowitz, Sadyebeth. *Young America's Story of Franklin D. Roosevelt, Man of Action*. Garden City, NY: Doubleday, Doran & Company, 1933.

Ludwig, Emil. *Roosevelt, a Study in Fortune and Power*. New York: Garden City Publishing Co., 1941.

Mackenzie, Compton. *Mr. Roosevelt*. New York: E. P. Dutton, 1944.

Maine, Basil. *Franklin Roosevelt, His Life and Achievement*. London: Nicholson & Watson, 1942.

Maney, Patrick J. *The Roosevelt Presence: A Biography of FDR*. New York: Twayne Publishers, 1992.

Manser, Richard L. *"Roosevelt and China: From Cairo to Yalta."* Ph.D. diss., Temple University, 1987. (DAI, 48:4, 1005A, UMI Order # DA8716382)

Marks, Frederick W., III. *Wind Over Sand: The Diplomacy of Franklin Roosevelt*. Athens, GA: University of Georgia Press, 1988.

Matloff, Maurice. *Mr. Roosevelt's Three Wars: FDR as War Leader*. Colorado Springs, CO: United States Air Force Academy, 1964.

McIntire, Ross T. in collaboration with George Creel. *White House Physician*. New York: G. P. Putnam's Sons, 1946.

McKown, Robin. *Roosevelt's America*. New York: Grosset & Dunlap, 1962. (juvenile)

Merriam, Eve. *The Real Book About Franklin D. Roosevelt*. Garden City, NY: Garden City Books, 1952. (juvenile)

Messer, Robert L. *The End of an Alliance: James F. Brynes, Roosevelt, Truman, and the Origins of the Cold War*. Chapel Hill, NC: University of North Carolina Press, 1982.

Miller, Nathan. *FDR, An Intimate History*. Garden City, NY: Doubleday, 1983.

______. *The Roosevelt Chronicles*. Garden City, NY: Doubleday, 1979.

Minnen, Charles A. Van and John F. Sears. *FDR and His Contemporaries: Foreign Perceptions of An American President*. New York: St. Martin's Press, 1991.

Montgomery, Mabel. *A Courageous Conquest: The Life Story of Franklin Delano Roosevelt*. Edited by Henry I. Christ. New York: Globe Book Co., 1951.

Moody, Frank Kennon. *"F.D.R. and His Neighbors: A Study of the Relationship Between Franklin D. Roosevelt and the Residents of Dutchess County."* Ph.D. diss., State University of New York at Albany, 1981. (DAI, 42:12, 5223A, UMI Order # DA8206805)

Mooney, Booth. *Roosevelt and Rayburn: A Political Partnership*. Philadelphia: Lippincott, 1971.

Morgan, Ted. *FDR: A Biography*. New York: Simon & Schuster, 1985.

Mortiner, Edward. *The World That FDR Built: Vision and Reality*. New York: Scribner's, 1988.

Morton, H. C. (Henry Canova). *Atlantic Meeting: An Account of Mr. Churchill's Voyage on H.M.S. Prince of Wales, in August 1941 and the Conference with President Roosevelt Which Resulted in the Atlantic Charter*. New York: Dodd, Mead & Co., 1943.

Moscow, Warren. *Roosevelt and Willkie*. Englewood Cliffs, NJ: Prentice-Hall, 1968.

Nadeau, Remi A. *Stalin, Churchill and Roosevelt Divide Europe*. New York: Praeger, 1990.

Nash, Gerald D., comp. *Franklin Delano Roosevelt*. Englewood Cliffs, NJ: Prentice-Hall, 1967.

Nave, Eric and James Rusbridger. *Betrayal at Pearl Harbor: How Churchill Lured Roosevelt Into World War II*. New York: Summit Books, 1991.

Nesbitt, Henrietta. *White House Diary*. Garden City, NY: Doubleday, 1948.

Nevins, Allan. *The Place of Franklin D. Roosevelt in History*. New York: Humanities Press, 1965.

Nisbet, Robert A. *Roosevelt and Stalin: The Failed Courtship*. Washington, DC: Regnery Gateway, 1988.

Nisenson, Samuel. *From Boyhood to President with Franklin Delano Roosevelt*. Cleveland: The World Syndicate Publishing Co., 1934.

Notaro, Carmen Anthony. "*Franklin D. Roosevelt and the American Communists: Peacetime Relations, 1932-1941*." Ph.D. diss., State University of New York at Buffalo, 1969. (DAI, 31:4, 1733A, UMI Order # 7017353)

O'Callaghan, D. B. (Dennis Brynley). *Roosevelt and the United States*. London: Longmans, 1966.

O'Connor, Edmund. *Roosevelt*. St. Paul, MN: Greenhaven Press, 1980. (juvenile)

O'Connor, Raymond G. *Diplomacy for Victory: FDR and Unconditional Surrender*. New York: Norton, 1971.

O'Neill, Herbert Charles. *Men of Destiny: Being Studies of the Four Who Rode the War and Made This Precarious Landfall*. London: Phoenix House, 1953.

Osinski, Alice K. *Franklin D. Roosevelt: Thirty-second President of the United States*. Chicago: Children's Press, 1987. (juvenile)

Parks, Lillian Rogers. *The Roosevelts: A Family in Turmoil*. Englewood Cliffs, NJ: Prentice-Hall, 1981.

Parrish, Thomas. *Roosevelt and Marshall: Partners in Politics and War*. New York: William Morrow, 1989.

Peare, Catherine Owens. *The FDR Story*. New York: Thomas Y. Crowell, 1962. (juvenile)

Perkins, Dexter. *The New Age of Franklin Roosevelt, 1932-1945.* Chicago: University of Chicago Press, 1957.

Perkins, Frances. *The Roosevelt I Knew.* New York: Viking Press, 1946.

Perlmutter, Amos. *FDR & Stalin: A Not So Grand Alliance, 1943-1945.* Columbia: University of Missouri Press, 1993.

Peterson, Hans Joachim. "*The Post-War German View of Franklin Delano Roosevelt.*" Ph.D. diss., University of Denver, 1966. (DAI, 27:6, 1891A, UMI Order # 6611770)

Pike, Fredrick B. *FDR's Good Neighbor Policy: Sixty Years of Generally Gentle Chaos.* Austin: University of Texas Press, 1995.

Pound, Ezra. *America, Roosevelt and the Causes of the Present War.* London: P. Russell, 1951.

Range, Willard. "*Franklin D. Roosevelt's Theory of International Relations.*" Ph.D. diss., The University of North Carolina at Chapel Hill, 1958. (DAI, 19:8, 2128, UMI Order # 585963)

______. *Franklin D. Roosevelt's World Order.* Athens, GA: University of Georgia Press, 1959.

Rauch, Basil. *Roosevelt: From Munich to Pearl Harbor. A Study in the Creation of A Foreign Policy.* New York: Barnes and Noble, 1967.

Rawcliffe, Michael. *The Roosevelt File.* London: Batsford Academic and Educational, 1980. (juvenile)

Ray, John Philip. *Roosevelt and Kennedy.* London: Heinemann Educational, 1970.

Reilly, Michael F. as told to William J. Slocum. *Reilly of the White House.* New York: Simon & Schuster, 1947.

Reynolds, Ernest Edwin. *Four Modern Statesmen: Winston S. Churchill, Franklin D. Roosevelt, Joseph Stalin, Chiang Kai-shek.* New York: Oxford University Press, 1944.

Richardson, Stewart, ed. *The Secret History of World War II: The Ultra-Secret Wartime Letters and Cables of Roosevelt, Stalin, and Churchill.* New York: Richardson & Steirman, 1986.

Roberts, Elizabeth Mauchline. *Roosevelt.* New York: Roy Publishers, 1970. (juvenile)

Robinson, Edgar E. *Roosevelt Leadership, 1933-1945.* Philadelphia: Lippincott, 1954.

______. *They Voted for Roosevelt: The Presidential Vote, 1932-1944.* Stanford, CA: Stanford University Press, 1947.

Rock, William R. *Chamberlain and Roosevelt: A British Foreign Policy and the United States, 1937-1940.* Columbus: The Ohio State University Press, 1988.

Rollins, Alfred B., ed. *Franklin D. Roosevelt and the Age of Action.* New York: Dell Publishing Co., 1960.

______. *Roosevelt and Howe*. New York: Knopf, 1962.

Roosevelt, Eleanor. *The Autobiography of Eleanor Roosevelt*. New York: Harper, 1961.

______. *This I Remember*. New York: Harper, 1949.

Roosevelt, Elliott. *As He Saw It*. New York: Duell, Sloan & Pearce, 1946.

______ and James Brough. *A Rendezvous with Destiny: The Roosevelts of the White House*. New York: Putnam, 1975.

______. *An Untold Story: The Roosevelts of Hyde Park*. New York: Putnam's Sons, 1973.

Roosevelt, Franklin D. *Addresses of Franklin D. Roosevelt and Winston Churchill*. Washington: U. S. Government Printing Office, 1942.

______. *Ah, That Voice: The Fireside Chats of Franklin Delano Roosevelt*. Compiled by Kenneth Yeilding and Paul Carlson. Odessa, TX: John Ben Shepperd, Jr. Library of the Presidents, Presidential Museum, 1974.

______. *The American Way: Selections from the Public Addresses and Papers of Franklin D. Roosevelt*. Edited by Dogobert D. Runes. New York: Philosophical Library, 1944.

______. *As FDR Said: A Treasury of His Speeches, Conversations and Writings*. Compiled by Frank Kingdon. New York: Duell, Sloan & Pearce, 1950.

______. *The Bible and the Nations: Excerpts from Letters and Addresses of Franklin Delano Roosevelt*. New York: American Bible Society, 1945.

______ and Winston Churchill. *Churchill and Roosevelt: The Complete Correspondence*. 3 volumes. Edited with commentary by Warren F. Kimball. Princeton, NJ: Princeton University Press, 1984.

______. *Complete Presidential Press Conferences of Franklin D. Roosevelt, (1933-1945)*. 12 Annual Volumes. New York: Da Capo Press, 1973.

______. *Development of United States Foreign Policy. Addresses and Messages of Franklin D. Roosevelt, Compiled from Official Sources, Intended to Present the Chronological Development of the Foreign Policy of the United States from the Announcement of the Good Neighbor Policy in 1933, Including the War Declarations*. Washington: Government Printing Office, 1942.

______. *Diary & Itineraries, 1933-1945*. New York: Clearwater, 1984. (14 microfiches. Originals held at FDR Library, Hyde Park, NY.)

______. *Essential Franklin Delano Roosevelt*. Edited by John Gabriel Hunt. New York: Gramercy Books, 1995.

_____ and Adolf Hitler. *Exchange of Communications Between the President of the United States and the Chancellor of the German Reich, April 1939*. New York: German Library of Information, 1939.

_____. *Executive Orders and Administrative Material: Covering, Important Presidential Proclamations, Selected Executive Orders from 1932 to November 1, 1944, Analysis and Comments on United States Boards and Agencies, Selected Administrative Rulings and Regulations, Abolished Agencies, Tables of Public Acts, Keyed to Federal Code Annotated, Table of Acts by Popular Names, Index*. Compiled and edited by the publisher's editorial staff. Indianapolis, IN: Bobbs-Merrill, 1945.

_____. *F.D.R. Columnist: The Uncollected Columns of Franklin D. Roosevelt*. Edited by Donald Scott Carmichael. Chicago: Pellegrini and Cudahy, 1947.

_____. *F.D.R.: His Personal Letters*. 4 volumes. Edited by Elliott Roosevelt, and others. New York: Duell, Sloan & Pearce, 1947-1950.

_____. *F.D.R. Lives On: The Great Speeches of President Roosevelt*. Edited by Michael B. Landis. Washington: Presidential Publishers, 1947.

_____. *The F.D.R. Memoirs*. As written by Bernard Abell. Garden City, NY: Doubleday, 1973.

_____. *FDR's Fireside Chats*. Edited by Russell D. Buhite and David W. Levy. Norman: University of Oklahoma Press, 1992.

_____. *For the President: Personal and Secret. Correspondence Between Franklin D. Roosevelt and William C. Bullitt*. Boston: Houghton Mifflin, 1972.

_____. *Franklin D. Roosevelt and Foreign Affairs*. Edited by Edgar B. Nixon. Volumes 1-3. Cambridge, MA: Harvard University Press, 1969. Volumes 4-17. New York: Clearwater Publishing Co., 1979.

_____. *Franklin D. Roosevelt: The Man, the Myth, the Era, 1882-1945*. Edited by Herbert A. Rosenbaum and Elizabeth Bartelme. New York: Greenwood Press, 1987.

_____. *Franklin D. Roosevelt: Usher Books*. 64 microfiche. Calendar appointments covering the FDR presidency. New York: Clearwater Pub. Co., 1984.

_____. *Franklin D. Roosevelt's Own Story. Told in His Own Words from His Private and Public Papers*. Selected by Donald Day. Boston: Little, Brown, 1951.

_____. *Franklin Delano Roosevelt: Selections from His Writings*. Edited by Philip S. Foner. New York: International Publishers, 1947.

______. *Franklin Delano Roosevelt, 1882-1945: Chronology, Documents, Bibliographical Aids*. Edited by Howard F. Bremer. Dobbs Ferry, NY: Oceana Publications, 1971.

______. *The Great Betrayal, President Roosevelt's Report on Japanese Aggression*. Washington, DC: American Council on Public Affairs, 1942.

______. *A Guide to the Map Room Messages of President Roosevelt (1939-1945): The Presidential Diaries of Henry Morganthau, Jr. (1938-1945)*. Compiled by John Gibson. Frederick, MD: University Publications of America, 1981.

______. *The Inaugural Addresses of Franklin D. Roosevelt, President of the United States*. Worcester: A. J. St. Onge, 1945.

______. *Index to the Complete Recorded Speeches of Franklin Delano Roosevelt: 278 Speeches Dating from 1920 to 1945*. North Hollywood, CA: n.p., 1974.

______. *The Living Words of F. D. Roosevelt*. Bombay: Thacker & Co. Ltd., 1946.

______. *Log of the President's Inspection Tour, 13-29 April, 1943*. n.p., 1943.

______. *Log of the President's Inspection Trip to the Pacific, July-August 1944*. n.p., 1944.

______. *Log of the President's Trip to Africa and the Middle East, November-December 1943*. n.p., 1943.

______. *Log of the President's Visit to Canada, 16 August, 1943 to 26 August 1943: 17-24 August, "Quadrant" Conference at Quebec, 25 August, Visit to Ottawa*. n.p., 1943.

______. *Log of the Trip of the President to the Casablanca Conference, 9-31 January 1943*. n.p., 1943.

______. *Map Room Files of President Roosevelt, 1939-1945. Map Room Army and Navy Messages, December 1941-May 1942*. Project Coordinator, Robert E. Lester. Bethesda, MD: University Publications of America, 1991. (microform)

______. *Map Room Files of President Roosevelt, 1939-1945. Map Room Conference and Special Files, 1942-1945*. Project Coordinator, Robert E. Lester. Bethesda, MD: University Publications of America, 1991. (microform)

______. *Map Room Files of President Roosevelt, 1939-1945. Map Room Military Subject Files, 1941-1945*. Project Coordinator, Robert E. Lester. Bethesda, MD: University Publications of America, 1991. (microfilm)

______. *Map Room Messages of President Roosevelt, 1939-1945.* Edited by Paul Keraris. Frederick, MD: University Publications of America, 1984. (9 microfilm reels)

______. *Memorable Quotations of Franklin D. Roosevelt.* Compiled by E. Taylor Parks and Lois F. Parks. New York: Crowell, 1965.

______ and Winston Churchill. *The Messages Between Franklin D. Roosevelt and Winston S. Churchill, 1939-1945: And Related Materials in the Franklin D. Roosevelt Library.* 6 reels of 35mm film. National Historical Publications Commission, Microform Publications Program, 1973.

______. *My Friends: Twenty-eight History Making Speeches.* Edited by Edward H. Kavinoky and Julian Park. Buffalo: Foster & Stewart, 1945.

______. *National Defense.* Washington: American Council on Public Affairs, 1940.

______. *Nothing to Fear: The Selected Addresses of Franklin Delano Roosevelt, 1932-1945.* Boston: Houghton Mifflin, 1946.

______. *On War Against Japan: Franklin D. Roosevelt's "Day of Infamy" Address of 1941.* Washington, DC: National Archives and Records Administration, 1988.

______. *Our Democracy in Action: The Philosophy of Franklin D. Roosevelt, as Found in His Speeches, Messages and Other Public Papers.* Washington, DC: National Home Library Foundation, 1940.

______. *"Our Nation at War": Log of the President's Inspection Trip, 1 September - 1 October 1942.* n.p., 1942.

______. *Our Sons Will Triumph: From the D-Day Prayer of the Commander in Chief of the Armed Forces of the United States, Franklin Delano Roosevelt, June Sixth, 1944.* Arranged by Jack Dixon. New York: Thomas Y. Crowell, 1944.

______. *Pearl Harbor: Speeches Before and After Pearl Harbor by Franklin Delano Roosevelt.* New York: Shaman & Schlick, 1946.

______. *President Franklin D. Roosevelt's Office Files, 1933-1945.* Project Coordinator, Robert E. Lester. Bethesda, MD: University Publications of America, 1990. (microform)

______. *President's Log for the 1944 Quebec Conference (Octagon) September 9-21, 1944.* n.p., 1944.

______. *The President's Trip to the Crimea Conference and Great Bitter Lake, Egypt, January 22 to February 28, 1945.* n.p., 1945.

______. *The Public Papers and Addresses of Franklin D. Roosevelt.* Volumes 1-9. New York: Random House, 1938. Volumes 10-13. New York: Macmillan, 1950.

_____. *Rendezvous with Destiny: Addresses and Opinions of Franklin Delano Roosevelt*. Selected and arranged by J. B. S. Hardman. New York: Dryden Press, 1944.

_____ and Winston Churchill. *Roosevelt and Churchill: Their Secret Wartime Correspondence*. Edited by Francis L. Loewenheim, and others. New York: Saturday Review Press, 1975.

_____. *Roosevelt and Daniels: A Friendship in Politics*. Edited by Carroll Kilpatrick. Chapel Hill, NC: University of North Carolina Press, 1952.

_____. *Roosevelt and Frankfurter: Their Correspondence, 1928-1945*. Annotated by Max Freedman. Boston: Little, Brown, 1967.

_____. *Roosevelt Letters, Being the Personal Correspondence of Franklin Delano Roosevelt*. 3 volumes. Edited by Elliott Roosevelt. London: G. G. Harrap, 1949-1952.

_____. *The Roosevelt Reader: Selected Speeches, Messages, Press Conferences and Letters of Franklin D. Roosevelt*. Edited with an introduction by Basil Rauch. New York: Holt, Rinehart & Winston, 1957.

_____. *Roosevelt's Foreign Policy, 1933-1941. Franklin D. Roosevelt's Unedited Speeches and Messages*. Compiled and collated by Douglas Lurton. New York: W. Funk, Inc., 1942.

_____. *Selected Speeches, Messages, Press Conferences, and Letters*. Edited by Basil Rauch. New York: Rinehart, 1957.

_____. *A Selection of President Franklin D. Roosevelt's Addresses*. New York: France Forever, 1943.

_____. *The Sunny Side of F.D.R.* Compiled and edited by M. S. Venkataramani. Athens, OH: Ohio University Press, 1973.

_____. *The War Message to the Nation and Congress Concerning the Involvement of the United States in A War with the Empire of Japan and Axis Powers*. Philadelphia: Ritten House, 1942.

_____. *War Messages of Franklin Delano Roosevelt, December 8, 1941 to October 12, 1942. The President's War Addresses to the People and to the Congress of the United States of America*. Washington, DC, n.p., 1942.

_____. *The War Messages of Franklin D. Roosevelt, December 8, 1941 to April 13, 1945: The President's War Addresses to the People and to the Congress of the United States of America*. Washington, DC, n.p., 1945.

_____. *Wartime Correspondence Between President Roosevelt and Pope Pius XII*. Edited by Myron Taylor. New York: Macmillan, 1947.

_____. *The Wisdom and Wit of Franklin D. Roosevelt*. Edited by Peter and Helen Beilenson. White Plains, NY: Peter Pauper Press, 1982.

______. *The Wisdom of FDR*. Edited by Dagobert D. Runes. New York: Carol Publishing Group, 1993.

______. *The Wit and Wisdom of Franklin D. Roosevelt*. Edited, with an introduction by Maxwell Meyersohn. Boston: Beacon Press, 1950.

Roosevelt, James and Sidney Shalett. *Affectionately, F.D.R.: A Son's Story of A Lonely Man*. New York: Harcourt, Brace, 1959.

______ with Bill Libby. *My Parents: A Differing View*. Chicago: Playboy Press, 1977.

Roosevelt, Sara Delano. *My Boy Franklin*. As told by Mrs. James Roosevelt to Isabel Leighton and Gabrielle Forbush. New York: R. Long and R. R. Smith, 1933.

Rosenau, James N., ed. *The Roosevelt Treasury*. Garden City, NY: Doubleday, 1951.

Rosenbaum, Herbert D. and Elizabeth Bartelme, Eds. *Franklin D. Roosevelt: The Man, the Myth, the Era, 1882-1945*. New York: Greenwood Press, 1987.

Rosenblum, Marcus. *The Story of Franklin D. Roosevelt*. New York: Simon and Schuster, 1949.

Rosenman, Samuel I. *Working with Roosevelt*. New York: Harper and Brothers, 1952.

Ross, Leland M. and Allen W. Grobin. *This Democratic Roosevelt: The Life Story of "F. D.": An Authentic Biography*. New York: E. P. Dutton & Co., 1932.

Rossi, Mario. *Roosevelt and the French*. Westport, CT: Praeger, 1994.

Ryan, Halford R. *Franklin D. Roosevelt's Rhetorical Presidency*. New York: Greenwood Press, 1988.

Sainsbury, Keith L. *Churchill and Roosevelt at War: The War They Fought and the Peace They Hoped to Make*. New York: Viking Press, 1994.

______. *The Turning Point: Roosevelt, Stalin, Churchill, and Chiang Kai-shek, 1943: The Moscow, Cairo, and Tehran Conferences*. Oxford: Oxford University Press, 1985.

Sandak, Cass R. *The Franklin Roosevelts*. New York: Crestwood House, 1992. (juvenile)

Savage, Sean J. *Roosevelt, the Party Leader, 1932-1945*. Lexington: University Press of Kentucky, 1991.

Schlesinger, Arthur M., Jr. *The Age of Roosevelt*. 3 volumes. Boston: Houghton Mifflin, 1957-1960.

______. *War and the Constitution: Abraham Lincoln and Franklin D. Roosevelt*. Gettysburg, PA: Gettysburg College, 1988.

Schoor, Gene. *The Picture Story of Franklin Delano Roosevelt*. New York: Fell, 1950.

Schoumatoff, Elizabeth. *FDR's Unfinished Portrait: A Memoir*. Pittsburgh: University of Pittsburgh Press, 1991.

Selfridge, John D. *Franklin D. Roosevelt, the People's President*. New York: Fawcett Columbine, 1990. (juvenile)

Shivanna, K. S. *Jawaharlal Nehru, Franklin D. Roosevelt, and America*. Bangalore: Sri Raghavendra Prakashana, 1982.

Shogan, Robert. *Hard Bargain. How FDR Twisted Churchill's Arm, Evaded the Law, and Changed the Role of the American Presidency*. New York: Scribner, 1995.

Simpson, Michael. *Franklin D. Roosevelt*. Oxford: B. Blackwell, 1989.

Smith, A. Merriman. *Thank You, Mr. President, A White House Notebook*. New York: Harper & Brothers, 1946.

Stettinius, Edward Reilly. *Roosevelt and the Russians: The Yalta Conference*. Garden City, NY: Doubleday, 1949.

Stewart, William J., comp. *The Era of Franklin D. Roosevelt: A Selected Bibliography of Periodical, Essay, and Dissertation Literature, 1945-1971*. Hyde Park, NY: Franklin D. Roosevelt Library, National Archives and Record Service, General Services Administration, 1974.

Sullivan, Wilson. *Franklin Delano Roosevelt*. New York: American Heritage Publishing Co., 1970.

Sweeny, Charles. *Pearl Harbor*. Salt Lake City, UT: Privately Printed by Arrow Press, 1946.

Tansill, Charles Callan. *Back Door to War: The Roosevelt Foreign Policy, 1933-1941*. Chicago: Henry Regnery, 1952.

Thomas, Henry. *Franklin Delano Roosevelt*. New York: Putnam, 1962. (juvenile)

Thompson, Kenneth W., ed. *The Roosevelt Presidency: Four Intimate Perspectives of FDR*. Washington, DC: University Press of America, 1982.

Thompson, Robert Smith. *A Time for War: Franklin D. Roosevelt and the Path to Pearl Harbor*. New York: Prentice Hall, 1991.

Thorne, Willis E. *The War Eternal of Predatory Greed and Self Preservation, with Special Reference to the Political Psychology and Technique of President Roosevelt*. Chicago, n.p., 1937.

Tittle, Walter. *Roosevelt as an Artist Saw Him: With Portraits and Illustrations*. New York: R. M. McBride, 1948.

Tugwell, Rexford G. *The Art of Politics, As Practiced by Franklin Delano Roosevelt, Luis Munoz Marin, and Fiorello La Guardia*. Garden City, NY: Doubleday, 1958.

______. *The Democratic Roosevelt: A Biography of Franklin D. Roosevelt*. Garden City, NY: Doubleday, 1957.

______. *FDR: Architect of An Era*. New York: Macmillan, 1967.

______. *In Search of Roosevelt*. Cambridge, MA: Harvard University Press, 1972.

Tully, Grace G. *F.D.R., My Boss*. New York: C. Scribner's Sons, 1949.

Van Everen, Brooks. "*Franklin D. Roosevelt and the German Problem, 1914-1945*." Ph.D. diss., University of Colorado, 1970. (DAI, 31:9, 4696A, UMI Order # 715944)

Venkataramani, M. S. and B. K. Shrivastava. *Roosevelt, Gandhi, Churchill: America and the Last Phase of India's Freedom Struggle*. New Delhi: Radiant Publishers, 1983.

Venn, Fiona. *Franklin D. Roosevelt*. London: Cardinal, 1990.

Viorst, Milton. *Hostile Allies: FDR and Charles De Gaulle*. New York: Macmillan, 1965.

Voss, Frederick. *FDR: The Early Years: An Exhibition at the National Portrait Gallery, January 28 to July 25, 1982*. Washington, DC: United States Government Printing Office, 1982.

Walker, Gregg B. "*Franklin D. Roosevelt as Summit Negotiator at Tehran, 1943 and Yalta, 1945*." Ph.D. diss., University of Kansas, 1983. (DAI, 44:11, 3207A, UMI Order # DA8403683)

Walker, Turnley. *Roosevelt and the Warm Springs Story*. New York: A. A. Wyn, 1953.

Waller, George Macgregor. *Pearl Harbor: Roosevelt and the Coming of War*. Boston: Heath, 1950.

Wann, A. J. *The President as Chief Administrator: A Study of Franklin D. Roosevelt*. Washington, DC: Public Affairs Press, 1968.

Ward, Geoffrey C. *A First-Class Temperament: The Emergence of Franklin Roosevelt*. New York: Harper & Row, 1989.

______. *Before the Trumpet: Young Franklin Roosevelt, 1882-1905*. New York: Harper & Row, 1985.

Weber, Mark. *President Roosevelt's Campaign to Incite War in Europe: The Secret Documents*. Brooklyn, NY: Revisionist Press, 1983.

Wehle, Louis Brandeis. *Hidden Threads of History: Wilson Through Roosevelt*. New York: Macmillan, 1953.

Weingast, David Elliott. *Franklin D. Roosevelt: Man of Destiny*. New York: Messner, 1952. (juvenile)

Weinrich, William Arthur. "*Business and Foreign Affairs: The Roosevelt Defense Program, 1937-1941*." Ph.D. diss., University of Oklahoma, 1971. (DAI, 32:7, 3940A, UMI Order # 723450)

Wharton, Don, ed. *The Roosevelt Omnibus*. New York: A. A. Knopf, 1934.

Whipple, Wayne. *The Story of Young Franklin Roosevelt*. Chicago: The Goldsmith Publishing Company, 1934.

White, Graham J. *FDR and the Press*. Chicago: University of Chicago Press, 1979.

White, William Smith. *Majesty and Mischief: A Mixed Tribute to F.D.R.* New York: McGraw-Hill, 1961.

Wilson, Theodore. *The First Summit: Roosevelt and Churchill at Placentia Bay*. Rev. ed. Lawrence, KS: University of Kansas Press, 1991.

Winfield, Betty Houchin. *FDR and the News Media*. Urbana: University of Illinois Press, 1990.

______. *"Roosevelt and the Press: How Franklin D. Roosevelt Influenced News Gathering, 1933-1941*." Ph.D. diss., University of Washington, 1978.   (Not available from UMI)

Wise, William. *Franklin Delano Roosevelt*. New York: Putnam, 1967. (juvenile)

Wittmer, Felix. *Yalta Betrayal: Data on the Decline and Fall of Franklin Delano Roosevelt*. Caldwell, ID: Caxton Printers Ltd., 1953.

Wolf, Ann M. *The Long Shadow of Franklin D. Roosevelt*. Philadelphia: Dorrance, 1974.

Wolfskill, George and John A. Hudson. *All But the People: Franklin D. Roosevelt and His Critics, 1933-39*. New York: Macmillan, 1969.

Woods, John A. *Roosevelt and Modern America*. New York: Macmillan, 1959.

Woods, Randall Bennett. *The Roosevelt Foreign Policy Establishment and the Good Neighbor: The United States and Argentina, 1941-1945*. Lawrence, KS: Regents Press of Kansas, 1979.

Woon, Basil Dillon. *Roosevelt, World Statesman*. London: P. Davies, 1942.

Young, James Capers. *Roosevelt Revealed*. New York: Farrar & Rinehart Inc., 1936.

Young, Lowell T. *"Franklin D. Roosevelt and Imperialism"*. Ph.D. diss., University of Virginia, 1970.   (DAI, 31:9, 4698A, UMI Order # 7026550)

Zavin, Howard S. *"Forward to the Land: Franklin D. Roosevelt and the City, 1882-1933*." Ph.D. diss., New York University, 1972.   (DAI, 33:2, 715A, UMI Order # 7221551)

4 President Harry S. Truman 1884-1972

United States of America

Harry S. Truman assumed the presidency upon the death of Franklin D. Roosevelt on 12 April 1945. The former Missouri senator, vice-president for only three months, was suddenly commander-in-chief and responsible for a host of situations, the most important being the final defeat of Nazi Germany and Imperial Japan.

When Roosevelt decided to run for a fourth term, Truman was selected as a compromise vice-presidential candidate to appease the different voting segments of the Democratic party. He had become well-known because of his work as chairman of the Senate investigation committee concerning fraud and corruption by government contractors. His committee saved the government millions of dollars and increased the production of war supplies.

By April 1945, Germany was in its last stages of resistance. On 30 April, Adolf Hitler shot himself. His successor, Admiral Karl Doenitz, surrendered all German forces on 7 May. Truman proclaimed 8 May as VE day. Though Germany was defeated, Japan remained a determined foe. Japanese leaders were unwilling to begin surrender negotiations even though their forces had been defeated in various island battles, most of the Imperial Navy had been destroyed, and destructive fire bomb raids conducted by the United States Army Air Force had burned major cities and killed thousands of civilians.

Truman's first important diplomatic duty occurred in July. He travelled to Potsdam, Germany, a suburb of Berlin, to meet with British Prime Minister Winston Churchill and Soviet Premier Josef Stalin. At the conference, they agreed upon the partition of Germany into four sections, each to be separately controlled by the United States, Great Britain, France, and the Soviet Union. Stalin also agreed to enter the war against Japan and his military forces invaded Manchuria in August.

At Potsdam, the Allies, specifically the United States, Great Britain, and China, issued an ultimatum to Japan to surrender or suffer the consequences. The ultimatum was issued after Truman received word that the first test of an atomic bomb had been successful at a site near Alamogordo, New Mexico. When the Japanese government failed to respond to the ultimatum, Truman ordered the first bomb to be dropped. The target chosen was Hiroshima and the city was destroyed. When the Japanese leaders still would not begin negotiations, a second bomb was dropped on Nagasaki with similar results. Finally, the Japanese government, at the prompting of Emperor Hirohito, agreed to surrender and ceased all resistance on 14 August 1945. Truman never regretted or made excuses for his decision to use atomic weapons. His decision was based upon the conditions of the situation at the time. The invasion of the Japanese home islands, slated for November 1945, would have resulted in massive Allied casualties. By using atomic weapons, he brought about a quick and decisive end to the war.

For the purpose of this bibliography, the year 1945 is the focal point, however, Truman served as president for nearly eight years, leaving office in January 1953. There are several excellent works on the life and career of Harry S. Truman. Recommended for reading are Robert J. Donovan's two-volume set, *Conflict and Crisis* and *Tumultuous Years*, Robert Ferrell's *Harry S. Truman*, Richard Hayne's *The Awesome Power*, Roy Jenkins' *Truman*, David McCullough's *Truman* (winner of the 1993 Pulitzer prize for biography), and Merle Miller's *Plain Speaking*. Harry S. Truman's *Memoirs* is also recommended as are any of the works concerning his personal letters and papers. These works and others are listed in the bibliography that follows.

Bibliography

Abel, Jules. *The Truman Scandals*. Chicago: Regnery, 1956.

Allen, Robert S. and William V. Shannon. *Truman Merry-Go-Round*. New York: Vanguard Press, 1950.

Allen, Thomas B. and Norman Polmar. *Code-Name Downfall: The Secret Plan to Invade Japan And Why Truman Dropped the Bomb*. New York: Simon & Schuster, 1995.

Ayers, Eben A. *Truman in the White House: The Diary of Eben A. Ayers*. Columbia: University of Missouri Press, 1991.

Bernstein, Barton J., ed. *Politics and Policies of the Truman Administration*. Chicago: Quadrangle Books, 1970.

_____ and Allan J. Matugow, eds. *The Truman Administration: A Documentary History*. New York: Harper, 1966.

Burns, Richard Dean, comp. *Harry S. Truman: A Bibliography of His Times and Presidency*. Wilmington: Scholarly Resources Inc., 1984.

Clemens, Cyril. *The Man From Missouri: A Biography of Harry S. Truman*. Webster Groves, MO: International Mark Twain Society. J. P. Didier of New York, distributor, 1945.

______. *Mark Twain and Harry S. Truman*. Webster Grove, MO: International Mark Twain Society, 1950.

Cochran, Bert. *Harry Truman and the Crisis Presidency*. New York: Funk & Wagnalls, 1973.

Coffin, Tristran. *Missouri Compromise*. Boston: Little, Brown, 1947.

Collins, David R. *Harry S. Truman: People's President*. Champaign, IL: Garrard Publishing Company, 1975. (juvenile)

______. *Harry S. Truman, 33rd President of the United States*. Ada, OK: Garrett Educational Corporation, 1988. (juvenile)

Crane, John de Murinelly Cirne. *The Pictorial Biography of Harry S. Truman, the Thirty-Third President of the United States*. Washington, n.p., 1948.

Daniels, Jonathan. *The Man of Independence*. Philadelphia: Lippincott, 1950.

Dayton, Eldorous L. *Give 'em Hell Harry: An Informal Biography of the Terrible Tempered Mr. T*. New York: Devin-Adair, 1956.

Donovan, Robert J. *Conflict and Crisis: The Presidency of Harry S. Truman, 1945-1948*. New York: Norton, 1977.

______. *Tumultuous Years: The Presidency of Harry S. Truman, 1949-1953*. New York: Norton, 1982.

Druks, Herbert. *Truman and the Russians*. Rev. 2nd ed. New York: Robert Speller and Sons, Publishers Inc., 1981.

Dunar, Andrew J. *The Truman Scandals and the Politics of Morality*. Columbia: University of Missouri Press, 1984.

Faber, Doris. *Harry Truman*. New York: Abelard-Schuman, 1973.

Farley, Karin Clafford. *Harry S. Truman: The Man from Independence*. Englewood Cliffs, NJ: J. Messner, 1989.

Feinberg, Barbara. *Harry S. Truman*. New York: F. Watts, 1994. (juvenile)

Ferrell, Robert H. *Choosing Truman: The Democratic Convention of 1944*. Columbia: University of Missouri Press, 1994.

______. *Harry S. Truman, A Life*. Columbia: University of Missouri Press, 1994.

______. *Harry S. Truman and the Modern American Presidency*. Boston: Little, Brown, 1983.

______. *Harry S. Truman: His Life on the Family Farms*. Worland, WY: High Plains Pub. Co., 1991.

______. *Truman, A Centenary Remembrance*. New York: Viking Press, 1984.

Fleming, Thomas. *Harry S. Truman*. New York: Walker, 1993. (juvenile)

Gallu, Samuel. *"Give 'em Hell, Harry." Reminiscences*. New York: Viking Press, 1975.

Gibson, Joan, comp. *A Guide to Map Room Messages of President Truman (1945-1946) and Potsdam Conference Documents (1945)*. Frederick, MD: University Publications of America, 1980.

Gies, Joseph. *Harry S. Truman: A Pictorial Biography*. Garden City, NY: Doubleday, 1968.

Giglio, James N. and Greg G. Thielen. *Truman in Cartoon and Caricature*. Ames: Iowa State University Press, 1984.

Gosnell, Harold Foote. *Truman's Crises: A Political Biography of Harry S. Truman*. Westport, CT: Greenwood Press, 1980.

Greenberg, Morrie. *The Buck Stops Here: A Biography of Harry Truman*. Minneapolis, MN: Dillon Press, 1989. (juvenile)

Hamby, Alonzo L. *Man of the People: A Life of Harry S. Truman*. New York: Oxford University Press, 1995.

Hargrove, Jim. *Harry S. Truman*. Chicago: Children's Press, 1987. (juvenile)

Harry S. Truman Library. *Historical Materials in the Harry S. Truman Library. 30th Anniversary Edition, 1957-1987*. Independence, MO: The Library, 1987.

Hayman, Le Roy. *Harry S. Truman: A Biography*. New York: Crowell, 1969. (juvenile)

Haynes, Richard F. *The Awesome Power: Harry S. Truman as Commander-in-Chief*. Baton Rouge, LA: Louisiana State University Press, 1973.

______. *"Truman as Commander-in-Chief: A Study of President Harry S. Truman's Concept and Exercise of the Military Function of the Presidency, 1945-1953."* (Volumes I and II.) Ph.D. diss., The Louisiana State University and Agricultural and Mechanical College, 1971. (DAI, 32:7, 3921A, UMI Order # 723495)

Hechler, Ken. *Working with Truman: A Personal Memoir of the White House Years*. New York: Putnam, 1982.

Hedley, Jon Hollister. *Harry S. Truman, The "Little" Man from Missouri*. Woodbury, NY: Barron's Educational Service, 1977.

Heindel, Richard H., ed. *An Introductory Anthology of President Truman*. Compiled by the staff of the American Library in London. London: Printed by the Reproduction Section, 1945.

Heller, Francis H., ed. *The Truman White House: The Administration of the Presidency, 1945-1953*. Lawrence, KS: University of Kansas Press, 1980.

Helm, William Pickett. *Harry Truman, A Political Biography*. New York: Duell, Sloan & Pearce, 1947.

Hersey, John. *Aspects of the Presidency*. New Haven: Ticknor & Fields, 1980.

Hua, Ching-chao. *From Yalta to Panmunjom: Truman's Diplomacy and the Four Powers, 1945-1953*. Ithaca, NY: East Asia Program, Cornell University, 1993.

Hudson, Wilma J. *Harry S. Truman: Missouri Farm Boy*. Indianapolis, IN: Bobbs-Merrill, 1973. (juvenile)

Huthmacher, J. Joseph, comp. *The Truman Years: The Reconstruction of Postwar America*. Hinsdale, IL: Dryden Press, 1973.

Jacobs, William Jay. *Truman*. Encino, CA: Glencoe Publishing Co., 1980.

Jenkins, Roy. *Truman*. New York: Harper & Row, 1986.

Kelton, Nancy. *Harry Four-Eyes*. Chicago: Children's Press, 1971. (juvenile)

Kirkendall, Richard S., ed. *The Harry S. Truman Encyclopedia*. Boston: G. K. Hall, 1989.

Lacey, Michael J., ed. *The Truman Presidency*. New York: Cambridge University Press, 1989.

Leavell, J. Perry, Jr. *Harry S. Truman*. New York: Chelsea House, 1988. (juvenile)

Lee, R. Alton. *Harry S. Truman: Where Did The Buck Stop?* New York: P. Lang, 1991.

Levantrosser, William F. *Harry S. Truman: The Man from Independence*. New York: Greenwood Press, 1986.

Lingham, Brian. *Harry Truman: The Man - His Music*. Kansas City: Published in cooperation with the Harry S. Truman Library Institute of Independence, Missouri and the Kansas City Symphony of Kansas City, Missouri, by the Lowell Press, 1985.

Loving, David W., comp. *A Guide to the Microform Edition of President Harry S. Truman's Office Files, 1945-1953*. Bethesda, MD: University Publications of America, 1989.

Maddox, Robert James. *From War to Cold War: The Education of Harry S. Truman*. Boulder, CO: Westview Press, 1988.

Martin, Ralph G. *President from Missouri: Harry S. Truman*. New York: J. Messner, 1964. (juvenile)

McCoy, Donald R. *The Presidency of Harry S. Truman*. Lawrence, KS: University Press of Kansas, 1984.

McCullough, David. *Truman*. New York: Simon & Schuster, 1992.

McNaughton, Frank and Walter Hehmeyer. *Harry Truman - President*. New York: McGraw-Hill, 1948.

_____ . *This Man Truman*. New York: McGraw-Hill, 1945.

Melton, David. *Harry S. Truman: The Man Who Walked with Giants*. Independence, MO: Independence Press, 1980. (juvenile)

Messer, Robert L. *The End of An Alliance: James F. Brynes, Roosevelt, Truman, and the Origins of the Cold War*. Chapel Hill: University of North Carolina Press, 1982.

Miklowitz, Gloria. *Harry Truman*. New York: G. P. Putnam's Sons, 1975. (juvenile)

Miller, Merle. *Plain Speaking: An Oral Biography of Harry S. Truman*. New York: Berkley Publishing Corporation. Distributed by Putnam of New York, 1974.

Miller, Richard Lawrence. *Truman: The Rise to Power*. New York: McGraw-Hill, 1986.

Mollman, John Peter. *Harry S. Truman: A Biography*. New York: Monarch Press, 1966.

Morris, Jeffrey Brandon. *The Truman Way*. Minneapolis: Lerner Publications, 1994. (juvenile)

O'Neal, Michael. *President Truman and the Atomic Bomb: Opposing Viewpoints*. San Diego: Greenhaven Press, 1990. (juvenile)

Parks, Arva M. *Harry Truman and the Little White House in Key West*. Miami: Centennial Press, 1991.

Pemberton, William E. *Harry S. Truman: Fair Dealer and Cold Warrior*. Boston: Twayne, 1989.

Phillips, Cabell. *The Truman Presidency: The History of A Triumphant Succession*. New York: Macmillan, 1966.

Powell, Eugene James. *Tom's Boy Harry: The First Complete Authentic Story of Harry Truman's Connection with the Pendergast Machine*. Jefferson City, MO: Hawthorn Publishing Company, 1948.

Reichard, Gary W. *Politics as Usual: The Age of Truman and Eisenhower*. Arlington Heights, IL: Harlan Davidson, 1988.

Richards, Kenneth G. *Harry S. Truman*. Chicago: Children's Press, 1968. (juvenile)

Robbins, Charles. *Last of His Kind: An Informal Portrait of Harry S. Truman*. New York: Morrow, 1979.

Robbins, Jhan. *Bess and Harry: An American Love Story*. New York: Putnam, 1980.

Roberts, Allen E. *Brother Truman: The Masonic Life and Philosophy of Harry S. Truman*. Highland Springs, VA: Anchor Communications, 1985.

Ryan, Halford Ross. *Harry S. Truman: Presidential Rhetoric*. Westport, CT: Greenwood Press, 1993.

Sand, G. W. (Gregory W.) *Truman in Retirement: A Former President Views the Nation and the World*. South Bend, IN: Justice Books, 1993.

Sandak, Cass R. *The Trumans*. New York: Crestwood House, 1992. (juvenile)

Schmidtlein, Eugene Francis. *"Truman the Senator."* Ph.D. diss., University of Missouri, 1962. (DAI, 23:12, 4668, UMI Order # 626421)

Smith, A. Merriman. *Thank You, Mr. President, A White House Notebook*. New York: Harper & Brothers, 1946.

Spencer, Cornelia. *Straight Furrow: The Biography of Harry S. Truman for Young People*. New York: John Day, 1949. (juvenile)

Stapleton, Margaret L. *The Truman and Eisenhower Years: A Selective Bibliography*. Metuchen, NJ: Scarecrow Press, 1973.

Steinberg, Alfred. *Harry S. Truman*. New York: Putnam, 1963. (juvenile)

______. *The Man from Missouri: The Life and Times of Harry S. Truman*. New York: Putnam, 1962.

Stone, I. (Isidor) F. *The Truman Era, 1945-1952*. New York: Monthly Review Press, 1953.

Theoharis, Athan, ed. *The Truman Presidency: The Origins of the Imperial Presidency and the National Security State*. Stanfordville, NY: Earl M. Coleman Enterprises Inc.,1979.

Thompson, Kenneth W. *The Truman Presidency: Intimate Perspectives*. Lanham, MD: University Press of America, 1984.

Thomson, David S. *A Pictorial Biography: Harry S. Truman*. New York: Grosset & Dunlap, 1973.

Truman, Harry S. *Addresses and Statements of Harry S. Truman, A Topical Record from January, 1935 to April, 1945*. Washington: The United States News, 1945.

______. *The Autobiography of Harry S. Truman*. Edited by Robert H. Ferrell. Boulder, CO: Colorado Associated University Press, 1980.

______. *Captain Harry. Harry Truman: A Selection of Historical Photographs and Documents Including a Handwritten Manuscript by Mr. Truman Reproduced in Its Entirety on Single Sheets and in the Actual Size of the Original: "The Military Career of A Missourian"*. Kansas City, MO: Harry S. Truman Good Neighbor Award Foundation, 1982.

______. *Cumulated Indexes to the Public Papers of the Presidents of the United States: Harry S. Truman, 1945-1953*. White Plains, NY: Kraus International Publications, 1979.

______. *Dear Bess: The Letters from Harry to Bess Truman, 1910-1959*. New York: Norton, 1983.

______. *Harry S. Truman in His Own Words*. Edited by William Hillman. New York: Bonanza Books, 1980.

______. *The Harry S. Truman Oral Histories Collection*. Frederick, MD: University Publications of America, 1990. (628 microfiche)

______. *The Harry S. Truman Oral History Collection. Index*. Bethesda, MD: University Publications of America, 1990.

______. *Harry S. Truman, 1884-: Chronology, Documents, Bibliographic Aids*. Edited by Howard B. Furer. Dobbs Ferry, NY: Oceana Publications, 1970.

______. *Harry Truman Speaks His Mind*. New York: Popular Library, 1960.

______. *Letters from Father: The Truman Family's Personal Correspondence*. Edited and annotated by Margaret Truman. South Yarmouth, MA: J. Curley, 1981.

______. *Letters Home*. Edited by Monte M. Poen. Boston: G. K. Hall, 1984.

______. *The Man from Missouri: The Memorable Words of the Thirty-Third President*. Selected and arranged by Ted Sheldon. Kansas City, MO: Hallmark Editions, 1970.

______. *Map Room Messages of President Truman (1945-1946)*. Edited by Paul Kesaris. Frederick, MD: University Publications of America, 1980. (5 microfilm reels)

______. *Memoirs of Harry S. Truman*. 2 volumes. Garden City, NY: Doubleday, 1955-1956.

______. *Mr. Citizen*. New York: Geis Associates. Distributed by Random House, 1960.

______. *Mr. President: The First Publication from the Personal Diaries, Private Letters, Papers, and Revealing Interviews of Harry S. Truman, 33rd President of the United States of America*. By William Hillman. New York: Farrar, Straus & Young, 1952.

______. *Off the Record: The Private Papers of Harry S. Truman*. Edited by Robert H. Ferrell. New York: Harper & Row, 1980.

______. *President Harry S. Truman's Office Files, 1945-1953*. Bethesda, MD: University Publications of America, 1990. (84 microform reels) (Original files are held in the Harry S. Truman Presidential Library, Independence, MO.)

______. *The Quotable Truman*. Compiled by David Gallen. New York: Carroll & Graf Publishers, 1994.

______. *Strictly Personal and Confidential: The Letters Harry Truman Never Mailed*. Edited by Monte E. Poen. Boston: Little, Brown, 1982.

______. *The Truman Administration: Its Principles and Practice*. Edited by Louis W. Koenig. New York: New York University Press, 1956.

______. *The Truman Program: Addresses and Messages*. Edited by M. B. Schnapper. Washington, DC: Public Affairs Press, 1949.

______. *Truman Speaks*. Edited by Cyril Clemens. Webster Groves, MO: International Mark Twain Society. J. P. Didier of New York, distributor, 1946.

______. *Truman Speaks: On the Presidency, the Constitution, and Statecraft*. New York: Columbia University Press, 1960.

______. *The Truman Wit*. Edited by Alex J. Goldman. New York: Citadel Press, 1966.

______. *The Truman Years*. Edited by Eleanora W. Schoenbaum. New York: Facts on File, 1978.

______. *The Truman Years: The Words and Times of Harry S. Truman*. By the editors of Country Beautiful. Waukesha, WI: Country Beautiful, 1976.

______. *Where the Buck Stops: The Personal and Private Writings of Harry S. Truman*. Edited by Margaret Truman. New York: Warner Books, 1989.

______. *The Words of Harry S. Truman*. New York: Newmarket Press, 1984.

Truman, Margaret. *Harry S. Truman*. New York: Morrow, 1973.

Ubriaco, Robert D., Jr. "*Harry S. Truman, The Politics of Yalta, and the Domestic Origins of the Truman Doctrine*." Ph.D. diss., University of Illinois at Urbana-Champaign, 1992. (DAI, 53:10, 3655A, UMI Order # DA9305718)

Underhill, Robert. *The Truman Persuasions*. Ames, IA: Iowa State University Press, 1981.

United States. Congress (93d, 1st session, 1973). *Memorial Services in the Congress of the United States and Tributes in Eulogy of Harry S. Truman, Late President of the United States*. Washington: U.S. Government Printing Office, 1973.

Walch, Timothy and Dwight W. Miller, eds. *Herbert Hoover and Harry S. Truman: A Documentary History*. Worland, WY: High Plains Pub. Co., 1992.

Wilk, Gerard H. *Truman and Berlin: Decisive Years Between the Potsdam Conference and Marshall Plan*. Berlin: Press and Information Office of the Land Berlin, 1986.

Williams, Herbert Lee. *The Newspaperman's President: Harry S. Truman*. Chicago: Nelson-Hall, 1984.

Wolfson, Victor. *The Man Who Cared: A Life of Harry S. Truman*. New York: Ariel Books, 1966. (juvenile)

5 Generalissimo Chiang Kai-shek 1887-1975

China

Chiang Kai-shek and his military forces battled Japanese invaders for eight years from 1937 to 1945. The brutal conflict killed millions of Chinese and left the country in ruins. The victory, which would not have been possible without massive military and economic assistance from the United States and Great Britain, was a hollow one for Chiang. Four more years of civil war against Mao Tse-tung's Communist forces ended in defeat and forced him to flee to the island of Formosa in 1949.

Chiang received his military training in China and Japan during the 1920s. While in Japan, he met Sun Yat-sen, the Chinese revolutionary. Upon learning about Sun's principles, he joined the Kuomintung or Nationalist party and rose quickly in the party hierarchy. When Sun died in 1925, Chiang emerged as the party leader and launched military operations against the warlords of northern China. By 1928, most of the warlords had been defeated and Chiang formed the National Government of China. Chiang's government tried to institute new economic reforms, but Mao's Communists were a continual threat, as were the Japanese. The "Manchurian Incident" at Mukden occurred in 1931, resulting in the loss of part of Manchuria to Japan. In 1937, the Japanese army invaded China to obtain much needed raw materials and agricultural land. The invasion caused Chiang and Mao to form an unfriendly alliance, one that would contribute to Chiang's downfall twelve years later.

The strategic military importance of China made Chiang a major member of the top Allied political leaders. American President Franklin D. Roosevelt and British Prime Minister Winston Churchill met with him in Cairo, Egypt in 1943. War aims were discussed and Chiang reiterated his need for more economic and military support to fight the Japanese. Agreement was reached because Roosevelt and Churchill needed China to remain in the war at all costs. The Chinese Army, though it did not fight well, kept large numbers of Japanese troops occupied and the Allies used Chinese airfields to launch planes to bomb Japan.

When the Second World War ended, the Chinese civil war began in earnest. Mao's Communist forces finally defeated Chiang's Nationalist forces and he fled to Formosa. He established a new government on the island and planned to return to the mainland, but never did. Chiang was re-elected numerous times as president, finally dying in office in 1975.

Unlike the other Allied political leaders, Chiang has not been a favourite subject of biographers. His life before the 1920s was shadowy and the man was aloof and uncooperative. Recommended for reading are Brian Crozier's *The Man Who Lost China*, Richard Curtis' *Chiang Kai-shek*, and Robert Payne's *Chiang Kai-shek*. Also recommended are any of the speeches Chiang made during the Second World War. These works and others are listed in the bibliography that follows.

Bibliography

Berkov, Robert. *Strong Man of China: The Story of Chiang Kai-shek*. Boston: Houghton Mifflin, 1938.

Chang, Hsin-hai. *Chiang Kai-shek: Asia's Man of Destiny*. Garden City, NY: Doubleday, Doran & Co., 1944.

Ch'en, Chieh-ju. *Chiang Kai-shek's Secret Past: The Memoir of His Second Wife*. Edited with an introduction by Lloyd E. Eastman. Boulder, CO: Westview Press, 1993.

Chi, Hsi-sheng. *Nationalist China at War: Military Defeats and Political Collapse, 1937-1945*. Ann Arbor, MI: University of Michigan Press, 1982.

Chiang Kai-shek. *All We Are and All We Have: Speeches and Messages Since Pearl Harbor, December 9, 1941-November 17, 1942*. New York: John Day, 1942.

______. *China's Destiny*. Translated by Wang Chung-hui. New York: Macmillan, 1947.

______. *Collected War-Time Messages of Generalissimo Chiang Kai-shek, 1936-1945*. Ministry of Information, Government of China. New York: John Day Company, 1946.

______. *Generalissimo Chiang Speaks: A Collection of His Addresses and Messages on the War of Resistance*. Hong Kong: The Pacific Publishing Company, 1939.

______. *In Memoriam the Free World Mourns President Chiang Kai-shek*. Taiwan: n.p., 1975.

______. *Resistance and Reconstruction: Messages During China's Six Years of War, 1937-1943*. 2nd ed. New York: Harper, 1943.

_____ and others. *The Sino-Japanese Undeclared War*. Providence, RI: Printed by the Chinese Consolidated and Benevolent Association of Rhode Island, 1938.

Chiang, Mei-ling. *General Chiang Kai-shek: The Account of the Fortnight in Sian When the Fate of China Hung in the Balance*. Garden City, NY: Doubleday, Doran & Co., 1937.

Chin, Hsiao-yi. *Mr. Chiang Kai-shek's Understanding and Implementation of Dr. Sun Yat-sen's Revolutionary Ideology and Programs*. Taipei, Taiwan: Conference on the History of the Republic of China, 1981.

China. *President Chiang Kai-shek, His Life Story in Pictures*. Taipei, Taiwan: Government Information Office, Republic of China, 1971.

Chook, Shiu Heng. *Chiang Kai-shek Close-up: A Personal View*. Oakland, CA: United California University Press, 1978.

Clark, Carter Blue, ed. *Chiang Kai-shek and the United States*. [United States]: IAHE Publishing Co., 1986.

Clark, Elmer T. *The Chiangs of China*. New York: Abingdon-Cokesbury Press, 1943.

Crozier, Brian. *The Man Who Lost China: The First Full Biography of Chiang Kai-shek*. New York: Scribner, 1976.

Curtis, Richard. *Chiang Kai-shek*. New York: Hawthorn Books, 1969.

Dolan, Sean. *Chiang Kai-shek*. New York: Chelsea House, 1988. (juvenile)

Elegant, Robert S. *Mao vs. Chiang: The Battle for China, 1925-1949*. New York: Grosset & Dunlap, 1972.

Furuya, Keiji, ed. *Chiang Kai-shek: His Life and Times*. Abridged English edition by Chun-ming Chang. New York: St. John's University, 1981.

Gibbons, David Sprague. "*Dominant Political Leadership and Political Integration in A Transitional Society: China, Chiang Kai-shek and Mao Tse-tung, 1935-1949.*" Ph.D. diss., Princeton University, 1968. (DAI, 29:8, 2765A, UMI Order # 692739)

Gibson, Michael Richard. "*Chiang Kai-shek's Central Army, 1924-1938.*" Ph.D. diss., The George Washington University, 1985. (DAI, 46:5, 1379A, UMI Order # DA8514496)

Gregory, J. S. (John Stradbroke). *Jiang Jie-shi, 1887-1975*. St. Lucia, Queensland: University of Queensland Press, 1982.

Hahn, Emily. *Chiang Kai-shek, an Unauthorized Biography*. Garden City, NY: Doubleday, 1955.

Hedin, Sven Anders. *Chiang Kai-shek, Marshal of China*. Translated from the Swedish by Bernard Norbelie. New York: John Day Co., 1940.

Hsiung, Shih-I. *Life of Chiang Kai-Shek*. London: Peter Davies, 1948.

Hu, P'u-yu, comp. *The Military Exploits and Deeds of President Chiang Kai-shek*. Translated by Chen Kuei-liang. 2nd ed. Taipei: Chung Wu Publishing Co., 1973.

Lattimore, Owen. *China Memoirs: Chiang Kai-shek and the War Against Japan*. Compiled by Fujikko Isono. Tokyo: University of Tokyo Press, 1990.

Linebarger, Paul M. A. *The China of Chiang Kai-shek: A Political Study*. Boston: World Peace Foundation, 1941.

Loh, Pichon Pei Yung. *The Early Chiang Kai-shek: A Study of His Personality and Politics, 1887-1924*. New York: Columbia University Press, 1971.

Mathews, Basil. *Wings over China*. New York: Friendship Press, 1940.

Miller, Basil. *Generalissimo and Madame Chiang Kai-shek: Christian Liberators of China*. 3rd ed. Grand Rapids, MI: Zondervan Publishing House, 1943.

Morwood, William. *Duel for the Middle Kingdom: The Struggle Between Chiang Kai-shek and Mao Tse-tung for Control of China*. New York: Everest House, 1980.

Payne, Robert. *Chiang Kai-shek*. New York: Weybright & Talley, 1969.

Reynolds, Ernest Edwin. *Four Modern Statesmen: Winston S. Churchill, Franklin D. Roosevelt, Joseph Stalin, Chiang Kai-shek*. New York: Oxford University Press, 1944.

Sainsbury, Keith. *The Turning Point: Roosevelt, Stalin, Churchill, and Chiang Kai-shek, 1943. The Moscow, Cairo, and Tehran Conferences*. Oxford: Oxford University Press, 1985.

Seps, Jerry Bernard. "*German Military Advisors and Chiang Kai-shek, 1927-1938*." Ph.D. diss., University of California, Berkeley, 1972. (Not available from UMI)

Spencer, Cornelia. *Chiang Kai-shek, Generalissimo of Nationalist China*. New York: John Day Co., 1968.

Tong, Hollington Kong. *Chiang Kai-shek, Soldier and Statesman: Authorized Biography*. London: Hurst & Blackett, 1938.

Walbert, Kate. *Chiang Kai-shek*. New York: Chelsea House Publishers, 1986.

Welch, Robert Henry Winborne. *Again, May God Forgive Us!* Belmont, MA: Belmont Pub. Co., 1971. (Includes a biographical sketch of Generalissimo Chiang Kai-shek.)

Wu, Chi-Wei David. "*A Rhetorical Analysis of Selected Speeches by Generalissimo Chiang Kai-shek During the War of Resistance Against Japanese Aggression, 1937-1945*." Ph.D. diss., Ohio University, 1986. (DAI, 47:5, 1531A, UMI Order # DA8618727)

Wu, Tien-wei. *The Sian Incident*. Ann Arbor: Center for Chinese Studies, University of Michigan, 1976.
Young, C. W. H. *New Life for Kiangsi*. Shanghai: The China Publishing Co., 1935.

6 General Charles De Gaulle 1890-1970

Free France

Charles De Gaulle was a career military officer when the Second World War began. After German military forces invaded France, he was given command of the 4th Armoured Division and had limited success. For this accomplishment, he was named Under Secretary for War just prior to the collapse of the French government. Rather than surrender, he went to England and established the "Free France" movement, vowing to continue to fight the Germans. He was given support by the American and British governments, but his relationship with the Allies was stormy at best. He never felt he was treated as a true ally and had little input in the political and military decision-making process.

When Paris was liberated in August 1944, De Gaulle returned to the capital and established a new government. However, he was not invited to the Yalta and Potsdam conferences where the top Allied political leaders met to decide Nazi Germany's fate.

De Gaulle led the French government until 1946 when he resigned. In 1958, he returned to politics and was elected president of the Fifth Republic, remaining in office until 1969. He died on 9 November 1970. Recommended for reading about the life and career of Charles De Gaulle are Don Cook's *Charles De Gaulle*, Brian Crozier's *De Gaulle*, and Jean Lacouture's two-volume set, *De Gaulle*. Also recommended is *The Complete War Memoirs of Charles De Gaulle, 1940-1946*. It should be noted that the works listed in the following bibliography concern De Gaulle's involvement in the Second World War or are biographical in nature. Works addressing his post-war political career are not included.

Bibliography

Aglion, Raoul. *Roosevelt and De Gaulle: Allies in Conflict. Personal Memoir*. New York: The Free Press, 1988.

Apsler, Alfred. *"Vive de Gaulle." The Story of Charles De Gaulle*. New York: J. Messner, 1973. (juvenile)

Aron, Robert. *An Explanation of De Gaulle*. Translated from the French by Marianne Sinclair. New York: Harper & Row, 1966.

______. *De Gaulle Before Paris: The Liberation of France, June-August 1944*. Translated by Humphrey Hare. London: Putnam, 1962.

Ashcroft, Edward. *De Gaulle*. London: Oldhams Press, 1962.

Baer, Barbara. *"British Foreign Policy Towards Charles De Gaulle, 1940-1944."* Ph.D. diss., Marquette University, 1976. (DAI, 38:4, 2288A, UMI Order # 7716752)

Banfield, Susan. *Charles De Gaulle*. New York: Chelsea House, 1985. (juvenile)

Barres, Philippe. *Charles De Gaulle*. Garden City, NY: Doubleday, Doran & Co., 1941.

Bernstein, Henry. *Charles de Gaulle and Joan of Arc*. New York: France Forever, 1943.

Brichant, Colette Dubois. *Charles de Gaulle, Artiste de L'Action*. New York: McGraw-Hill, 1969.

Clark, Stanley F. *The Man Who is France: The Story of General Charles De Gaulle*. New York: Dodd, Mead, 1960.

Cook, Don. *Charles De Gaulle, A Biography*. New York: Putnam, 1983.

Crawley, Aidan. *De Gaulle: A Biography*. Indianapolis, IN: Bobbs-Merrill Co., 1969.

Crozier, Brian. *De Gaulle*. New York: Scribner, 1973.

De Gaulle, Charles. *The Army of the Future*. Philadelphia: Lippincott, 1941.

______. *The Complete War Memoirs of Charles De Gaulle, 1940-1946*. New York: Simon & Schuster, 1964.

______. *De Gaulle: Implacable Ally*. Edited by Roy C. Macridis. New York: Harper & Row, 1966.

______. *Edge of the Sword*. Translated from the French by Gerard Hopkins. London: Faber & Faber, 1960. Originally published in France in 1932.

______. *Memoirs of Hope: Renewal and Endeavor*. Translated from the French by Terence Kilmartin. New York: Simon & Schuster, 1971.

______. *The Speeches of General De Gaulle [June 18, 1940 - Dec. 1942]*. London: Oxford University Press, 1944.

______. *Two Speeches by General Charles de Gaulle... An Address to the Provisional Assembly, March 18, 1944, and A Broadcast to the People of France, April 4, 1944*. New York: France Forever, 1944.

De Menil, Lois Patterson. *Who Speaks for Europe? The Vision of Charles de Gaulle*. New York: St. Martin's Press, 1978.

Debray, Regis. *Charles de Gaulle: Futurist of A Nation.* Translated by John Howe. London: Verso, 1994.

DePorte, A. (Anton) W. *De Gaulle's Foreign Policy, 1944-1946.* Cambridge, MA: Harvard University Press, 1968.

Epstein, Sam and Beryl Epstein. *Charles De Gaulle, Defender of France.* Champaign, IL: Garrard Pub. Co., 1973. (juvenile)

Eunson, Ruby. *When France was De Gaulle.* New York: Watts, 1971.

Funk, Arthur. *Charles De Gaulle: The Crucial Years, 1943-1944.* Norman, OK: University of Oklahoma Press, 1959.

Galante, Pierre. *The General!* New York: Random House, 1968.

"Gallicus", pseud. *General de Gaulle, The Hope of France.* London: W. Collins Sons & Co. Ltd., 1941.

Giangreco, D. M. *Roosevelt, de Gaulle, and the Posts: Franco-American War Relations Viewed Through Their Effects on the French Postal System, 1942-1944.* Bonita, CA: Joseph V. Bush, Inc., 1986.

Gordon, Philip H. *A Certain Idea of France: French Security Policy and the Gaullist Legacy.* Princeton, NJ: Princeton University Press, 1993.

Gough, Hugh and John Horne. *De Gaulle and Twentieth-Century France.* New York: Edward Arnold, 1994.

Grinnell-Milne, Duncan William. *The Triumph of Integrity: A Portrait of Charles de Gaulle.* New York: Macmillan, 1962.

Harrity, Richard and Ralph G. Martin. *Man of Destiny: De Gaulle of France.* New York: Duell, Sloan & Pearce, 1961.

Hatch, Alden. *The De Gaulle Nobody Knows: An Intimate Biography of Charles De Gaulle.* New York: Hawthorn Books Inc., 1960.

Hessenstein, Alfred A. *A Giant in the Age of Steel: The Story of General De Gaulle.* New York: Hutchinson & Co. Ltd., 1944.

Hoffman, Stanley. *Decline or Renewal? France Since the 1930s.* New York: Viking Press, 1974.

Hough, Sandra Jean Wurth. *"A Conceptual Analysis for Predicting International Behavior: A Person-Centered Pretheory of Political Leadership - Charles De Gaulle."* Ph.D. diss., The University of Oklahoma, 1975. (DAI, 36:8, 5527A, UMI Order # 763104)

Kerillis, Henri de. *I Accuse De Gaulle.* Translated by Harold Rosenberg. New York: Harcourt, Brace & Co., 1946.

Kersaudy, Francois. *Churchill and De Gaulle.* New York: Antheneum, 1981.

Kettle, Michael. *De Gaulle and Algeria, 1940-1960: From Mers-el-Kabir to the Algiers Barricades.* London: Quartet Books, 1993.

Lacouture, Jean. *De Gaulle.* Translated by Francis K. Price. New York: New American Library, 1966.

_____. *De Gaulle: The Rebel, 1890-1944*. Translated from the French by Patrick O'Brian. New York: Norton, 1990.

_____. *De Gaulle: The Ruler, 1945-1970*. Translated from the French by Alan Sheridan. New York: Norton, 1991.

Launay, Jacques de. *De Gaulle and His France: A Psychopolitical and Historical Portrait*. Translated by Dorothy Albertyn. New York: Julian Press, 1968.

Ledwidge, Bernard. *De Gaulle*. New York: Stein & Day, 1982.

Lester, John. *De Gaulle: King Without A Crown*. New York: Hawthorne Books, 1968. (juvenile)

Malraux, Andre. *The Case for De Gaulle: A Dialogue Between Andre Malraux and James Burnham*. Translated by Spencer Byard. New York: Random House, 1948.

_____. *Felled Oaks: Conversation with De Gaulle*. Translated from the French by Irene Clephone. Revised by Linda Asher. New York: Holt, Rinehart & Winston, 1972.

Masson, Phillipe. *De Gaulle*. New York: Ballantine Books, 1972.

Mauriac, Claude. *The Other De Gaulle: Diaries, 1944-1954*. Translated by Moura Budberg and Gordon Latta. New York: John Day Company, 1973.

Mauriac, Francois. *De Gaulle*. Translated from the French by Richard Howard. Garden City, NY: Doubleday, 1966.

Mengin, Robert. *No Laurels for De Gaulle*. Translated from the French by Jay Allen. New York: Farrar, Straus & Giroux, 1966.

Molchanov, Nikolai. *General De Gaulle: His Life and Work*. Translated from the Russian by Sergei Syrovatkin. Moscow: Progress Publishers, 1985.

Monticone, Ronald C. *Charles De Gaulle*. New York: Twayne Publishers, 1975.

Paxton, Robert O. and Nicholas Wahl, eds. *De Gaulle and the United States: A Centennial Reappraisal*. Providence, RI: Berg, 1993.

Plume, Christian and Pierre Demaret. *Target de Gaulle: The Thirty-one Attempts to Assassinate the General*. Translated from the French by Richard Barry. London: Corgi, 1976.

Rebhorn, Marlette Diane Olsen. "*De Gaulle's Rise to Power: The Failure of American Diplomacy, 1942-1944*." Ph.D. diss., University of Texas at Austin, 1971. (DAI, 32:11, 6350A, UMI Order # 7215819)

Riveloup, Andre. *The Truth About De Gaulle*. New York: Arco Publishing Co., 1944.

Schoenbrun, David. *The Three Lives of Charles De Gaulle*. New York: Atheneum, 1966.

Serfaty, Simon. *France, De Gaulle, and Europe: The Policy of the Fourth and Fifth Republics Toward the Continent*. Baltimore: Johns Hopkins Press, 1968.

Shennan, Andrew. *De Gaulle*. London: Longman, 1993.

Spears, Edward Louis. *Two Men Who Saved France: Petain and De Gaulle*. New York: Stein & Day, 1966.

Steele, Ross. *The Death and the Legend of Charles de Gaulle*. North Ryde, NSW: Macquarie University, 1972.

Sulzberger, C. L. (Cyrus Leo). *The Last of the Giants*. London: Weidenfeld & Nicolson, 1972.

Thody, Philip. *The Achievements of Charles de Gaulle*. Bangor: Headstart History, 1991.

Thompson, Robert Smith. *Pledge to Destiny: Charles De Gaulle and the Rise of the Free French*. New York: McGraw-Hill, 1974.

Thomson, David. *Two Frenchmen: Pierre Laval and Charles De Gaulle*. London: Cresset Press, 1951.

Todd, James Everett. "*Charles De Gaulle: His Role in the Military. Controversies of the 1930's and in the Formation of the Free French Movement in the Summer of 1940*." Ph.D. diss., University of Colorado, 1964. (DAI, 28:7, 2633A, UMI Order # 654220)

Tournoux, Jean Raymond. *Sons of France: Petain and De Gaulle*. Translated by Oliver Coburn. New York: Viking Press, 1966.

Viorst, Milton. *Hostile Allies: FDR and Charles De Gaulle*. New York: Macmillan, 1965.

Wachtel, Dennis Fay. "*De Gaulle and the Invasion of North Africa*." Ph.D. diss., St. Louis University, 1964. (DAI, 25:8, 4678, UMI Order # 6413485)

Wainwright, William Harvey. "*De Gaulle and Indochina, 1940-1945*." Ph.D. diss., Fletcher School of Law and Diplomacy, Tufts University, 1972. (Not available from UMI)

Werth, Alexander. *De Gaulle: A Political Biography*. Baltimore: Penguin, 1965.

White, Dorothy S. *Seeds of Discord: De Gaulle, Free France, and the Allies*. Syracuse, NY: Syracuse University Press, 1964.

White, Sam. *De Gaulle*. London: Harrap, 1984.

Whitelaw, Nancy. *A Biography of General Charles de Gaulle: "I Am France"*. New York: Dillon Press, 1991. (juvenile)

Willis, F. (Frank) Ray, ed. *De Gaulle: Anachronism, Realist, or Prophet?* New York: Holt, Rinehart & Winston, 1967.

PART II

AXIS POLITICAL LEADERS

7 Fuehrer Adolf Hitler 1889-1945

Nazi Germany

Adolf Hitler is most responsible for the wave of destruction that engulfed the world during the Second World War. Because of his actions, other leaders had to respond. He put Germany on a war footing in the 1930s and attempted to become the first ruler of a thousand year reich.

Hitler was born in Austria, but always associated himself with Germany. When the First World War began, he enlisted in the German Army rather than the Austrian Army. His principle duty was that of a messenger, an extremely dangerous task. He was wounded once, won two medals for bravery, and was gassed in 1918. Temporarily blinded, he was in a hospital when the war ended. Like many Germans, he could not believe the German Army had been defeated. There had to be an explanation other than the fact that Germany had been beaten by a superior opponent.

Hitler, like millions of others, was unemployed at the conclusion of the war. After recovering from the effects of the gas, he accepted a job to spy on a small, radical political party. When he discovered that the party's views were similar to his own, he joined and rapidly moved up the party hierarchy because of his ability as an organizer and speaker. Soon he was elected chairman of the organization that he would rule for the remainder of his life: the Nazi party.

In 1923, Hitler believed he had enough support and strength to overthrow the Bavarian state government. The Beer Hall Putsch failed and he was sent to Landsberg prison. While in prison, he took the opportunity to write his autobiography, *Mein Kampf* (*My Struggle*). In the rambling and stiff text, he outlined his dreams and plans for a great Germanic state, one that would unite all German speaking peoples and exclude all that were not racially pure. He particularly emphasized his hatred of Communism and the Jewish race.

Most people who read *Mein Kampf* saw it merely as the poor work of a small-time politician who would remain forever on the fringe of society. However, Hitler did not intend to disappear from the political scene. He continued to recruit supporters and in his speeches, he railed against the Weimar government, the Communists, and the Jews. The Jews, especially, were singled out. They were held responsible for Germany's defeat in 1918 as well as the economic problems that were present in Germany. In 1932, Hitler arrived as a political force. The Nazi party received forty percent of the votes cast in the fall election. Though not a majority, Hitler was given permission by President Paul von Hindenberg to form a coalition government. Hitler accepted the position of chancellor.

Once in office, Hitler moved quickly to consolidate his power. When a fire destroyed the Reichstag (capitol building), Hitler was granted emergency dictatorial powers. He never relinquished those powers. Soon, all other political parties were banned. He began employing out-of-work Germans, mainly by enlarging the armed forces and building or expanding armaments and munitions factories. All these actions were in direct violation of the Versailles Treaty signed by Germany in 1919. He took action against the Jewish population by revoking their citizenship. Dachau, the first concentration camp, was opened to house political prisoners and other nonconformists.

Hitler began his territorial expansion in 1936 when he ordered the German Army to re-occupy the Rhineland, another violation of the Versailles Treaty. Even though the German military commanders did not believe the army could successfully resist a military challenge from the Allies, they obeyed his orders. In retrospect, the German officers were probably correct. If Great Britain and France had confronted the German Army when it marched into the Rhineland in 1936, the Germans would have lost. Hitler, though, took the gamble that his opponents would not act and he was correct. He gained more public support when Austria joined the German reich in 1937 and when he obtained the Sudetenland from Czechoslovakia. The remainder of Czechoslovakia joined the Third Reich in early 1939. Hitler also signed a non-aggression pact with his most hated enemy, Premier Josef Stalin, in August 1939. The pact, in principle, divided Poland between Germany and the Soviet Union.

By the summer of 1939, Hitler was a riding a huge wave of popularity. To this point, all of his territorial conquests had been bloodless. He now decided to unleash his armed forces against Poland even though some of his generals thought the armed forces were not ready to fight. Nevertheless, on 1 September 1939, Hitler's military forces invaded Poland, and to the surprise of everyone, including many of his generals, the Polish forces were destroyed in a matter of weeks. In turn, Hitler was shocked when France and Great Britain, in accordance with their treaty obligations with Poland, declared war on Germany. Hitler had assumed that they would do nothing this time as they had in the past.

However, Hitler held the upper hand. His troops were battle-tested and possessed the blitzkrieg strategy. In the spring of 1940, German armed forces assaulted western Europe and destroyed the French Army in six weeks and drove the British Expeditionary Force from the continent. Hitler controlled most of Europe by July 1940, but the new British prime minister was far tougher than Neville Chamberlain. Winston Churchill vowed to continue fighting and immediately sought aid from the United States and President Franklin D. Roosevelt.

When the German Army invaded the Soviet Union on 22 June 1941, the German generals' worst fears were finally realized. Their forces were not strong enough. Despite early victories, Germany was finally ground down in fighting on the Eastern front, the North African front, the northwest and southern European fronts, and in the air and on the sea. Hitler could never accept anything but the annihilation of his enemies, and they, in turn, granted him no quarter. Germany finally surrendered in May 1945 with many of its cities and towns in ruins, its people destitute, and its fuehrer dead in the destroyed capital of Berlin. Hitler had stated in 1933 that no power on earth would remove him from his position as chancellor while he was alive. His statement proved correct.

Adolf Hitler was the catalyst for change in Europe in the 1930s. He made all the initial movements and others reacted to them. By his own powerful and driven personality, he attempted to create a Germany that would last a thousand years. However, his thirst for conquest and extreme racial bigotry united many nations against him. He moved too far, too fast and Germany was not prepared to withstand the massive retaliation that was directed against it by the Allied nations.

There are many outstanding works on the life and career of Adolf Hitler. A few recommendations are Alan Bullock's *Hitler, A Study in Tyranny*, James Duffy's *Hitler Slept Late and Other Blunders That Cost Him the War*, Charles Flood's *Hitler: The Path to Power*, Joachim Fest's *Hitler*, Franz Halder's *Hitler As Warlord*, Robert Herzstein's *Adolf Hitler and the German Trauma*, Ronald Lewin's *Hitler's Mistakes*, Robert Payne's *The Life and Death of Adolf Hitler*, William Shirer's *The Rise and Fall of the Third Reich*, John Toland's *Adolf Hitler*, and H. R. Trevor-Roper's *The Last Days of Hitler*. Two excellent works that psychoanalyze Hitler's personality are Walter Langer's *The Mind of Adolf Hitler* and Robert G. L. Waite's *The Psychopathic God*. Finally, Hitler's autobiography, *Mein Kampf*, should be read to understand the goals he set for himself and Germany. These works and others are listed in the bibliography that follows.

Bibliography

Abel, Theodore Fred. *Why Hitler Came to Power*. New York: Prentice-Hall, 1938.

Abend, Murray. *"Hitler's Racial Theory and Practice."* Ph.D. diss., Syracuse University, 1955. (DAI, 15:12, 2561, UMI Order # 15042)

Altshuler, David A. *Hitler's War Against the Jews*. A young reader's version of *The War Against the Jews* by Lucy S. Dawidowicz. New York: Behrman House, 1978. (juvenile)

American Jewish Congress. *The Case of Civilization Against Hitlerism, Presented Under the Auspices of the American Jewish Congress at Madison Square Garden, New York, March 7, 1934*. New York: R. O. Ballou, 1934.

Anders, Wladyshaw. *Hitler's Defeat in Russia*. Chicago: H. Regnery, 1953.

Angebert, Jean Michel. *The Occult and the Third Reich: The Mystical Origins of Nazism and the Search for the Holy Grail*. Translated by Lewis A. M. Sumberg. New York: Macmillan, 1974.

Ansel, Walter. *Hitler and the Middle Sea*. Durham, NC: Duke University Press, 1972.

______. *Hitler Confronts England*. Durham, NC: Duke University Press, 1960.

App, Austin Joseph. *A Straight Look at the Third Reich: Hitler and National Socialism, How Right, How Wrong?* Takoma Park, MD: Boniface Press, 1974.

Appel, Benjamin. *Hitler: From Power to Ruin*. New York: Grosset & Dunlap, 1964.

Armstrong, Hamilton F. *Hitler's Reich: The First Phase*. New York: Macmillan, 1933.

Arndt, Robert. *The Women in Hitler's Life*. New York: Herald Pub. Co., 1944.

Askenasy, Hans. *Hitler's Secret*. Laguna Beach, CA: H. Askenasy, 1984.

Bacon, Eugene Hayward. *American Press Opinion of Hitler, 1932-1937*. Washington, DC: n.p., 1948.

Bailey, Thomas A. and Paul B. Ryan. *Hitler vs Roosevelt: The Undeclared Naval War*. New York: The Free Press, 1979.

Baldwin, Peter, ed. *Reworking the Past: Hitler, the Holocaust, and the Historians' Debate*. Boston: Beacon Press, 1990.

Bardakjian, Kevork B. *Hitler and the Armenian Genocide*. Cambridge, MA: Zoryan Institute, 1985.

Barnes, James J. and Patience P. Barnes. *Hitler's Mein Kampf in Britain and America: A Publishing History, 1930-1939*. New York: Cambridge University Press, 1980.

Barnett, Correlli, ed. *Hitler's Generals*. New York: Grove Weidenfeld, 1989.

Baross, Gabor. *Hungary and Hitler*. Toronto: Sovereign Press, 1964.

Barrett, Michael B., ed. *Proceedings of the Citadel Symposium on Hitler and the National Socialist Era, 24-25 April 1980*. Charleston, SC: Citadel Development Foundation, 1982.

Baur, Hans. *Hitler at My Side*. Translated by Lyndel Butler. Houston: Eichler Pub. Corp., 1986.

Bayles, William D. *Caesars in Goose Step*. New York: Harper, 1940.

Baynes, H. G. *Germany Possessed*. London: J. Cape, 1941.

Bender, Roger James. *The Hitler Albums*. Mountain View, CA: R. J. Bender Co., 1970.

Bendersky, Joseph W. *A History of Nazi Germany*. Chicago: Nelson-Hall, 1984.

Berman, Sylvan Marine. *"Hitler: A Study of Ideology and 'Realpolitik' in German-Soviet Relations, 1938-1941."* Ph.D. diss., The American University, 1962. (DAI, 23:5, 1764, UMI Order # 624522)

Bezymenski, Lev. *The Death of Adolf Hitler: Unknown Documents from Soviet Archives*. New York: Harcourt, Brace & World, 1968.

Bildendienst, Zigaretten. *Adolf Hitler: Pictures of the Life of the Fuehrer*. Lakeville, MN: Northstar Books Division, U.S.M., Inc., 1979.

Billinger, Karl, pseud. *Hitler is No Fool*. New York: Modern Age Books Inc., 1939.

Binion, Rudolph. *Hitler Among the Germans*. New York: Elsevier, 1976.

Boehm, Eric Hartzell. *"Policy-Making of the Nazi Government: A Study in the Determination of Decisions of State."* Ph.D. diss., Yale University, 1952. (DAI, 30:1, 239A, UMI Order # 6911347)

Boldt, Gerhard. *Hitler: The Last Ten Days*. Translated by Sandra Bance. New York: Coward, McCann & Geoghegan, 1973.

Bracher, Karl Dietrich. *The German Dictatorship: The Origins, Structure and Effects of National Socialism*. Translated from the German by Jean Steinberg. New York: Praeger, 1970.

Bradley, Catherine. *Hitler and the Third Reich*. New York: Gloucester Press, 1990. (juvenile)

Braun, Eva. *The Private Life of Adolf Hitler: The Intimate Notes and Diary of Eva Braun*. London: Aldus Publications, 1949.

Breiting, Richard. *Secret Conversations with Hitler: The Two Newly Discovered 1931 Interviews*. Edited by Edouard Calic. Translated from the German by Richard Barry. New York: John Day Co., 1971.

Bromberg, Norbert and Verna Volz Small. *Hitler's Psychopathology*. New York: International Universities Press, 1983.

Brooman, Josh. *Hitler's Germany, 1933-1945*. Harlow: Longman, 1985.

Brossard, Chandler. *The Insane World of Adolf Hitler: Told in Searing Unforgettable Photographs and Text*. New York: Fawcett Publications, 1966.

Broszat, Martin. *Hitler and the Collapse of Weimar Germany*. Translated with a Foreword by V. R. Berghahn. New York: St. Martin's Press, 1987.

_____. *The Hitler State: The Foundation and Development of the Internal Structure of the Third Reich*. Translated by John W. Hiden. New York: Longman, 1981.

Browne, Harry. *Hitler and the Rise of Nazism*. New York: Roy, 1969.

Buechner, Howard A. and Wilhelm Bernhart. *Adolf Hitler and the Secrets of the Holy Lance*. Metairie, LA: Thunderbird Press, 1988.

Bullock, Alan. *Hitler, A Study in Tyranny*. Rev. ed. New York: Harper & Row, 1964.

_____. *Hitler and Stalin: Parallel Lives*. Toronto: McClelland & Stewart, 1991.

Bunting, James. *Adolf Hitler*. Folkestone: Bailey & Swinfen, 1973.

Burrin, Philippe. *Hitler and the Jews: The Genesis of the Holocaust*. Translated by Saul Friedlander. London: Edward Arnold, 1994.

Carr, William. *Hitler: A Study in Personality and Politics*. New York: St. Martin's Press, 1979.

Casmir, Fred Lutz. *"Hitler: A Study in Persuasion."* Ph.D. diss., The Ohio State University, 1961. (DAI, 22:11, 4116, UMI Order # 622125)

Cecil, Robert. *Hitler's Decision to Invade Russia, 1941*. London: Davis-Poynter, 1975.

Churchill, Allan, ed. *Eyewitness Hitler: The Nazi Fuehrer and His Times as Seen by Contemporaries, 1930-1945*. New York: Walker, 1979.

Clapham, Noel Pavitt. "*Anglo-French Influence on Hitler's Northern Policy, September 1, 1939 - April 1, 1940.*" Ph.D. diss., University of Nebraska, 1968. (DAI, 29:7, 2175A, UMI Order # 6818013)

Clark, Robert Thomson. *The Fall of the German Republic: A Political Study*. New York: Russell & Russell, 1964.

Compton, James V. *The Swastika and the Eagle: Hitler, the United States, and the Origins of World War II*. Boston: Houghton Mifflin, 1967.

Cross, Colin. *Adolf Hitler*. London: Hodder & Stoughton, 1973.

Cullen, Emma Lucille. "*Chamberlain and Hitler: Failure of Appeasement.*" Ph.D. diss., St. John's University, 1943. (Not available from UMI)

Dahlerus, Birger. *The Last Attempt*. London: Hutchinson, 1948.

Dalton, Hugh. *Hitler's War, Before and After*. New York: Penguin, 1940.

David, Claude. *Hitler's Germany*. Translated by Anne-Marie Geoghegan. New York: Walker, 1963.

Davidson, Eugene. *The Making of Adolf Hitler*. New York: Macmillan, 1977.

Davis, John Williams. "*Hitler and the Versailles Settlement.*" Ph.D. diss., The University of Wisconsin, 1964. (DAI, 25:4, 2470, UMI Order # 6410225)

Dawidowicz, Lucy S. *The War Against the Jews, 1933-1945*. New York: Holt, Rinehart & Winston, 1975.

Dayton, Eldorous L. *Secret Life of Adolf Hitler*. New York: Citadel Press, 1960.

De Jaeger, Charles. *The Linz File: Hitler's Plunder of Europe's Art*. Exeter, England: Webb & Bower, 1981.

De Luca, Anthony R. *Personality, Power and Politics: Observations on the Historical Significance of Napoleon, Bismarck, Lenin, and Hitler*. Cambridge, MA: Schenkman Pub. Co., 1983.

Deakin, Frederick William. *The Brutal Friendship: Mussolini, Hitler, and the Fall of Italian Fascism*. Rev. ed. Garden City, NY: Doubleday, 1962.

Degrelle, Leon. *Hitler: Born at Versailles*. Costa Mesa, CA: Institute for Historical Review, 1987.

Deuel, Wallace R. *Hitler and Nazi Germany*. Chicago: Reprinted from The Chicago Daily News, 1941.

Deutsch, Harold C. *The Conspiracy Against Hitler in the Twilight War*. Minneapolis, MN: University of Minnesota Press, 1968.

______. *Hitler and His Generals: The Hidden Crisis, January-June 1938*. Minneapolis, MN: University of Minnesota Press, 1974.

Devaney, John. *Hitler: Mad Dictator of World War II*. New York: Putnam, 1978. (juvenile)

Dietrich, Otto. *Hitler*. Translated by Richard and Clara Winston. Chicago: H. Regnery, 1955.

______. *With Hitler on the Road to Power. Personal Experiences with My Leader*. London: n.p, 1934.

Dolan, Edward F. *Adolf Hitler: A Portrait in Tyranny*. New York: Dodd, Mead, 1981.

Dornberg, John. *Munich 1923: The Story of Hitler's First Grab for Power*. New York: Harper & Row, 1982.

Duffy, James P. *Hitler Slept Late and Other Blunders That Cost Him the War*. New York: Praeger, 1991.

______ and Vincent L. Ricci. *Target Hitler: The Plots to Kill Adolf Hitler*. New York: Praeger, 1992.

Dupuy, Trevor Nevitt, and others. *Hitler's Last Gamble: The Battle of the Bulge, December 1944-January 1945*. New York: HarperCollins, 1994.

______. *The Military Life of Adolf Hitler, Fuehrer of Germany*. New York: F. Watts, 1969. (juvenile)

Eimerl, Sarel. *Hitler Over Europe: The Road to World War II*. Boston: Little, Brown, 1972.

Einzig, Paul. *Hitler's "New Order" in Europe*. London: Macmillan, 1941.

Elliott, B. J. (Brendan John). *Hitler and Germany*. 2nd ed. London: Longman, 1990.

Engelmann, Bernt. *In Hitler's Germany: Daily Life in the Third Reich*. Translated by Krishna Winston. New York: Pantheon Books, 1986.

Ensor, Robert Charles Kirkwood. *Herr Hitler's Self-Discourse in Mein Kampf*. Oxford: The Clarendon Press, 1939.

______. *Who Hitler Is*. Oxford: The Clarendon Press, 1939.

Eskew, Margaret Hodges. *The Syntactic Preferences of Adolf Hitler in His Declaration of War on Poland*. New York: P. Lang, 1992.

Feder, Gottfried. *Hitler's Official Programme and Its Fundamental Ideas*. New York: H. Fertig, 1971.

Fenyo, Mario D. *Hitler, Horthy, and Hungary: German-Hungarian Relations, 1941-1944*. New Haven, CT: Yale University Press, 1972.

______. *"Horthy, Hitler, and Hungary: A Contribution to the Study of German Hungarian Relations from June 1941 to the Fall of the Horthy Regime in October 1944."* Ph.D. diss., The American University, 1969. (DAI, 30:3, 1104A, Order # 6914173)

Fest, Joachim C. *Hitler*. Translated from the German by Richard and Clara Winston. New York: Harcourt Brace Jovanovich, 1974.

FitzGibbon, Constantine. *To Kill Hitler*. London: Tom Stacey Ltd., 1972.

Fleming, Gerald. *Hitler and the Final Solution*. Berkeley, CA: University of California Press, 1984.

Flood, Charles Bracelen. *Hitler: The Path to Power*. Boston: Houghton Mifflin, 1989.

Forman, James. *Nazism*. New York: F. Watts, 1978. (juvenile)

Francois-Poncet, Andre. *The Fateful Years, Memoirs of a French Ambassador in Berlin, 1931-1938*. Translated from the French by Jacques Leclercq. New York: H. Fertig, 1946.

Frank, Robert Henry. "*Hitler and the National Socialist Coalition, 1924-1932*." Ph.D. diss., The Johns Hopkins University, 1969. (DAI, 32:12, 6889A, UMI Order # 7216845)

Friedlander, Saul. *Prelude to Downfall: Hitler and the United States, 1939-41*. Translated from the French by Alice B. and Alexander Werth. New York: Knopf, 1967.

Fuchs, Thomas. *The Hitler Fact Book*. Los Angeles: Fountain Books, 1990.

Galante, Pierre. *Operation Valkyrie: The German Generals' Plot Against Hitler*. Translated from the French by Mark Howson and Cary Ryan. New York: Harper & Row, 1981.

______ and Eugene Silianoff. *Voices from the Bunker: The True Account of Hitler's Last Days*. Translated from the French by Jan Dalley. New York: G. P. Putnam's Sons, 1989.

Geary, Richard. *Hitler and Nazism*. London: Routledge, 1993.

Genri, Ernst. *Hitler Over Europe*. New York: Simon & Schuster, 1934.

______. *Hitler Over Russia? The Coming Fight Between Fascist and Socialist Armies*. Translated by Michael Davidson. New York: Simon & Schuster, 1936.

Gerber, Albert Benjamin. *The Life of Adolf Hitler, 1889-1945*. Philadelphia: Mercury Books, 1961.

Gervasi, Frank. *Adolf Hitler*. New York: Hawthorn Books, 1974.

Gilbert, Felix, comp. *Hitler Directs His War: The Secret Record of His Daily Military Conferences*. New York: Oxford University Press, 1950.

Gilfond, Henry. *The Reichstag Fire, February 1933: Hitler Utilizes Arson to Extend His Dictatorship*. New York: Watts, 1973. (juvenile)

Gisevius, Hans Bernd. *To the Bitter End*. Translated from the German by Richard and Clara Winston. Boston: Houghton Mifflin, 1947.

Goebbels, Josef, and others. *Adolf Hitler: Pictures from the Life of the Fuehrer, 1931-1935*. Translated from the 1936 edition by Carl Underhill Quinn. New York: Peebles Press, 1978. Distributed by Bobbs-Merrill.

Golding, Louis. *Hitler Through the Ages*. London: Sovereign Books Ltd., 1939.

Gordon, Harold J. *Hitler and the Beer Hall Putsch*. Princeton, NJ: Princeton University Press, 1972.

Gordon, Sarah. *Hitler, Germans, and the "Jewish Question"*. Princeton, NJ: Princeton University Press, 1984.

Granatstein, J. L. *The Era of the Third Reich*. Toronto: Macmillan of Canada, 1970.

Granzow, Brigitte. *A Mirror of Nazism: British Opinion and the Emergence of Hitler*. London: V. Gollancz, 1964.

Gray, Ronald D. *Hitler and the Germans*. New York: Cambridge University Press, 1981.

Grunfeld, Frederic V. *The Hitler File: A Social History of Germany and the Nazis, 1918-1945*. New York: Random House, 1974.

Grzesinski, Albert Carl. *Inside Germany*. Translated by Alexander S. Lipschitz. New York: Dutton, 1939.

Gun, Nerin E. *Eva Braun: Hitler's Mistress*. New York: Meredith Press, 1968.

Gunther, John. *The High Cost of Hitler*. London: H. Hamilton, 1939.

Hackett, Francis. *What Mein Kampf Means to America*. New York: Reynal & Hitchcock, 1941.

Haffner, Sebastian. *The Meaning of Hitler*. Translated by Ewald Osers. New York: Macmillan, 1979.

Halder, Franz. *Hitler As War Lord*. Translated from the German by Paul Findlay. London: Putnam, 1950.

Hamilton, Charles. *The Hitler Diaries: Fakes That Fooled the World*. Lexington, KY: University Press of Kentucky, 1991.

Hamilton, Richard F. *Who Voted for Hitler?* Princeton, NJ: Princeton University Press, 1982.

Hance, Jesse S. *When Hitler Lived in the United States*. New York: Vantage Press, 1968.

Handel, Michael I. *The Diplomacy of Surprise: Hitler, Nixon, Sadat*. Cambridge, MA: Center for International Affairs, Harvard University, 1981.

Hanfstaengl, Ernst. *Hitler: The Missing Years*. London: Eyre & Spottiswoode, 1957.

Hanser, Richard. *Putsch! How Hitler Made Revolution*. New York: P. H. Wyden, 1970.

Hanstaengl, Ernst Franz Sedgwick. *Unheard Witness*. Philadelphia: Lippincott, 1937.

Harris, Robert. *Selling Hitler*. New York: Penguin Books, 1986.

Hauner, Milan. *Hitler, A Chronology of His Life and Time*. New York: St. Martin's Press, 1983.

Heiber, Helmut. *Adolf Hitler*. Translated from the German by Lawrence Wilson. Chester Springs, PA: Dutour Publications, 1961.

Heiden, Konrad. *Der Fuehrer: Hitler's Rise to Power*. Translated by Robert Manheim. Boston: Houghton Mifflin, 1944.

_____. *A History of National Socialism*. Translated from the German. New York: Octagon Books, 1971.

_____. *Hitler: A Biography*. Translated from the German by Winifred Ray. New York: A. A. Knopf, 1936.

_____. *One Man Against Europe*. New York: Penguin Books Ltd., 1940.

Heinz, Heinz A. *Germany's Hitler*. London: Hurst & Blackett, 1934.

Hershman, D. Jablow and Julian Lieb. *A Brotherhood of Tyrants: Manic Depression and Absolute Power*. Amherst, NY: Prometheus Books, 1994.

Herzstein, Robert Edwin. *Adolf Hitler and the German Trauma, 1933-1945: An Interpretation of the Nazi Phenomenon*. New York: Putnam, 1974.

_____. *Adolf Hitler and the Third Reich, 1933-1945*. Boston: Houghton Mifflin, 1971.

_____. *Roosevelt and Hitler: Prelude to War*. New York: Paragon House, 1989.

_____. *The War Hitler Won: The Most Infamous Propaganda Campaign in History*. New York: Putnam, 1978.

Hesse, Fritz. *Hitler and the English*. London: A. Wingate, 1954.

Heston, Leonard L. *The Medical Casebook of Adolf Hitler: His Illnesses, Doctors, and Drugs*. New York: Stein & Day, 1979.

Heyes, Eileen. *Adolf Hitler*. Brookfield, CT: Millbrook Press, 1993. (juvenile)

Hiden, John and John Farquharson. *Explaining Hitler's Germany: Historians and the Third Reich*. Totowa, NJ: Barnes & Noble, 1983.

_____. *Germany and Europe, 1919-1939*. New York: Longman, 1977.

Higgins, Trumbull. *Hitler and Russia: The Third Reich in A Two Front War, 1937-1943*. New York: Macmillan, 1966.

Hills, C. A. R. *The Hitler File*. London: Batsford, 1980.

Hilton, Stanley E. *Hitler's Secret War in South America, 1939-1945: German Military Espionage and Allied Counterespionage in Brazil*. Baton Rouge: Louisiana State University Press, 1981.

Hinsley, F. H. (Francis Harry). *Hitler's Strategy: The Naval Evidence*. England: University Press, 1951.

Hirsch, Phil, comp. *Hitler and His Henchmen*. New York: Pyramid Books, 1967.

Hitler, Adolf. *Adolf Hitler's Quotations*. [United States]: Hammer, 1990.

_____. *The Art of Lying*. (Microform). London: 1943. New Haven, CT: Yale University Library, 1990.

_____. *Fuehrer Conferences on Naval Affairs, 1939-1945*. Translated from the German. Annapolis, MD: Naval Institute Press, 1990.

_____. *Fuehrer Directives and Other Top-Level Directives of the German Armed Forces*. Washington, DC: U.S. Navy Department, 1948.

_____. *Germany Declares for Peace*. Berlin: Liebheit & Thiesen, 1933.

_____. *Hitler: Speeches and Proclamations, 1932-1945. The Chronicle of A Dictatorship*. 4 volumes. Edited by Max Domarus. Translated from the German by Mary Fran Gilbert. London: Tauris, 1990.

_____. *Hitler Step by Step, 1933-1939. A Calendar of Aggression*. London: Times Publishing Company. Reprinted from The Times, London, Tuesday, Sept. 26, 1939.

_____. "Hitler to Mussolini." Translation of a letter Adolf Hitler sent to Benito Mussolini, outlining his reasons for invading the Soviet Union, dated June 21, 1941, with comment by Stefan T. Possony. *Infantry Journal* 61 (August 1947): 14-17.

_____. *Hitler, Volume 3: June 1928-September 1930*. New Providence, NJ: K. G. Saur, 1993.

_____. *Hitler, Volume 4: October 1930-November 1931*. New Providence, NJ: K. G. Saur, 1993.

_____. *Hitler's Secret Book*. Translated by Salvator Attanasio. New York: Grove Press, 1962. Translation of a manuscript dictated by Adolf Hitler in 1928.

_____. *Hitler's War Directives, 1939-1945*. Edited by H. R. Trevor-Roper. London: Sidgwick & Nicolson, 1964.

_____. *Hitler's Words*. Edited by Gordon Prange. Washington, DC: American Council on Public Affairs, 1944.

_____. *Mein Kampf*. Boston: Houghton Mifflin, 1939.

_____. *My Battle*. Abridged and translated by E. T. S. Dugdale. Boston: Houghton Mifflin, 1933.

_____. *My New Order*. New York: Reynal & Hitchcock, 1941.

_____. *The New Germany Desires Work and Peace*. Speeches by Reich Chancellor Adolf Hitler, The Leader of the New Germany. Berlin: Liebheit & Thiesen, 1933.

_____. *Poland: British and German Foreign Policy. Speeches by Adolf Hitler and Lord Halifax*. Westminster: Friends of Europe, 1939.

_____. *Secret Conversations, 1941-1944*. Translated by Norman Cameron and R. H. Stevens. New York: Farrar, Straus & Young, 1953.

_____. *The Speeches of Adolf Hitler, April 1922-August 1939*. Arranged and edited by Norman H. Baynes. New York: Oxford University Press, 1942.

_____. *The Testament of Adolf Hitler: The Hitler-Bormann Documents, February-April 1945*. Los Angeles: World Service, 1978.

Hitler, Bridget Elizabeth. *My Brother-in-Law Adolf*. Unpublished. Manuscript in New York City Public Library.

Hoffman, Peter. *Hitler's Personal Security*. Cambridge, MA: MIT Press, 1989.

Hoffmann, Heinrich. *Hitler: The Hoffmann Photographs*. Edited by Ray R. Cowdery. Lakeville, MN: USM, 1990.

_____. *Hitler Was My Friend*. Translated by R. H. Stevens. London: Burke, 1955.

Holden, Matthew. *Hitler*. London: Wayland, 1974.

Hoover, Calvin B. *Germany Enters the Third Reich*. New York: Macmillan, 1933.

Hoyt, Edwin P. *Hitler's War*. New York: McGraw-Hill, 1988.

Hulbert, Roy Joseph. "*Hitler's Idea of 'Legal Revolution' and the Triumph of Nazism: A Study of Politics and Moral Anarchy*." Ph.D. diss., University of Washington, 1975. (DAI, 37:2, 1157A, UMI Order # 7617505)

Infield, Glenn B. *Eva and Adolf*. New York: Grosset & Dunlap, 1974.

_____. *Hitler's Secret Life: The Mysteries of the Eagle's Nest*. New York: Stein & Day, 1979.

_____. *The Private Lives of Eva and Adolf*. New York: Grosset & Dunlap, 1978.

Irving, David. *Hitler's War*. New York: Viking Press, 1977.

_____. *The War Path: Hitler's Germany, 1933-1939*. New York: Viking Press, 1978.

Italia, Bob. *The Story of Adolf Hitler*. Edina, MN: Abdo & Daughters, 1990. (juvenile)

Jablonsky, David. *Churchill and Hitler: Essays on the Political-Military Direction of Total War*. Portland, OR: International Specialized Book Services, 1994.

_____. *The Nazi Party in Dissolution: Hitler and the Verbotzeit, 1923-1925*. Totowa, NJ: F. Cass, 1989.

_____. *Strategic Rationality is Not Enough: Hitler and the Concept of Crazy States*. Carlisle Barracks, PA: Strategic Studies Institute, U.S. Army War College, 1991.

Jackel, Eberhard. *David Irving's Hitler: A Faulty History Dissected, Two Essays*. Translation and comments by H. David Kirk. Port Angeles, WA: Ben-Simons Publications, 1993.

_____. *Hitler in History*. Hanover, NH: University of New England Press, 1984.

_____. *Hitler's World View: A Blueprint for Power*. Translated from the German by Herbert Arnold. Cambridge, MA: Harvard University Press, 1981.

Jacobs, William Jay. *Hitler*. Beverly Hills, CA: Benziger, 1976.

Jacobsen, Hans Adolf. *Germans Against Hitler, July 20, 1944*. Bonn: Press and Information Office of the Federal Government of Germany, 1969.

Jenks, William Alexander. *Vienna and the Young Hitler*. New York: Columbia University Press, 1960.

Jetzinger, Franz. *Hitler's Youth*. Translated from the German by Lawrence Wilson. London: Hutchinson, 1958.

Jones, F. (Frederick) Elwyn. *Hitler's Drive in the East*. New York: E. P. Dutton, 1937.

Jones, J. Sydney. *Hitler in Vienna, 1907-1913: Clues to the Future*. New York: Stein & Day, 1983.

Jukes, Geoffrey. *Hitler's Stalingrad Decisions*. Berkeley, CA: University of California Press, 1985.

Kahle, Hans. *They Plotted Against Hitler: The Story Behind the Attempt on Hitler's Life*. London: I.N.G. Publications, 1944.

Kalow, Gert. *The Shadow of Hitler: A Critique of Political Consciousness*. London: Rapp & Whiting, 1967.

Katz, Robert. *Adolf Hitler: A Biography*. New York: Monarch Press, 1966.

Kellock, James. *Germany and Nazism: Philosophy of Mein Kampf*. Bombay: National War Front, 1944.

Kelly, Maurice E., comp. *Adolf Hitler*. Translated by Inge Christl. Sydney, NSW: View Productions, 1985.

Kempowski, Walter, comp. *Did You Ever See Hitler? German Answers*. Translated by Michael Roloff. New York: Avon Books, 1975.

Kepler, Norman William. "*A Psychohistorical Examination of Adolf Hitler*." Ph.D. diss., United States International University, 1985. (DAI, 46:6, 2067B, UMI Order # DA8516337)

Kershaw, Ian. *Hitler*. New York: Longman, 1991.

______. *The "Hitler Myth": Image and Reality in the Third Reich*. New York: Oxford University Press, 1987.

Kestenberg, Louis. "*The Governing Ideology of Frederick II of Prussia and Hitler*." Ph.D. diss., University of Colorado at Boulder, 1943. (Not available from UMI)

Kindermann, Gottfried Karl. *Hitler's Defeat in Austria, 1933-1934: Europe's First Containment of Nazi Expansionism*. Translated by Sonia Brough and David Taylor. Boulder, CO: Westview Press, 1988.

King-Hall, Stephen. *Three Dictators: Mussolini, Hitler, and Stalin*. London: Faber & Faber, 1964. (juvenile)

Klein, Mina C. and H. Arthur Klein. *Hitler's Hang Ups: An Adventure in Insight*. New York: Dutton, 1976. (juvenile)

Koch, H. W., ed. *Aspects of the Third Reich*. London: Macmillan, 1985.

Koch-Weser, Erich Friedrich Ludwig. *Hitler and Beyond, A German Testament*. New York: A. A. Knopf, 1945.

Koenigsberg, Richard A. *Hitler's Ideology: A Study in Psychoanalytic Sociology*. New York: Library of Social Science, 1975.

Krueger, Kurt. *I Was Hitler's Doctor*. New York: Biltmore Publishing Co., 1943.

______. *Inside Hitler*. New York: Avalon Press Inc., 1942.

Kubizek, August. *The Young Hitler I Knew*. Translated from the German by E. V. Anderson. Boston: Houghton Mifflin, 1954.

Laing, Stuart, ed. *The Illustrated Hitler Diary, 1917-1945*. New York: Galahad, 1980.

Lang, Joachem von. *Adolf Hitler: Faces of A Dictator*. New York: Harcourt, Brace & World, 1969.

Langer, Walter C. *The Mind of Adolf Hitler: The Secret Wartime Report*. New York: Basic Books, 1972.

Laurie, Arthur Pillans. *The Case for Germany: A Study of Modern Germany*. Berlin: International Verlag, 1939.

Layton, Geoff. *Germany: The Third Reich, 1933-45*. London: Hodder & Stoughton, 1992.

Lengyel, Emil. *Hitler*. New York: The Dial Press, 1932.

Leonhard, Wolfgang. *Betrayal: The Hitler-Stalin Pact of 1939*. New York: St. Martin's Press, 1983.

Lewin, Ronald. *Hitler's Mistakes*. New York: William Morrow, 1986.

Lewis, Brenda Ralph. *Hitler and Nazi Germany*. London: Evans Brothers, 1979.

Lewis, Wyndham. *Hitler*. London: Chatto & Windus, 1931.

______. *The Hitler Cult*. London: Dent, 1939.

______. *Hitler, the Germans, and the Jews*. New York: Gordon Press Publishers, 1973.

Lichtenberger, Henri. *The Third Reich*. Translated from the French by Koppel S. Pinson. New York: Greystone Press, 1937.

Lorimer, Emily. *What Hitler Wants*. Harmondsworth, Middlesex, England: Penguin Books Ltd., 1939.

Ludecke, Kurt. *I Knew Hitler: The Story of A Nazi Who Escaped the Blood Purge*. New York: Charles Scribner's Sons, 1937.

Ludwig, Emil. *Three Portraits: Hitler, Mussolini, Stalin*. New York: Alliance Book Corporation, Longmans, Green & Co., 1940.

Lukacs, John. *The Duel. 10 May - 31 July 1940: The Eighty-Day Struggle Between Churchill and Hitler*. New York: Ticknor & Fields, 1991. Distributed by Houghton Mifflin.

Macksey, Kenneth, ed. *The Hitler Options: Alternative Decisions of World War II*. London, PA: Greenhill Books, 1995.

Maier, Charles S., ed., and others. *The Rise of the Nazi Regime: Historical Reassessments*. Boulder, CO: Westview Press, 1986.

Manning, Jonathan R., ed. *Adolf Hitler*. Authored by His Ministers of the Third Reich, Hermann Goering, and others. Phoenix, AZ: T.H.E. Publishing Co., 1973.

Manvell, Roger. *Adolf Hitler: The Man and the Myth*. Rev. ed. London: Panther, 1978.

______ and Heinrich Fraenkel. *The Hundred Days to Hitler*. New York: St. Martin's Press, 1974.

______. *The July Plot: The Attempt in 1944 on Hitler's Life and the Men Behind It*. London: Bodley Head, 1964.

Marrin, Albert. *Hitler*. New York: Puffin Books, 1993. (juvenile)

Martienssen, Anthony K. *Hitler and His Admirals*. New York: E. P. Dutton, 1949.

Maser, Werner. *Hitler: Legend, Myth, and Reality*. Translated from the German by Peter and Betty Ross. New York: Harper & Row, 1973.

______. *Hitler's Letters and Notes*. Translated from the German by Arnold Pomerans. New York: Harper & Row, 1974.

______. *Hitler's Mein Kampf: An Analysis*. Translated from the German by R. H. Barry. London: Faber, 1970.

Mason, Herbert Molloy, Jr. *To Kill the Devil: The Attempts on the Life of Adolf Hitler*. New York: W. W. Norton & Co., 1978.

Matanle, Ivor. *Adolf Hitler: A Photographic Documentary*. New York: Cresent Books, 1983.

Maugham, Frederic. *Lies as Allies or Hitler at War*. New York: Oxford University Press, 1941.

McCabe, Joseph. *Hitler and His Gang: The True Story of the Greatest Crime in History*. Girard, KS: Haldeman-Julius Publications, 1944.

McGuire, Michael Dennis. *"Mythic Rhetoric: A Case Study of Adolf Hitler's 'Mein Kampf.'"* Ph.D. diss., The University of Iowa, 1975. (DAI, 36:8, 4851A, UMI Order # 762152)

McKale, Donald M. *Hitler: The Survival Myth*. New York: Stein & Day, 1980.

______. *The Nazi Party Courts: Hitler's Management of Conflict in His Movement, 1921-1925*. Lawrence, KS: University Press of Kansas, 1974.

McKnight, Gerald. *The Strange Loves of Adolf Hitler*. London: Sphere, 1978.

McRandle, James H. *The Track of the Wolf: Essays on National Socialism and Its Leader, Adolf Hitler*. Evanston, IL: Northwestern University Press, 1965.

McSherry, James E. *Stalin, Hitler, and Europe*. Cleveland, OH: World Publishing Co., 1968.

Meinecke, Friedrich. *The German Catastrophe, Reflections and Recollections*. Translated by Sydney B. Fay. Boston: Beacon Press, 1963.

Metcalfe, Philip. *1933*. London: Bantam Press, 1989.

Mitchell, Otis C. *Hitler Over Germany: The Establishment of the Nazi Dictatorship, 1918-1934*. Philadelphia: Institute for the Study of Human Issues, 1983.

______. *Hitler's Nazi State: The Years of Dictatorial Rule, 1934-1945*. New York: P. Lang, 1988.

______. *Nazism and the Common Man: Essays in German History (1929-1939)*. Minneapolis, MN: Burgess Pub. Co., 1972.

Moore, Herbert and James W. Barrett, eds. *Who Killed Hitler?* New York: Booktab Press, 1947.

Morell, Theodor Gilbert. *The Secret Diaries of Hitler's Doctor*. Edited by David Irving. New York: Macmillan, 1983.

Moriarty, David M., comp. and ed. *A Psychological Study of Adolf Hitler*. St. Louis: W. H. Green, 1993.

Mott, Francis J. *Hitler Right and Wrong*. New York: Society of Life, 1935.

Musman, Richard. *Hitler and Mussolini*. London: Chatto & Windus, 1968.

Musmanno, Michael A. *Ten Days to Die*. Garden City, NY: Doubleday, 1950.

Myklebust, Svein Lorents. "*The Greatest Deception in the History of Warfare: Hitler's Deceptive Operations in the Months Prior to the Attack on Russia in June 1941*." Ph.D. diss., The University of Wisconsin-Madison, 1980.   (DAI, 41:5, 2253A, UMI Order # 8015221)

Neumann, Robert. *The Pictorial History of the Third Reich*. New York: Bantam Books, 1962.

Nicholls, A. J. (Anthony James). *Weimar and the Rise of Hitler*. 3rd ed. London: Macmillan, 1991.

______. and Erich Mathias, eds. *German Democracy and the Triumph of Hitler: Essays in Recent Germany History*. New York: St. Martin's Press, 1972.

Nova, Fritz. "*The National Socialist Fuehrerprinzip and Its Background in German Thought*." Ph.D. diss., University of Pennsylvania, 1943. (Not available from UMI)

O'Donnell, James Preston. *The Bunker: The History of the Reich Chancellery Group*. Boston: Houghton Mifflin, 1978.

Ohquist, Johannes Vilhelm. *The Reich of the Fuehrer: The Ideology and Development of National Socialism as Seen by a Foreigner*. Germany: Max Schmersow, 1942.

Olden, Rudolf. *Hitler*. Translated by Walter Ettinghausen. New York: Covici, Friede, 1936.

O'Neill, Herbert Charles. *Men of Destiny: Being Studies of the Four Who Rode the War and Made This Precarious Landfall*. London: Phoenix House, 1953.

Orlow, Dietrich. *The History of the Nazi Party, 1933-1945*. Pittsburgh: University of Pittsburgh Press, 1973.

Owen, Frank. *The Three Dictators: Mussolini, Stalin, Hitler*. London: G. Allen & Unwin Ltd., 1940.

Palumbo, Michael Vincent. "*The Uncertain Friendship: Hitler and Mussolini, 1922-1933*." Ph.D. diss., City University of New York, 1979. (Not available from UMI)

Parkinson, Roger. *Hitler*. New York: St. Martin's Press, 1974. (juvenile)

Pauley, Bruce F. *Hitler and the Forgotten Nazis: A History of Austrian National Socialism*. Chapel Hill: University of North Carolina Press, 1981.

Payne, Robert. *The Life and Death of Adolf Hitler*. New York: Praeger, 1973.

Pearson, Eileen. *Hitler's Reich*. St Paul, MN: Greenhaven Press, 1977. (juvenile)

Pelz, Werner and Lotte Pelz. *I am Adolf Hitler*. London: SCM Press, 1969.

Peterson, Edward N. *The Limits of Hitler's Power*. Princeton, NJ: Princeton University Press, 1969.

Phillips, D. M. *Hitler and the Rise of the Nazis*. London: Edward Arnold, 1968. (juvenile)

Phillips, Leona Rasmussen. *Adolf Hitler and the Third Reich: An Annotated Bibliography*. New York: Gordon Press, 1977.

Picker, Henry and Heinrich Hoffman. *Hitler Closeup*. Translated from the German by Nicholas Fry. New York: Macmillan, 1973.

Plehwe, Friedrich-Karl von. *The End of An Alliance: Rome's Defection from the Axis in 1943*. Translated from the German by Eric Mosbacher. London: Oxford University Press, 1971.

Pollock, James Kerr and Harlow J. Heneman. *The Hitler Decrees*. Ann Arbor, MI: G. Wahr, 1934.

Pool, James. *Who Financed Hitler: The Secret Funding of Hitler's Rise to Power, 1919-1933*. New York: Dial Press, 1978.

Prange, Gordan William. *Hitler's Speeches and the United States*. New York: Oxford University Press, 1941.

Price, Billy F. *Adolf Hitler, the Unknown Artist*. Houston: B.F. Price Publishing Co., 1984.

Pridham, Geoffrey. *Hitler's Rise to Power: The Nazi Movement in Bavaria, 1923-1933*. New York: Harper & Row, 1973.

Pullar Smith, Margaret A. *Hitler and Mussolini: The Western Dictators*. Glasgow: Blackie, 1978.

Ratcliffe, A. *The Truth About Hitler and the Roman Catholic Church*. Brooklyn, NY: The Revisionist Press, 1982.

Rauschning, Hermann. *Hitler Speaks: A Series of Political Conversations with Adolf Hitler on His Real Aims*. London: T. Butterworth, 1939.

Ray, John. *Hitler and Mussolini*. London: Heinemann Educational, 1970.

Read, Anthony and David Fisher. *The Deadly Embrace: Hitler, Stalin, and the Nazi-Soviet Pact, 1939-1941*. New York: Norton, 1988.

Remak, Joachim, ed. *The Nazi Years: A Documentary History*. Englewood Cliffs, NJ: Prentice-Hall, 1969.

Reynolds, Rothay. *When Freedom Shrieked*. London: V. Gollancz, 1939.

Rhodes, James M. *The Hitler Movement: A Modern Millenarian Revolution*. Stanford, CA: Hoover Institution Press, 1980.

Rich, Norman. *Hitler's War Aims*. New York: Norton, 1973.

Roberts, Geoffrey. *The Unholy Alliance: Stalin's Pact with Hitler*. London: Tauris, 1989.

Roberts, Stephen H. *The House that Hitler Built*. London: Methuen, 1937.

Robertson, Esmonde M. *Hitler's Pre-War Policy and Military Plans, 1933-1939*. New York: Citadel Press, 1963.

Rohl, J. C. G. *From Bismarck to Hitler: The Problem of Continuity in German History*. London: Longman, 1970.

Rosenfeld, Alvin H. *Imagining Hitler*. Bloomington, IN: Indiana University Press, 1985.

Rosio, Bob. *Hitler and the New Age*. Lafayette, LA: Huntington House Publishers, 1993.

Rubenstein, Joshua. *Adolf Hitler*. New York: F. Watts, 1982. (juvenile)

Rutherford, Ward. *Hitler's Propaganda Machine*. New York: Grosset & Dunlop, 1978.

Sapinsley, Barbara. *From Kaiser to Hitler: The Life and Death of A Democracy, 1919-1933*. New York: Grosset & Dunlap, 1968.

Scherger, George L. *Men of the Hour: Mussolini, Gandhi, Stalin, Hitler*. Chicago: Popular Interest Series Publishing Co., 1933.

Schlabrendorff, Fabian von. *They Almost Killed Hitler*. New York: Macmillan, 1947.

Schmeller, Helmut J. *Hitler and Keitel: An Investigation of the Influence of Party Ideology on the High Command of the Armed Forces of Germany Between 1938 and 1945*. Hays, KS: Fort Hays State College, 1970.

______. "Hitler's View of History." Ph.D. diss., Kansas State University, 1975. (DAI, 37:2, 1161A, UMI Order # 7617122)

Schmidt, Paul. *Hitler's Interpreter*. Edited by R. H. C. Steed. New York: Macmillan, 1951.

Schoenbaum, David. *Hitler's Social Revolution: Class and Status in Nazi Germany, 1933-1939*. Garden City, NY: Doubleday, 1966.

Schramm, Percy. *Hitler: The Man and the Military Leader*. Translated, edited, with an introduction by Donald S. Detwiler. Chicago: Quadrangle Books, 1971.

Schuman, Frederick L. *The Nazi Dictatorship: A Study in Social Pathology and the Politics of Fascism.* New York: A. A. Knopf, 1935.

Schwaab, Edleff H. *Hitler's Mind: A Plunge Into Madness.* New York: Praeger, 1992.

Schwarzwaller, Wulf. *The Unknown Hitler: His Private Life and Fortune.* Bethesda, MD: National Press Books, 1988.

Seward, Desmond. *Napoleon and Hitler: A Comparative Biography.* New York: Viking Press, 1989.

Shirer, William L. *The Rise and Fall of Adolf Hitler.* New York: Random House, 1961. (juvenile)

_____. *The Rise and Fall of the Third Reich: A History of Nazi Germany.* New York: Simon & Schuster, 1960.

Short, K. R. M. and S. Dolezel, eds. *Hitler's Fall: The Newsreel Witness.* London: Croom Helm, 1988.

Shuster, George N. *Strong Man Rules: An Interpretation of Germany Today.* New York: D. Appleton-Century Company Inc., 1934.

Simpson, Amos E., comp. with the assistance of Sarah Cain Neitzel. *Why Hitler?* Boston: Houghton Mifflin, 1971.

Simpson, William. *Hitler and Germany.* Cambridge: Cambridge University Press, 1991.

Skipper, G. C. *The Death of Hitler.* Chicago: Children's Press, 1980. (juvenile)

Smith, Bradley F. *Adolf Hitler: His Family, Childhood, and Youth.* Stanford, CA: Hoover Institute on War, Revolution, and Peace, 1967.

Smith, Gene. *The Horns of the Moon: A Short Biography of Adolf Hitler.* New York: Charterhouse, 1974.

Snell, John L., ed. *The Nazi Revolution: Hitler's Dictatorship and the German Nation.* Lexington, MA: Heath, 1973.

Snyder, Louis Leo. *Hitler and Nazism.* New York: F. Watts, 1961.

_____. *Hitlerism: The Iron Fist in Germany.* New York: The Mohawk Press, 1932.

_____. *Hitler's Third Reich: A Documentary History.* Chicago: Nelson-Hall, 1981.

Sognnaes, Reidar F. *Dental Evidence in the Postmortem Identification of Adolf Hitler, Eva Braun, and Martin Bormann.* New York: Appleton-Century-Crofts, 1977.

Spielvogel, Jackson J. *Hitler and Nazi Germany: A History.* 2nd ed. Englewood Cliffs, NJ: Prentice-Hall, 1992.

Stachura, Peter D. *The Weimar Era and Hitler, 1918-1933: A Critical Bibliography.* Oxford: Clio Press Ltd., 1977.

Staudinger, Hans. *The Inner Nazi: A Critical Analysis of Mein Kampf.* Baton Rouge, LA: Louisiana State University Press, 1981.

Steed, Wickham. *Hitler: Whence and Whither?* London: Nisbit & Co. Ltd., 1934.

______. *Our War Aims.* London: Secker and Warburg, 1939.

______. *That Bad Man: A Tale for the Young and All Ages.* London: Macmillan & Co. Ltd., 1942.

Steeh, Judith. *The Rise and Fall of Adolf Hitler.* New York: Galahad Books, 1980.

Steel, Johannes. *Hitler as Frankenstein.* London: Wishart & Co., 1933.

Stein, George. H., ed. *Hitler.* Englewood Cliffs, NJ: Prentice-Hall, 1968.

Stern, Fritz Richard. *Germany 1933: Fifty Years Later.* New York: Leo Baeck Institute, 1984.

Stern, J. P. (Joseph Peter). *Hitler: The Fuehrer and the People.* Berkeley, CA: University of California Press, 1978.

Stevens, Lawrence. *Hitler and Fascism: Mini-Play and Activities.* Stockton, CA: Stevens & Shea Publishers, 1981.

Stewart, Gail B. *Hitler's Reich.* San Diego: Lucent Books, 1994. (juvenile)

Stierlin, Helm. *Adolf Hitler: A Family Perspective.* New York: Psychohistory Press, 1976.

Stoakes, Geoffrey. *Hitler and the Quest for World Domination.* New York: Berg, 1986.

Stone, Norman. *Hitler.* Boston: Little, Brown, 1980.

Strasser, Otto. *Hitler and I.* Boston: Houghton Mifflin, 1940.

Strawson, John. *Hitler's Battles for Europe.* New York: Scribner, 1971.

Suster, Gerald. *Hitler, the Occult Messiah.* New York: St. Martin's Press, 1981.

Sutton, Antony C. *Wall Street and the Rise of Hitler.* Sudbury, England: Bloomfield Books, 1976.

Syberberg, Hans Jurgen. *Hitler, a Film about Germany.* Translated by Joachim Neugroschel. New York: Farrar, Straus & Giroux, 1982.

Tames, Richard. *Hitler: An Illustrated Life of Adolf Hitler.* Aylesburg, England: Shire Publications, 1974.

Taylor, Gordon. *Hitler: A Biography.* London: Pilot Press, 1939.

Taylor, Simon. *The Rise of Hitler: Revolution and Counterrevolution in Germany, 1918-1933.* New York: Universe Books, 1983.

Tell, Rolf. *The Eternal Ger-maniac.* London: G. Allen & Unwin Ltd., 1942.

Thyssen, Fritz. *I Paid Hitler*. New York: Farrar & Rinehart, Inc., 1941.

Time-Life Book eds. *The Center of the Web*. Alexandria, VA: Time-Life Books, 1990.

______. *Storming to Power*. Alexandria, VA: Time-Life Books, 1989.

______. *The Twisted Dream*. Alexandria, VA: Time-Life Books, 1991.

Toland, John. *Adolf Hitler*. Garden City, NY: Doubleday, 1976.

______. *Hitler, the Pictorial Documentary of His Life*. Garden City, NY: Doubleday, 1978.

Tolischus, Otto D. *They Wanted War*. New York: Reynal & Hitchcock, 1940.

Tolstoy, Nikolai. *Night of the Long Knives*. New York: Ballantine Books, 1972.

Toynbee, Arnold and Veronica Toynbee, eds. *Hitler's Europe*. New York: Oxford University Press, 1954.

Trevor-Roper, H. R. (Hugh Redwald), ed. *Blitzkrieg to Defeat: Hitler's War Directives, 1939-1945*. New York: Holt, Rinehart & Winston, 1964.

______. *The Last Days of Hitler*. New York: Macmillan, 1947.

Trotskii, Lev. *What Hitler Wants*. New York: The John Day Company, 1933.

Turner, Henry Ashby, Jr. *German Big Business and the Rise of Hitler*. New York: Oxford University Press, 1985.

Van Creveld, Martin L. *Hitler's Strategy, 1940 to 1941: The Balkan Clue*. New York: Cambridge University Press, 1973.

Von Maltitz, Horst. *The Evolution of Hitler's Germany: The Ideology, the Personality, the Moment*. New York: McGraw-Hill, 1973.

Wagener, Otto. *Hitler: Memoirs of a Confident*. Edited by Henry Ashby Turner, Jr. Translated by Ruth Hein. New Haven, CT: Yale University Press, 1985.

Wagner, Ludwig. *Hitler, Man of Strife: A Biography*. New York: W. W. Norton & Co., 1942.

Waite, Robert G. L., ed. *Hitler and Nazi Germany*. New York: Holt, Rinehart & Winston, 1969.

______. *The Psychopathic God - Adolf Hitler*. New York: Basic Books, 1977.

Waldman, Morris David. *Sieg Heil, the Story of Adolf Hitler*. Dobbs Ferry, NY: Oceana Publications, 1962.

Walker, Malvin. *Chronological Encyclopedia of Adolf Hitler and the Third Reich*. New York: Charlton Press, 1978.

Walther, Herbert, ed. *Der Fuehrer: The Life and Times of Adolf Hitler*. Secaucus, NJ: Chartwell Books Inc., 1978.

_____, ed. *Hitler*. New York: Fell, 1978.

Weinberg, Gerhard L. *The Foreign Policy of Hitler's Germany: Diplomatic Revolution in Europe, 1933-1936*. Chicago: University of Chicago Press, 1970.

_____. *The Foreign Policy of Hitler's Germany: Starting World War II, 1937-1939*. Chicago: University of Chicago Press, 1980.

_____. *Germany, Hitler and World War II*. New York: Cambridge University Press, 1995.

Weinstein, Fred. *The Dynamics of Nazism: Leadership, Ideology, and the Holocaust*. New York: Academic Press, 1980.

Wepman, Dennis. *Adolf Hitler*. New York: Chelsea House, 1985. (juvenile)

Wertheimer, Mildred Salz. *Germany Under Hitler*. New York: Foreign Association. Boston: World Peace Foundation, 1935.

Whealey, Robert H. *Hitler and Spain: The Nazi Role in the Spanish Civil War, 1936-1939*. Lexington, KY: University of Kentucky Press, 1989.

Wheaton, Eliot Barculo. *Prelude to Calamity: The Nazi Revolution, 1933-35, with a Background Survey of the Weimar Era*. Garden City, NY: Doubleday, 1968.

Wilkie, Richard William. "*A Quantitative Analysis of Rhetorical Invention in Selected Speeches Delivered by Adolf Hitler in 1936*." Ph.D. diss., The University of Michigan, 1962. (DAI, 23:2, 753, UMI Order # 623271)

Williams, Simon. *The Rise and Fall of Hitler's Germany*. Basingstoke: Macmillan, 1986.

Williamson, D. G. *The Third Reich*. 2nd ed. London: Longman, 1995.

Wilt, Alan F. *Nazi Germany*. Arlington Heights, IL: H. Davidson, 1994.

Wiskemann, Elizabeth. *The Rome-Berlin Axis: A Study of the Relations Between Hitler and Mussolini*. New & rev. ed. London: Collins, 1966.

Wistrich, Robert. *Hitler's Apocalypse: Jews and the Nazi Legacy*. New York: St. Martin's Press, 1985.

Wolfe, Burton H. *Hitler and the Nazis*. New York: Putnam, 1970.

Wolfe, Henry Cutler. *The German Octopus: Hitler Bids for World Power*. Garden City, NY: Doubleday, Doran & Co., 1938.

Wolfe, Robert, intro. *A Man Called A. H.* New York: Garland Pub., 1989.

Wolman, Benjamin B., ed. *Psychoanalytic Interpretation of History*. New York: Basic Books, 1971.

World Committee for the Victims of German Fascism. *The Brown Book of the Hitler Terror and the Burning of the Reichstag*. New York: Knopf, 1933.

Wulff, Wilhelm. *Zodiac and Swastika: How Astrology Guided Hitler's Germany*. New York: Coward, McCann & Geoghegan, 1973.

Wykes, Alan. *Hitler*. New York: Ballantine Books, 1971.

Zalampas, Michael. *Adolf Hitler and the Third Reich in American Magazines, 1923-1939*. Bowling Green, OH: Bowling Green State University Popular Press, 1989.

Zalampas, Sherree Owens. *Adolf Hitler: A Psychological Interpretation of His Views on Architecture, Art, and Music*. Bowling Green, OH: Bowling Green University Popular Press, 1990.

Zeman, Zbynek. *Heckling Hitler: Caricatures of the Third Reich*. 2nd ed. Hanover, NH: University Press of New England, 1987.

Zepp-La Rouche, Helga, ed. *The Hitler Book: A Schiller Institute Study*. New York: New Benjamin Franklin House, 1984.

8 Il Duce Benito Mussolini 1883-1945

Fascist Italy

Benito Mussolini was the world's first Fascist dictator, coming to power in Italy in 1922. His appointment as head of the government was quasi-legal and welcomed by most Italians. Once in office, he banned all other political parties and nationalized under strict government control the police force, major industries, and newspapers. His reign in the 1920s was marked with some success, but his desire to build a new Roman empire greatly exceeded the abilities of Italy's military forces and industries, ultimately resulting in his downfall and death.

In his early years, Mussolini was a Socialist, but when the First World War began, he switched his politics and called for Italy's involvement on the side of the Allies. Mussolini loved to orate. With his ability to speak and his wise use of the newspaper media, he effectively delivered his message to the Italian people. At one time, he was editor of the *Avanti*, the leading Socialist newspaper. When he was expelled from the Socialist party, he founded his own paper, *Il Popolo d' Italia*. His urging for Italy to join the war was a contributing factor in Italy entering the conflict in 1915. Mussolini joined the army and served two years before being wounded in 1917. When the war ended and he had recovered from his wound, he founded the Fascist party. By 1922, he had gained enough support from the middle and upper classes to compel the King of Italy to name him prime minister. He soon established a dictatorship based on the principles of Fascism.

The naming of Adolf Hitler as chancellor of Germany in 1933 gave Mussolini the perfect partner. In the first few years of their relationship, Mussolini was the dominant member. While Hitler consolidated his power, Mussolini embarked on the first step of his plan to create a new Roman empire. His military forces, equipped with tanks, planes, and machine guns, invaded Ethiopia and slaughtered an enemy armed with bows and arrows. The first phase of his plan was a success.

The Spanish Civil War was used as a testing ground for military forces from Italy, Germany, and the Soviet Union. The war also marked the last real success Mussolini would enjoy. Though Italian military equipment did not perform well in combat, the support given to General Francisco Franco by Mussolini, and predominately Hitler, enabled Franco to win the war.

By the late 1930s, Hitler emerged as the true force in Europe, replacing Mussolini as the dominant partner because of Germany's bloodless territorial victories in Austria and Czechoslovakia. The two dictators signed the Pact of Steel on 22 May 1939, pledging to come to the aid of the other if attacked. Franco declined the invitation from Hitler to join. Mussolini, though, aligned himself with a man bent on war. On 27 September 1940, Japan joined the alliance with the signing of the Tripartite Pact.

When German armed forces invaded France in May 1940, Mussolini declared war on France and Great Britain and ordered the Italian Army to invade southern France. As a portend of events to come, Italian units did not perform well even though the French were greatly demoralized because of the German Army's lightning advances in northern France.

Once France fell and Hitler was master of Europe, Mussolini was determined to show he was Hitler's equal. The Italian Army invaded Greece in the fall of 1940, but the operation was a disaster for the Italians. In the spring of 1941, Hitler had to send several of his crack Panzer divisions to destroy the Greek Army and drive the British Expeditionary Force out of Greece and onto Crete. German airborne forces then invaded Crete, and though the assault was successful, casualties were extremely heavy for the airborne troops.

After 1941, Mussolini was not a force in the Axis partnership. His troops in North Africa were soundly defeated by the British Eighth Army, the last units surrendering in May 1943 along with the German forces still present. Troops serving on the Eastern front fared even worse as Premier Josef Stalin's Red Army destroyed division after division.

In the fall of 1943, the Fascist Grand Council decided to surrender. Mussolini was arrested and his replacement, Marshal Pietro Badoglio, entered into negotiations with the Allies. Italian authorities incarcerated Mussolini at a mountaintop resort, but he was rescued by German commandos and escorted safely to Berlin to meet Hitler. The German dictator still had use for his old ally, naming him head of a puppet government in northern Italy, the only part of Italy still fully under German control.

By 1944, Mussolini had little interest in the events occurring around him. In 1945, the war turned totally against the Axis powers. In April, Mussolini and his mistress, Clara Petacci, attempted to escape to Austria, but were caught by Italian partisans and shot. Their bodies were hung by their heels at a gas station in Milan. Mussolini was a bombastic dictator whose dreams of a new Roman empire far exceeded his ability and means to achieve it. Italy did not have the industrial base or the military forces to compete with Great Britain, the Soviet Union, and the United States.

There are several good works on the life and career of Benito Mussolini. Recommended for reading are Laura Fermi's *Mussolini*, A. James Gregor's *Young Mussolini and the Intellectual Origins of Fascism*, Christopher Hibbert's *Il Duce*, Ivone Kirkpatrick's *Mussolini*, MacGregor Knox's *Mussolini Unleashed, 1939-1941*, Esmonde Robertson's *Mussolini As Empire Builder, 1932-1936*, and Denis Mack Smith's *Mussolini*. It is also recommended that any of Mussolini's works be read to obtain an insightful look at the man's own view of his life. Of special note is *The Fall of Mussolini*. These works and others are listed in the bibliography that follows.

Bibliography

Absalom, R. N. L. (Roger Neil Lewis). *Mussolini and the Rise of Italian Fascism*. New York: Roy Publishers, 1969.

Adams, Henry. *Italy at War*. Alexandria, VA: Time-Life Books, 1982.

Archer, Jules. *Twentieth Century Caesar, Benito Mussolini*. New York: J. Messner, 1964. (juvenile)

Bayne-Jardine, Colin Charles. *Mussolini and Italy*. New York: McGraw-Hill, 1966. (juvenile)

Blinkhorn, Martin. *Mussolini and Fascist Italy*. 2nd ed. London: Routledge, 1994.

Bolitho, William. *Italy Under Mussolini*. New York: Macmillan, 1926.

Bond, John. *Mussolini: Wild Man of Europe*. Washington, DC: Independent Publishing Co., 1929.

Borghi, Armando. *Mussolini: Red and Black*. Translated by Dorothy Daudley. New York: Haskell House Publishers, 1974. (Reprint of 1938 edition.)

Bosworth, R. J. B. *Benito Mussolini and the Fascist Destruction of Liberal Italy, 1900-1945*. Adelaide: Rigby, 1973.

Box, Pelham Horton. *Three Master Builders and Another*. Freeport, NY: Books for Libraries Press, 1968. (Reprint of 1925 edition.)

Bradford, Gamaliel. *The Quick and the Dead*. Boston: Houghton Mifflin, 1931.

Bulmer-Thomas, Ivor. *Who Mussolini Is*. London: Oxford University Press, 1942.

Cannistraro, Philip V. and Brian R. Sullivan. *Il Duce's Other Woman*. New York: Morrow, 1993.

Cappuccilli, Ralph Michael. "*The Speaking of Benito Mussolini from 1922-1936*." Ph.D. diss., Purdue University, 1967. (DAI, 28:6, 2364A, UMI Order # 6716623)

Cassels, Alan. *Mussolini's Early Diplomacy*. Princeton, NJ: Princeton University Press, 1970.

______. "*Mussolini's Foreign Policy: The First Years, 1922-1924*." Ph.D. diss., University of Michigan, 1961. (DAI, 21:1, 3434, UMI Order # 611893)

Ciano, Edda Mussolini. *My Truth*. Translated from the Italian by Eileen Finletter. New York: Morrow, 1977.

Collier, Richard. *Duce! A Biography of Benito Mussolini*. New York: Viking Press, 1971.

Cresswell, C. M. *The Keystone of Fascism: A Study of the Ascendancy of Discipline*. London: Besant & Co. Ltd., 1929.

Dabrowski, Roman. *Mussolini: Twilight and Fall*. Translated by H. C. Stevens. New York: Roy Publishers, 1956.

Darrah, David. *Hail, Caesar!* Boston: Hale, Cushman & Fint, 1936.

De Cola, Thomas Guido. "*Roosevelt and Mussolini: The Critical Years, 1938-1941*." Ph.D. diss., Kent State University, 1967. (DAI, 28:11, 4568A, UMI Order # 686205)

Deakin, Frederick William. *The Brutal Friendship: Mussolini, Hitler, and the Fall of Italian Fascism*. Rev. ed. Garden City, NY: Doubleday, 1962.

______. *The Six Hundred Days of Mussolini*. Revised by the author. Garden City, NY: Anchor Books, 1966.

DeSanti, Louis Aldo. "*United States Relations With Italy Under Mussolini, 1922-1941: A Study Based on the Records of the Department of State and Documents from the Captured Files of Mussolini*." Ph.D. diss., Columbia University, 1951. (DAI, 12:1, 89, UMI Order # 3332)

Diggins, John P. *Mussolini and Fascism: The View from America*. Princeton, NJ: Princeton University Press, 1972.

______. "*Mussolini's Italy: The View from America*." Ph.D. diss., University of Southern California, 1964. (DAI, 25:2, 1170, UMI Order # 649150)

Ebenstein, William. *Fascism at Work*. London: M. Hopkinson, 1934.

Fermi, Laura. *Mussolini*. Chicago: University of Chicago Press, 1961.

Finer, Herman. *Mussolini's Italy*. New York: Holt, 1935.

Fiori, Vittorio, E. de. *Mussolini: The Man of Destiny*. Translated by Mario A. Pei. New York: E. P. Dutton & Co., 1928.

Freeman, Marian. *Mussolini and Fascist Italy*. London: Bell & Hyman, 1984.

Gallo, Max. *Mussolini's Italy: Twenty Years of the Fascist Era*. Translated by Charles Lam Markmann. New York: Macmillan, 1973.

Gelb, Alan. *Mussolini*. New York: Pocket Books, 1985.

Godden, Gertrude M. *Mussolini: The Birth of the New Democracy*. New York: P. J. Kenedy, 1923.

Gorgolini, Pietro. *The Fascist Movement in Italian Life*. Translated and edited with an introduction by M. D. Petre. Boston: Little, Brown, 1923.

Gourlay, Jack. *Benito Mussolini: A Biography*. New York: Monarch Press, 1966.

Gregor, A. James. *Young Mussolini and the Intellectual Origins of Fascism*. Berkeley, CA: University of California Press, 1979.

Halperin, Samuel William. *Mussolini and Italian Fascism*. Princeton, NJ: Van Nostrand, 1964.

Hartenian, Lawrence Raymond. *Benito Mussolini*. New York: Chelsea House, 1988. (juvenile)

Herder, John Hart. "*A Human Relations Study of Roosevelt and Mussolini: A Comparative Study of the Principles and Practices of Democratic Conference Leadership as Represented by Franklin Roosevelt and of Autocratic Conference Leadership as Represented by Benito Mussolini.*" Ph.D. diss., New York University, 1954. (DAI, 14:10, 1830, UMI Order # 9312)

Herrstrom, William Dewey. *Mussolini and Fascism*. Wichita, KS: Defender Publishers, 1937.

Hibbert, Christopher. *Il Duce: The Life of Benito Mussolini*. Boston: Little, Brown, 1962.

_____. *Mussolini*. New York: Ballantine Books, 1972.

Howard, Milford W. *Fascism: A Challenge to Democracy*. New York: Fleming H. Revell Co., 1928.

Hoyt, Edwin P. *Mussolini's Empire: The Rise and Fall of Fascism in Europe*. New York: J. Wiley, 1994.

Hullinger, Edwin Ware. *The New Fascist State: A Study of Italy Under Mussolini*. New York: Rae D. Henkle Co. Inc., 1928.

Iezzi, Frank. "*Selected Political Addresses of Benito Mussolini: Translations, Notes and Rhetorical Analysis.*" Ph.D. diss., The University of Wisconsin, 1954. (Not available from UMI)

Italia, Bob. *Benito Mussolini*. Minneapolis, MN: Abdo & Daughters, 1990. (juvenile)

Jacobs, William Jay. *Mussolini*. Encino, CA: Glencoe Publishing Co., 1980. (juvenile)

Joes, Anthony James. *Mussolini*. New York: F. Watts, 1982.

Jones, Spencer John. *Benito Mussolini, An Introduction to the Study of Fascism*. London: Hunter & Longhurst Ltd., 1927.

Jordan, Laylon Wayne. "*America's Mussolini: The United States and Italy, 1919-1936*." Ph.D. diss., University of Virginia, 1972. (DAI, 33:4, 1648A, UMI Order # 7223429)

Kemechey, L. "*Il Duce": The Life and Work of Benito Mussolini*. Translated from the Hungarian by Magda Vamos. New York: R. R. Smith Inc., 1930.

Kent, Peter C. *The Pope and the Duce: The International Impact of the Lateran Agreements*. New York: St. Martin's Press, 1981.

King-Hall, Stephen. *Three Dictators: Mussolini, Hitler, and Stalin*. London: Faber & Faber, 1964. (juvenile)

Kirkpatrick, Ivone. *Mussolini: A Study in Power*. New York: Hawthorn, 1964.

Knox, MacGregor. *Mussolini Unleashed, 1939-1941: Politics and Strategy in Fascist Italy's Last War*. New York: Cambridge University Press, 1982.

______. "*1940. Italy's Parallel War. Part I. From Non-Belligerence to the Collapse of France*." Ph.D. diss., Yale University, 1976. (DAI, 41:8, 3691A, UMI Order # 8103067)

Leeds, Christopher. *Italy Under Mussolini*. New York: Putnam, 1972.

Ludwig, Emil. *Three Portraits: Hitler, Mussolini, Stalin*. New York: Alliance Book Corporation, Longmans, Green & Co., 1940.

Lussu, Emilio. *Enter Mussolini*. London: Metheun & Co. Ltd., 1936.

Lyttle, Richard B. *Il Duce: The Rise and Fall of Benito Mussolini*. New York: Antheneum, 1987. (juvenile)

Macarthy, Maxwell H. H. *One Man Alone: The History of Mussolini and the Axis*. London: Chatto & Windus, 1944.

MacGregor-Hastie, Roy. *The Day of the Lion: The Life and Death of Fascist Italy, 1922-1945*. New York: Coward-McCann, 1963.

Mack Smith, Denis. *Mussolini*. New York: Knopf, 1982.

______. *Mussolini As A Military Leader*. Reading, England: University of Reading, 1974.

______. *Mussolini's Roman Empire*. New York: Viking Press, 1976.

Mangione, Jerre Gerlando. *Mussolini's March on Rome, October 30, 1922: A Dictator in the Making Achieves Political Power in Italy*. New York: Watts, 1975. (juvenile)

Marriott, J. A. R. (John Arthur Ransome). *The Makers of Modern Italy: Napoleon - Mussolini*. Oxford: The Clarendon Press, 1931.

Megaro, Gaudens. *Mussolini in the Making*. Boston: Houghton Mifflin, 1938.

Michaelis, Meir. *Mussolini and the Jews: German-Italian Relations and the Jewish Question, 1922-1945*. New York: Oxford University Press, 1978.

Millsap, Mary Ruth. "*Mussolini and the United States: Italo-American Relations, 1934-1941*." Ph.D. diss., University of California at Los Angeles, 1972. (DAI, 3:4, 1655A, UMI Order # 7225813)

Missiroli, Mario. *What Italy Owes to Mussolini*. London: J. Heritage, 1938.

Monelli, Paolo. *Mussolini: The Intimate Life of A Demagogue*. Translated from the Italian by Brigid Maxwell. New York: Vanguard Press, 1954.

Mulvihill, Margaret. *Mussolini and Italian Fascism*. New York: Franklin Watts, 1990. (juvenile)

Munro, Ion S. *Through Fascism to World Power: A History of Revolution in Italy*. Freeport, NY: Books for Libraries Press, 1971.

Musman, Richard. *Hitler and Mussolini*. London: Chatto & Windus, 1968.

Mussolini, Benito. *The Doctrine of Fascism*. 3rd ed. Translated by E. Cope. Firenze: Vallecchi, 1938.

______. *The Fall of Mussolini: His Own Story*. Translated from the Italian by Frances Frenaye. New York: Farrar, Straus, 1948.

______. *Memoirs, 1942-43*. Translated by Frances Lobb. London: G. Weidenfeld & Nicolson, 1949.

______. *Mussolini As Revealed in His Political Speeches (November 1914 - August 1923)*. Selected, translated, and edited by Barone Bernardo Quaranta di San Severino. New York: H. Fertig, 1976.

______. *My Autobiography*. Westport, CT: Greenwood Press, 1970. (Reprint of 1928 edition).

______. *Talks with Mussolini*. Interviewed by Ludwig Emil. Translated from the German by Eden and Cedar Paul. Boston: Little, Brown, 1933.

Mussolini, Rachele. *Mussolini: An Intimate Biography*. New York: Morrow, 1974.

Mussolini, Vittorio. *Mussolini: The Tragic Women in His Life*. Translated from the Italian by Graham Snell. New York: Dial Press, 1973.

Nelson, Elizabeth Jean. "*To Ethiopia and Beyond: The Primacy of Struggle in Mussolini's Public Discourse*." Ph.D. diss., The University of Iowa, 1988. (DAI, 49:11, 3202A, UMI Order # 8903957)

Ogle, Marbury B., Jr. "*The Political Theory of Benito Mussolini.*" Ph.D. diss., The Ohio State University, 1937. (Not available from UMI)

Owen, Frank. *The Three Dictators: Mussolini, Stalin, Hitler*. London: G. Allen & Unwin Ltd., 1940.

Paley, Alan L. *Benito Mussolini: Fascist Dictator of Italy*. Charlottesville, NY: SamHar Press, 1975.

Palumbo, Michael Vincent. "*The Uncertain Friendship: Hitler and Mussolini, 1922-1933.*" Ph.D. diss., City University of New York, 1979. (Not available from UMI)

Petrie, Charles Alexander. *Mussolini*. London: The Holme Press, 1931.

Pini, Giorgio. *The Official Life of Benito Mussolini*. London: Hutchinson & Co., 1939.

Plehwe, Friedrich-Karl von. *The End of an Alliance: Rome's Defection from the Axis in 1943*. Translated from the German by Eric Mosbacher. London: Oxford University Press, 1971.

Pound, Ezra. *Jefferson and/or Mussolini; L'idea statale; Fascism As I Have Seen It*. New York: Liveright, 1936.

Pullar Smith, Margaret A. *Hitler and Mussolini: The Western Dictators*. Glasgow: Blackie, 1978.

Ray, John. *Hitler and Mussolini*. London: Heinemann Educational, 1970.

Robertson, Alexander. *Mussolini and the New Italy: Head of the Italian Government, Duce of the Fascisti*. New York: Fleming H. Revell, 1928.

Robertson, Esmonde M. *Mussolini as Empire Builder: Europe and Africa, 1932-1936*. New York: St. Martin's Press, 1977.

Ruark, Lawrence Bernard. "*Admiration for Mussolini Among German Intellectuals, 1922-1932.*" Ph.D. diss., Boston University Graduate School, 1970. (DAI, 31:5, 2321A, UMI Order # 7022380)

Sarfatti, Margherita. *The Life of Benito Mussolini*. London: Thorton Butterworth Ltd., 1925.

Sbacchi, Alberto. *Ethiopia Under Mussolini: Fascism and the Colonial Experience*. London: Zed, 1985.

Scherger, George L. *Men of the Hour: Mussolini, Gandhi, Stalin, Hitler*. Chicago: Popular Interest Series Publishing Co., 1933.

Seldes, George. *Sawdust Caesar: The Untold Story of Mussolini and Fascism*. New York: AMS Press, 1978. Reprint of 1935 edition.

Sherrill, Charles H. *Bismarck and Mussolini*. Boston: Houghton Mifflin, 1931.

Skipper, G. C. *Benito Mussolini: A Dictator Dies*. Chicago: Children's Press, 1981. (juvenile)

Sullivan, Brian R. *"A Thirst for Glory: Mussolini, the Italian Military and the Fascist Regime, 1922-1936."* Ph.D. diss., Columbia University, 1984. (DAI, 45:3, 915A, UMI Order # DA8413037)

Tubby, Cecil S. *Mussolini, The Marvel Man, Is He the Predicted Super-Man?* Springfield, MO: n.p., 1929.

Turati, Augusto. *A Revolution and Its Leader*. London: Alexander-Ouseley Limited, 1930.

Urgo, Louis Anthony. *"British Newspaper Reaction to the Rise of Mussolini: August 1922 - August 1923."* Ph.D., diss., Georgetown University, 1967. (DAI, 28:8, 3129A, UMI Order # 681897)

Villari, Luigi. *Italian Foreign Policy Under Mussolini*. New York: Devin-Adair, 1956.

Whittle, Peter. *One Afternoon at Mezzegra*. Englewood Cliffs, NJ: Prentice-Hall, 1969.

Wiskemann, Elizabeth. *The Rome-Berlin Axis: A Study of the Relations Between Hitler and Mussolini*. New and rev. ed. London: Collins, 1966.

Wolfson, Robert. *Benito Mussolini and Fascist Italy*. London: Edward Arnold, 1984.

9 Marshal Henri Philippe Petain 1856-1951

Vichy France

Marshal Petain was the hero of Verdun, the ferocious six month battle fought during the First World War in 1916. The German plan was to bleed the French Army dry. In the resulting carnage, over three hundred thousand French soldiers became casualties, but so did approximately the same number of Germans. The German high command stopped the fighting when it became apparent that the French line would hold fast.

In 1939, Petain was ambassador to Spain. When the German Army invaded France in May 1940, he was recalled and appointed deputy premier by Premier Paul Reynaud. When the French Army and the British Expeditionary Force failed to stop the blitzkrieg tactics employed by the German panzer divisions, Petain felt it was best for France to distance itself from Great Britain and sue for a separate peace. Other members of the French cabinet agreed with him, causing Reynaud to resign on 16 June 1940. Petain then arranged an armistice with the German adversary. The armistice papers were signed on 22 June 1940 in the same railroad car that the Germans signed their papers at the conclusion of the First World War. Petain was then permitted to form a new French government at Vichy. The Vichy government was allowed to govern the interior portions of France and collaborated with the Germans until the Allied invasion of North Africa in November 1942. After the invasion, Adolf Hitler became suspicious of the Vichy government's intentions and ordered German armed forces to occupy all of France. In August 1944, Petain was sent to Germany after the Allies invaded France. He returned in 1945 to stand trial for treason. He was sentenced to death, but Charles De Gaulle commuted his sentence to life imprisonment. Petain died on the Ile d' Yeu at the age of 95 in 1951.

Marshal Petain was 84 years old when Germany invaded France. The heavy responsibility of leading his nation during such turbulent times must have been an immense burden for him to bear. He chose the path of collaboration believing that this choice was the best he could make for his defeated country. Recommended for reading about the life and career of Marshal Petain are Richard Griffith's *Petain*, Herbert R. Lottman's *Petain: Hero or Traitor, The Untold Story*, Jules Roy's *Trial of Marshal Petain*, Stephen Ryan's *Petain the Soldier* and Paul Webster's *Petain's Crime*. These works and others are listed in the bibliography that follows.

Bibliography

Anonymous. *Petain-Laval: The Conspiracy*. Translated by Michael Sadleir. London: Constable & Co. Ltd., 1942.

Barnes, Harry E. *Crucifying the Savior of France: Petain*. Cambridge, MA: Harvard University Library, 1945.

Bilger, Edeltraut Luise. "*The Reconstruction of France: Marshal Petain's Policies, 1940-1942, As Evaluated by American Journalists and Scholars*." Ph.D. diss., Oklahoma State University, 1984. (DAI, 45:9, 3968A, UMI Order # DA8427643)

Bolton, Glorney. *Petain*. London: Allen & Unwin, 1957.

Flanner, Janet. *Petain, the Old Man of France*. New York: Simon & Schuster, 1944.

Geraud, Andre. *The Gravediggers of France: Gamelin, Daladier, Reynaud, Petain, and Lavel: Military Defeat, Armistice, Counterrevolution*. Garden City, NY: Doubleday, Doran, 1944.

Griffiths, Richard. *Petain, A Biography of Marshal Philippe Petain of Vichy*. Garden City, NY: Doubleday, 1972.

Guedalla, Philip. *The Two Marshalls: Bazaine, Petain*. New York: Reynal & Hitchcock, 1943.

Huddleston, Sisley. *Petain, Patriot or Traitor?* London: A. Dakers, 1951.

Lottman, Herbert R. *Petain, Hero or Traitor: The Untold Story*. New York: Morrow, 1985.

Martel, Francis. *Petain: Verdun to Vichy*. New York: Dutton, 1943.

Paxton, Robert O. *Parades and Politics at Vichy: The French Officer Corps Under Marshall Petain*. Princeton, NJ: Princeton University Press, 1966.

Rousso, Henry. *The Vichy Syndrome: History and Memory in France Since 1944*. Translated by Arthur Goldhammer. Cambridge, MA: Harvard University Press, 1991.

Roy, Jules. *Trial of Marshal Petain*. Translated from the French by Robert Baldick. New York: Harper & Row, 1967.

Ryan, Stephen. "*Petain and French Military Planning, 1900-1940.*" Ph.D. diss., Columbia University, 1961. (DAI, 22:8, 2777, UMI Order # 615480)

_____. *Petain the Soldier*. South Brunswick, NJ: A. S. Barnes, 1969.

Smith, Gene. *The Ends of Greatness: Haig, Petain, Rathenau, and Eden. Victims of History*. New York: Crown Publishers, 1990.

Spears, Edward Louis. *Two Men Who Saved France: Petain and De Gaulle*. New York: Stein & Day, 1966.

Szaluta, Jacques. "*Marshal Petain Between Two Wars, 1918-1940: The Interplay of Personality and Circumstance.*" Ph.D. diss., Columbia University, 1969. (DAI, 33:1, 263A, UMI Order # 7219091)

_____. *Petain: For and Against*. New York: Vantage, 1973.

Tournoux, Jean Raymond. *Sons of France: Petain and De Gaulle*. Translated by Oliver Coburn. New York: Viking Press, 1966.

Webster, Paul. *Petain's Crime: The Full Story of French Collaboration in the Holocaust*. London: Macmillan, 1990.

10 Prime Minister Hideki Tojo 1884-1948

Imperial Japan

General Hideki Tojo was prime minister of Japan from October 1941 until July 1944 when he was finally removed after a series of military defeats, the most recent being the loss of Saipan in the Marianas. Tojo devoted his life to the military. In 1935, he was named Chief of Staff of the Kwangtung Army stationed in Manchuria and played a large role in the various "incidents" that expanded Japan's influence in the region. Later, when army officers revolted in both Japan and Manchuria, Tojo moved quickly to arrest the ringleaders in the Kwangtung Army. When the revolt was suppressed, the government was extremely grateful for the role he played in curbing the crisis.

When the Marco Polo Bridge incident widened into outright warfare in 1937, Tojo rushed more troops into Manchuria and northern China and guided his units to several victories. As a reward, he was named Vice-Minister of War in the government, but only lasted six months due to his outspoken views on expansion issues. However, when a new government was formed in 1940, he was named Minister of War. By his prompting, the Japanese government entered into a formal alliance with Hitler and Benito Mussolini of Italy in September 1940. The agreement was called the Tripartite Pact which established, in theory, a new world order. Japan would dominate Asia while Germany and Italy would rule Europe and Africa.

The oil embargo imposed in 1941 by American President Franklin D. Roosevelt to restrict Japanese aggression in China and South-east Asia actually helped propel Japan toward total war. When the government of Prince Fumimaro Konoye resigned, Tojo was asked to form a new government. Tojo felt that military action must be taken against the United States and Great Britain immediately to relieve the now-stalemated war in China and to eliminate Western influence in Asia.

As well as being prime minister, Tojo retained his position as war minister, but he was not a dictator like his counterparts, Hitler and Mussolini. Though personally vain and arrogant, his position, in accordance with the Japanese constitution, was more like being chairman of the board. During his time as prime minister, he never implemented a single overall strategy for conducting the war effort and never gained control of the actions of the Imperial Navy, of which he was a bitter enemy. At the end of the war, Tojo attempted to kill himself, but failed. He was tried at the War Crimes Trials in Tokyo, convicted, and hanged on 23 December 1948.

Tojo was a major catalyst in the 1930s that caused Japan to attempt the implementation of the Greater East Asian Co-Prosperity Plan. When the war against China had not been won after four years of costly fighting, the Japanese government embarked on an expansionist plan in Southeast Asia and the Philippines that involved direct confrontation with the United States. This plan of expansion, designed to resolve the China problem, was grossly nearsighted and brought a hail of destruction upon Japan the likes of which had not been seen before. Defeat was decisive and total. Recommended for reading about the life and career of Hideki Tojo are Courtney Browne's *Tojo*, Robert Butow's *Tojo and the Coming of the War*, and Edwin Hoyt's *Warlord*. These works and others are listed in the bibliography that follows.

Bibliography

Browne, Courtney. *Tojo: The Last Banzai*. New York: Holt, Rinehart & Winston, 1967.

Butow, Robert Joseph. *Tojo and the Coming of the War*. Princeton, NJ: Princeton University Press, 1961.

Coox, Alvin D. *Tojo*. New York: Ballantine Books, 1975.

Deverall, Richard L. G. *The Imperial Japanese Army: Hideki Tojo's Military Socialism*. Bangalore, India: Deccan Harold Press, 1951.

Hoyt, Edwin P. *Warlord: Tojo Against the World*. Lanham, MD: Scarborough House, 1993.

11 Emperor Hirohito 1901-1989

Imperial Japan

Hirohito became Showa emperor in 1926. He is included in this bibliography because, as emperor, he gave final approval to all decisions made by the Japanese government. In the 1920s and 1930s, Japan experienced many economic and political changes. During the period, the militarists gained increasing control of the government and demanded that Japan extend its influence in Asia to satisfy the growing need for raw materials and land. Much of the militarists' attention was directed toward China.

Many times Hirohito opposed the expansionist ideas of the government, but his court advisors cautioned him not to speak out against the militarists for fear of retaliation. Assassination was a tool used in Japan at the time. Regardless, Hirohito had very little legal power. His role consisted, in accordance with the constitution, of giving final approval to all projects presented to him. He did not have any type of veto power. Since approval was always given, many Westerners believed that Hirohito was a strong proponent of expansionism and war.

Though Hirohito did little in opposing the start of the war, he was instrumental in ending the conflict. On 15 August 1945, a few days after two atomic bombs had destroyed Hiroshima and Nagasaki, his pre-recorded message was broadcast to the Japanese nation over the radio. In the message, he asked the people to cease all resistance and accept the surrender terms of the Allies. After the war, he was forced by General Douglas MacArthur to revoke his right of divinity and in the new constitution was denied any privilege of political input. He was allowed to remain as emperor. Hirohito lived the longest of the Second World War leaders. He died in January 1989.

Recommendations for reading about the life of Emperor Hirohito are Edward Behr's *Hirohito*, David Bergamini's *Japan's Imperial Conspiracy*, Edwin P. Hoyt's *Hirohito*, Toshiaki Kawahara's *Hirohito and His Times*, Leonard Mosley's *Hirohito, Emperor of Japan*, and

Jerrold Packard's *Sons of Heaven*. These works and others are listed in the bibliography that follows.

Bibliography

Behr, Edward. *Hirohito: Behind the Myth*. New York: Villard Books, 1989.

Bergamini, David. *Japan's Imperial Conspiracy*. New York: Morrow, 1971.

Crump, Thomas. *The Death of An Emperor: Japan at the Crossroads*. Oxford: Oxford University Press, 1991.

Field, Norma. *In the Realm of A Dying Emperor*. New York: Vintage Books, 1993.

Gluck, Carol and Stephen R. Graubard, eds. *Showa: The Japan of Hirohito*. New York: Norton, 1990.

Hirohito. *The Emperor and the End of the War*. Translated at General Headquarters, Far East Command, Military Intelligence Section, General Staff, Allied Translator and Interpreter Service, n.d.

______. *Emperor Hirohito: A Pictorial History*. Tokyo: Kodansha International, 1975. Distributed in the United States by Harper & Row.

Honjo, Shigeru. *Emperor Hirohito and His Chief Aide de Camp. The Honjo Diary, 1933-36*. Tokyo: University of Tokyo Press, 1982.

Hoobler, Dorothy. *Showa: The Age of Hirohito*. New York: Walker, 1990. (juvenile)

Hoyt, Edwin P. *Hirohito: The Emperor and the Man*. New York: Praeger, 1992.

Irokawa, Daikichi. *The Age of Hirohito: In Search of Modern Japan*. New York: The Free Press, 1995.

Italia, Bob. *The Story of Emperor Hirohito*. Edina, MN: Abdo & Daughters, 1990. (juvenile)

Kanaji, Isamu. *Japan's Compassionate Emperor*. Translated by John Carroll and Iwase Takao. Tokyo: Kao Corporation, 1989.

Kanroji, Osanaga. *Hirohito: An Intimate Portrait of the Japanese Emperor*. Los Angeles: Gateway Publishers, 1975. Distributed in the U.S. by Japan Publications Trading Co.

Kawahara, Toshiaki. *Hirohito and His Times: A Japanese Perspective*. New York: Kodansha International, 1990.

Large, Stephen S. *Emperor Hirohito and Showa Japan: A Political Biography*. New York: Routledge, 1992.

Manning, Paul. *Hirohito: The War Years*. New York: Dodd, Mead, 1986.

Mosley, Leonard. *Hirohito, Emperor of Japan*. Englewood Cliffs, NJ: Prentice-Hall, 1966.

Packard, Jerrold M. *Sons of Heaven: A Portrait of the Japanese Monarchy*. New York: Scribner, 1987.

Price, Willard. *Japan and the Son of Heaven*. New York: Duell, Sloan & Pearce, 1945.

Severns, Karen. *Hirohito*. New York: Chelsea House, 1988.

Williams, David. *Reporting on the Death of Emperor Showa*. Oxford: Nissan Institute of Japanese Studies, 1990.

PART III

ALLIED MILITARY COMMANDERS

12 American Commanders

This chapter presents short biographical profiles and bibliographies of works about and by the top-ranking military commanders of the United States armed forces. During the course of the Second World War, American military commanders led the mightiest armies, navies, and air forces ever assembled by one country. Under their direction, American armed forces, in conjunction with Soviet and British armed forces and other Allied contingents, defeated the Axis powers of Nazi Germany, Fascist Italy, and Imperial Japan. Officers are listed in alphabetical order by their last name.

General of the Air Force Henry Harley Arnold
United States Army Air Force
1886-1950

Arnold was an early proponent of the application of airplanes for military purposes. He was the top-ranking officer in the United States Army Air Corps prior to the start of the Second World War. During the war, he commanded the US Army Air Force. He was a strong advocate of strategic bombing and under his direction, American air power became the most powerful air force on earth by the end of the war. His friendly personality helped smooth relations with the British high command whenever disagreements in strategy occurred. Arnold can rightly be called the father of the United States Air Force and was its first five star general. Recommended for reading are General Arnold's memoir, *Global Mission*, Thomas Coffey's *Hap*, Dewitt Copp's *A Few Great Captains*, and Flint DuPre's *Hap Arnold*.

Bibliography

Arnold, Henry and Ira C. Eaker. *Army Flyer*. New York: Harper & Brothers, 1942.

______. *Global Mission*. New York: Harper & Brothers, 1949.

______ and Ira C. Eaker. *This Flying Game*. 3rd ed. New York: Funk & Wagnalls, 1943.

______. *The War Reports of General of the Army George C. Marshall, Chief of Staff, General of the Army H. H. Arnold, Commanding General, Army Air Forces and Fleet Admiral Ernest J. King, Commander-in-Chief, United States Fleet and Chief of Naval Operations*. Philadelphia: Lippincott, 1947.

______ and Ira C. Eaker. *Winged Warfare*. New York: Harper & Brothers, 1941.

Coffey, Thomas M. *Hap. The Story of the U.S. Air Force and the Man Who Built It: General Henry "Hap" Arnold*. New York: Viking Press, 1982.

Copp, Dewitt S. *A Few Great Captains: The Men and Events That Shaped the Development of U.S. Air Power*. Garden City, NY: Doubleday, 1980.

DuPre, Flint O. *Hap Arnold: Architect of American Air Power*. New York: Macmillan, 1972.

Jahns, Robert L. *Franklin Roosevelt and General Hap Arnold: The Statesman and the Strategist Build an Air Force*. Carlisle Barracks, PA: U.S. Army War College, 1990.

United States. Army Air Forces. *Air War. Official Report of the Commanding General of the Army Air Forces to the Secretary of War, January 4, 1944*. Washington: The United States News, 1944.

Vice Admiral Gerald Francis Bogan
United States Navy
1894-1973

Bogan was a carrier admiral during the Second World War. His Task Force 38.2 participated in the Battle of Leyte Gulf in October 1944, considered by many military historians to be the greatest sea battle of all time. Overall US commander was Admiral William Halsey who commanded the Third Fleet. Admiral Marc Mitscher commanded Task Force 38. Combined attacks by surface ships, carrier planes, and submarines sank 26 Japanese ships, including the giant battleship

Musashi and the aircraft carrier *Zuikaku*, the last carrier to be sunk that participated in the raid on Pearl Harbor nearly three years earlier. The battle left the Japanese Imperial Navy unable to mount any credible offensive threat for the remainder of the war and sealed the fate of all Japanese land forces still operating in the Philippines. Contact your library's interlibrary loan department for the availability of Admiral Bogan's *Reminiscences*.

Bibliography

Bogan, Gerald Francis. *Reminiscences of Vice Admiral Gerald F. Bogan, U.S. Navy (Retired)*. Annapolis, MD: U.S. Naval Institute, 1986. Originally issued in 1970, Oral History Program (Navy).

General of the Army Omar Nelson Bradley
United States Army
1893-1981

Bradley was not flamboyant in the style of General George Patton or General Douglas MacArthur. However, lack of this characteristic did not inhibit him from becoming an outstanding general, one who was much respected by his fellow officers and the troops who served under him. By the end of the Second World War, he commanded four armies in Europe totalling more than a million men. After the war, he became chairman of the Joint Chiefs of Staff. General Bradley has always been characterized as being a soft-spoken, quiet man who took orders uncomplainingly and without question. This image is true to a point, but he also had strong opinions about his superiors and other general officers which he revealed in his autobiography, *A General's Life*. Recommended for reading are General Bradley's *A General's Life* (completed by Clay Blair), Bradley's earlier work, *A Soldier's Story*, and Charles Whiting's *Bradley*.

Bibliography

Bradley, Omar N. *The Collected Writings of General Omar N. Bradley*. 5 volumes. Washington, DC: n.p., 1967-1971.

_____. *Magazine Articles*. 4 volumes. Washington: Defense Printing Office, 1970-1971. (Articles written by and about General Omar Bradley, 1943-1971.)

_____. *A Soldier's Story*. New York: Holt, 1951.

_____ and Clay Blair. *A General's Life: An Autobiography*. New York: Simon & Schuster, 1983.

Kirkpatrick, Charles Edward. *Omar Nelson Bradley: The Centennial*. Washington, DC: U.S. Army, 1992.

Lusey, Rodney S. "*Operational Principles: A Study of General Omar Bradley and Field Marshal Eric von Mainstein in World War II*." M.M.A.S. thesis, U.S. Army Command and General Staff, 1985.

Pratt, Fletcher. "The Tactician of the West. Infantry Specialist. Part One." *Infantry Journal* 61 (December 1947): 4-14.

_____. "The Tactician of the West. Tactical Commander. Part Two." *Infantry Journal* 62 (January 1948): 52-59.

_____. "The Tactician of the West. Poor Man's War. Part Three." *Infantry Journal* 62 (February 1948): 19-25.

Reeder, Red. *Omar Nelson Bradley: The Soldier's General*. Champaign, IL: Garrard Pub. Co., 1969.

Whiting, Charles. *Bradley*. New York: Ballantine Books, 1971.

Lieutenant General Lewis Hyde Brereton
United States Army Air Force
1890-1967

Brereton was in command of all American air units in the Far East when the war began, but most of his planes were destroyed when Japanese armed forces invaded the Philippines. He was then transferred to India and given command of the US Middle East Air Force. His principle duties were to train pilots and acquire much needed supplies. He was transferred again in October 1942 to command the US Ninth Army Air Force. His air units performed very well in support of ground troops during the Tunisian campaign in North Africa. In fall of 1943, he was sent to Great Britain to prepare the Ninth Army Air Force to deliver close tactical air support for Operation Overlord, the upcoming invasion of France. Once again, his units performed admirably, destroying bridges and other targets in France. In August 1944, Brereton was given command of the First Allied Airborne Army. He was heavily involved in planning airborne operations for the remainder of the war. The most notable was Field Marshal Bernard Montgomery's Operation Market

Garden, which called for the seizure of several key bridges in Holland by paratroopers. The most important bridge was at Arnhem, which spanned the Rhine River and would give the Allies entry into Germany. The plan was too ambitious and had only limited success. One end of the Arnhem bridge was held for a short time, but British armoured units could not break through and the paratroopers had to retreat. *The Brereton Diaries* are recommended for reading.

Bibliography

Brereton, Lewis H. *The Brereton Diaries: The War in the Air in the Pacific, Middle East, and Europe, 30 October 1941-8 May, 1945*. New York: Morrow, 1946.

Admiral Arleigh Albert Burke
United States Navy
1901-1996

Burke gained fame as a destroyer squadron commander during the war. In November 1943, he obtained the nickname '31-Knot' Burke for his actions during the battles of Empress Augusta Bay and Cape St. George in the Solomons. His destroyers sank numerous Japanese ships. In March 1944, Burke was promoted to chief of staff under Admiral Marc Mitscher and coordinated all naval tactical operations during the Battle of the Philippine Sea, Leyte Gulf, and Okinawa. Admiral Burke also made many contributions to the post-war navy. He became Chief of Naval Operations in 1955 and held the post until 1961. He was a proponent of high technology and the use of nuclear power and guided the post-war navy in that direction. His innovations and plans were implemented during the Vietnam War. Recommended for reading are John Jones' and Hubert Kelly, Jr's *Admiral Arleigh (31-Knot) Burke* and E. B. Potter's *Admiral Arleigh Burke*.

Bibliography

Burke, Arleigh A. *The Best of Burke: Selections from the War-time Dispatches, Battle Reports, Admonitions and Reflections of Admiral Arleigh A. Burke, USN (Ret.).* Fredericksburg, TX: The Admiral Nimitz Foundation, 1986.

______. *Reminiscences of Admiral Arleigh Burke, USN, Retired: Special Series on Selected Subjects.* Annapolis, MD: U.S. Naval Institute, 1979.

Jones, John Kenneth and Hubert Kelly, Jr. *Admiral Arleigh (31-Knot) Burke: Story of A Fighting Sailor.* Philadelphia: Chilton Books, 1962.

______. *Destroyer Squadron 23: Combat Exploits of Arleigh Burke's Gallant Force.* Philadelphia: Chilton Co., 1959.

Potter, E. B. (Elmer Belmont). *Admiral Arleigh Burke.* New York: Random House, 1990.

Lieutenant General John Kenneth Cannon
United States Army Air Force
1892-1955

Cannon spent his war years in the North African and Mediterranean Theatres of Operations. His first assignment was as Commanding General, XII Air Support Command during Operation Torch, the invasion of North Africa. He then commanded XII Bomber Command and was Deputy Commanding General, Allied Tactical Air Force during Operation Husky, the invasion of Sicily, and during Operation Avalanche, the invasion of Italy which immediately followed the conclusion of Husky. In 1944, he was in command of all air force units that participated in Operation Anvil-Dragoon, the invasion of southern France. In March 1945, he was appointed Commander-in-Chief of Allied Air Forces in the Mediterranean Theatre of Operations. The only source found for General Cannon was his *Papers*.

Bibliography

Cannon, John Kenneth. *Papers, 1930-1954.* n.p., n.d.

Lieutenant General Claire Lee Chennault
United States Army Air Force
1893-1958

Chennault achieved his fame while commanding the famous Flying Tigers. After retiring from the US Army Air Corps, Chennault went to China in 1937 and attempted to train Chinese pilots, but his efforts were generally unsuccessful. In 1941, he returned to the United States and recruited approximately one hundred American pilots to fight for China. Under the official title of American Volunteer Group (AVG), the Flying Tigers became operational in late 1941 and by April 1942, when they were disbanded, had destroyed several hundred Japanese planes. At this time, Chennault returned to active duty and was given command of the China Air Task Force. In July 1943, he commanded the Fourteenth Army Air Force. He had frequent clashes with General Joseph Stilwell over strategic planning and finally resigned his post in July 1945. Chennault was a tough, independent airman who cared deeply for his men and the Chinese people and was always attempting to obtain more supplies and equipment for his air units. Recommended for reading are General Chennault's memoir, *Way of a Fighter*, Daniel Ford's *Flying Tigers*, Jack Samson's *Chennault*, and Duane Schultz's *The Maverick War*.

Bibliography

Archibald, Joe. *Commander of the Flying Tigers: Claire Lee Chennault*. New York: Messner, 1966.

Ayling, Keith. *Old Leatherface of the Flying Tigers: The Story of General Chennault*. Indianapolis, IN: Bobbs-Merrill, 1945.

Bauer, Boyd Heber. "*General Claire Lee Chennault and China, 1937-1958: A Study of Chennault, His Relationship with China, and Selected Issues in Sino-American Relations*." Ph.D. diss., The American University, 1973. (DAI, 35:1, 550A, UMI Order # 7414855)

Byrd, Martha. *Chennault: Giving Wings to the Tiger*. Tuscaloosa: University of Alabama Press, 1987.

Chennault, Anna. *Chennault and the Flying Tigers*. New York: P. S. Eriksson, 1963.

_____. *A Thousand Springs: The Biography of A Marriage*. Middlebury, CT: P. S. Eriksson, 1982.

Chennault, Claire Lee. *The Role of Defensive Pursuit*. n.p., 1935. (microform)

______. *Way of a Fighter: The Memoirs of Claire Lee Chennault*. Edited by Robert Hotz. New York: G. P. Putnam's Sons, 1949.

Cornelius, Wanda and Thayne Short. *Ding Hao, America's Air War in China, 1937-1945*. Gretna, LA: Pelican Pub. Co., 1980.

Ford, Daniel. *Flying Tigers: Claire Chennault and the American Volunteer Group*. Washington, DC: Smithsonian Institution Press, 1991.

Heiferman, Ronald. *Flying Tigers: Chennault in China*. New York: Ballantine Books, 1971.

Hessen, Robert, ed. *General Claire Lee Chennault: A Guide to His Papers in the Hoover Institution Archives*. Stanford, CA: Hoover Institution Press, 1983.

Hotz, Robert B. *With General Chennault: The Story of the Flying Tigers*. New York: Coward-McCann, 1943.

Johnson, Wayne G. and Don Van Cleve, eds. *Chennault's Flying Tigers: A Commemorative History of the American Volunteer Group, The Original Flying Tigers, China Air Task Force, 14th Air Force, 1941-1945*. Silver Bay, MN: 14th Air Force Association, 1982.

Mims, Sam. *Chennault of the Flying Tigers*. Philadelphia: Macrae Smith Co., 1943.

Nalty, Bernard C. *Tigers Over Asia*. New York: Elsevier-Dutton, 1978.

Rosholt, Malcolm. *Claire L. Chennault: A Tribute*. Rosholt, WI: Flying Tigers of the 14th Air Force, 1983.

Samson, Jack. *Chennault*. New York: Doubleday, 1987.

Schultz, Duane P. *The Maverick War: Chennault and the Flying Tigers*. New York: St. Martin's Press, 1987.

Scott, Robert Lee. *Flying Tiger: Chennault of China*. Garden City, NY: Doubleday, 1959.

Smith, Robert Moody assisted by Philip D. Smith. *With Chennault in China: A Flying Tiger's Diary*. Blue Ridge Summit, PA: Tab Books, 1984.

Toland, John. *The Flying Tigers*. New York: Random House, 1963.

Rear Admiral Joseph James Clark
United States Navy
1893-1971

Clark commanded the new aircraft carrier *Hornet* in Admiral Marc Mitscher's Task Force 58. The first *Hornet* was sunk during the Battle of Santa Cruz in October 1942. Clark's planes raided air bases on Iwo Jima and Chichi Jima just prior to the Saipan landings in the Marianas in June 1944. The Japanese planes his pilots destroyed could have been a serious threat for naval and Marine units involved in the campaign. Clark returned to Task Force 58 in time to participate in the Battle of the Philippine Sea, which naval pilots dubbed the "Great Marianas Turkey Shoot." Pilots from the *Hornet* accounted for many of the nearly 500 Japanese planes that were destroyed. Admiral Clark's *Carrier Admiral* is recommended for reading.

Bibliography

Clark, J. J. (Joseph James) with Clark G. Reynolds. *Carrier Admiral*. New York: David McKay, 1967.
____ and Dwight H. Barnes. *Sea Power and Its Meaning*. Rev. ed. New York: F. Watts, 1968.

General Mark Wayne Clark
United States Army
1896-1984

Clark was one of the United States Army's highest ranking officers during the Second World War, but has received less attention than his counterparts. Perhaps the reason is because he was involved in the Italian campaign (September 1943-May 1945), a campaign that is not as well remembered as the campaign in Northwest Europe (June 1944-May 1945) despite the heavy fighting that occurred. Clark's first duties in the war came during the planning of Operation Torch, the invasion of North Africa in November 1942. When the Allies invaded Italy in September 1943, he commanded the US Fifth Army. His forces captured Rome in early June 1944. In November 1944, he was named commander of the 15th Army Group, replacing Field Marshal Sir Harold Alexander. When the war ended in May 1945, his units had advanced into the northern regions of Italy. Recommended for reading are Martin Blumenson's *Mark Clark* and General Clark's memoir, *Calculated Risk*.

Bibliography

Blumenson, Martin. *Mark Clark*. New York: Congdon & Weed, 1984. Distributed by St. Martin's Press.

Clark, Mark Wayne. *Calculated Risk: The Story of the War in the Mediterranean*. New York: Harper & Brothers, 1950.

Clark, Maurine. *Captain's Bride, General's Lady: The Memoirs of Mrs. Mark W. Clark*. New York: McGraw-Hill Co. Inc., 1956.

General Lucius D. Clay
United States Army
1897-1978

Clay was a military engineer before the start of the Second World War. In 1942, he was given command of the US Army's procurement program. The job of logistics is often overlooked in the running of an army in wartime, but it is a vital function that must be administered effectively or else the fighting component can be rendered useless and placed in great peril. Clay was outstanding in the execution of his duties. For the Normandy invasion, General Dwight Eisenhower named him supply base commander and later deputy director of the Office of Mobilization. He held the latter position until April 1945 when he became Eisenhower's deputy for the military occupation of Germany. After the war, as military governor, Clay worked vigorously for the restoration of a civilian German government. Recommended for reading are General Clay's *Decision in Germany*, John Backer's *Winds of History*, and Jean Smith's *Lucius D. Clay*.

Bibliography

Backer, John H. *Winds of History: The German Years of Lucius DuBignon Clay*. New York: Van Nostrand Reinhold, 1983.

Clay, Lucius D. *Decision in Germany*. Garden City, NY: Doubleday & Company Inc., 1950.

______. *Germany and the Fight for Freedom*. Cambridge: Harvard University Press, 1950.

______. *Lucius D. Clay*. Glen Rock, NJ: Microfilming Corporation of America, 1977. Columbia University Oral History Collection. (microfiche)

_____. *The Papers of General Lucius D. Clay, Germany, 1945-1949*. 2 volumes. Bloomington, IN: Indiana University Press, 1974.

Schmitt, Hans A., ed. *U.S. Occupation in Europe After World War II: Papers and Reminiscences from the April 23-24, 1976 Conference Held at the George C. Marshall Research Foundation, Lexington, Virginia*. Lawrence: Regents Press of Kansas, 1978.

Smith, Jean Edward. *Lucius D. Clay: An American Life*. New York: Holt, 1990.

St. Onge, Robert J. *General Lucius D. Clay: A Case Study of Strategic Leadership and Vision*. Carlisle Barracks, PA: U.S. Army War College, 1991.

General Joseph Lawton Collins
United States Army
1896-1963

Collins saw combat action in both the Pacific and European Theatres of Operations during the Second World War. His 25th Infantry Division landed on Guadalcanal in December 1942 to relieve the 1st Marine Division. The 25th mopped up the remaining Japanese units that had not been evacuated or killed during the heavy fighting with the 1st Marine Division. In charge of the XIV Corps, his troops invaded New Guinea in January 1943 and cleared the island of Japanese troops. Collins was transferred to the European Theatre of Operations in December 1943 and was given command of the VII Corps. He trained his troops hard for the upcoming invasion of France. On D-Day, 6 June 1944, his troops landed at Utah Beach. They moved quickly inland and captured Cherbourg on 24 June. After closing the Falise Gap, his units moved into Belgium. During the Battle of the Bulge, Collins' tanks and infantry led a counterattack from the north, recapturing Houffalize. In the spring, the VII Corps crossed the Rhine River and moved deep into Germany, linking up with the Red Army along the Elbe River during the last days of the war. Collins is recognized as one of the US Army's best ground commanders during the war. Collins remained in the Army following the conclusion of the war, serving until 1956. General Collins' autobiography, *Lightning Joe*, is recommended for reading.

Bibliography

Collins, Joseph Lawton. *Lightning Joe: An Autobiography*. Baton Rouge,
    LA: Louisiana State University Press, 1979.
Wade, Gary. *Conversations with General J. Lawton Collins*. Fort
    Leavenworth, KS: Combat Studies Institute, U.S. Army Command
    and General Staff College, 1983.

General Jacob Loucks Devers
United States Army
1887-1979

Devers, despite his high military rank, is one of the lesser known
generals that commanded an army group during the Second World War.
In September 1942, he was promoted to the rank of lieutenant general
and in May 1943, was named Commanding General, European Theatre
of Operations, US Army. In December 1943, he replaced General
Dwight Eisenhower as Commanding General, North Africa Theatre of
Operations, US Army. In addition to this position, he became Deputy
Supreme Allied Commander, Mediterranean Theatre of Operations. He
was in command of Operation Anvil-Dragoon, the invasion of southern
France in August 1944. Excellent progress was made by the US Seventh
Army and the First French Army. In September 1944, these two armies
became the 6th Army Group with Devers in overall command. After
heavy fighting in the Alsace region, the 6th Army Group moved into
southern Germany during the late stages of the war, capturing Munich
and Adolf Hitler's mountain retreat, Berchtesgaden. Devers was
promoted to full general in March 1945. The only source found
concerning the career of General Devers was *Report of Operations in
France and Germany, 1944-1945*. Contact your library's interlibrary
loan department for its availability.

Bibliography

Seventh US Army. *Report of Operations in France and Germany,
    1944-1945*. 3 volumes. Heidelberg: Aloys Graf, 1946.

Lieutenant General James Harold Doolittle
United States Army Air Force
1896-1993

Doolittle is best remembered for leading a flight of sixteen B-25 bombers that raided Tokyo on 18 April 1942. The planes flew off the deck of the aircraft carrier *Hornet*, an extremely difficult task. The bombing raid did little physical damage to Japan, but was a tremendous morale booster for America. Doolittle was more than just a bomber pilot. He was involved in the task of converting a portion of the automobile industry to the manufacturing of airplanes and helped invent instruments to aid flying. He was commander of the Twelfth Air Force and the Northwest Strategic Air Force in North Africa. In December 1943, he was given command of the Eighth Air Force. His units bombed V1 and V2 rocket factories, railroads, and synthetic oil refineries in France and Germany, greatly aiding ground units involved in Operation Overlord, the invasion of Normandy, France. Recommended for reading are General Doolittle's memoir, *I Could Never Be So Lucky Again*, Carroll Glines' *Jimmy Doolittle*, and Lowell Thomas' and Edward Jablonski's *Doolittle*.

Bibliography

Cohen, Stan. *Destination Tokyo: A Pictorial History of Doolittle's Tokyo Raid, April 8, 1942*. Missoula, MT: Pictorial Histories Publishing Co., 1983.

Doolittle, James H. *Board on Officer-Enlisted Man Relationships. The Complete Doolittle Report*. Washington: Infantry Journal Press, 1946.

_____ with Carroll V. Glines. *I Could Never Be So Lucky Again: The Memoirs of General James H. Doolittle*. New York: Bantam Books, 1991.

_____. *Reminiscences of General James H. Doolittle, U.S. Air Forces (Retired)*. Annapolis, MD: U. S. Naval Institute, 1987. Oral History Program (Navy).

Glines, Carroll V., Jr. *The Doolittle Raid: America's Daring First Strike Against Japan*. New York: Orion Books, 1988.

_____. *Doolittle's Tokyo Raiders*. Princeton, NJ: Van Nostrand, 1964.

_____. *Jimmy Doolittle: Daredevil Aviator and Scientist*. New York: Macmillan, 1972.

_____. *Jimmy Doolittle, Master of the Calculated Risk*. New York: Van Nostrand Reinhold Co., 1980.

Mann, Carl. *Lightning in the Sky: The Story of Jimmy Doolittle*. New York: R. M. McBride & Company, 1943.

Merrill, James M. *Target Tokyo: The Halsey-Doolittle Raid*. Chicago: Rand-McNally, 1984.

Reynolds, Quentin James. *The Amazing Mr. Doolittle: A Biography of Lieutenant-General James H. Doolittle*. New York: Appleton-Century-Crofts, 1953.

Schultz, Duane P. *The Doolittle Raid*. New York: St. Martin's Press, 1988.

Thomas, Lowell and Edward Jablonski. *Doolittle - A Biography*. Garden City, NY: Doubleday, 1976.

General Ira Clarence Eaker
United States Army Air Force
1896-1987

Eaker was a strong proponent of precision strategic air bombardment. He led the first US Army Air Force bombing raid against Germany on 17 August 1943. The target was the railroad yards at Rouen. In command of the Eighth US Army Air Force, he attended the Casablanca Conference in January 1943 and convinced the Combined Chiefs of Staff that daylight precision bombing would work in conjunction with the Royal Air Force's nighttime bombing. In June 1943, he was promoted to lieutenant general and in 1944, succeeded Air Chief Marshal Sir Arthur Tedder as Commander-in-Chief of Mediterranean Air Command. Based in Italy, his planes struck targets in Italy, Germany, and the Balkans. Eaker was involved in one of the most controversial bombing operations of the war. He designed the plan for the bombing of the Italian monastery at Monte Cassino. The monastery was reduced to rubble. He also commanded all air operations during Operation Anvil-Dragoon, the invasion of southern France. Recommended for reading are Dewitt Copp's *A Few Great Captains*, and James Parton's *"Air Force Spoken Here"*.

Bibliography

Copp, Dewitt S. *A Few Great Captains: The Men and Events That Shaped the Development of U.S. Air Power*. Garden City, NY: Doubleday, 1980.

Eaker, Ira C. and Henry H. Arnold. *Army Flyer*. New York: Harper & Brothers, 1942.

______. *Interview of Lt. Gen. Ira C. Eaker*. Interviewed by Hugh N. Ahmann, February 10-11, 1975. Maxwell Air Force Base, AL: Albert F. Simpson Historical Research Center, Office of Air Force History, Headquarters USAF, 1980.

______ and Henry H. Arnold. *This Flying Game*. 3rd ed. New York: Funk & Wagnalls, 1943.

______ and ______. *Winged Warfare*. New York: Harper & Brothers, 1941.

Parton, James. *"Air Force Spoken Here": General Ira Eaker and the Command of the Air*. Bethesda, MD: Adler & Adler, 1986.

General Robert Lawrence Eichelberger
United States Army
1886-1961

Eichelberger served under General Douglas MacArthur in the Pacific Theatre of Operations during the Second World War. His I Corps won a victory on Buna during the New Guinea campaign that helped reverse the tide of Japanese expansion toward Australia. His forces captured Hollandia in April 1944. He was in command of the US Eighth Army during the invasion and conquest of the Philippines in 1944-45. Recommended for reading are General Eichelberger's *Our Jungle Road to Tokyo*, Paul Chwialkowski's *In Caesar's Shadow*, and John Shortal's *Forged by Fire*.

Bibliography

Chwialkowski, Paul. *"A 'Near Great' General: The Life and Career of Robert L. Eichelberger."* Ph.D. diss., Duke University, 1991. (DAI, 52:8, 3045A, UMI Order # DA9202484)

______. *In Caesar's Shadow: The Life of General Robert Eichelberger*. Westport, CT: Greenwood Press, 1993.

Eichelberger, Robert L. *Dear Miss Em: General Eichelberger's War in the Pacific, 1942-1945*. Edited by Jay Luvaas. Westport, CT: Greenwood Press, 1972.

______. *Our Jungle Road to Tokyo*. New York: Viking Press, 1950.

______. *The Robert L. Eichelberger Papers*. n.p., n.d.

McNeill, Dan K. *Eichelberger in Mindandao: Leadership in Joint Operations*. Carlisle Barracks, PA: U.S. Army War College, 1989.

Shortal, John F. *Forged by Fire: General Robert L. Eichelberger and the Pacific War*. Columbia, SC: University of South Carolina Press, 1987.

______. "*Robert L. Eichelberger: The Evolution of A Combat Commander*." Ph.D. diss., Temple University, 1985. (DAI, 46:8, 2422A, UMI Order # DA8521144)

General of the Army Dwight David Eisenhower
United States Army
1890-1969

Eisenhower rose quickly in rank at the outset of the Second World War. By the war's end, he had achieved the rank of Supreme Allied Commander and had directed the Allied military forces that, in concert with the Soviet Union's Red Army, defeated Nazi Germany. He is probably best known for his ability to keep his generals fighting the Germans rather than among themselves as they were inclined to do. He had to discipline George Patton on several occasions and Bernard Montgomery was always trying to run the war effort the way he desired. Eisenhower's quick smile and likeable personality, as well as his tremendous military success, made him America's most popular general and paved the way for his election to the presidency in 1952. Given Eisenhower's rank and achievements, he has had a multitude of biographers. Highly recommended are the works by Stephen Ambrose. Recommended titles are *The Supreme Commander*, *Eisenhower*, Volumes 1 and 2 or *Eisenhower: Soldier and President*, a condensed version of the two-volume work. Also recommended are Michael Beschloss' *Eisenhower*, David Eisenhower's *Eisenhower at War, 1943-45*, Merle Miller's *Ike, the Soldier*, and E. K. G. Sixsmith's *Eisenhower As Military Commander*. Eisenhower, himself, published numerous books and his personal papers have been published. Recommended for reading are *Crusade in Europe*, *In Review: Pictures I've Kept*, and *The Papers of Dwight David Eisenhower*, Volumes I-IX. The works listed in the following bibliography deal primarily with Eisenhower's military career and not with his years as president.

Bibliography

Allied Forces. Supreme Headquarters. *Eisenhower's Own Story of the War*. New York: Arco Publishing Co., 1946.

Altman, Frances. *Dwight D. Eisenhower: Crusader for Peace*. Minneapolis, MN: T. S. Denison & Company Inc., 1970.

Ambrose, Stephen E. *Eisenhower and Berlin, 1945: The Decision to Halt at the Elbe*. New York: Norton, 1967.

______. *Eisenhower: President and Elder Statesman, 1952-1969*. Volume 2. New York: Simon & Schuster, 1984.

______. *Eisenhower: Soldier and President*. Revised edition. New York: Simon & Schuster, 1990. (Condensed version of an earlier two-volume work, *Eisenhower: Soldier, General of the Army, President-Elect, 1890-1952* and *Eisenhower: President and Elder Statesman, 1952-1969*.)

______. *Eisenhower: Soldier, General of the Army, President-Elect, 1890-1952*. Volume 1. New York: Simon & Schuster, 1983.

______. *Ike: Abilene to Berlin. The Life of Dwight D. Eisenhower from His Childhood in Abilene, Kansas Through His Command of the Allied Forces in Europe in World War II*. New York: Harper & Row, 1973.

______. *Ike's Spies: Eisenhower and the Espionage Establishment*. Garden City, NY: Doubleday & Co., 1981.

______. *The Supreme Commander: The War Years of General Dwight D. Eisenhower*. Garden City, NY: Doubleday, 1970.

American Heritage Editors. *Eisenhower, American Hero: The Historical Record of His Life*. New York: American Heritage Publishing Co., 1969.

Archer, Jules. *Battlefield President: Dwight D. Eisenhower*. New York: J. Messner, 1967. (juvenile)

Army Times, eds. *The Challenge and the Triumph: The Story of General Dwight D. Eisenhower*. New York: Putnam, 1966.

Beckhard, Arthur J. *The Story of Dwight D. Eisenhower*. New York: Grosset & Dunlap, 1970. (juvenile)

Bender, Mark C. *Watershed at Leavenworth: Dwight D. Eisenhower and the Command and General Staff School*. Fort Leavenworth, KS: U.S. Army Command and General Staff College, 1990.

Beschloss, Michael R. *Eisenhower: A Centennial Life*. New York: Harper & Row, 1990.

Birkner, Michael J., ed. *Eisenhower and the Art of Leadership*. Lectures by Fred I. Greenstein, George C. Herring, and Stephen E. Ambrose. Gettysburg, PA: Gettysburg College, 1990.

Bischof, Gunter and Stephen E. Ambrose. *Eisenhower: A Centenary Assessment*. Baton Rouge: Louisiana State University Press, 1995.

_____. *Eisenhower and the German POWs: Facts Against Falsehood*. Baton Rouge: Louisiana State University Press, 1992.

Blumenson, Martin. *Eisenhower*. New York: Ballantine Books, 1972.

Bohanan, Robert D., comp. *Dwight D. Eisenhower: A Selected Bibliography of Periodical and Dissertation Literature*. Abilene, KS: Eisenhower Library, 1981.

Brendon, Piers. *Ike: The Life and Times of Dwight D. Eisenhower*. London: Secker & Warburg, 1987.

Burk, Robert F. *Dwight D. Eisenhower, Hero and Politician*. Boston: Twayne Publishers, 1986.

Butcher, Harry Cecil. *My Three Years with Eisenhower: The Personal Diary of Captain Harry C. Butcher, USNR, Naval Aide to General Eisenhower, 1942 to 1945*. New York: Simon & Schuster, 1946.

Cannon, Marian G. *Dwight David Eisenhower: War Hero and President*. New York: Watts, 1990. (juvenile)

Carpenter, Allan. *Dwight David Eisenhower, the Warring Peacemaker*. Vero Beach, FL: Rourke Publications, 1987. (juvenile)

Childs, Marquis. *Eisenhower, Captive Hero: A Critical Study of the General and the President*. New York: Harcourt, Brace, 1958.

Clemens, Cyril. *Mark Twain and Dwight D. Eisenhower*. Webster Groves, MO: International Mark Twain Society, 1953.

Cook, Blanche Wiesen. *The Declassified Eisenhower: A Divided Legacy*. Garden City, NY: Doubleday, 1981.

Darby, Jean. *Dwight D. Eisenhower: A Man Called Ike*. Minneapolis, MN: Leaner Publications, 1989. (juvenile)

David, Lester and Irene David. *Ike and Mamie: The Story of the General and His Lady*. New York: G. P. Putnam's Sons, 1981.

Davis, Kenneth S. *General Eisenhower, Soldier of Democracy: From Boyhood to Supreme Commander*. Rev. ed. Garden City, NY: Doubleday, 1952.

Deitch, Kenneth M. and JoAnne B. Weisman. *Dwight D. Eisenhower, Man of Many Hats*. Lowell, MA: Discovery Enterprises, 1990. (juvenile)

Donovan, Robert J. *Confidential Secretary: Ann Whitman's 20 Years with Eisenhower and Rockefeller*. New York: Dutton, 1988.

Dwight D. Eisenhower Library. *Historical Materials in the Dwight D. Eisenhower Library*. Abilene, KS: The Library, 1981.

Eisenhower, David. *Eisenhower at War, 1943-1945*. New York: Vantage Books, 1987.

Eisenhower, Dwight D. *At Ease: Stories I Tell to Friends*. Garden City, NY: Doubleday, 1967.

______. *Crusade in Europe*. Garden City, NY: Doubleday, 1948.

______. *Dear General: Eisenhower's War Time Letters to Marshall*. Edited by Joseph Patrick Hobbs. Baltimore: Johns Hopkins Press, 1971.

______. *Dwight D. Eisenhower, 1890-1969: Chronology, Documents, Bibliographical Aids*. Edited by Robert I. Vexler. Dobbs Ferry, NY: Oceana Publications, 1970.

______. *Eisenhower Diaries*. Edited by Robert H. Ferrell. New York: W. W. Norton & Co., 1981.

______. *Eisenhower: Soldier, President, Statesman*. Edited by Joann P. Krieg. New York: Greenwood Press, 1987.

______. *Eisenhower Speaks: Dwight D. Eisenhower in His Messages and Speeches*. Selected and edited by Rudolph L. Treuenfels. New York: Farrar, Straus, 1948.

______. *Ike, A Great American*. Selected by Don Ramsey. Kansas City: Hallmark, 1972.

______. *Ike's Letters to a Friend, 1941-1958*. Edited by Robert Griffith. Lawrence, KS: University Press of Kansas, 1984.

______. *In Review: Pictures I've Kept. A Concise Pictorial Autobiography*. Garden City, NY: Doubleday, 1969.

______. *Letters to Mamie*. Garden City, NY: Doubleday, 1978.

______. *The Papers of Dwight David Eisenhower. Volumes I-V: The War Years*. Alfred A. Chandler, Jr., ed., and others. Baltimore: Johns Hopkins Press, 1970.

______. *The Papers of Dwight David Eisenhower. Volume VI: Occupation, 1945*. Alfred D. Chandler, Jr. and Louis Galambos, eds. Baltimore: Johns Hopkins Press, 1979.

______. *The Papers of Dwight David Eisenhower. Volumes VII-IX: The Chief of Staff*. Louis Galambos, ed. Baltimore: Johns Hopkins Press, 1979.

______. *The Quotable Dwight D. Eisenhower*. Compiled by Elsie Gollagher and the staff of Quote. Anderson, SC: Droke House, 1967. Distributed by Grosset & Dunlap of New York.

______. *Report by the Supreme Commander to the Combined Chiefs of Staff on the Operations in Europe of the Allied Expeditionary Force, 6 June 1944 to 8 May 1945*. Washington, DC: Government Printing Office, 1946.

______. *Selected Speeches of Dwight David Eisenhower, 34th President of the United States. Selected from Three Principal Periods of His Life: As Supreme Allied Commander in Europe During the War Years, As Supreme NATO Commander and As President.* Washington, DC: U.S. Government Printing Office, 1970.

______. *What Eisenhower Thinks.* Edited and Interpreted by Allan Taylor. New York: Crowell, 1952.

______. *The Wisdom of Dwight D. Eisenhower: Quotations from Ike's Speeches and Writings, 1939-1969.* Selected by Stephen E. Ambrose. New Orleans: Eisenhower Center, 1990.

Eisenhower Foundation. *D-Day: The Normandy Invasion in Retrospective.* Abilene, KS: Eisenhower Center, 1971.

Faber, Doris. *Dwight Eisenhower.* New York: Abelard-Schuman, 1977. (juvenile)

Field, Rudolph. *Ike, The Man of the Hour.* New York: Universal, 1952.

______. *Mr. American, Dwight David Eisenhower: An Evaluation.* New York: R. Field Co., 1952.

Friedman, Irving I. *Meet General Ike: A Pictorial Profile of General Dwight D. Eisenhower.* New York: Virson Pub. Co., 1948.

Gelb, Norman. *Ike and Monty: Generals at War.* New York: William Morrow & Company, Inc., 1994.

Gunther, John. *Eisenhower, the Man and the Symbol.* New York: Harper, 1952.

Hargrove, Jim. *Dwight D. Eisenhower.* Chicago: Children's Press, 1987. (juvenile)

Harris, Jack C. *Dwight D. Eisenhower: A Great American Hero.* New York: Golden Books, 1990. (juvenile)

Hatch, Alden. *General Eisenhower: A Biography of Dwight D. Eisenhower.* London: Skeffington & Son, 1946.

______. *General Ike: A Biography of Dwight D. Eisenhower.* Rev. ed. New York: Holt, 1952.

______. *Young Ike.* New York: Messner, 1953. (juvenile)

Hendrix, Sue. *Dwight Eisenhower, Planner, Leader, President.* Mankato, MN: Creative Education, 1974. (juvenile)

Hicks, Wilson, ed. *This is Ike: A Picture Story of the Man.* New York: Holt, 1952.

Hudson, Wilma J. *Dwight D. Eisenhower: Young Military Leader.* Indianapolis, IN: Bobbs-Merrill, 1970. (juvenile)

Jacobs, William Jay. *Dwight David Eisenhower.* New York: Watts, 1995. (juvenile)

Jameson, Henry B. *They Still Call Him Ike*. New York: Vantage Press, 1972.

Kinnard, Douglas. *Ike, 1890-1990: A Pictorial History*. Washington, DC: Brassey's Defence, 1990.

Krieg, Joann P., ed. *Dwight D. Eisenhower, Soldier, President, Statesman*. New York: Greenwood Press, 1987.

Lee, R. Alton, comp. *Dwight D. Eisenhower: A Bibliography of His Times and Presidency*. Wilmington, DE: Scholarly Resources Inc., 1991.

______. *Dwight D. Eisenhower: Soldier and Statesman*. Chicago: Nelson-Hall, 1981.

Longgood, William F. *Ike: A Pictorial Biography*. Picture Editor, Daro Gossner. New York: Time-Life Books, 1969.

Lovelace, Delos Wheeler. *'Ike' Eisenhower: Statesman and Soldier of Peace*. Rev. ed. New York: Crowell, 1969. (juvenile)

Lyon, Peter. *Eisenhower: Portrait of A Hero*. Boston: Little, Brown, 1974.

Maurious, Andre. *Eisenhower, the Liberator*. Translated by Eileen Lane Kinney. New York: Didier, 1945.

Mayer, S. L. *Great American Generals of World War 2: MacArthur, Eisenhower, Patton*. New York: Gallery Books, 1984.

McCann, Kevin. *Man from Abilene*. Garden City, NY: Doubleday, 1952.

McKeogh, Michael James and Richard Lockridge. *Sgt. Mickey and General Ike*. New York: G. P. Putnam's Sons, 1946.

Mehurst, Martin. *Eisenhower's War of Words: Rhetoric and Leadership*. East Lansing: Michigan State University Press, 1993.

Miller, Francis Trevelyan. *Eisenhower: Man and Soldier*. Philadelphia: John C. Winston Co., 1944.

Miller, Merle. *Ike, the Soldier: As They Knew Him*. New York: Putnam's Sons, 1987.

Moos, Malcolm. *Dwight D. Eisenhower*. New York: Random House, 1964. (juvenile)

Morgan, Kathleen Summersby. *Past Forgetting: My Love Affair with Dwight D. Eisenhower*. New York: Simon & Schuster, 1976.

Morin, Relman. *Dwight D. Eisenhower: A Gauge of Greatness*. New York: Simon & Schuster, 1969.

Murray, G. E. Patrick. "*Eisenhower and Montgomery: Broad Front Versus Single Thrust, The Historiography of the Debate Over Strategy and Command, August 1944 - April 1945*." Ph.D. diss., Temple University, 1991. (DAI, 52:10, 3704A, UMI Order # DA9207885)

Nadich, Judah. *Eisenhower and the Jews*. New York: Twayne Publishers, 1953.

Neal, Steve. *The Eisenhowers: Reluctant Dynasty*. Garden City: Doubleday & Co., 1978.

Nicolay, Helen. *Born to Command: The Story of General Eisenhower*. New York: Appleton-Century Co., 1945.

Odom, Charles B. *General George S. Patton and Eisenhower*. New Orleans: World Picture Productions, Rose Printing Co., 1985.

Pinkley, Virgil with James F. Scheer. *Eisenhower Declassified*. Old Tappan, NJ: Revill, 1979.

Puryear, Edgar F., Jr. *19 Stars: A Study in Military Character and Leadership*. (George Marshall, Dwight Eisenhower, Douglas MacArthur, and George Patton.) Washington, DC: Coiner Publications, 1971.

Radford, Ruby L. *Dwight D. Eisenhower*. New York: Putnam, 1970. (juvenile)

Reeder, Red. *Dwight D. Eisenhower: Fighter for Peace*. Champaign, IL: Garrard Publishing Co., 1968. (juvenile)

Rostow, W. W. (Walt Whitman). *Pre-Invasion Bombing Strategy: General Eisenhower's Decision of March 25, 1944*. Austin: University of Texas Press, 1981.

Russell, Don. *Invincible Ike: The Inspiring Story of Dwight D. Eisenhower*. Chicago: Successful Living Publications, 1952.

Russoli, Edward and Candace Russoli. *Dwight D. Eisenhower: General, President, and Cook*. Allentown, PA: Benedettini Books, 1990.

Sandak, Cass R. *The Eisenhowers*. New York: Crestwood, 1993. (juvenile)

Sandberg, Peter Lars. *Dwight D. Eisenhower*. New Haven, CT: Chelsea House, 1986. (juvenile)

Sherman, Diane. *The Boy from Abilene: The Story of Dwight D. Eisenhower*. Philadelphia: Westminister Press, 1968.

Sixsmith, E. K. G. (Eric Kerr Gilborne). *Eisenhower as Military Commander*. New York: Stein & Day, 1972.

Slater, Ellis D. *The Ike I Knew*. Material collected by Ernestine Durr. Edited and typed by Elsie Maki. Ellis D. Slater Trust, 1980.

Smith, A. Merriman. *Meet Mr. Eisenhower*. New York: Harper, 1955.

Smith, Walter Bedell. *Eisenhower's Six Great Decisions: Europe, 1944-1945*. New York: Longmans, Green, 1956.

Snyder, Marty with Glenn D. Kittler. *My Friend Ike*. New York: Frederick Fell Inc., 1956.

Steinberg, Alfred. *Dwight D. Eisenhower*. New York: Putnam, 1968.

Summersby, Kathleen. *Eisenhower Was My Boss*. Edited by Michael Kearns. New York: Prentice-Hall, 1948.

Thomas, Henry. *Dwight D. Eisenhower: General, President*. New York: Putnam, 1969. (juvenile)

United States Army Center of Military History. *Dwight David Eisenhower*. Washington, DC: U.S. Army Center of Military History, 1990.

United States. Department of Defense. *Journey to Victory: Dwight D. Eisenhower, 1890-1990*. Washington, DC: Department of Defense, 1990.

United States. 91st Congress, 1st Session, 1969. *Memorial Services in the Congress of the United States and Tributes in Eulogy of Dwight David Eisenhower, Late A President of the United States*. Compiled under the direction of the Joint Committee on Printing. Washington, DC: U.S. Government Printing Office, 1970.

Van Gelder, Lawrence. *Ike: A Soldier's Crusade*. New York: Universal Publishing & Distributing Co., 1969.

Vexler, Robert I., ed. *Dwight D. Eisenhower, 1890-1969: Chronology, Documents, Bibliographic Aids*. Dobbs Ferry, NY: Oceana Publications, 1970.

Whitney, David C. *The Picture Life of Dwight D. Eisenhower*. New York: F. Watts, 1968.

Wykes, Alan. *The Biography of Dwight D. Eisenhower*. New York: Galley Press, 1982.

Rear Admiral James Fife
United States Navy
1897-1975

Fife was involved in submarine warfare during the Second World War. In 1944, he assumed command of all US Navy submarine operations in the Pacific Theatre of Operations. During the war, submarines attacked Japanese shipping and naval vessels, inflicting heavy losses on the merchant fleet and Imperial Navy. Admiral Fife retired from active duty in 1955. Contact your library's interlibrary loan department for the availability of Admiral Fife's *Reminiscences*.

Bibliography

Fife, James. *The Reminiscences of James Fife*. Glen Rock, NJ: Microfilming Corp. of America, 1972.

Vice Admiral Frank Fletcher
United States Navy
1885-1973

Fletcher was at sea when the Japanese Imperial Navy attacked the US Naval base at Pearl Harbor, Hawaii. He commanded the carrier *Yorktown* during the Pacific war's two most crucial sea battles: Coral Sea and Midway. During the Coral Sea battle in May 1942, US naval planes sunk one carrier and inflicted enough damage on other ships to force the Japanese to postpone their planned invasion of Port Moseby, New Guinea. The battle was considered a tactical draw because both sides lost a carrier (the US Navy lost the *Lexington* and the *Yorktown* was damaged), but a strategic victory for the Americans because the Japanese tide of expansion was halted, at least temporarily. Coral Sea was the first engagement at sea during which opposing ships did not come into contact with each other. Fletcher was in overall command of the two American task forces that laid in wait for the Japanese fleet during the Battle of Midway in June 1942. However, early in the battle, the *Yorktown* was hit by bombs and disabled. Command of the operation shifted to Admiral Raymond Spruance. Planes from his carriers *Enterprise* and *Hornet* attacked and sank four Japanese carriers. During the aftermath of the battle, the *Yorktown* was sunk by a Japanese submarine as it was being towed back to Pearl Harbor. Fletcher was in command of a task force during the Guadalcanal campaign of 1942-43 until he was wounded in action on board the carrier *Saratoga*. After recovering, he was given command of north Pacific naval forces for the remainder of the war. Stephen Regan's *The Bitter Tempest* is recommended for reading.

Bibliography

Regan, Stephen D. *The Bitter Tempest: The Biography of Admiral Frank Jack Fletcher*. Ames: Iowa State University Press, 1994.

Lieutenant General James Maurice Gavin
United States Army
1907-1990

Gavin saw action as a paratrooper during the Second World War. He commanded the 505th Parachute Infantry Regiment during the conquest of Sicily in July-August 1943. In September 1943, he was promoted to temporary brigadier general and fought at Salerno, Italy. In June 1944, during the first weeks of Operation Overlord, the invasion of France, he and his paratroopers fought behind enemy lines without relief. In August 1944, he was given command of the 82nd Airborne Division and participated in Operation Market Garden, an airborne operation designed to seize a number of bridges leading to the Rhine River at Arnhem, Holland. The mission was only partially successful. In October 1944, he was promoted to major general. His 82nd Airborne played an important role during the Battle of the Bulge in December 1944-January 1945, helping seal off the northern sector of the bulge. In February 1945, the 82nd crossed the Seigfried Line and moved into northern Germany, reaching the Elbe River in late April 1945. General Gavin remained in the US Army until 1958, holding numerous chief of staff positions in Europe and at the Pentagon. Recommended for reading are General Gavin's autobiography, *On to Berlin*, Bradley Biggs' *Gavin*, and T. Michael Booth's and Duncan Spencer's *Paratrooper*.

Bibliography

Biggs, Bradley. *Gavin*. Hamden, CT: Archon Books, 1980.
Booth, T. Michael and Duncan Spencer. *Paratrooper: The Life of General James M. Gavin*. New York: Simon & Schuster, 1994.
Gavin, James M. *Airborne Warfare*. Washington: Infantry Journal Press, 1947.
_____. *On to Berlin: Battles of an Airborne Commander, 1943-1946*. New York: Viking Press, 1978.

Major General Roy Stanley Geiger
United States Marine Corps
1885-1947

Geiger saw combat action on Guadalcanal in 1942 before being recalled to the United States to become Director of Marine Aviation. However, Geiger felt he was best suited for combat command and in November 1943, was given command of the 1st Marine Amphibious Corps. His Marines landed on Bougainville of the Solomon Islands in November 1943. Fighting was very heavy, but gradually the Marines secured the upper hand by April 1944, controlling large portions of the island along with US Army troops. In July 1944, Geiger commanded the III Marine Amphibious Corps, formerly the I Marine Amphibious Corps, which assaulted Guam of the Marianas. The US Army's 77th Infantry Division was also involved in the heavy fighting. Nearly all the Japanese defenders were killed during the campaign to secure the island. Geiger commanded the III Marine Amphibious Corps during the last large amphibious assault in the Pacific theatre, the invasion of Okinawa. Overall commander for the operation was US Army Lieutenant General Simon Buckner, US Tenth Army, who was killed during the fighting. The invasion began on 1 April 1945 and most Japanese resistance ceased by the end of June. Marine and Army units suffered nearly 40 000 casualties, including over 7 600 killed. The US Navy was also hard hit, primarily by kamikaze planes, incurring over 10 000 casualties with many ships damaged or sunk. The Japanese, though defeated, did not die to the last man as they usually did during earlier island battles. Nearly 7 000 surrendered, but over 125 000 were killed. The only biography located on the career of General Geiger was written by Roger Willock which was privately published in 1968. It was reprinted in 1983 by the Marine Corps Association located at Quantico, Virginia. It should be available through interlibrary loan.

Bibliography

Willock, Roger. *Unaccustomed to Fear: A Biography of the Late General Roy S. Geiger, U.S.M.C.* Princeton, NJ: n.p., 1968.

Major General Leslie Richard Groves
United States Army
1896-1970

Groves was a military engineer before the start of the Second World War. When the government gave the military permission to begin working on the atomic bomb, Groves was placed in charge of the operation, code named the Manhattan Project. Groves did not have any formal education in nuclear physics and left that portion of the project to the scientists. He dealt mainly with security, administrative management, and any additional problems that arose from such a massive scientific project. He also chose the site of Los Alamos, New Mexico where much of the research and testing was conducted. Groves strongly believed that the atomic bomb was a weapon that should be developed and used against the enemy to shorten the war and save American lives. Recommended for reading are General Groves' *Now It Can Be Told* and William Lawren's *The General and the Bomb*.

Bibliography

Groves, Leslie R. *Now It Can Be Told: The Story of the Manhattan Project*. New York: Harper, 1962.

Lawren, William. *The General and the Bomb: General Leslie R. Groves, Director of the Manhattan Project*. New York: Dodd, Mead, 1988.

Admiral John Lesslie Hall, Jr.
United States Navy
1891-1978

Hall excelled at amphibious landings in the Mediterranean, Northwest Europe, and Pacific Theatres of Operations. He was in command of Dime Force which landed the 1st Infantry Division at Gela, Sicily on 10 July 1943. Naval gunfire from his ships played a crucial role in stopping an enemy tank attack against forward units of the 1st Division. His next assignment was as Southern Attack Force commander during the Salerno, Italy landings in September 1943. Enemy resistance was heavier than during the Sicilian landings and naval gunfire helped suppress the defenders, allowing the VI Corps to get ashore and establish a beachhead. Admiral Hall had even more responsibility during Operation Overlord, the invasion of Normandy, France. His naval units landed the V Corps on Omaha beach despite heavy resistance. Hall was also in charge of all off-shore bombardment both before and during the invasion. When units of the V Corps were trapped behind the seawall, naval gunfire supported the troops and aided them as they finally breached the shore defences.   Hall later transferred to the Pacific Theatre of Operations, landing the XXIV Corps on Okinawa in April 1945. Susan Godson's *Viking of Assault* is recommended for reading.

Bibliography

Godson, Susan Hall. *The Development of Amphibious Warfare in World War II: As Reflected in the Campaigns of Admiral John Lesslie Hall, Jr., USN*. Washington, DC: American University, 1979. (Not available for interlibrary loan)
______. *Viking of Assault: Admiral John Lesslie Hall, Jr., and Amphibious Warfare*. Washington, DC: University Press of America, 1982.
Hall, John Lesslie, Jr. *Oral History of Admiral John L. Hall, USN (Ret.)*. Interviewed by John T. Mason. New York: Columbia University Oral History Research Office, 1963.

Fleet Admiral William Frederick Halsey, Jr.
United States Navy
1882-1959

"Bull" Halsey was in command of United States Navy carrier operations in the Pacific Ocean when the war began on 7 December 1941. He and his carriers were at sea when Japanese aircraft attacked Pearl Harbor, Hawaii. He also missed the greatest carrier battle of the war at Midway due to a skin disease which developed a painful rash all over his body. He was in command of naval operations off the island of Guadalcanal as American military forces stopped Japanese expansion and put the enemy on the defensive. In October 1944, while commanding the Third Fleet, his ships engaged the Japanese Imperial Navy in the largest naval action in maritime history, the Battle of Leyte Gulf. At the conclusion, the Japanese navy was finished as a credible fighting force and the few remaining ships fled back to Japan. In 1945, Halsey commanded all naval operations off Okinawa as Marines and US Army troops invaded and captured the island. In December 1945, he was promoted to the rank of fleet admiral, a rank held by only a few men in the history of the United States Navy. Halsey was aggressive, possibly overly aggressive at times, but he felt the way to win was to engage the enemy and destroy him with superior firepower. He was the navy's best carrier admiral, knowing full well the potential aviation held in the Pacific war. Recommended for reading are Admiral Halsey's memoir, *Admiral Halsey's Story*, James Merrill's *A Sailor's Admiral*, and E. B. Potter's *Bull Halsey*.

Bibliography

Blassingame, Wyatt. *William F. Halsey, Five Star Admiral*. Champaign, IL: Garrard Pub. Co., 1970. (juvenile)

Frank, Benis. *Halsey*. New York: Ballantine Books, 1974.

Halsey, William Frederick and J. Bryan Halsey III. *Admiral Halsey's Story*. New York: Whittlesey House, 1947.

Jordan, Ralph B. *Born to Fight: The Life of Admiral Halsey*. Philadelphia: David McKay Company, 1946.

Keating, Lawrence A. *Fleet Admiral: The Story of William F. Halsey*. Philadelphia: Westminster Press, 1965.

Library of Congress Manuscript Division. *William Frederick Halsey, Jr., Ernest Joseph King, Herbert Bain Knowles: A Register of Their Papers in the Library of Congress*. Washington: Library of Congress Manuscript Division, 1983.

Merrill, James M. *A Sailor's Admiral: A Biography of William F. Halsey*. New York: Crowell, 1976.

_____. *Target Tokyo: The Halsey-Doolittle Raid*. Chicago: Rand-McNally, 1964.

Montman, James H. *The Military Strategies of Spruance and Halsey*. Maxwell Air Force Base, AL: Air Command and Staff College, Air University, 1984.

Pearl, Jack. *Admiral "Bull" Halsey*. Derby, CT: Monarch Books, 1962.

Potter, E. B. (Elmer Belmont). *Bull Halsey*. Annapolis, MD: Naval Institute Press, 1985.

Whipple, Chandler. *William F. Halsey: Fighting Admiral*. New York: Putnam, 1968. (juvenile)

Major General Ernest Nason Harmon
United States Army
1894-1979

Harmon saw action as a tank commander during the Second World War. In November 1942, his 2nd Armoured Division landed on North African soil in Morocco and fought during the Tunisian campaign. In April 1943, he was given command of the 1st Armoured Division. In September, his division landed at Salerno, Italy. The 1st Armoured reached the Anzio beachhead in January 1944 and led the breakout in May. By June, forward units were beyond Rome. Harmon returned to the United States in July to take command of the XIII Corps, but by October 1944, he was in Belgium, again commanding the 2nd Armoured Division. His tanks cracked the Seigfried Line in October and in January 1945, helped repel the German assault in the Ardennes. In February, he was given command of the XXII Corps which he retained until January 1946 when he assumed command of the VI Corps, a military police unit responsible for the entire US zone of occupation. General Harmon's autobiography, *Combat Commander*, is recommended for reading.

Bibliography

Harmon, Ernest N. with Milton MacKaye and William Ross MacKaye. *Combat Commander: Autobiography of A Soldier*. Englewood Cliffs, NJ: Prentice-Hall, 1970.

Admiral Thomas Charles Hart
United States Navy
1877-1971

Hart was in command of the US Navy's Asiatic Fleet when the Pacific war began. The Asiatic Fleet was very small in size and did not oppose the Japanese landings in the Philippines. In late December 1941, Hart evacuated his headquarters in Manila Bay and moved to Java. In February 1942, just prior to the start of the Battle of the Java Sea, Hart was replaced by Dutch Admiral C. E. L. Helfrich as commander of the multi-national naval force. During the battle, most of the Allied ships were sunk as they tried to stop the Japanese invasion of the Dutch East Indies. Hart returned to the United States and served on the Navy's

General Board until his retirement in February 1945. James Leutze's *A Different Kind of Victory* is recommended for reading.

Bibliography

Hart, Thomas Charles. *Narrative of Events, Asiatic Fleet Leading Up to War and 8 December 1941 to 15 February 1942*. Washington, DC: n.p., 1946.

______. *The Reminiscences of Thomas C. Hart*. Glen Rock, NJ: Microfilming Corp of America, 1972. (microfiche)

Leutze, James. *A Different Kind of Victory: A Biography of Admiral Thomas C. Hart*. Annapolis: Naval Institute Press, 1981.

Admiral Henry Kent Hewitt
United States Navy
1887-1972

Hewitt spent his war years in the North African and Mediterranean Theatres of Operations. He was one of the US Navy's most experienced amphibious landing experts. He was in command of naval units that landed US Army troops during Operation Torch, the invasion of North Africa, Operation Husky, the invasion of Sicily, Operation Avalanche, the assault at Salerno, Italy, and Operation Anvil-Dragoon, the invasion of southern France. Contact your library's interlibrary loan department for the availability of the sources listed in the following bibliography.

Bibliography

Clagett, John. *Admiral H. Kent Hewitt: United States Navy*. Newport, RI: Naval War College, 1975.

Hewitt, H. Kent. "Executing Operation Anvil-Dragoon." *United States Naval Institute Proceedings* 78 (August 1954): 897-911.

______. *The Reminiscences of Admiral H. Kent Hewitt*. Glen Rock, NJ: Microfilming Corporation of America, 1972. (microfiche)

Vice Admiral Harry Wilbur Hill
United States Navy
1890-1971

Hill commanded Battleship Division 4 which provided naval gunnery support during the Guadalcanal campaign in 1942. In 1943 and 1944, he commanded Amphibious Group 2 during the invasions of Tarawa, Eniwetok, and Tinian. He was deputy commander of the Iwo Jima Task Force and was commander of 5th Amphibious Force during the Okinawa campaign. Contact your library's interlibrary loan department for the availability of Admiral Hill's *Reminiscences*.

Bibliography

Hill, Harry Wilbur. *The Reminiscences of Harry W. Hill, USN*. Glen Rock, NJ: Microfilming Corp. of America, 1975.

Vice Admiral John Howard Hoover
United States Navy
1887-1970

Hoover commanded the Caribbean Sea Frontier at the beginning of the war. He later transferred to the Pacific and commanded land-based air operations during the Gilberts, Marshalls, and Marianas campaigns. His duties expanded in 1944 to include the Forward Areas of the Pacific. His units supported US invasion forces that landed in the Philippines and conducted bombing operations against the Japanese main islands. Contact your library's interlibrary loan department for the availability of Admiral Hoover's *Reminiscences*.

Bibliography

Hoover, John Howard. *The Reminiscences of Admiral John H. Hoover*. Glen Rock, NJ: Microfilming Corp. of America, 1972.

Admiral Royal Eason Ingersoll
United States Navy
1883-1976

Ingersoll held both ship commands and staff positions before the Second World War. In 1940, he was named assistant to Admiral Harold Stark, the Chief of Naval Operations. In January 1942, he was promoted to vice admiral and given command of the Atlantic Fleet. His principle responsibilities included convoy protection, enemy submarine detection, and protection of the eastern seaboard of the United States. In November 1944, he was given command of the Western Sea Frontier. Along with this position, he was made Deputy Chief of Naval Operations and deputy commander of the US Fleet. He held these positions until his retirement in 1946. J. M. Worthington's *Biography of Admiral Ingersoll* is recommended for reading.

Bibliography

Ingersoll, Royal E. *The Reminiscences of Admiral Royal E. Ingersoll*. New York: Columbia University Oral History Research Office, 1965.

Worthington, J. M. *Biography of Admiral Ingersoll*. 2 volumes. Annapolis, MD: Naval War College, United States Naval Academy, 1988.

General George Churchill Kenney
United States Army Air Force
1889-1977

Kenney was General Douglas MacArthur's air commander from 1942 to 1945. He commanded Allied Air Forces, Southwest Pacific Areas for the duration of the war. In addition, he commanded the Fifth Air Force until June 1944. At that time, he was named commander of the Far East Air Forces which included the Fifth, Seventh, and Thirteenth Air Forces. His units provided strategic and tactical air support for MacArthur's ground troops during the New Guinea, the Solomons, the Bismarcks, the Admiralities, the Moluccas, and the Philippines campaigns. General Kenney's autobiography, *General Kenney Reports*, is recommended for reading.

Bibliography

Caine, Steven A. *Needed, Decisive Airpower Leaders: General George C. Kenney, A Role Model*. Carlisle Barracks, PA: U.S. Army War College, 1991.

Kenney, George C. *General Kenney Reports: A Personal History of the Pacific War*. New York: Duell, Sloan & Pearce, 1949.

______. *The MacArthur I Know*. New York: Duell, Sloan & Pearce, 1951.

Admiral Husband Edward Kimmel
United States Navy
1882-1968

Kimmel was in command of the US Pacific Fleet stationed at Pearl Harbor, Hawaii when it was attacked by Japanese Navy carrier aircraft on 7 December 1941. He was removed from command on 17 December 1941 and was censured by the Roberts Commission which investigated the attack. After the war, a congressional inquiry absolved Kimmel of earlier charges. Kimmel is one of the more controversial figures of the Second World War. Some historians see him as a scapegoat for the Roosevelt administration, having been left in the dark concerning the deterioration of diplomatic relations with the Japanese government. Others perceived Kimmel as being too lax in his command and felt he should have been better prepared as a matter of course. Recommended for reading are Admiral Kimmel's *Admiral Kimmel's Story* and David Brownlow's *The Accused*.

Bibliography

Brownlow, Donald Grey. *The Accused: The Ordeal of Rear Admiral Husband Kimmel, U.S.N.* New York: Vantage Press, 1968.

Kimmel, Husband Edward. *Admiral Kimmel's Story*. Chicago: H. Regnery, 1955.

United States. Navy Department. Pearl Harbor Court of Inquiry. *Finding of Facts*. Washington: n.p., 1945.

Fleet Admiral Ernest Joseph King
United States Navy
1878-1956

King was Commander-in-Chief of the Fleet when carrier planes of the Japanese Imperial Navy attacked Pearl Harbor, Hawaii on 7 December 1941. In March 1942, he was named Chief of Naval Operations. He held both posts for the duration of the war. He was also a member of the Joint Chiefs of Staff. Being the highest ranking naval officer, his power and influence was immense. All during the war, he was the leading advocate of a Japan-first strategy rather than a Germany-first strategy as was held by President Franklin D. Roosevelt, other members of the Joint Chiefs of Staff, and the British high command. Though the British did not agree with King's Japan-first strategy, they, as well as others, recognized his considerable ability as a strategist and the way he handled the problem of logistics in fighting a two-ocean war. Recommended for reading are Thomas Buell's *Master of Sea Power* and Admiral King's memoir, *Fleet Admiral King*.

Bibliography

Barnes, Gary I. *Great Warriors of World War II, Admiral Ernest King, Admiral Chester W. Nimitz*. Maxwell Air Force Base, AL: Air Command and Staff College, Air University, 1984.

Buell, Thomas B. *Master of Sea Power: A Biography of Fleet Admiral Ernest J. King*. Boston: Little, Brown, 1980.

Graybar, Lloyd. "Admiral King's Toughest Battle." *Naval War College Review* 32 (February 1979): 38-45.

King, Ernest J. and Walter Muir Whitehill. *Fleet Admiral King: A Naval Record*. New York: Norton, 1952.

______. *The Official Papers of Fleet Admiral Ernest J. King*. Wilmington, DE: Scholarly Resources Inc., 1991. (microfiche)

______. *Our Navy at War. A Report to the Secretary of the Navy, Covering Our Peacetime Navy and Our Wartime Navy and Including Combat Operations up to March 1, 1944*. Washington: United States News, 1944.

______. *U.S. Navy at War, 1941-1945. Official Reports to the Secretary of the Navy*. Washington: United States Navy Department, 1946.

______. *United States Navy at War. Final Official Report to the Secretary of the Navy, Covering the Period March 1, 1945, to October 1, 1945*. Washington: The United States News, 1945.

_____. *United States Navy at War. Second Official Report to the Secretary of the Navy, Covering Combat Operations March 1, 1944 to March 1, 1945*. Washington: The United States News, 1945.

_____. *The War Reports of General of the Army George C. Marshall, Chief of Staff, General of the Army H. H. Arnold, Commanding General, Army Air Forces and Fleet Admiral Ernest J. King, Commander-in-Chief, United States Fleet and Chief of Naval Operations*. Philadelphia: Lippincott, 1947.

Library of Congress. Manuscript Division. *William Frederick Halsey, Jr., Ernest Joseph King, Herbert Bain Knowles: A Register of Their Papers in the Library of Congress*. Washington: Library of Congress, Manuscript Division, 1983.

Reynolds, Clark. "Admiral Ernest J. King and the Strategy for Victory in the Pacific." *Naval War College Review* (Winter 1976): 57-67.

Admiral Thomas Cassin Kinkaid
United States Navy
1888-1972

Kinkaid was in command of Task Force 16 during the Battle of Santa Cruz Island on 16 October 1942. One of his carriers, the *Hornet*, was sunk, but his planes inflicted serious casualties on the opposing Japanese planes and pilots. After the battle, he was given command of Task Force 67. He trained the cruiser squadron in night fighting tactics to interdict and destroy Japanese ships (the Tokyo Express) that were bringing supplies to Japanese troops stationed in the Solomons. Kinkaid was commander of the Seventh Fleet during the invasion of the Philippines in October 1944. Shortly after the landings, a portion of Kinkaid's naval units, the escort carrier group of Rear Admiral Thomas Sprague, came under heavy attack during the Battle of Leyte Gulf. The carriers and destroyer escorts put up a tremendous defence in the face of nearly overwhelming odds. Their tactics resulted in the loss of only one carrier and three destroyers. Gerald Wheeler's *Kinkaid of the Seventh Fleet* is recommended for reading.

Bibliography

Kinkaid, Thomas Cassin. *Reminiscences of Thomas Cassin Kinkaid.* New York: Columbia University, 1961.

Wheeler, Gerald F. *Kinkaid of the Seventh Fleet: A Biography of Admiral Thomas C. Kinkaid, U.S. Navy.* Washington: Naval Historical Center, Department of the Navy, 1994.

Admiral Alan Goodrich Kirk
United States Navy
1888-1963

Kirk commanded amphibious landing task forces during the war. In July 1943, he was in command of Cent Force during Operation Husky, the invasion of Sicily. His naval units landed the 45th Infantry Division at Scoglitti despite rough coastal conditions. Kirk was commander of the Western Naval Task Force during Operation Overlord, the invasion of Normandy, France. On 6 June 1944, his naval units landed US Army troops on Utah and Omaha beaches in the face of determined resistance, especially on Omaha beach. Kirk continued to supervise resupply missions as the infantry units moved inland. Contact your library's interlibrary loan department for the availability of Admiral Kirk's *Reminiscences*.

Bibliography

Kirk, Alan Goodrich. *The Reminiscences of Alan Goodrich Kirk.* Glen Rock, NJ: Microfilming Corp. of America, 1972.

General Walter Krueger
United States Army
1881-1967

Krueger was one of General Douglas MacArthur's best ground commanders in the Pacific Theatre of Operations. He commanded the US Sixth Army from 1943 to the conclusion of the war. He fought campaigns in New Guinea, New Britain, the Admiralities, and the

Moluccas islands. Sixth Army units landed on Leyte, a southern island of the Philippines, in October 1944. The island was secured by December. The Sixth Army was then given the task of liberating the island of Luzon and Manila, the capital of the Philippines, in January 1945. The fighting was fierce. Japanese troops and naval units fighting as infantry added to the carnage by deliberately massacring thousands of innocent civilians. Most organized Japanese resistance ended by March 1945 and Krueger spent the remainder of the war commanding his troops in mopping up operations around Luzon. General Krueger's autobiography, *From Down Under to Nippon*, is recommended for reading.

Bibliography

Krueger, Walter. *From Down Under to Nippon: The Story of the Sixth Army in World War II*. Washington, DC: Combat Forces Press, 1953.

______. *The Walter Krueger Papers*. n.p., n.d.

U.S. Sixth Army. *The Sixth Army in Action, A Photo History, January 1943 - June 1945*. Kyoto, Japan, 1945. Published by the 8th Information and Historical Service, United States Sixth Army, December 1945.

Fleet Admiral William Daniel Leahy
United States Navy
1875-1959

Leahy was President Franklin D. Roosevelt's personal military advisor and chief of staff during the Second World War. In this capacity, he presided over the meetings of the Joint Chiefs of Staff. He had daily conferences with the president and presented Roosevelt's position on military matters to the Joint Chiefs. Because of the personal friendship he developed with Roosevelt, he was privy to the president's thoughts and ideas. This knowledge proved to be invaluable after Roosevelt died in April 1945. Leahy was able to brief President Harry Truman on all ongoing operations in great detail and offered excellent counsel during the last months of the war. Admiral Leahy's autobiography, *I Was There*, provides excellent insight on the day-to-day activities of the White House during the Second World War. Henry Adams' *Witness to Power* is also recommended.

Bibliography

Adams, Henry H. *Witness to Power: The Life of Fleet Admiral William D. Leahy*. Annapolis, MD: Naval Institute Press, 1985.

Holmes, James Houghton. *"Admiral Leahy in Vichy France."* Ph.D. diss., George Washington University, 1974. (DAI, 35:4, 2175A, UMI Order # 7422256)

Leahy, William D. *I Was There*. New York: Whittlesey House, 1950.

______. *William D. Leahy Diaries*. n.p., n.d. (microfilm)

McClain, Linda. *"The Role of Admiral W. D. Leahy in U.S. Foreign Policy."* Ph.D. diss., University of Virginia, 1986. (DAI, 46:7, 2065A, UMI Order # 8515520)

Reed, Donald A. *Admiral Leahy at Vichy*. Chicago: Adams Press, 1968.

General Curtis Emerson LeMay
United States Army Air Force
1906-1990

LeMay was one of America's most controversial and outstanding commanders. He was one of the leading architects of air bombing operations against Germany and Japan during the Second World War. He later became the United States Air Force Chief of Staff before retiring in 1965. His personal bravery is unquestioned, having led many bombing attacks against Germany. One of the controversies surrounding LeMay was the strategy he devised against Japan while commanding the XXI Bomber Command. Because Japanese industry consisted largely of cottage-type operations located in or near residential areas, LeMay believed that the best way to halt production was by using incendiary devices dropped from low altitudes by B-29 bombers. His plan was approved and instituted. In one raid in March 1945, over 16 square miles of Tokyo were destroyed as huge fires consumed homes made mostly of wood. Estimates were that over 150 000 civilians died in this single raid. LeMay never attempted to defend his actions to his critics. He believed that his top priority was to defeat the enemy by using all means available to him. Recommended for reading are Thomas Coffey's *Iron Eagle* and General LeMay's autobiography, *Mission with LeMay*.

Bibliography

Coffey, Thomas M. *Iron Eagle: The Turbulent Life of General Curtis LeMay*. New York: Crown Publishers, 1986.

Kohn, Richard H. and Joseph Harahan, eds. *Strategic Air Warfare: An Interview with Generals Curtis E. LeMay, Leon W. Johnson, David Burchinal and Jack L. Catton. Washington, DC: Office of Air Force History, U.S. Air Force, 1988.*

LeMay, Curtis E. and Bill Yenne. *Superfortress: The Story of the B-29 and American Air Power*. New York: McGraw-Hill, 1988.

_____ with MacKinley Kantor. *Mission with LeMay: My Story*. Garden City, NY: Doubleday, 1965.

General of the Army Douglas MacArthur
United States Army
1880-1964

MacArthur was one of three Allied Supreme Commanders during the Second World War. The others were General Dwight Eisenhower and Admiral Lord Louis Mountbatten. MacArthur was in command of all Far Eastern land forces when the war began. His American and Filipino troops fought a valiant campaign before being defeated in May 1942. Before the fall of the Philippines, MacArthur was ordered by President Franklin D. Roosevelt to go to Australia. During the next three years, MacArthur perfected the strategy of "island hopping". Only selected islands were assaulted and then used as staging areas and air bases as the Allies moved closer to Japan. New Guinea was captured in 1943 and MacArthur made good his promise to return to the Philippines when his troops invaded in October 1944. In September 1945, as Supreme Commander, he conducted the Japanese surrender ceremonies aboard the USS battleship *Missouri*. Being one of America's most well-known, respected, and at the same time, controversial generals, MacArthur has had many biographers. D. Clayton James has written the definitive biography of MacArthur's career. The three-volume set is entitled *The Years of MacArthur*. Other recommendations are Clay Blair, Jr.'s *MacArthur*, Frazier Hunt's *The Untold Story of Douglas MacArthur*, Gavin Long's *MacArthur as Military Commander*, William Manchester's *American Caesar*, and Michael Schaller's *Douglas MacArthur*. Also recommended are MacArthur's memoir, *Reminiscences*, and *A Soldier Speaks*, a four-volume set of his papers and speeches.

Bibliography

Altman, Frances. *General Douglas MacArthur, Military Genius*. Minneapolis, MN: Denison, 1973. (juvenile)

Archer, Jules. *Front-line General: Douglas MacArthur*. New York: Messner, 1963. (juvenile)

Army Times eds. *The Banners and the Glory: The Story of General Douglas MacArthur*. New York: Putnam, 1965.

Beck, John Jacob. *MacArthur and Wainwright: Sacrifice of the Philippines*. Albuquerque: University of New Mexico Press, 1974.

Bein, Peter J. *General MacArthur and the Yamashita Decision, September 1944-February 1946*. Carlisle Barracks, PA: U.S. Army War College, 1989.

Blair, Clay, Jr. *MacArthur*. Garden City, NY: Doubleday, 1977.

Breuer, William B. *MacArthur's Undercover War*. New York: J. Wiley & Sons, 1995.

Burns, Martin. *MacArthur, the Real Story*. New York: Universal Pub. & Distributive Corp., 1951.

Choate, Joseph. *Douglas MacArthur As I Knew Him*. Los Angeles: J. Choate, 1986.

Cochran, Alexander S. *MacArthur, ULTRA, and the Pacific War, 1942-1944*. n.p., 1983.

Considine, Bob. *General Douglas MacArthur*. Greenwich, CT: Fawcett, 1964.

_____. *MacArthur the Magnificent*. Philadelphia: David McKay Co., 1942.

Costello, John. *Days of Infamy: MacArthur, Roosevelt, Churchill: The Shocking Truth Revealed*. New York: Pocket Books, 1994.

Darby, Jean. *Douglas MacArthur*. Minneapolis, MN: Lerner Publications, 1989. (juvenile)

Devaney, John. *Douglas MacArthur: Something of a Hero*. New York: Putnam, 1979. (juvenile)

Drea, Edward J. *MacArthur's ULTRA: Codebreaking and the War Against Japan, 1942-1945*. Lawrence: University Press of Kansas, 1991.

Egeberg, Roger Olaf. *The General, MacArthur, and the Man He Called "Doc"*. New York: Hippocrene Books, 1983.

Eyre, James Kline. *The Roosevelt-MacArthur Conflict*. 2d ed. Chambersburg, PA: Printed for AMG Publications by the Craft Press, 1965.

Finklestein, Norman. *The Emperor General: A Biography of Douglas MacArthur*. Minneapolis, MN: Dillon Press, 1989. (juvenile)

Finn, Richard B. *Winners in Peace: MacArthur, Yoshida, and Postwar Japan*. Berkeley: University of California Press, 1991.

Fredricks, Edgar J. *MacArthur: His Mission and Meaning*. Philadelphia: Whitmore Pub. Co., 1968.

Ganoe, William Addleman. *MacArthur Closeup: Much Then and Some Now*. New York: Vantage, 1962.

Gunther, John. *The Riddle of MacArthur: Japan, Korea, and the Far East*. New York: Harper, 1951.

Hastings, Howard Livingston. *General Douglas MacArthur in Picture and Story*. New York: Hampton Publishing Co., 1942.

Hersey, John. *Men on Bataan*. New York: A. A. Knopf, 1953.

Hoyt, Edwin P. *MacArthur's Navy: The Seventh Fleet and the Battle for the Philippines*. New York: Jove Books, 1991.

_____. *MacArthur's Return*. New York: Avon Books, 1992.

Huff, Sidney L. with Joe Alex Morris. *My Fifteen Years with General MacArthur*. New York: Paperback Library, 1964.

Hunt, Frazier. *MacArthur and the War Against Japan*. New York: Charles Scribner's Sons, 1944.

_____. *The Untold Story of Douglas MacArthur*. New York: Devin-Adair Co., 1954.

James, D. Clayton. *The Years of MacArthur. Volume I: 1880-1941*. Boston: Houghton Mifflin, 1970.

_____. *The Years of MacArthur. Volume II: 1941-1945*. Boston: Houghton Mifflin, 1975.

_____. *The Years of MacArthur. Volume III: 1945-1964*. Boston: Houghton Mifflin, 1985.

Julian, Allen Phelps. *MacArthur: The Life of a General*. Des Moines, IA: Meredith Press, 1963. (juvenile)

Kelley, Frank and Cornelius Ryan. *MacArthur: Man of Action*. Garden City, NY: Doubleday, 1950.

Kelley, William A. *MacArthur: Hero of Destiny*. Greenwich, CT: Fawcett Publications, 1942.

Kenney, George C. *The MacArthur I Know*. New York: Duell, Sloan & Pearce, 1951.

Lee, Clark and Richard Henschel. *Douglas MacArthur*. New York: Holt, 1952.

Long, Gavin. *MacArthur as a Military Commander*. Princeton, NJ: Van Nostrand, 1969.

Long, Laura. *Douglas MacArthur, Young Protector*. Indianapolis: Bobbs-Merrill, 1965. (juvenile)

Luszki, Walter A. *A Rape of Justice: MacArthur and the New Guinea Hangings*. Lanham, MD: Madison Books, 1991.

MacArthur, Douglas. *A Collection of Speeches, Messages, Press Releases and Other Public Statements Dating from VJ Day to October 14, 1947*. n.p., 1947.

______. *Courage was the Rule: General Douglas MacArthur's Own Story*. New York: Whittlesley-McGraw, 1965.

______. *Duty, Honor, Country: A Pictorial Autobiography*. New York: McGraw-Hill, 1965.

______. *Duty, Honor, Country: Two Memorable Addresses*. New York: Rolton House Publishers, 1962.

______. *History of Intelligence Activities Under General Douglas MacArthur, 1942-1950. The Intelligence Series: G2, USAFFE, SWPA, AFPAC, FEC, SCAP*. Wilmington, DE: Scholarly Resources, 1983. (8 microfilm reels)

______. *"I Shall Return."* n.p., n.d.

______. *MacArthur on War: His Military Writings*. Edited by Frank C. Waldrop. New York: Duell, Sloan & Pearce, 1942.

______. *Reminiscences*. New York: McGraw-Hill, 1964.

______. *Reports of General MacArthur*. 2 volumes. Prepared by his general staff. Charles, A. Willoughby, editor-in-chief. Washington, DC: Government Printing Office, 1966.

______. *Revitalizing a Nation: A Statement of Beliefs, Opinions, and Policies Embodied in the Public Pronouncements of General of the Army Douglas MacArthur*. Chicago: Heritage Foundation Inc., 1952.

______. *A Soldier Speaks: Public Papers and Speeches of General of the Army Douglas MacArthur*. 4 volumes. Edited by Vorin E. Whan, Jr. Washington, DC: U.S. Department of the Army, 1966.

Manchester, William. *American Caesar*. New York: Dell, 1978. (juvenile)

______. *American Caesar, Douglas MacArthur, 1880-1964*. Boston: Little, Brown, 1978.

Martin, William B. *An Analysis of the Military Strategy of General Douglas MacArthur*. Maxwell Air Force Base, AL: Air Command and Staff College, 1984.

Mattern, Carolyn Jane. *"The Man on the Dark Horse: The Presidential Campaigns for General Douglas MacArthur, 1944-1948."* Ph.D. diss., The University of Wisconsin-Madison, 1976. (DAI, 37:6, 3856A, UMI Order # 7620677)

Mayer, S. L. (Sydney L.) *The Biography of General of the Army, Douglas MacArthur*. Northbrook, IL: Book Value International, 1981.

______. *Great American Generals of World War 2: MacArthur, Eisenhower, Patton*. New York: Gallery Books, 1984.

______. *MacArthur*. New York: Ballantine Books, 1971.

Miller, Frances Trevelyan. *General Douglas MacArthur, Fighter for Freedom*. Philadelphia: John C. Winston Co., 1942.

______. *General Douglas MacArthur, Soldier-Statesman*. Philadelphia: John C. Winston Co., 1951.

Muggah, Mary Gates and Paul H. Raihle. *The MacArthur Story*. Chippewa Falls, WI: Chippewa Falls Book Agency, 1945.

Newlon, Clarke. *The Fighting Douglas MacArthur*. New York: Dodd, Mead, 1965.

Nicolay, Helen. *MacArthur of Bataan*. New York: D. Appleton-Century Co., 1942.

Palmer, Billy J. *MacArthur in Japan: Viceroy with a Dream*. Maxwell Air Force Base, AL: Air War College, Air University, 1978.

Pearl, Jack. *General Douglas MacArthur*. Derby, CT: Monarch, 1961.

Petillo, Carol Morris. *Douglas MacArthur: The Philippine Years*. Bloomington, IN: Indiana University Press, 1981.

______. *"Douglas MacArthur: The Philippine Years."* Ph.D. diss., Rutgers University, The State University of New Jersey, 1979. (DAI, 40:7, 4197A, UMI Order # 7928436)

Phillips, William S., Jr. *Douglas MacArthur: A Modern Knight-Errant*. Philadelphia: Dorrance, 1978.

Puryear, Edgar F., Jr. *19 Stars: A Study in Military Character and Leadership*. (George Marshall, Dwight Eisenhower, Douglas MacArthur, and George Patton.) Washington, DC: Coiner Publications, 1971.

Rasor, Eugene L., ed. *General Douglas MacArthur, 1880-1964: Historiography and Annotated Bibliography*. Westport, CT: Greenwood Press Inc., 1994.

Rhoades, Weldon E. *Flying MacArthur to Victory*. College Station, TX: Texas A&M University Press, 1987.

Rice, Edward E. *General Douglas MacArthur*. New York: Dell Publishing Company Inc., 1942.

Richards, Norman. *Douglas MacArthur*. Chicago: Children's Press, 1967. (juvenile)

Robb, Stephen. *"Fifty Years of Farewell: Douglas MacArthur's Commemorative and Deliberative Speaking."* Ph.D. diss., Indiana University, 1967. (DAI, 28:9, 3812A, UMI Order # 682348)

Rogers, Paul P. *The Bitter Years: MacArthur and Sutherland*. New York: Praeger, 1991.

______. *The Good Years: MacArthur and Sutherland*. New York: Praeger, 1990.

Schaller, Michael. *Douglas MacArthur: The Far Eastern General*. New York: Oxford University Press, 1989.

Schoor, Gene. *General Douglas MacArthur: A Pictorial Biography*. New York: R. Field, 1951.

Sebald, William J. with Russell Brines. *With MacArthur in Japan: A Personal History of the Occupation*. New York: W. W. Norton, 1965.

Skipper, G. C. *MacArthur and the Philippines*. Chicago: Children's Press, 1982. (juvenile)

Steinberg, Alfred. *Douglas MacArthur*. New York: Putnam, 1961. (juvenile)

Steinberg, Rafael and the Editors of Time-Life Books. *The Return to the Philippines*. Alexandria, VA: Time-Life Books, 1980.

Taylor, Lawrence. *A Trial of Generals: Homma, Yamashita, MacArthur*. South Bend, IN: Icarus, 1981.

Walker, James Allen. *General Douglas MacArthur and the Philippine Army*. Norfolk: Walker, 1975.

Whitney, Courtney. *MacArthur: His Rendezvous with History*. New York: Knopf, 1955.

Willoughby, Charles A. and John Chamberlain. *MacArthur, 1941-1951*. New York: McGraw-Hill, 1954.

Wittner, Lawrence S., comp. *MacArthur*. Englewood Cliffs, NJ: Prentice-Hall, 1971.

General of the Army George Catlett Marshall
United States Army
1880-1959

Marshall was the top-ranking United States Army officer during the Second World War. He was chiefly responsible, along with President Franklin D. Roosevelt, for expanding the US Army and for dividing it into three primary areas (army ground forces, army air forces, and army service forces) for better manageability. He established the Joint Chiefs of Staff and was its first chairman. Though he had hoped to lead the Allied invasion of Europe in 1944, President Roosevelt felt he was too indispensable to leave Washington. General Dwight Eisenhower was selected for the position. Probably more than any other officer, Marshall fostered the unity between the American and British high commands that was necessary to defeat the Axis powers. After the war, he was appointed Secretary of State by President Harry S. Truman and created the Marshall Plan which gave economic aid to the ravaged western European countries during the early years of the Cold War. Given his status, Marshall has had numerous biographers. Forrest Pogue has written the definitive biography of Marshall's career. It consists of four volumes, each entitled *George C. Marshall*. Other works recommended for reading are Ed Cray's *General of the Army George C. Marshall, Soldier and Statesman*, Leonard Mosley's *Marshall*, Robert Payne's *The Marshall Story*, and Mark Stoler's *George C. Marshall*. Also recommended are the *Papers of George Catlett Marshall*. Currently, three volumes have been published, spanning the years 1880 to 1943. Three additional volumes will be published to complete the project.

Bibliography

Cray, Ed. *General of the Army George C. Marshall, Soldier and Statesman*. New York: W. W. Norton, 1990.

Davis, Forrest. *Did Marshall Prolong the Pacific War?* Orange, CT: The Freeman, 1951.

Dooley, Joseph C. *George C. Marshall: A Study in Mentorship*. Carlisle Barracks, PA: U.S. Army War College, 1990.

Faber, Harold. *Soldier and Statesman: General George C. Marshall*. New York: Ariel Books, 1964.

Ferrell, Robert H. *George C. Marshall*. New York: Cooper Square Publishers, 1966.

Frye, William. *Marshall, Citizen Soldier*. Indianapolis, IN: Bobbs-Merrill, 1947.

Gorman, Paul F. *The Secret of Future Victories*. Alexandria, VA: Institute for Defense Analyses, 1993.

Higginbotham, Don. *George Washington and George Marshall: Some Reflections on the American Military Tradition*. Colorado Springs, CO: U.S. Air Force Academy, 1984.

Jacob, John N. *George C. Marshall Papers, 1932-1960: A Guide*. Lexington, VA: George C. Marshall Research Foundation, 1987.

Lubetkin, Wendy. *George Marshall*. New York: Chelsea House, 1989. (juvenile)

Marshall, George C. *Demobilization of the Army*. Washington, DC: U.S. Government Printing Office, 1945.

______. *General Marshall's Report, The Winning of the War in Europe and the Pacific*. Washington, DC. Published for the War Department in cooperation with the Council on Books in Wartime by Simon & Schuster, 1945.

______. *General Marshall's Victory Report*. Corpus Christi, TX: Edward B. Harney Chapter No. 12, Disabled American Veterans, 1947.

_____. *George C. Marshall. Interviews and Reminiscences for Forrest C. Pogue*. Rev. ed. Lexington, VA: George C. Marshall Research Foundation, 1991.

_____. *Memoirs of My Services in the World War, 1917-1918*. Boston: Houghton Mifflin, 1976.

_____. *The Papers of George C. Marshall: Selected World War II Correspondence*. Robert E. Lester, project ed. Bethesda, MD: University Publications of America, 1992. (microform)

_____. *The Papers of George Catlett Marshall. Volume 1: "The Soldierly Spirit," December 1880-June 1939*. Larry I. Bland and Sharon Ritenour, eds. Baltimore: Johns Hopkins Press, 1981.

_____. *The Papers of George Catlett Marshall. Volume 2: "We Cannot Delay," July 1, 1939-December 6, 1941*. Larry I. Bland, ed., and others. Baltimore: Johns Hopkins Press, 1986.

_____. *The Papers of George Catlett Marshall. Volume 3: "The Right Man for the Job," December 7, 1941-May 31, 1943*. Larry I. Bland and Sharon Ritenour Stevens, eds. Baltimore: Johns Hopkins Press, 1991.

_____. *Report on the Army. July 1, 1939 to June 30, 1943. Biennial Report of General George C. Marshall, Chief of Staff of the United States Army to the Secretary of War*. Washington, DC: The Infantry Journal, 1943.

_____. *Selected Papers and Speeches of General of the Army George C. Marshall*. Edited by H. A. DeWeerd. Washington, DC: Infantry Journal, 1945.

_____. *Strengthening the National Defense*. Washington, DC: U.S. Government Printing Office, 1941.

_____. *The United States at War, Official Report by Gen. George C. Marshall, Chief of Staff, U.S. Army*. Washington, DC: The United States News, 1943.

_____. *"Victory is Certain," Being the Biennial Report of the Chief of Staff of the U.S. Army, General George C. Marshall, July 1, 1941, to June 30, 1943, to the Secretary of War*. New York: National Educational Alliance, 1943.

_____. *The War Reports of General of the Army George C. Marshall, Chief of Staff, General of the Army H. H. Arnold, Commanding General, Army Air Forces, and Fleet Admiral Ernest J. King, Commander-in-Chief, United States Fleet and Chief of Naval Operations*. Philadelphia: J. B. Lippincott, 1947.

_____. *The Winning of the War in Europe and the Pacific. The Biennial Reports of the Chief of Staff for the Period July 1943 to June 1945*. Washington, DC: Published by the War Department, 1945.

Marshall, Katherine Tupper. *Together: Annuals of an Army Wife*. Atlanta: Tupper & Love Inc., 1946.

McCarthy, Joseph. *America's Retreat from Victory: The Story of George Catlett Marshall*. New York: Devin-Adair, 1951.

Mosley, Leonard. *Marshall: Hero for Our Times*. New York: Hearst Books, 1982.

Nelson, John T. *General George C. Marshall: Strategic Leadership and the Challenges of Reconstituting the Army, 1939-41*. Carlisle Barracks, PA: Strategic Studies Institute, U.S. Army War College, 1993.

Parrish, Thomas. *Roosevelt and Marshall: Partners in Politics and War*. New York: W. Morrow, 1989.

Payne, Robert. *The Marshall Story: A Biography of General George C. Marshall*. New York: Prentice-Hall, 1951.

Pogue, Forrest C. *George C. Marshall: Education of a General, 1882-1939*. New York: Viking Press, 1963.

______. *George C. Marshall: Global Commander*. Colorado Springs, CO: United States Air Force Academy, 1968.

______. *George C. Marshall: Ordeal and Hope, 1939-1942*. New York: Viking Press, 1966.

______. *George C. Marshall: Organizer of Victory, 1943-1945*. New York: Viking Press, 1973.

______. *George C. Marshall: Statesman, 1945-1959*. New York: Viking Press, 1987.

Puryear, Edgar F., Jr. *19 Stars: A Study in Military Character and Leadership*. (George Marshall, Dwight Eisenhower, Douglas MacArthur, and George Patton.) Washington, DC: Coiner Publications, 1971.

Stoler, Mark A. *George C. Marshall: Soldier-Statesman of the American Century*. Boston: Twayne Publishers, 1989.

Wilson, Rose Page. *General Marshall Remembered: The Recollections of a Forty-Year Friendship with A Great Soldier-Statesman*. Englewood Cliffs, NJ: Prentice-Hall, 1968.

Lieutenant General Lesley J. McNair
United States Army
1883-1944

McNair reached the rank of brigadier general at the age of 36 at the conclusion of the First World War. After the war, he reverted back to major and finally regained his star in 1937. McNair is generally regarded as the man who trained the US Army for its combat role during the Second World War. His training methods consisted of near-combat conditions and were rigorous in their scope and deployment. In 1939, he was commandant of the Command and General Staff School. He achieved the rank of lieutenant general in 1941 and was commander of Army Ground Forces, one of the three components of the US Army created by President Franklin D. Roosevelt and General George Marshall. McNair's duties included activation, training, and evaluation of all US Army combat divisions. General McNair was killed on 25 July 1944 while visiting the front lines during the start of Operation Cobra, the Allied attempt to break out from the Normandy beachhead. He was killed when US bombers dropped their bombs short of the forward German lines and among the staging areas of the US combat divisions. Only two sources were found concerning the career of General McNair.

Bibliography

Gorman, Paul F. *The Secret of Future Victories*. Alexandria, VA: Institute for Defense Analyses, 1993.
Kahn, Ely Jacques. *McNair: Educator of an Army*. Washington, DC: The Infantry Journal, 1945.

Lieutenant General Troy H. Middleton
United States Army
1889-1976

Middleton first saw combat in the First World War during the Meuse-Argonne campaign in September-October 1918. He left the US Army in 1937 to work at Louisiana State University. Recalled to duty in January 1942, he was promoted to major general and given command of the 45th Infantry Division in July 1942. The 45th landed on Sicily on 10 July 1943, and was involved in heavy fighting as the island was cleared of German defenders. In September 1943, the 45th landed at Salerno, Italy and saw constant combat for six weeks before going into reserve. Middleton then returned to the United States for treatment of a recurring knee injury. In March 1944, he was given command of the VIII Corps. The VIII Corps first saw action in France during Operation Cobra in July 1944. This operation signalled the breakout of Allied forces from the Normandy beachhead. Middleton's units captured

Brittany and the city of Brest. The VIII Corps was stationed in the Ardennes in December 1944 when the German Army counterattacked in hope of splitting the Allied armies in two and capturing the port city of Antwerp, Belgium. Initial gains were made, but Middleton reacted very well to the crisis. He recommended that the 101st Airborne Division be sent to Bastogne. This manoeuvre greatly upset the German high command's timetable and gave other Allied divisions time to close off the flanks and begin counterattacks to eliminate the bulge.   General Middleton was one of the US Army's best ground commanders during the Second World War. Frank Price's *Troy H. Middleton* is recommended for reading.

Bibliography

Middleton, Troy H. *An Oral History with Troy H. Middleton.* Interviewed by Dr. Orley B. Caudill. Baton Rouge, LA, April 16, 1973.

Price, Frank James. *Troy H. Middleton: A Biography*. Baton Rouge, LA: Louisiana State University Press, 1974.

Admiral Marc Andrew Mitscher
United States Navy
1887-1947

Mitscher was the US Navy's leading aviation expert during the Second World War and saw nearly continuous action from April 1942 to the end of the war. He was in command of the USS carrier *Hornet* from which Lieutenant Colonel (later Lieutenant General) Jimmy Doolittle's B-25 bombers took off to raid Tokyo. After April 1943, he was in command of all naval air operations in the Guadalcanal area and in January 1944, was given command of Task Force 58, a fast carrier group. During the next ten months, his task force ranged over the Pacific, amassing an amazing record of almost 800 ships sunk and shooting down over 4 400 enemy planes. The task force provided air cover during amphibious and land operations in the Marshalls, Hollandia, the Marianas, the Philippines, Iwo Jima, and Okinawa. During the Marianas campaign, Mitscher's carrier group took part in the Battle of the Philippine Sea. The engagement resulted in the destruction of three Japanese carriers and the loss of over 450 Japanese air crews. The Japanese Navy's carrier force was effectively broken during the battle, which was dubbed the "Great Marianas Turkey Shoot" by American naval pilots. Theodore Taylor's *The Magnificent Mitscher* is recommended for reading.

Bibliography

Taylor, Theodore. *The Magnificent Mitscher*. New York: Norton, 1954.

Fleet Admiral Chester William Nimitz
United States Navy
1885-1966

Nimitz replaced Admiral Husband Kimmel as Commander-in-Chief of the Pacific Fleet shortly after the US naval base at Pearl Harbor, Hawaii was attacked by Japanese Imperial Navy carrier aircraft. During his tenure as head of all naval operations in the Pacific, a position second only to that of Fleet Admiral Ernest King, the combined forces he commanded won victory after victory at Midway, Guadalcanal, the Gilberts, the Marshalls, the Marianas, Leyte Gulf, Iwo Jima, and Okinawa. Admiral Nimitz is regarded as one of the greatest admirals in naval history. Recommended for reading are Edwin Hoyt's *How They Won the War in the Pacific* and E. B. Potter's *Nimitz*.

Bibliography

Barnes, Gary I. *Great Warriors of World War II, Admiral Ernest King, Admiral Chester W. Nimitz*. Maxwell Air Force Base, AL: Air Command and Staff College, Air University, 1984.

Driskill, Frank A. and Dede W. Casad. *Admiral of the Hills: Biography of Chester W. Nimitz*. Austin, TX: Eakin Press, 1983.

Hoyt, Edwin P. *How They Won the War in the Pacific: Nimitz and His Admirals*. New York: Weybright & Talley, 1970.

Joan of Arc, Sister. *My Name is Nimitz*. San Antonio, TX: Standard Print Co., 1948.

Lamar, H. Arthur. *I Saw Stars*. Fredericksburg, TX: Admiral Nimitz Foundation, 1975.

Nimitz, Chester W. *Nimitz: Reflections on Pearl Harbor*. Fredericksburg, TX: Admiral Nimitz Foundation, 1971.

______. *Reminiscences of Admiral Chester W. Nimitz*. New York: New York Times Oral History Program, 1967.

______. *Some Thoughts to Live By: Philosophy of Fleet Admiral Chester Nimitz of Fredericksburg, Texas*. Fredericksburg, TX: Admiral Nimitz Foundation, 1991.

______, ed., and others. *Triumph in the Atlantic: The Naval Struggle Against the Axis*. Englewood Cliffs, NJ: Prentice-Hall, 1960.

Potter, E. B. (Elmer Belmont) and Chester W. Nimitz. *The Great Sea War: The Story of Naval Action in World War II*. Englewood Cliffs, NJ: Prentice-Hall, 1960.

______. *Nimitz*. Annapolis, MD: Naval Institute Press, 1976.

United States Navy. Pacific Fleet. *Admiral Nimitz Command Summary: Running Estimate and Summary, 1941-1945*. Wilmington, DE: Scholarly Resources, 1984. (microfilm)

Lieutenant General Alexander McCarrell Patch
United States Army
1889-1945

Patch first saw action during the Second World War on the island of Guadalcanal in the Solomon Islands chain. His US Army units relieved US Marine forces in November 1942 and ended the last Japanese resistance in February 1943. At the conclusion of the Guadalcanal campaign, Patch returned to the United States to command the Desert Training Centre. In 1944, he was promoted to lieutenant general and given command of the US Seventh Army. His forces participated in Operation Anvil-Dragoon, the invasion of southern France in August 1944. In September 1944, the Seventh Army and the First French Army were formed into the 6th Army Group with General Jacob Devers in overall command. The Seventh Army fought well, capturing Alsace and advancing to the Rhine River by late March 1945. The Seventh Army crossed the Rhine on 26 March 1945 and moved into southern Germany, routing German army units before they could form an organized line of resistance. Patch accepted the surrender of Army Group G from General Hermann Balck on 5 May 1945. William Wyant's *Sandy Patch* is recommended for reading.

Bibliography

Patch, Alexander M. "Some Thoughts on Leadership." *Military Review* 22 (December 1943).
Wyant, William K. *Sandy Patch: A Biography of Lt. Gen. Alexander M. Patch*. New York: Praeger, 1991.

General George Smith Patton, Jr.
United States Army
1885-1945

Patton was one of the US Army's most famous and controversial generals. He is recognized as one of the foremost authorities on the application of armour in warfare. His troops performed magnificently under his direction in North Africa, Sicily, and France, inflicting more battle casualties on the German Army than any other units employed by the Western Allies. Patton's career was turbulent. He had to work very hard to overcome dyslexia while at Virginia Military Institute and West Point. This handicap, plus the self-imposed pressure to measure up to the heroic deeds of his ancestors, placed many psychological burdens on Patton that lasted a lifetime. Several times he was reprimanded by General Dwight Eisenhower for misconduct, the most famous being the slapping incidents in Sicily involving two soldiers who were suffering from battle fatigue. Patton would not recognize any psychological reasons for failure to perform in combat though he, at numerous times, also showed the effects of mental tension due to combat strain. He died in December 1945 from injuries and complications incurred from an automobile accident near Mannheim, Germany. Recommended for reading are Martin Blumenson's *Patton* and *The Patton Papers*. Blumenson was editor of the two-volume *Patton Papers* and was the historian for Patton's US Third Army at the conclusion of the war. Also recommended are H. Esseme's *Patton*, Ladislas Farago's *The Last Days of Patton* and *Patton*, George Forty's *Patton's Third Army at War*, and Charles Whiting's *Patton's Last Battle*. Finally, General Patton's diary, *War As I Knew It*, published as a memoir, is recommended. In 1947, Patton's widow, Beatrice, decided to edit and publish his diary. She was assisted in the endeavor by Colonel Paul Harkins.

Bibliography

Allen, Robert. *Lucky Forward: The History of Patton's Third U.S. Army*. New York: Vanguard Press, 1947.

Army Times Editors. *Warrior: The Story of General George S. Patton*. New York: Putnam, 1967.

Ayer, Fred, Jr. *Before the Colors Fade: Portrait of a Soldier, George S. Patton, Jr*. Boston: Houghton Mifflin, 1964.

Baron, Richard, and others. *Raid: The Untold Story of Patton's Secret Mission*. New York: Putnam, 1981.

Blumenson, Martin. *The Many Faces of George S. Patton, Jr*. Colorado Springs, CO: United States Air Force Academy, 1972.

______. *Patton*. New York: Quill Books, 1994.

______. *Patton: The Man Behind the Legend, 1885-1945*. New York: Morrow, 1985.

Carpenter, Allan. *George Smith Patton, Jr.: The Lost Romantic*. Vero Beach, FL: Rourke Publications, 1987. (juvenile)

Codman, Charles R. *Drive*. Boston: Little, Brown, 1957.

D'Este, Carlo. *Patton: A Genius for War*. New York: HarperCollins, 1995.

Devaney, John. *"Blood and Guts": The True Story of General George S. Patton, USA*. New York: Messner, 1982. (juvenile)

Essame, H. (Hubert). *Patton: A Study in Command*. New York: Scribner, 1974.

Farago, Ladislas. *The Last Days of Patton*. New York: McGraw-Hill, 1981.

______. *Patton: Ordeal and Triumph*. New York: I. Oblensky, 1964.

Finke, Blythe Foote. *General Patton: Fearless Military Leader*. Charlottesville, NY: SamHar Press, 1972. (juvenile)

Forty, George. *Patton's Third Army at War*. New York: Charles Schribner's Sons, 1978.

Frankel, Nat and Larry Smith. *Patton's Best: An Informal History of the 4th Armored Division*. New York: Hawthorn Books, 1978.

Harkins, Paul Donal. *When the Third Cracked Europe: The Story of Patton's Incredible Army*. Harrisburg, PA: Stackpole Books, 1969.

Hatch, Alden. *George Patton, General in Spurs*. New York: Messner, 1950.

Higgins, George A. *"The Operational Tenets of General Heinz Guderian and George S. Patton, Jr."* M.M.A.S. thesis, U.S. Army Command and General Staff, 1986.

Hogg, Ian V. *The Biography of General George S. Patton*. New York: Gallery Press, 1982.

Janes, Terry D. *Patton's Troubleshooters II*. Kansas City, MO: Opinicus Pub. Co., 1990.

______, comp. and ed. *Patton's Troubleshooters Photo Album*. Kansas City, MO: Opinicus Pub. Co., 1989.

Landry, Vincent J. *Blitzkrieg Masters: Guderian and Patton*. Maxwell Air Force Base, AL: Air Command and Staff College, Air University, 1985.

Mayer, S. L. *Great American Generals of World War 2: MacArthur, Eisenhower, Patton*. New York: Gallery Books, 1984.

Mellor, William Bancroft. *General Patton: The Last Cavalier*. New York: Putnam, 1971. (juvenile)

______. *Patton, Fighting Man*. New York: G. P. Putnam's Sons, 1946.

Nye, Roger H. *The Patton Mind: The Professional Development of An Extraordinary Leader*. Garden City Park, NY: Avery, 1993.

Odom, Charles B. *General George S. Patton and Eisenhower*. New Orleans: World Picture Productions, Rose Printing Co., 1985.

Patton, George Smith, Jr. *The Patton Papers*. 2 volumes. Edited by Martin Blumenson. Boston: Houghton Mifflin, 1972-1974.

______. *The Poems of General George S. Patton, Jr.: Lines of Fire*. Edited, annotated, and introduced by Carmine A. Prioli. Lewiston, NY: Edwin Mellen Press, 1991.

______. *Pure Patton*. Edited by Charles M. Province. San Diego, CA: Province Publishing, 1979.

______. *War As I Knew It*. Annotated by Colonel Paul D. Harkins. Edited by Beatrice Ayer Patton. Boston: Houghton Mifflin, 1947.

Patton, Robert H. *The Pattons: A Personal History of an American Family*. New York: Crown, 1994.

Pearl, Jack. *Blood-and-Guts Patton: The Swashbuckling Life of America's Most Daring and Controversial General*. Derby, CT: Monarch Books, 1961.

Peck, Ira. *Patton*. New York: Scholastic Book Services, 1970.

Peifer, Charles. *Soldier of Destiny: A Biography of George Patton*. Minneapolis, MN: Dillon Press, 1989. (juvenile)

Perry, Milton F. and Barbara W. Parke. *Patton and His Pistols: The Favorite Side Arms of George S. Patton, Jr*. Harrisburg, PA: Stackpole, 1957.

Province, Charles. *Patton's Third Army: A Chronology of Third Army Advance, August 1944-May 1945*. New York: Hippocrene Books, 1994.

______. *The Unknown Patton*. New York: Hippocrene Books, 1982.

Puryear, Edgar F., Jr. *19 Stars: A Study in Military Character and Leadership*. (George Marshall, Dwight Eisenhower, Douglas MacArthur, and George Patton.) Washington, DC: Coiner Publications, 1971.

Rohmer, Richard H. *Patton's Gap: An Account of the Battle for Normandy, 1944*. New York: Beaufort Books, 1981.

Semmes, Harry Hodges. *Portrait of Patton*. New York: Appleton-Century-Crofts, 1955.

Shapiro, Milton J. *Tank Command: General George S. Patton's 4th Armored Division*. New York: McKay, 1979. (juvenile)

Skubik, Stephen J. *The Murder of General Patton*. Bennington, NH: S. J. Skubik, 1993.

Wallace, Brenton G. *Patton and His Third Army*. Harrisburg, PA: Military Service Publishing Co., 1946.

Wellard, James. *General George S. Patton, Jr: Man Under Mars*. New York: Dodd, Mead & Co., 1946.

White, D. J. *Patton: Leadership by Design*. Quantico, VA: Marine Corps Command and Staff College, 1986.

Whiting, Charles. *Patton*. New York: Ballantine Books, 1970.

_______. *Patton's Last Battle*. New York: Stein & Day, 1987.

Williams, Vernon L. *Lieutenant Patton and the American Army in the Mexican Punitive Expedition, 1915-1916*. Dubuque, IA: Kendall, Hunt Pub. Co., 1992.

Lieutenant General Elwood R. Quesada
United States Army Air Force
1904-1993

Quesada was one of the US Army's aviation experts during the pre-war years. After the Second World War began, he rose rapidly in rank, becoming a brigadier general in 1942. In 1943, he was given command of the 12th Fighter Command located in North Africa. In October 1943, he went to England to command the 9th Tactical Air Command. His air units provided close air support for the bombers and air cover for ground troops once landings were made on the French coast in June 1944 and during the battle for Germany. Quesada remained in the service after the end of the war, holding a variety of posts until his retirement in 1961. Thomas Hughes' *Over Lord* is recommended for reading.

Bibliography

Hughes, Thomas. *Over Lord: General Pete Quesada and the Triumph of Tactical Air Power in World War II*. New York: Free Press, 1995.

Quesada, Elwood. *The Reminiscences of General Elwood Quesada*. Glen Rock, NY: Microfilming Corporation of America, 1979. Columbia University Oral History Collection (microfiche).

Admiral James O. Richardson
United States Navy
1878-1974

Richardson was Commander-in-Chief of the US Fleet from 1940 until January 1941 when he was relieved of command by President Franklin D. Roosevelt and replaced by Admiral Husband Kimmel. Richardson had a difference of opinion with the president concerning the deployment of the Pacific Fleet to Pearl Harbor, Hawaii. The admiral felt that the presence of the fleet at Pearl Harbor did not deter the Japanese government from aggressive behaviour because the fleet was undermanned and unready for combat due to lack of training and inadequate resupply facilities. He wanted the fleet stationed on the west coast of the United States so it could be refitted, upgraded, and accompanied by a supply train of support ships if war occurred with Japan. Richardson made his position clearly known during a meeting with Roosevelt in October 1940. Three months later he was relieved of command. After the attack on Pearl Harbor, Richardson was very critical of the Roosevelt administration, contending that the government failed to adequately alert the military commanders in Hawaii of the seriousness of the diplomatic situation. Richardson's memoir, *The Treadmill to Pearl Harbor*, concentrates mainly on the years 1939 to 1941 and is recommended for readers interested in the pre-war Navy just prior to the attack on Pearl Harbor.

Bibliography

Richardson, James O. *On the Treadmill to Pearl Harbor: The Memoirs of Admiral James O. Richardson, USN (Retired)*. As told to Vice Admiral George C. Dyer, USN (Retired). Washington, DC: Naval History Division, Department of the Navy, 1973.

Lieutenant General Robert Charlwood Richardson, Jr.
United States Army
1882-1954

Richardson was involved in primarily administrative duties during his war career. In 1944, he was named Commanding General, US Army Forces in the Pacific Ocean Areas, but was mostly concerned with logistics and the training of US Army units. His after action reports should be of interest to readers who want to learn about U.S. Army operations during the Pacific campaigns of 1944 and 1945.

Bibliography

Richardson, Robert C., Jr. *Participation in the Final Phase of the Pacific War by the United States Army Forces, Middle Pacific, 21 June-2 September 1945*. Headquarters United States Army Forces, Pacific Ocean Areas, Office of the Commanding General, 1946.

______. *Participation in the Iwo Jima Operation by the United States Army Forces, Pacific Ocean Areas, February-March 1945*. Headquarters United States Army Forces, Middle Pacific, Office of the Commanding General, 1946.

______. *Participation in the Okinawa Operation by the United States Army Forces, Pacific Ocean Areas, April-June 1945*. Headquarters United States Army Forces, Middle Pacific, Office of the Commanding General, 1946.

______. *Participation in the Western Carolines and Central Philippines Operations by the United States Army Forces, Pacific Ocean Areas, September-November 1944*. Headquarters United States Army Forces, Middle Pacific, Office of the Commanding General, 1945.

General Matthew Bunker Ridgway
United States Army
1895-1993

Ridgway was one of the US Army's leading tactical experts on paratroop deployment during the Second World War. He planned the airborne portion of Operation Husky, the invasion of Sicily in July 1943. Overall, the execution of the plan was not considered successful due to bad weather, inexperienced pilots, and friendly anti-aircraft fire which caused many casualties. Ridgway commanded the 82nd Airborne Division for most of the war until he was given command of the XVIII Airborne Corps. After Operation Husky, he saw action in Italy and in Northwest Europe. The most notable campaigns were Operation Overlord, the invasion of Normandy, France, the Cotentin Peninsula campaign, and Operation Market Garden in Holland. Ridgway remained in the US Army after the conclusion of the war. During the Korean War, in 1951, he replaced General Douglas MacArthur as supreme commander of Allied forces in the Far East, and in 1952, was named supreme commander of Allied forces in Europe. General Ridgway's memoir is recommended for reading about Allied airborne operations during the Second World War. Clay Blair's *Ridgway's Paratroopers* is also recommended.

Bibliography

Blair, Clay. *Ridgway's Paratroopers: The American Airborne in World War II*. Garden City, NY: Dial Press, 1985.

Burns, Julian H. *The Education of Matthew Ridgway in Generalship*. Carlisle Barracks, PA: U.S. Army War College, 1989.

Edwards, Paul M., comp. *General Matthew B. Ridgway: An Annotated Bibliography*. Westport, CT: Greenwood Press, 1993.

Ridgway, Matthew. *Soldier: The Memoirs of Matthew B. Ridgway*. As told to Harold H. Martin. New York: Harper, 1956.

General William Hood Simpson
United States Army
1888-1980

Simpson was an outstanding US Army commander during the Second World War. He was promoted to lieutenant general in September 1943 and in 1944 was given command of the US Ninth Army. After the invasion of France, his units fought under the command of General Omar Bradley's 12 Army Group or Field Marshal Bernard Montgomery's 21st Army Group depending on the combat situation. Simpson's units captured Brest in late September and moved into the Ardennes Forest in October 1944. After the battle of the Bulge, the Ninth Army moved from the Roer River to the Rhine River, crossing Germany's last natural barrier on 24 March 1945. When the war ended, his combat units were poised on the banks of the Elbe River. Berlin was only fifty miles to the east. Simpson was promoted to full general upon his retirement. The only works found concerning the career of General Simpson were a Ph.D. dissertation and a US Army War College paper. Contact your library's interlibrary loan department about their availability.

Bibliography

Stone, Thomas Richardson. "*He Had the Guts to Say No: A Military Biography of General William Hood Simpson.*" Ph.D. diss., Rice University, 1974. (DAI, 35:4, 2198A, UMI Order # 7421342)
______. *Never Send an Infantryman Where You Can Send an Artillery Shell: Individual Study Project*. Carlisle Barracks, PA: U.S. Army War College, 1980.

General Holland McTyeire Smith
United States Marine Corps
1882-1967

"Howlin' Mad" Smith is considered to be the creator of US Marine amphibious operations doctrine which called for close cooperation of air, land, and sea forces. From 1941 to 1944, he commanded the V Amphibious Corps. His Marine units saw action on numerous islands including Tarawa, Makin, Kwajalein, Eniwetok, Saipan, and Tinian. In August 1944, he was named commanding general of Fleet Marine Force Pacific and directed amphibious assaults against Guam, Iwo Jima, and Okinawa. Smith had very high standards concerning performance of duty. As a result, he had numerous run-ins and disputes with his US Army counterparts. Recommended for reading are General Smith's *Coral and Brass* and Harry Gailey's *Howlin' Mad vs. the Army*.

Bibliography

Cooper, Norman V. *A Fighting General: The Biography of Gen. Holland M. "Howlin' Mad" Smith*. Quantico, VA: Marine Corps Association, 1987.
Gailey, Harry A. *Howlin' Mad vs. the Army: Conflict in Command, Saipan, 1944*. Novato, CA: Presidio Press, 1986.

Smith, Holland M. and Percy Finch. *Coral and Brass*. New York: Scribner, 1949.

_____. *The Development of Amphibious Tactics in the U.S. Navy*. Washington, DC: History and Museums Division, Headquarters, U.S. Marine Corps, 1992.

Lieutenant General Julian Constable Smith
United States Marine Corps
1885-1975

Smith was an early proponent of amphibious warfare. In November 1943, he commanded the 2nd Marine Division during the invasion of Tawara in the Gilbert Islands. Despite many unanticipated obstacles, his Marines forced their way ashore and on the second day, attacked the Japanese defenders. By the end of the third day, the island was occupied, but the Marines suffered nearly 1 000 dead and 2 000 wounded. Only a handful of Japanese survived of the 5 000 engaged. The experiences learned on Tawara taught the Marines many valuable lessons that aided their training for future amphibious operations. Smith next conducted amphibious assaults in the southern Palaus and at Ulithi. In December 1944, he returned to the United States as Commander of the Department of the Pacific until his retirement in February 1946. Contact your library's interlibrary loan department about the availability of General Smith's oral history.

Bibliography

Smith, Julian Constable. *Lieutenant-General Julian C. Smith, U.S. Marine Corps, (Retired)*. Washington, DC: Historical Division, Headquarters, U.S. Marine Corps, Oral History Program, 1973.

General Walter Bedell Smith
United States Army
1895-1961

Smith's wartime duties kept him behind the front lines, but he performed a valuable role as General Dwight Eisenhower's chief of staff from

September 1942 to the conclusion of the war. Among his many duties, he negotiated the surrender of Italy in September 1943 and of all German armed forces in May 1945. After the war, he held several government positions, including ambassador to the Soviet Union and director of the Central Intelligence Agency. D. K. R. Crosswell's *Chief of Staff* is recommended for reading.

Bibliography

Crosswell, D. K. R. (Daniel K. R.) *Chief of Staff: The Military Career of General Walter Bedell Smith*. New York: Greenwood Publishing Group, 1991.

Smith, Walter Bedell. *Eisenhower's Six Great Decisions: Europe, 1944-1945*. New York: Longmans' Green, 1956.

_____. *My Three Years in Moscow*. Philadelphia: J.B. Lippincott Company, 1950.

General Brehon Burke Somervell
United States Army
1892-1955

During the Second World War, there were many officers who performed extremely essential duties, but received little public recognition for their efforts. Somervell was one such individual. From 1942 to the conclusion of the war, he was Commanding General of US Army Service Forces and served as military advisor to President Franklin D. Roosevelt. He was also the creator of the Pentagon, the headquarters of the US military service in Washington, DC. In his capacity as head of Army Service Forces, his primary concerns were troop mobilization and war production which included the procurement and shipment of supplies and equipment from the factories to the numerous war fronts. This task was truly gigantic in scope and operation. The logistical branch of the military forces was of vital importance because combat personnel could not fight if they were not properly supplied and equipped. John Ohl's *Supplying the Troops* is recommended for reading.

Bibliography

Millett, John D. *The Organization and the Role of the Army Service Forces. United States Army in World War II. The Army Services*. Washington, DC: U.S. Government Printing Office, 1954.

Ohl, John Kennedy. *Supplying the Troops: General Somervell and American Logistics in WWII*. De Kalb: Northern Illinois University Press, 1994.

Somervell, Brehon B., et al. *Administrative Management in the Army Services Forces*. Chicago, IL: Public Administrative Services, 1944.

______. *Speeches, 1941-1945*. (Privately published). n.p., n.d.

General Carl Andrew Spaatz
United States Army Air Force
1891-1974

Spaatz was one of the US Army Air Force's top air commanders during the Second World War. In July 1942, he went to Great Britain to lead the Eighth Air Force in the strategic bombing of Germany. He was a proponent of daytime, precision bombing and believed that bombers could defend themselves while attacking specific targets. However, losses were heavy until P-51 Mustang fighters began accompanying the bombers. In late 1942, Spaatz was sent to North Africa to command the Twelfth Air Force and Eastern Air Command. His air units, collectively known as the Northwest Africa Air Force, performed very well during the Tunisian and Sicilian campaigns in 1943. By January 1944, he was back in Great Britain, preparing for the invasion of Normandy, France. His new position was Commanding General of the Strategic Air Command. Primary targets were sites in Normandy, German petroleum facilities, and railroad networks. In March 1945, he was transferred to the Pacific Theatre of Operations and commanded the Strategic Air Force of the Pacific. His B-29 bombers raided Japanese cities, doing tremendous damage. Two of his bombers dropped atomic bombs on Hiroshima and Nagasaki in August 1945. Recommended for reading are Richard Davis' *Tempering the Blade* and David Mets' *Master of Airpower*.

Bibliography

Copp, Dewitt S. *A Few Great Captains: The Men and Events That Shaped The Development of U.S. Air Power*. Garden City, NY: Doubleday, 1980.

Davis, Richard G. "*The Bomber Baron: Carl Andrew Spaatz and the Army Air Forces in Europe, 1942-1945*." Ph.D. diss., George Washington University, 1986. (DAI, 47:4, 1458A, UMI Order # DA8615747)

______. *Carl A. Spaatz and the Air War in Europe*. Washington, DC: Office of Air Force History, U.S. Air Force, 1992.

______. *Tempering the Blade: General Carl Spaatz and American Tactical Air Power in North Africa, November 8, 1942-May 14, 1943*. Washington, DC: Office of Air Force History, 1989.

Eppley, Samuel M. *General Carl A. Spaatz*. Maxwell Air Force Base, AL: Air University, 1965.

Library of Congress. *The General Spaatz Collection*. Washington, DC: U.S. Government Printing Office, 1949.

Mets, David R. *Master of Airpower: General Carl A. Spaatz*. Novato, CA: Presidio Press, 1988.

Admiral Raymond Ames Spruance
United States Navy
1886-1969

Spruance was in command during two of the US Navy's most important victories of the war: Midway and the Battle of the Philippine Sea. He was in charge of Task Force 16 during the Battle of Midway in June 1942. He assumed command of all naval forces participating in the action after Vice Admiral Frank Fletcher's flagship, the carrier *Yorktown*, was put out of action by Japanese planes. Spruance directed air attacks against the Japanese fleet, resulting in the sinking of four carriers. Midway is considered to be the turning point of the naval war in the Pacific. After Midway, Spruance was promoted to chief of staff for Admiral Chester Nimitz and participated in strategic planning during the next year. He returned to sea duty in August 1943 to command the Fifth Fleet. His naval units shelled Tawara during pre-invasion operations. The Fifth Fleet performed the same duties at Kwajalein in January 1944 and at Saipan in June 1944. During the Saipan engagement, the remainder of the Japanese carrier fleet ventured forth to do battle. Spruance sent Admiral Marc Mitscher's task force to deal with the threat. Combined submarine and air attacks sank three Japanese carriers and American airmen shot down over 450 Japanese planes. The battle effectively ended the Japanese Navy's carriers as offensive weapons. Spruance directed naval operations during the Iwo Jima campaign and led the first carrier strike against Tokyo. When the war ended, he was planning the naval portion of the proposed invasion of Japan. Thomas Buell's *The Quiet Warrior* is recommended for reading.

Bibliography

Buell, Thomas B. *The Quiet Warrior: A Biography of Admiral Raymond A. Spruance*. Annapolis, MD: Naval Institute Press, 1974.

Cherpak, Evelyn M., comp. *Register of the Papers of Raymond A. Spruance*. Newport, RI: Naval Historical Collection, Naval War College, 1986.

Forrestel, E. (Emmet) P. *Admiral Raymond A. Spruance: A Study in Command*. Washington, DC: Government Printing Office, 1966.

Montman, James H. *The Military Strategies of Spruance and Halsey*. Maxwell Air Force Base, AL: Air Command and Staff College, Air University, 1984.

Admiral Harold Raynsford Stark
United States Navy
1880-1972

Stark was appointed Chief of Naval Operations in 1939. He was publicly criticized by a congressional inquiry after the attack on the US naval base at Pearl Harbor, Hawaii. He was replaced as CNO by Admiral Ernest King and given command of all US naval forces in the European Theatre of Operations. This position was more diplomatic than military in nature and he served as a mediator between some of the more volatile factions on both the American and British sides as the two Allied nations planned Operation Overlord, the invasion of Normandy, France. B. Mitchell Simpson's *Admiral Harold R. Stark* is recommended for reading.

Bibliography

Simpson, B. Mitchell, III. *Admiral Harold R. Stark: Architect of Victory, 1939-1945*. Columbia, SC: University of South Carolina Press, 1989.
United States. Navy Department. Pearl Harbor Court of Inquiry. *Finding the Facts*. Washington, DC: n.p., 1945.

General Joseph Warren Stilwell
United States Army
1883-1946

Stilwell was the highest ranking American officer in the China-Burma-India Theatre of Operations during the Second World War. Before the war, he was the military attache at the United States embassy in Peking so he was familiar with the Chinese government when he was appointed Generalissimo Chiang Kai-shek's commander-in-chief of military forces in 1942. Stilwell's command was marked with both victories and defeats. Burma was lost in 1943 and was not fully regained until 1945. Stilwell's main goal was for Chiang's army to engage the Japanese in combat in China, but Chiang continually resisted, fearing that any defeat would weaken his power base in his conflict with Mao Tse-tung's Communist forces. Finally, Chiang had Stilwell recalled in October 1944 after the Japanese captured many Chinese airfields. The United States Army Air Force had used these bases to launch air attacks against targets in Japan. Stilwell was an excellent strategist, but his personality was very abrasive. His low opinions of the British constantly caused him problems with his superiors. His nickname, "Vinegar Joe", was well earned. Though the China-Burma-India theatre is not as well known as other theatres of operation, Allied troops confronted and contained over one million Japanese troops for the duration of the war. Recommended for reading are Charles Romanus' and Riley Southerland's *Stilwell's Command Problems*, Barbara Tuchman's *Stilwell and the American Experience in China*, and General Stilwell's *Papers*.

Bibliography

Anders, Leslie. *The Ledo Road: General Joseph W. Stilwell's Highway to China*. Norman, OK: University of Oklahoma Press, 1965.
Belden, Jack. *Retreat with Stilwell*. New York: A. A. Knopf, 1943.

Bellah, James W. "Stilwell's Chinese Offensive." *Infantry Journal*, 55 (July 1944): 41-43.

Bidwell, Shelford. *The Chindit War: Stilwell, Wingate and the Campaign in Burma, 1944*. New York: Macmillan, 1979.

Dorn, Frank. *Walkout: With Stilwell in Burma*. New York: Crowell, 1971.

Eldridge, Fred. *Wrath in Burma: The Uncensored Story of General Stilwell and International Maneuvers in the Far East*. Garden City, NY: Doubleday, 1946.

Hunter, Charles Newton. *Galahad*. San Antonio, TX: Naylor Co., 1963.

Liang, Ching-Chaun. *General Stilwell in China, 1942-1944: The Full Story*. New York: St. John's University Press, 1972.

Romanus, Charles F. and Riley Southerland. *Stilwell's Command Problems*. Washington, DC: Office of the Chief of Military History, 1956.

______. *Stilwell's Mission to China*. Washington, DC: Office of Military History, Department of the Army, 1952.

Rooney, Douglas David. *Stilwell*. New York: Ballantine Books, 1971.

Stilwell, Joseph Warren. *The Stilwell Papers*. Arranged and edited by Theodore H. White. New York: W. Sloane Associates, 1948.

______. *Stilwell's Personal File - China, Burma, India, 1942-1944*. Edited by Riley Southerland and Charles F. Romanus. Wilmington, DE: Scholarly Resources, 1976.

Tuchman, Barbara. *Stilwell and the American Experience in China, 1911-1945*. New York: Macmillan, 1970.

Rear Admiral Robert Alfred Theobald
United States Navy
1884-1957

Theobald was Chief of Staff, US Fleet from 1939 to 1940. He saw action as Commander of Destroyers of the Pacific Fleet from December 1941 to May 1942 and then commanded Northern Pacific Force until 1943 when he became Commandant, First Naval District. He retired from the US Navy in February 1945. In his book, *The Final Secret of Pearl Harbor*, he contends that President Franklin D. Roosevelt and members of his administration did not adequately warn the military commanders in Hawaii of a possible surprise attack. Theobald also states that government officials in Washington denied the military commanders access to Magic, which deciphered the Japanese government's coded transmission signals. Theobald said he wrote his book to reveal the errors in judgement made by the Roosevelt administration and the administration's subsequent coverup and shifting of blame to the military commanders at Pearl Harbor.

Bibliography

Theobald, Robert A. *The Final Secret of Pearl Harbor: The Washington Contribution to the Japanese Attack*. New York: Devin-Adair, 1954.

General Lucian King Truscott, Jr.
United States Army
1895-1965

Truscott organized and trained US Army Ranger units for commando-type operations during the early part of the war. He was involved in the raid on Dieppe, France on 19 August 1942. Even though heavy casualties were incurred, many valuable lessons were learned that greatly aided future amphibious operations. His next operation involved his Rangers capturing Port Lyautey in French Morocco during Operation Torch, the invasion of North Africa. In March 1943, he transferred to the infantry, taking command of the 3rd Infantry Division. His division participated in Operation Husky, the invasion of Sicily, and performed very well, capturing Palermo and Messina. The 3rd Division next went ashore at Salerno, Italy as reinforcements. In January 1944, the 3rd Division landed at Anzio. When the Allied command was not pleased with the performance of the VI Corps commander, Major General John Lucas, Truscott replaced him in February 1944. After consolidating positions and building up reserves, Truscott's forces broke out of the beachhead in May and advanced toward Rome. After the breakout, the VI Corps was pulled out of the line to rest and prepare for the upcoming invasion of southern France. Truscott remained in command of the VI Corps until December 1944 when he was promoted and given command of General Mark Clark's Fifth Army in Italy. The Fifth Army attacked across the Po River Valley during the final days of the war, capturing Bologna on 21 April 1945. After the conclusion of hostilities, Truscott succeeded General George Patton as commander of the US Third Army, stationed in Bavaria. General Truscott's *Command Missions* is recommended for reading.

Bibliography

Truscott, Lucian K. *Command Missions: A Personal Story*. New York: Dutton, 1954.

_____. *The Twilight of the U.S. Cavalry: Life in the Old Army, 1917-1942*. Lawrence, KS: University Press of Kansas, 1989.

Admiral Richmond Kelly Turner
United States Navy
1885-1961

Turner first experienced combat during the Battle of Savo Island. His naval units were surprised and defeated by their Japanese counterparts. Turner next directed naval operations during the New Guinea and Gilbert Islands campaigns. He later landed ground forces during the Marshalls, Marianas, and Iwo Jima operations. By the conclusion of the war, Admiral Turner was a leading expert in amphibious warfare. George Dyer's *The Amphibians Came to Conquer* is recommended for reading.

Bibliography

Dyer, George Carroll. *The Amphibians Came to Conquer: The Story of Admiral Richmond Kelly Turner*. 2 volumes. Washington, DC: Government Printing Office, 1971.

General Nathan Farragut Twining
United States Army Air Force
1897-1982

Twining was an early proponent of strategic air bombardment. In 1942-43, he served as General Douglas MacArthur's chief of staff of the Army Air Forces, South Pacific. In July 1943, he assumed the position of Commander, Air Forces, Southwest Pacific as well as commanding the Thirteenth Air Force. He transferred to the Mediterranean Theatre of Operations in 1944 and commanded the Fifteenth Air Force in Italy. In a highly controversial operation, his bombers levelled the abbey at Monte Casino which resulted in much world protest and ultimately made reduction of the German defences much harder to achieve. Twining finished his tour of duty back in the Pacific Theatre of Operations as commander of the Twentieth Air Force. From 1953 to 1957, he served as chief of staff of the US Air Force and from 1957 to 1960, was chairman of the Joint Chiefs of Staff. The only source found concerning the career of General Twining is J. Britt McCarley's Ph.D. dissertation. Contact your library's interlibrary loan department about its availability.

Bibliography

McCarley, J. Britt. "*General Nathan Farragut Twining: The Making of A Disciple of American Strategic Air Power, 1897-1953.*" Ph.D. diss., Temple University, 1989. (DAI, 50:4, 1068A, UMI Order # DA8912456)

General Alexander Archer Vandegrift
United States Marine Corps
1887-1973

Vandegrift was the highest-ranking Marine by the end of the Second World War. In August 1942, he led the 1st Marine Division onto Guadalcanal as American military forces began the task of retaking the Pacific islands from Japanese military forces. After several months of furious fighting, the Marines emerged victorious. Vandegrift was sent back to the United States and given command of the newly formed 1st Marine Amphibious Corps. He saw action again in November 1943 when the Marines invaded Bougainville. In 1944, he was promoted to Commandant of the Marine Corps and was instrumental in increasing enlistments to replace the men lost in the numerous battles the Marines were fighting in the Pacific Theatre of Operations. Vandegrift's memoirs, *Once a Marine*, as told to Robert Asprey, is an excellent account of the duties he performed and of the role the Marine Corps played during the Second World War. John Foster's *Guadalcanal General* is also recommended.

Bibliography

Foster, John T. *Guadalcanal General: The Story of A. A. Vandegrift, USMC*. New York: Morrow, 1966.

Shaw, Henry I., Jr. *First Offensive: The Marine Campaign for Guadalcanal*. Washington, DC: History and Museums Division, Headquarters, U.S. Marine Corps. Superintendent of Documents, U.S. Government Printing Office, Distributor, 1992.

Vandegrift, Alexander Archer. *Once a Marine: The Memoirs of General A. A. Vandegrift, United States Marine Corps*. As told to Robert B. Asprey. New York: Norton, 1964.

General Hoyt S. Vandenberg
United States Army Air Force
1899-1954

Vandenberg split his war service between staff and combat commands. At the beginning of the war, he helped plan air operations during Operation Torch, the invasion of North Africa. Next, he helped organize the Twelfth Air Force which flew combat missions in the North African and Mediterranean Theatre of Operations. In August 1943, he returned to Washington to be Deputy Chief of the Air Staff. He spent the next months planning air operations for Overlord, the invasion of France. In August 1944, he assumed command of the Ninth Air Force operating in the European Theatre of Operations. Promoted to lieutenant general in March 1945, he returned one more time to the United States to resume staff duties. After the war, he served as Chief of Staff of the United States Air Force. Phillip Meilinger's *Hoyt S. Vandenberg, The Life of A General* is recommended for reading.

Bibliography

Meilinger, Phillip S. *Hoyt S. Vandenberg, the Life of a General*. Bloomington, IN: Indiana University Press, 1989.

______. *"Hoyt S. Vandenberg: Life of a General."* Ph.D. diss., University of Michigan, 1985. (DAI, 46:11, 3470A, UMI Order # 8600501)

Reynolds, Jon Anzuena. *"Education and Training for High Command: General Hoyt S. Vandenberg's Early Career."* Ph.D. diss., Duke University, 1980. (DAI, 41:3, 1189A, UMI Order # 8019332)

General Jonathan Mayhew Wainwright
United States Army
1881-1953

Wainwright served in the Philippines in the early 1900s and saw action in France during the First World War. After General Douglas MacArthur was ordered to Australia by President Franklin D. Roosevelt, Wainwright commanded the American and Filipino troops that fought invading Japanese forces in the Philippines in early 1942. Despite the tremendous odds against him, Wainwright fought a masterful defence and greatly upset the Japanese timetable for the conquest of the Philippines. Wainwright finally gave permission to his troops on Bataan to surrender in early April 1942. One month later, he surrendered his remaining forces on Corrigedor after Japanese troops landed on the island following a heavy artillery barrage that stunned the defenders. Wainwright was a prisoner of war for over three years. He was released in time to witness the signing of the surrender papers by Japanese government delegates on the deck of the USS battleship *Missouri*. Wainwright performed his duties in the Philippines in 1942 with outstanding valour despite the unfavourable military situation. During his captivity, he never lost his respect or military bearing. His *Papers* and memoir, *General Wainwright's Story*, are recommended for reading. Duane Schultz's *Hero of Bataan* is also recommended.

Bibliography

Beck, John Jacob. *MacArthur and Wainwright: Sacrifice of the Philippines*. Albuquerque: University of New Mexico Press, 1974.

Schultz, Duane P. *Hero of Bataan: The Story of General Jonathan M. Wainwright*. New York: St. Martin's Press, 1981.

Wainwright, Jonathan Mayhew. *General Wainwright's Story: The Account of Four Years of Humiliating Defeat, Surrender, and Captivity*. Edited by Robert Considine. Garden City, NY: Doubleday & Co., 1946.

______. *The Wainwright Papers*. Edited by Celedonio A. Ancheta. Quezon City, Philippines: New Day Publishers, 1980. Distributed by Cellar Door Book Shop, Detroit, MI.

General Albert Coady Wedemeyer
United States Army
1897-1992

Wedemeyer served in the War Department from 1941 to 1943. In 1943, he was named deputy chief of staff to Lord Louis Mountbatten in the South East Asia Command. When General Joseph Stilwell was removed as Chiang Kai-shek's chief of staff in October 1944, Wedemeyer replaced him. Previously, Stilwell had conducted military operations against the Japanese forces in China, but Chiang rarely agreed with him on strategy. Chiang was afraid to use his units against the Japanese for fear it would weaken his position against Mao Tse-tung's Communist forces. President Franklin D. Roosevelt directed Wedemeyer to concentrate on strengthening the relationship between Chiang and Mao because the military situation in China was fairly hopeless by the end of 1944. General Wedemeyer's memoir, *Wedemeyer Reports!*, is recommended for reading.

Bibliography

Wedemeyer, Albert. *Wedemeyer Reports!* New York: Holt, 1958.

13 British Commanders

This chapter presents short biographical profiles and bibliographies of works about and by the top-ranking military commanders in the British high command including those from the commonwealth nations, Australia and New Zealand. Unlike their American counterparts who saw the war as a great crusade in which the outcome was never really in doubt, British military commanders viewed the conflict as a life and death struggle that might not result in victory if hasty decisions were made. Thus, the British commanders advanced with caution during the course of the war to avoid a devastating defeat or a possible bloody stalemate as was the case during the First World War. The commanders profiled are listed in alphabetical order by their last name.

Earl Alexander of Tunis
Field Marshal Earl Alexander
(Harold Alexander)
British Army
1891-1969

Alexander was one of Great Britain's top field commanders during the Second World War. He commanded a division and later a corps during the campaign in France in 1940. His units were the last to evacuate the European continent at Dunkirk, Belgium. In January 1942, he was sent to Burma, but the retreat was already underway when he arrived and he had to regroup his forces in India. In August 1942, he was appointed commander-in-chief of all forces in North Africa. He was in command when General (later Field Marshal) Bernard Montgomery's British Eighth Army won the Battle of El Alamein in November 1942 and when combined American and British forces captured all German and Italian forces in Tunisia in May 1943. After the successful conclusion of the North

African campaign, he was named Deputy Supreme Commander and later Supreme Allied Commander of the Mediterranean Theatre of Operations after General Dwight Eisenhower was appointed Supreme Commander of the Allied Expeditionary Force. Alexander is well remembered for his ability to foster Allied cooperation. Many times he had to settle disputes between his American and British officers and was always considered fair in his judgement and evaluation. Recommended for reading are Field Marshal Alexander's *The Alexander Memoirs*, W. G. F. Jackson's *Alexander of Tunis, As Military Commander* and Nigel Nicholson's *Alex: The Life of Field Marshal Earl Alexander of Tunis*.

Bibliography

Alexander, Harold Rupert. *The Alexander Memoirs, 1940-1945*. Edited by John North. New York: McGraw-Hill, 1962.

_____. *Report by the Supreme Allied Commander Mediterranean, Field Marshal the Viscount Alexander of Tunis to the Combined Chiefs of Staff on the Italian Campaign, 12 December 1944 to 2nd May 1945*. London: n.p., 1951.

Blaxland, Gregory. *Alexander's Generals: The Italian Campaign, 1944-45*. London: W. Kimber, 1979.

Hillson, Norman. *Alexander of Tunis: A Biographical Portrait*. London: W. H. Allen, 1952.

Jackson, W. G. F. (William Godfrey Fothergill). *Alexander of Tunis, As Military Commander*. New York: Dodd, Mead, 1971.

Nicolson, Nigel. *Alex: The Life of Field Marshal Earl Alexander of Tunis*. New York: Atheneum, 1973.

General Kenneth A. N. Anderson
British Army
1891-1959

Anderson was not one of the better known British Army generals during the Second World War, but was a competent battlefield commander. He commanded the 3rd Division of the British Expeditionary Force during the final days of the Battle of France in May/June 1940. He and his men were evacuated at Dunkirk. For the remainder of 1940 to 1942, he served with the Home Forces in the British Isles. In late 1942, he was given command of the British First Army. Infantry units landed in North Africa in November 1942 during Operation Torch and the First Army participated in the defeat and capture of all German and Italian forces in North Africa by May 1943. Originally, Anderson was slated to command the Second Army during the invasion of France in 1944, but was replaced in January 1944 by Lieutenant General Miles Dempsey, who led the army in Northwest Europe for the remainder of the war. In 1945, Anderson was given the East African Command. After the war, he served ably as Governor of Gibraltar from 1947 to 1952. He was promoted to the rank of general in 1949. The only source found on the career of General Anderson was Gregory Blaxland's *The Plain Cook and the Great Showman: The First and Eighth Armies in North Africa*. It is recommended for reading.

Bibliography

Blaxland, Gregory. *The Plain Cook and the Great Showman: The First and Eighth Armies in North Africa*. London: Kimber, 1977.

Field Marshal Sir Claude Auchinleck
British Army
1884-1981

Auchinleck was one of the British Army's most well-liked and respected general officers. He commanded the IV Corps when the war began in 1939. In 1941, he was named commander-in-chief of British forces in India. When General (later Field Marshal) Archibald Wavell's Operation Battleaxe failed to defeat the German Afrika Korps on the Egyptian-Libyan frontier, Prime Minister Winston Churchill replaced Wavell with Auchinleck, naming him Commander-in-Chief, Middle East. Auchinleck's first major operation was Crusader. It was launched in November 1941. The battle was hard fought with the British Eighth Army emerging victorious and the siege of Tobruk lifted. However, the commander of the Afrika Korps, General (later Field Marshal) Erwin Rommel, did not give the British time to rest and refit. In January 1942, he attacked and advanced deep into Libya, finally stopping near Gazala. Rommel renewed his offensive in late May 1942, and after a series of fierce desert battles, forced the Eighth Army to retreat back into Egypt where Auchinleck was able to prepare defensive positions near El

Alamein. With the retreat of the Eighth Army, the port of Tobruk was, once again, besieged. This time Rommel immediately attacked the garrison, forcing its surrender on 21 June 1942. Rommel then pressed on to engage the Eighth Army in an attempt to break through to Alexandria and the Suez Canal. This time, the British held. Rommel incurred such heavy losses in men and armour that he could not continue the attack and withdrew to regroup and refit. Even though Auchinleck had held his positions and stopped Rommel's advance to the Suez Canal, Churchill relieved him of command, replacing him with General (later Field Marshal) Harold Alexander and placing General (later Field Marshal) Bernard Montgomery in command of the Eighth Army. Churchill was still stung by the loss of Tobruk and Auchinleck's inability to defeat Rommel decisively. Auchinleck returned to India as commander-in-chief of the Indian Army where he remained until his retirement in 1947. Recommended for reading are John Connell's *Auchinleck*, Alexander Greenwood's *Field-Marshal Auchinleck*, Roger Parkinson's *The Auk*, John Robertson's *Auchinleck*, and Philip Warner's *Auchinleck*.

Bibliography

Brownlow, Donald Grey. *Checkmate at Ruweisat: Auchinleck's Finest Hour*. North Quincy, MA: Christopher Pub. House, 1977.

Connell, John. *Auchinleck: A Biography of Field-Marshal Sir Claude Auchinleck*. London: Cassell, 1959.

Greenwood, Alexander. *Field-Marshal Auchinleck: A Biography of Field-Marshal Sir Claude Auchinleck*. Witton le Wear, Durham, England: Pentland Press, 1990.

O'Brien, G. and P. Roebuck, eds. *Nine Ulster Lives*. Belfast: Ulster Historical Foundation, 1992. (One chapter concerns the career of Claude Auchinleck.)

Parkinson, Roger. *The Auk: Auchinleck, Victor at Alamein*. New York: Hart-David MacGibbon, 1977.

Robertson, John Henry. *Auchinleck, A Biography of Field-Marshal Sir Claude Auchinleck*. London: Cassell, 1959.

Robinson-Horley, E. W. *Last Post: An Indian Army Memoir*. London: Leo Cooper in association with Secker & Warburg, 1985.

Warner, Philip. *Auchinleck: The Lonely Soldier*. London: Buchan and Enright, 1981.

Wright, Margaret M. *The Military Papers, 1940-48, of Field Marshal Sir Claude Auchinleck: A Calendar and Index*. Manchester: John Rylands University Library of Manchester, 1988.

Field Marshal Sir Thomas Blamey
Australian Army
1884-1951

Blamey was Australia's top-ranking commander during the Second World War. In February 1940, he commanded the Australian Imperial Forces, Middle East during the final stages of the first Libyan desert campaign. In 1941, his Anzac Corps was transferred to Greece. When the fighting went badly, he commanded the evacuation from Greece and later from Crete. He returned to Egypt and was named Deputy Commander-in-Chief, Middle East. In March 1942, he returned to Australia to assume command of the Australian Army and to serve under General Douglas MacArthur's command in the South Pacific area of operations. He personally led troops during the New Guinea and Buna campaigns in late 1942 and 1943. After 1943, his role in the war was greatly reduced as the Japanese threat to Australia faded. Recommended for reading are Norman Carlson's *I Remember Blamey* and John Hetherington's *Blamey, Controversial Soldier*.

Bibliography

Carlyon, Norman D. *I Remember Blamey*. South Melbourne: Macmillan, 1980.
Hetherington, John. *Blamey, Controversial Soldier: A Biography of Field Marshal Sir Thomas Blamey, G.B.E., K.C.B., C.M.G., D.S.O., E.D.* Canberra: Australian War Memorial and the Australian Government Printing Service, 1973.

Field Marshal Viscount Alanbrooke
(Alan Brooke)
British Army
1883-1963

Brooke was one of Great Britain's finest officers. He first saw combat on the Western Front during the First World War. Twenty-one years later, he was back in France in command of the 2nd Corps of the British Expeditionary Force. He trained his troops hard once the war began in September 1939. When the Germans invaded France and the Low Countries in May 1940, his corps performed very well. When the

Belgian Army capitulated, his units covered the open left flank of the BEF. If they had not held, the entire BEF could have been lost. As the BEF retreated to Dunkirk, Brooke personally assumed command of the evacuation. As a result, over 300 000 troops were saved to fight again. After the fall of France, he was named Commander-in-Chief, Home Forces and prepared his units to repel a possible German invasion of the British Isles, a daunting task considering most of the British Army's armour and artillery were left behind during the evacuation from the European continent. In December 1941, he was promoted to the top-ranking position in the British Army, Chief of the Imperial General Staff, replacing Field Marshal Sir John Dill. During his tenure as CIGS, he brought stability, strength, and direction to the post. Because of his calm demeanor and attitude, he was the ideal counterpart to Prime Minister Winston Churchill, who often was rash and impetuous. Brooke's one major disappointment occurred when he was not chosen to be Supreme Allied Commander for the invasion of France in 1944. Instead, the position went to General Dwight Eisenhower. Recommended for reading are Arthur Bryant's two volume set, *The Turn of the Tide* and *Triumph in the West*, and David Fraser's *Alanbrooke*.

Bibliography

Bryant, Arthur. *Triumph in the West: A History of the War Years Based on the Diaries of Field Marshal Lord Alanbrooke, Chief of the Imperial General Staff. Volume II.* Garden City, NY: Doubleday, 1959.

_____. *The Turn of the Tide: A History of the War Years Based on the Diaries of Field Marshal Lord Alanbrooke, Chief of the Imperial General Staff. Volume I.* Garden City, NY: Doubleday, 1957.

Fraser, David. *Alanbrooke.* New York: Atheneum, 1982.

Air Marshal Sir Arthur Coningham
Royal Air Force
1895-1948

Coningham was one of the RAF's best tactical air commanders. He is considered to be the creator of tactical air support for ground operations. From 1941 to 1943, he commanded the Western Desert Air Force. His fighters provided air support to the British Eighth Army during the El

Alamein and Tripoli campaigns. In 1943, he assumed command of the First Allied Tactical Air Force. His combat forces participated in the conclusion of the North African campaign, the invasion and conquest of Sicily, and the invasion of the Italian mainland. In June 1944, he led the Second Tactical Air Force during the Normandy invasion and subsequent operations in Northwest Europe until the conclusion of the war. Vincent Orange's *Coningham* is recommended for reading.

Bibliography

Orange, Vincent. *Coningham: A Biography of Air Marshal Sir Arthur Coningham, K.C.B., K.B.E., D.S.O., M.C., D.F.C., A.F.C.* London: Methuen, 1990.

Cunningham of Hyndhope
Admiral of the Fleet Sir Andrew Browne Cunningham
Royal Navy
1883-1963

Cunningham was acting commander of the Mediterranean Fleet when the war began in 1939. The Royal Navy's principle foe in the Mediterranean was the Italian Navy. When the Italians would not leave port, Cunningham devised a masterful plan of attack on the ships anchored at Taranto. In November 1940, bi-plane torpedo bombers were launched from a carrier and their attacks were very successful, sinking or damaging many battleships and cruisers. The Italian fleet was not a major factor during the remainder of the war. One indirect result of the attack was that officers of the Japanese Imperial Navy reviewed the outcome and decided that an attack on the American naval base at Pearl Harbor, Hawaii would be feasible. Cunningham also commanded the Mediterranean fleet in action during the German invasion of Crete, suffering heavy losses to his cruisers and destroyers. In 1942, he was named commander of all naval forces for Operation Torch, the invasion of North Africa, and for Operation Husky in 1943, the invasion of Sicily. In the fall of 1943, following the death of Admiral Sir Dudley Pound, Cunningham was appointed First Sea Lord of the Admiralty, the top-ranking position in the Royal Navy. Recommended for reading are Sir Cunningham's autobiography, *A Sailor's Odyssey*, and Oliver Warner's *Admiral of the Fleet*.

Bibliography

Cunningham, Andrew Browne. *A Sailor's Odyssey: The Autobiography of Admiral of the Fleet, Cunningham of Hyndhope*. New York: Dutton, 1951.

Ollard, Richard Lawrence. *Fisher and Cunningham: A Study in the Personalities of the Churchill Era*. London: Constable, 1991.

Pack, S. W. C. *Cunningham the Commander*. London: B. T. Batsford, 1974.

Warner, Oliver. *Admiral of the Fleet: Cunningham of Hyndhope, The Battle for the Mediterranean, A Memoir*. Athens, OH: Ohio University Press, 1967.

Major General Sir Francis De Guingand
British Army
1900-1979

De Guingand served in military intelligence before he assumed the post of chief of staff of the British Eighth Army in July 1942. In August, General (later Field Marshal) Bernard Montgomery assumed command of the Eighth Army and the two immediately got along very well. Montgomery had such confidence in De Guingand's planning abilities that De Guingand planned the initial stages of the Eighth Army's role in Operation Husky, the invasion of Sicily, while Montgomery concentrated on the campaign in Tunisia. When Montgomery assumed command of the 21st Army Group in Northwest Europe, De Guingand came with him as his chief of staff. De Guingand spent much of his time serving as a mediator between Montgomery and General Dwight Eisenhower, Supreme Allied Commander of the Allied Expeditionary Force. The two commanders had decidedly different opinions concerning the strategic operations to liberate Europe and defeat Nazi Germany. Any of the works published by General De Guingand are recommended for reading. They relate his exploits during the Second World War and of the contact he had with the Allies' top military commanders. Charles Richardson's *Send for Freddie* is also recommended.

Bibliography

De Guingand, Francis. *From Brass Hat to Bowler Hat*. London: N. Hamilton, 1979.
_____. *Generals at War*. London: Hodder & Stoughton, 1964.
_____. *Operation Victory*. New York: Charles Scribner's Sons, 1947.
Richardson, Charles. *Send for Freddie: The Story of Monty's Chief of Staff, Major-General Sir Francis de Guingand*. London: Kimber, 1987.

Field Marshal Sir John Greer Dill
British Army
1881-1944

Dill commanded the Ist Corps of the British Expeditionary Force when the war began in 1939. In April 1940, he returned to England to become Deputy Chief of the Imperial General Staff. In May 1940, he became Chief of the Imperial General Staff, the same month that Germany invaded France and the Low Countries. During his tenure as CIGS, he was constantly at odds with Prime Minister Winston Churchill. Dill urged caution in strategic planning and rarely favoured Churchill's plans of action which he considered to be risky and dangerous. The pressures of the post finally forced Dill to resign in December 1941. He was replaced by Field Marshal Sir Alan Brooke. Dill then became the top-ranking British member of the Allied Combined Chiefs of Staff. He achieved great cooperation with his American counterparts during the time he served, especially with President Franklin D. Roosevelt, General George Marshall, and Admiral Ernest King. Unfortunately, Dill died in November 1944 and did not see the successful conclusion of the war. Because of Dill's special relationship with his American Allies, the president and the US military arranged for him to be buried in Arlington National Cemetery. Alex Danchev's *Very Special Relationship* is recommended for reading about the career of Field Marshal Sir John Dill.

Bibliography

Danchev, Alex. *Very Special Relationship: Field Marshal Sir John Dill and the Anglo-American Alliance, 1941-44.* London: Brassey's Defence Publishers, 1986.

Dykes, Vivian. *Establishing the Anglo-American Alliance.* London: Brassey's, 1990.

Parker, Sally Lister. "*Attendant Lords: A Study of the British Joint Staff Mission in Washington, 1941-1945.*" Ph.D. diss., University of Maryland, 1984. (DAI, 46:2, 500A, UMI Order # DA8508512)

Douglas of Kirtleside, 1st Baron
Marshal of the Royal Air Force Baron Sholto Douglas
Royal Air Force
1893-1969

Douglas replaced Air Chief Marshal Sir Hugh Dowding as Commander-in-Chief Fighter Command following the Battle of Britain in November 1940. Douglas commanded the fighters until January 1943 when he transferred to the Middle East, assuming the commander-in-chief position there. In 1944, he was head of the Coastal Command and helped plan air operations for Operation Overlord, the invasion of France. At the conclusion of the war, he was the British member on the Allied Control Council for Germany. His duty was to confirm the death sentences of Nazi war criminals tried at Nuremberg. Ultimately, he reached the rank of Marshal of the Royal Air Force. Marshal Douglas' *Years of Command* is recommended for reading.

Bibliography

Douglas, Sholto. *Years of Combat: The First Volume of the Autobiography of Sholto Douglas.* London: Collins, 1963.

______. *Years of Command: The 2nd Volume of the Autobiography of Sholto Douglas, Marshal of the Royal Air Force, Lord Douglas of Kirtleside, G.C.B., M.C., D.F.C.* London: Collins, 1966.

Lord Dowding of Bentley Priory
Air Chief Marshal Sir Hugh C. T. Dowding
Royal Air Force
1882-1970

Dowding is most remembered for his leadership during the Battle of Britain in 1940. His flying career began during the First World War when he served in the Royal Flying Corps in France. After the war, he was instrumental in the conversion from bi-wing to mono-wing aircraft and the installation of radar stations along the English coast. Both the new planes and the radar stations played major roles during the Battle of Britain. From 1936 to 1940, Dowding was Air Officer Commander-in-Chief Fighter Command. During the Battle of France, he denied Prime Minister Winston Churchill's repeated requests to send more planes to Europe. Dowding believed the fighters would be needed for the defence of Great Britain. The RAF did fly in support of the Dunkirk evacuation. When the Battle of Britain began in late summer 1940, Dowding worked tirelessly as he positioned his fighters to attack the invading German Luftwaffe. The air victory achieved by the RAF halted the threat of a seaborne invasion by the German Army. Shortly after the conclusion of the Battle of Britain, Dowding was replaced by Air Marshal Sir Sholto Douglas. Dowding retired from active service in 1942. Only after the war did Dowding receive the credit he merited for his leadership during the Battle of Britain. Recommended for reading are Basil Collier's *Leader of the Few*, Lord Dowding's *Twelve Legions of Angels*, and Robert Wright's *The Man Who Won the Battle of Britain*.

Bibliography

Collier, Basil. *Leader of the Few: The Authorized Biography of Air Chief Marshal the Lord Dowding of Bentley Priory, G.C.B., G.C.V.O., C.M.G.* London: Jarrolds, 1957.

Dowding, Hugh C. T. *Twelve Legions of Angels*. London: Jarrolds, 1946.

Wright, Robert. *The Man Who Won the Battle of Britain*. New York: Scribner, 1969.

1st Baron of Wellington and Munstead
Lieutenant General Lord Freyberg
(Bernard Freyberg)
New Zealand Army
1889-1963

Freyberg's remarkable military career began during the First World War. He received the Victoria Cross for gallantry in action in December 1917. He was wounded a total of twelve times during his many years of combat in both world wars.   During the Second World War, he fought campaigns in North Africa, Greece, Crete, Sicily, and Italy. His New Zealand troops inflicted heavy casualties against German paratroopers during the Crete campaign. One controversial episode of his career was his insistence that the Monte Cassino abbey in Italy be bombed. The centuries-old abbey was destroyed and the Germans later used the ruins as defensive positions. The fight to evict them was very hard. Still, Freyberg was very popular with his troops, very brave in battle, and had a remarkable career that spanned two world wars. Recommended for reading are Laurie Barber's and John Tonkin-Covell's *Freyberg* and Paul Freyberg's *Bernard Freyberg, VC*.

Bibliography

Barber, Laurie and John Tonkin-Covell. *Freyberg: Churchill's Salamander*. Auckland: Century Hutchinson, 1989.

Freyberg, Paul. *Bernard Freyberg, VC: Soldier of Two Nations*. London: Hodder & Stoughton, 1991.

Hercus, Alan. *Lieutenant-General Sir Bernard Freyberg*. Wellington: A. H. & A. W. Reed, 1946.

Singleton-Gates, Peter. *General Lord Freyberg, VC: An Unofficial Biography*. London: M. Joseph, 1963.

Stevens, W. (William) G. *Freyberg: The Man, 1939-1945*. Wellington: A. H. and A. W. Reed, 1965.

Field Marshal Viscount Gort
(John Gort)
British Army
1886-1946

Gort won several medals for bravery during the First World War. In 1937, he was named Chief of the Imperial General Staff and served until September 1939 when he relinquished the position to Field Marshal Sir Edmund Ironside. Gort was in command of the British Expeditionary Force in France when the Second World War began. Though the BEF was driven from the continent during the Battle of France, Gort's decision to move two British divisions to cover the left flank after the Belgian Army surrendered most likely saved the entire BEF from destruction. He was Inspector General from 1940 to 1941 and then was Commander-in-Chief Gibraltar until 1942. His next post was as Commander-in-Chief Malta. During his time as C-in-C Malta, the intense German aerial bombardment killed or wounded nearly 5 000 civilians and military personnel. The attacks finally ceased in 1943 when all German armed forces surrendered in Tunisia. Gort was promoted to field marshal in 1943, and in 1944, became Commander-in-Chief Palestine. J. R. Colville's *Man of Valour* is recommended for reading.

Bibliography

Colville, J. R. (John Rupert). *Man of Valour: The Life of Field Marshal the Viscount Gort*. London: Collins, 1972.
Kennedy, Joseph P. with James M. Landis. *The Surrender of King Leopold, with an Appendix Containing the Keys-Gort Correspondence*. New York: n.p., 1950.

Marshal of the Royal Air Force Sir Arthur Harris
Royal Air Force
1892-1984

Harris was one of the Second World War's most controversial military commanders. He was promoted to command the Royal Air Force's Bomber Command in 1942 and quickly discarded the method of precision bombing and adopted the method of area or saturation bombing. He became famous for the thousand plane raids he launched against German cities. The purpose was to destroy German industry and demoralize the populace. The raids usually resulted in large civilian casualties. In February 1945, the entire city of Dresden was consumed in a firestorm as a result of air attacks and atmospheric conditions. Harris had many critics of his bombing tactics and of the heavy losses suffered by his bombing crews. His detractors also believed that the large loss of civilian lives was counterproductive and that new bomb-sight technology made saturation bombing obsolete. Recommended for reading are Marshal Harris' memoir, *Bomber Offensive*, Charles Messenger's *"Bomber" Harris and the Strategic Bombing Offensive, 1939-1945*, and Dudley Saward's *Bomber Harris*.

Bibliography

Harris, Arthur Travers. *Bomber Offensive*. New York: Macmillan Co., 1947.

Messenger, Charles. *"Bomber" Harris and the Strategic Bombing Offensive, 1939-1945*. New York: St. Martin's Press, 1984.

Saward, Dudley. *Bomber Harris: The Story of Sir Arthur Harris, Marshal of the Royal Air Force*. Garden City, NY: Doubleday, 1984.

Lieutenant General Sir Brian Horrocks
British Army
1895-1985

Horrocks served as XIII Corps commander, and later X Corps commander, in the British Eighth Army during the North African campaigns until he was wounded. After recovering, General (later Field Marshal) Bernard Montgomery, commander of the British 21st Army Group in Northwest Europe, gave Horrocks command of XXX Corps in August 1944. Horrocks' units made excellent progress in Belgium and Holland after the breakout from the Normandy beachhead until the start of Operation Market Garden. The airborne assault on a series of bridges leading to Arnhem, Holland was overly ambitious and Horrocks' armoured units could not break through to the beleaguered paratroopers fighting for the Rhine River bridge in Arnhem. The paratroopers finally had to withdraw after suffering heavy casualties. In the spring of 1945, after defeating eleven German divisions during the Battle of the Reichwald, XXX Corps crossed the Rhine River and advanced into northern Germany, participating in the final defeat of Nazi Germany. Horrocks was a very energetic commander who led from the front and Montgomery had great confidence in his ability. All the works by Sir Brian Horrocks are recommended for reading. Philip Warner's *Horrocks* is also recommended.

Bibliography

Horrocks, Brian with Eversley Belfield and H. E. Esseme. *Corps Commander*. New York: Scribner, 1977.
_____. *Escape to Action: An Autobiography*. New York: St. Martin's Press, 1960.
_____. *A Full Life*. Rev. ed. London: L. Cooper, 1974.
Warner, Philip. *Horrocks: The General Who Led from the Front*. London: Hamilton, 1984.

Field Marshal Lord Ironside
(William Edmund Ironside)
British Army
1880-1959

Ironside had a distinguished military career prior to the start of the Second World War. In September 1939, he replaced Sir John Gort as Chief of the Imperial General Staff. Gort went on to command the British Expeditionary Force, a position that Ironside coveted, but never received. After the defeat of the BEF in France in May/June 1940, Ironside was replaced as CIGS by Sir John Dill and named Commander-in-Chief, Home Forces. Ironside's diary is recommended for those who wish to learn more about the British General Staff during the years just prior to the Second World War and the first year of the conflict in Europe.

Bibliography

Ironside, Edmund. *The Ironside Diaries, 1937-1940*. Edited by Roderick Macleod and Denis Kelly. London: Constable, 1962.

General Lord Ismay
(Hastings Ismay)
British Army
1887-1965

Ismay was deputy military secretary to the War Cabinet in 1939. When Winston Churchill became prime minister in May 1940, Ismay was named chief of staff to the War Cabinet and held this position until 1945. Ismay performed a vitally important function as liaison between Churchill and the Chiefs of Staff. He handled his duties in a most diplomatic and tactful manner, smoothing over any rough spots that happened to occur, as they inevitably did. In reality, he ran the British war machine from 1940 to 1945. After the war, he was named the first Secretary General of NATO and held the position from 1953 to 1957. Recommended for reading are Lord Ismay's *Memoirs of General Lord Ismay* and Ronald Wingate's *Lord Ismay*.

Bibliography

Ismay, Hastings. *The Memoirs of General Lord Ismay*. New York: Viking, 1960.
Wingate, Ronald. *Lord Ismay: A Biography*. London: Hutchinson, 1970.

Lieutenant General Sir Oliver Leese
British Army
1894-1978

Leese was deputy chief of staff of the British Expeditionary Force in 1940. In 1942, after promotion to lieutenant general, he commanded a corps in the British Eighth Army in North Africa. His units performed very well in the victory at El Alamein and during the subsequent defeat of German forces in Africa in May 1943. He led his corps again during the invasion and conquest of Sicily in July/August 1943 and the invasion of Italy in September 1943. When General (later Field Marshal) Bernard Montgomery left the Eighth Army to return to England to help plan the invasion of France, Leese assumed command. He later left the Eighth Army to be Commander-in-Chief, Allied Landing Forces Southeast Asia. He held this position until the end of the war. Rowland Ryder's *Oliver Leese* is recommended for reading.

Bibliography

Leese, Oliver. *Brief History of the Operation in Burma*. Delhi: n.p., n.d.
Ryder, Rowland. *Oliver Leese*. London: H. Hamilton, 1987.

Montgomery of Alamein, 1st Viscount
Field Marshal Viscount Montgomery
(Bernard Law Montgomery)
British Army
1887-1976

Montgomery is recognized as the most successful of all British generals who commanded armies during the Second World War. After a series of limited victories and defeats in North Africa, Prime Minister Winston Churchill appointed Montgomery field commander of the British Eighth Army in August 1942. After another limited victory at Alam Halfa against the German Afrika Korps, Montgomery built up his army until he achieved overwhelming superiority in armour and artillery. In November 1942, he launched a classic set-piece battle at El Alamein and drove all German and Italian forces into Tunisia. The victory was a stunning achievement, restoring faith in the Churchill administration and giving the soldiers of the Eighth Army confidence in themselves. In the spring of 1943, in concert with other British and American forces, the Eighth Army defeated the German Panzer Army Afrika. Montgomery then played a pivotal role during the planning of the invasion of Sicily. He would not cooperate until his plan was approved. Sicily was conquered in August 1943, but many German troops escaped to Italy via the Straits of Messina to fight again.

During the initial stages of the invasion of France in June 1944, Montgomery controlled all Allied ground forces until General Dwight Eisenhower moved his headquarters to the continent. Montgomery then commanded the British 21st Army Group, consisting of the Canadian First Army and the British Second Army. Fighting was heavy in the British sector and the Americans made bigger gains in the opening months of the campaign, but Montgomery's forces engaged large numbers of German armour and infantry. The one time Montgomery abandoned his cautious character, the operation ended in failure. Airborne forces under his command tried to capture a series of bridges in Holland, the last being at Arnhem. The purpose was to secure passage over the Rhine River into Germany for advancing British armour units. Montgomery had hoped to end the war in the fall of 1944. His forces later assisted those of General Omar Bradley's 12th Army Group during the Battle of the Bulge in December 1944. British troops crossed the Rhine in late March 1945 and controlled northern Germany when the war ended. Montgomery was cautious, extremely methodical in his planning and execution of his strategy, and rarely lost his set-piece battles. He always felt his first obligation was to the men under his command. He was also vain and egotistical and did not get along well with his American Allies or some of his fellow British officers.

Field Marshal Montgomery's *Memoirs*, while possibly over-complimentary of his achievements, is an asset to the field of military history. Regardless of one's opinion of Montgomery, his memoir should be read by anyone interested in the major British land battles in North Africa, Sicily, and Northwest Europe. Nigel Hamilton has written the definitive biography of Montgomery. Hamilton had complete access to Montgomery's private papers which have not been made available to the public. Other works recommended for reading are Arthur Chalfont's *Montgomery of Alamein*, Alistair Horne's and David Montgomery's *Monty*, Ronald Lewin's *Montgomery as Military Commander*, Alan Moorehead's *Montgomery*, and R. W. Thompson's *Montgomery, the Field Marshal*.

Bibliography

Bailey, Eva. *Montgomery of Alamein*. London: H. Hamilton, 1985. (juvenile)

Bellamy, Frank. *High Command: The Stories of Sir Winston Churchill and General Montgomery*. Dragon's Dream. Distributed by Quick Fox, 1981.

Blaxland, Gregory. *The Plain Cook and the Great Showman: The First and Eighth Armies in North Africa*. London: Kimber, 1977.

Brett-James, Antony. *Conversations with Montgomery*. London: Kimber, 1984.

Chalfont, Arthur. *Montgomery of Alamein*. New York: Atheneum, 1976.

Clark, Ronald William. *Montgomery of Alamein*. New York: Roy Publishers, 1960. (juvenile)

Cummins, Howard W. *Mao, Hsiao, Churchill, and Montgomery: Personal Values and Decision Making*. Beverly Hills, CA: Sage Publications, 1974.

D'Este, Carlo. *Decision in Normandy*. New York: Dutton, 1983.

Fisher, John O. H. *Montgomery of Alamein: The General Who Never Lost A Campaign*. London: Hodder & Stoughton, 1981.

Gelb, Norman. *Ike and Monty: Generals at War*. New York: William Morrow & Company Inc., 1994.

Hamilton, Nigel. *Master of the Battlefield: Monty's War Years, 1942-1944*. New York: McGraw-Hill, 1983.

______. *Monty: Final Years of the Field Marshal, 1944-1976*. New York: McGraw-Hill, 1986.

______. *Monty: The Battles of Field Marshal Bernard Montgomery*. New York: Random, 1994.

______. *Monty: The Making of A General, 1887-1942*. New York: McGraw-Hill, 1981.

______. *Monty: The Man Behind the Legend*. Wheathampstead: Lennard, 1987.

Horne, Alistair and David Montgomery. *Monty: The Lonely Leader, 1944-1945*. New York: HarperCollins Publishers, 1994.

Howarth, T. E. B., comp. *Monty at Close Quarters: Recollections of the Man*. London: Leo Cooper in association with Secker & Warburg, 1985.

James, Meydrich Edward Clifton. *I Was Monty's Double*. London: Rider, 1954.

Jewell, Derek, ed. *Alamein and the Desert War*. New York: Ballantine Books, 1967.

Lamb, Richard. *Montgomery in Europe, 1943-1945: Success or Failure?* New York: Watts, 1983.

Larson, Melvin G. *Field Marshal Bernard L. Montgomery, Man of Prayer*. Grand Rapids, MI: Zondervan Publishing House, 1945.

Lewin, Ronald. *Montgomery as Military Commander*. New York: Stein & Day, 1971.

McGill, Michael C. *Montgomery, Field-Marshal: An Ulster Tribute*. Belfast: The Quota Press, 1946.

McMahon, Timothy L. *Operational Principles: The Operational Art of Erwin Rommel and Bernard Montgomery*. Fort Leavenworth, KS: U.S. Army Command and General Staff College, 1985.

Montgomery, Bernard Law. *Despatch Submitted by Field Marshal Viscount Montgomery of Alamein to the Secretary of State for War, Describing the Part Played by the 21st Army Group, and the Armies Under His Command from D-Day to VE Day*. New York: British Information Services, 1946.

______. *El Alamein to the River Sangro*. New York: E. P. Dutton, 1949.

______. *Forward to Victory: Speeches and Addresses*. London: Hutchinson & Co., 1948.

______. *A History of Warfare*. London: Janes, 1982.

______. *Memoirs*. Cleveland, OH: World Publishing Co., 1958.

______. *Military Leadership*. London, G. Cumberlege: Oxford University Press, 1946.

______. *Montgomery and the Eighth Army: A Selection from the Diaries, Correspondence and Other Papers of Field Marshal Montgomery of Alamein, August 1942 to December 1943*. Edited by Stephen Brooks. London: Bodley Head for the Army Records Society, 1991.

______. *Normandy to the Baltic*. Boston: Houghton Mifflin, 1948.

______. *Organization for War in Modern Times*. Royal United Service Institution Lecture, 12 October, 1955.

______. *The Path to Leadership*. New York: Putnam, 1961.

Montgomery, Brian. *A Field Marshal in the Family: A Personal Biography of Montgomery of El Alamein*. New York: Taplinger, 1974.

______. *Monty, A Life in Photographs: Family, Life, and the Times of Field Marshal the Viscount Montgomery of Alamein, 1887-1976*. Poole, Dorset: Blandford Press, 1985.

Moorehead, Alan. *Montgomery: A Biography*. New York: Coward-McCann, 1946.

Murray, G. E. Patrick. "*Eisenhower and Montgomery: Broad Front Versus Single Thrust, The Historiography of the Debate Over Strategy and Command, August 1944-April 1945.*" Ph.D. diss., Temple University, 1991. (DAI, 52:10, 3704A, UMI Order # DA9207885)

Musgrave, Victor. *Montgomery: His Life in Pictures*. London: Sagall Press, 1947.

Peacock, Irene Cynthia. *Field-Marshal Viscount Montgomery: His Life Told Mainly for the Young Reader*. London: Hutchinson, 1951. (juvenile)

Seth, Ronald. *Montgomery of Alamein*. London: Cassell, 1961.

Somerville, Donald. *Monty: A Biography of Field Marshal Montgomery*. New York: Smithmark, 1992.

Sweet, John J. T. *Mounting the Threat: The Battle of Bourguebus Ridge, 18-23 July 1944*. San Rafael, CA: Presidio Press, 1977.

Thompson, R. W. (Reginald William). *Montgomery*. New York: Ballantine Books, 1974.

______. *The Montgomery Legend*. London: George Allen & Unwin Ltd., 1967.

_____. *Montgomery, the Field Marshal: The Campaigns in North-West Europe, 1944-45*. New York: Scribner, 1969.
Whiting, Charles. *The Last Battle: Montgomery's Campaign, April-May 1945*. Marlborough: Crowood, 1989.

General Sir Frederick Morgan
British Army
1894-1967

Morgan is known for his abilities as an operations planner. In 1942, he was assigned to General Dwight Eisenhower's staff to plan a possible Allied landing in France to coincide with the Torch landings in North Africa. He then worked on the plans for Operation Husky, the invasion of Sicily. After Husky, he was named chief of staff to the Supreme Allied commander who had yet to be chosen. Morgan's task was to begin preparations for a cross-channel assault to land somewhere in France. Initially, Morgan had difficulty because a commander had not been selected. Once General Eisenhower was named, Morgan was able to plan the assault in better detail. Eisenhower also made many suggestions and changed portions of the plan to give it more strength and a better chance of success. Both of Sir Frederick Morgan's works, *Overture to Overlord* and *Peace and War*, are recommended for reading.

Bibliography

Morgan, Frederick Edgworth. *Overture to Overlord*. Garden City, NY: Doubleday, 1950.
_____. *Peace and War: A Soldier's Life*. London: Hodder & Stoughton, 1961.

Earl Mountbatten of Burma
Admiral of the Fleet Lord Louis Mountbatten
Royal Navy
1900-1979

Lord Louis Mountbatten, a member of Great Britain's royal family, was an outstanding military leader during and after the Second World War.

When the war began, he was commander of a Royal Navy destroyer flotilla and aided the evacuation of British troops from Norway when that operation went awry. He next saw action off the coast of Crete in the Mediterranean Sea during which his flagship, HMS *Kelly*, was torpedoed. Afterward, he was named Chief of Combined Operations. He planned the coastal raids at Dieppe and St. Nazairre and contributed to the planning of Operation Torch, the invasion of North Africa in November 1942. In 1943, he was named Supreme Allied Commander of Southeast Asia. Forces under his overall command began a land campaign that finally drove the Japanese out of Burma permanently by early 1945. At war's end, he accepted the surrender of over 750 000 Japanese troops at Singapore. After the war, he was the last Viceroy of India as that nation gained its independence. He later became First Sea Lord of the Admiralty and helped shape Britain's post-war military structure. He was assassinated in 1979 by terrorists of the Irish Republican Army. Recommended for reading are Lord Mountbatten's *Personal Diary*, Richard Hough's *Mountbatten*, John Terraine's *The Life and Times of Lord Mountbatten*, and Philip Ziegler's *Mountbatten*.

Bibliography

Baker, George. *Mountbatten of Burma*. London: Cassell, 1959.

Campbell-Johnson, Alan. *Mission with Mountbatten*. New York: E. P. Dutton, 1953.

Deacon, Richard. *The Greatest Tension: The Bizarre Story of Hollis, Liddell and Mountbatten*. London: Century, 1990.

Dennis, Peter. *Troubled Days of Peace: Mountbatten and South East Asia Command, 1945-46*. Manchester: Manchester University Press, 1987.

Dobson, Julia. *Mountbatten: Sailor Hero*. New York: MacRae Books, 1982. (juvenile)

Dulat, J. S. *Partners in Victory: Mountbatten, Slim and the Campaign in Burma, 1942-1945*. New Delhi: ABC Publishing, 1983.

Evans, William. *My Mountbatten Years: In the Service of Lord Lewis*. Leicester: Charnwood, 1989.

Hatch, Alden. *The Mountbattens: The Last Success Story*. New York: Random House, 1965.

Hough, Richard. *Bless Our Ship: Mountbatten and the Kelly*. London: Hodder & Stoughton, 1991.

_____. *Louis and Victoria: The Family History of the Mountbattens*. 2nd ed. London: Weidenfield & Nicolson, 1984.

_____. *Mountbatten*. New York: Random House, 1981.

Lambton, Antony. *The Mountbattens: The Battenburgs and Young Mountbatten*. London: Constable, 1989.

Mitchell, L. M., ed., and others. *A Summary Catalogue of the Papers of Earl Mountbatten of Burma*. Southampton: University of Southampton, 1991.

Mountbatten, Earl of Burma. *From Shore to Shore: The Final Years. The Diaries of Earl Mountbatten of Burma, 1953-1979*. Edited by Philip Ziegler. London: Collins, 1989.

_____. *Mountbatten: Eighty Years in Pictures*. London: Macmillan, 1981.

_____. *Personal Diary of Admiral The Lord Louis Mountbatten, Supreme Allied Commander, South-East Asia, 1943-1946*. Edited by Philip Ziegler. London: Collins, 1988.

_____. *Post Surrender Tasks: Section E of the Report to the Combined Chiefs of Staff by the Supreme Allied Commander, South East Asia, 1943-1945, Vice Admiral the Earl Mountbatten of Burma*. London: Her Majesty's Stationery Office, 1969.

_____. *Report to the Combined Chiefs of Staff by the Supreme Allied Commander, South-East Asia, 1943-1945*. London: His Majesty's Stationery Office, 1951.

_____. *The Strategy of the South East Asia Campaign: A Lecture Given by Admiral, the Viscount Mountbatten of Burma to the Royal United Service Institution on Wednesday, 9th Oct. 1946*. Ludhiana: Pabreja, 1946.

Murphy, Ray. *Last Viceroy: The Life and Times of Rear-Admiral the Earl Mountbatten of Burma*. London: Jarrolds, 1948.

Pattinson, William. *Mountbatten and the Men of the "Kelly"*. Wellingbough: P. Stephens, 1986.

Ross, Josephine. *Lord Mountbatten*. London: Hamish Hamilton, 1981.

Smith, Charles. *Lord Mountbatten: His Butler's Story*. New York: Stein & Day, 1980.

Swinson, Arthur. *Mountbatten*. New York: Ballantine Books, 1971.

Terraine, John. *The Life and Times of Lord Mountbatten: An Illustrated Biography Based on the Television History*. New York: Holt, Rinehart & Winston, 1980.

Villa, Brian Loring. *Unauthorized Action: Mountbatten and the Dieppe Raid*. Don Mills, Ont.: Oxford University Press, 1989.

Werstein, Irving. *The Supremo: Lord Louis Mountbatten and the Testing of Democracy*. Philadelphia: Macrae-Smith Co., 1971. (juvenile)

Ziegler, Philip. *Mountbatten: A Biography*. New York: A. A. Knopf, 1985.

General Sir Richard O'Connor
British Army
1889-1981

O'Connor was one of the British Army's most aggressive combat commanders. He was in command of the Western Desert Force in 1940 when the Italians invaded Egypt from Libya. O'Connor, under orders from Field Marshal Sir Archibald Wavell, launched a brilliant offensive against the Italians in December 1940. In a campaign that lasted until February 1941, O'Connor's forces captured nearly 80 000 Italians and advanced from Egypt all the way to Agheila, Libya, some 650 miles to the west, capturing the strategic ports of Tobruk and Benghazi along the way. The campaign was a stunning victory for Great Britain and caused the Axis powers to reassess the military situation in North Africa. Adolf Hitler decided to send General (later Field Marshal) Erwin Rommel to North Africa along with several German divisions. When Rommel went on the offensive, General O'Connor was captured as he visited front line positions in April 1941. He was sent to Italy and remained there until he escaped in December 1943. O'Connor was back in command during the land battles in Northwest Europe, leading the VIII Corps until the end of the war. Recommended for reading are C. N. Barclay's *Against All Odds*, John Baynes' *The Forgotten Victor*, and George Forty's *The First Victory*.

Bibliography

Barclay, C. (Cyril) N. *Against All Odds: The Story of the First Offensive in Libya in 1940-41, The First British Victory in the Second World War, Including Many Entrants from the Personal Account by Sir Richard N. O'Connor*. London: Sifton, Praed, 1955.

Baynes, John. *The Forgotten Victor: General Sir Richard O'Connor, K.T., G.C.B., D.S.O., M.C.* London: Brassey's, 1989.

Forty, George. *The First Victory: General O'Connor's Desert Triumph, Dec 1940-Feb 1941*. Turnbridge Wells, England: Nutshell, 1990.

Air Chief Marshal Sir Keith Park
Royal Air Force
1892-1975

Park commanded No. 11 Group during the Battle of Britain in 1940. He and Air Chief Marshal Sir Hugh Dowding deserve the lion's share of praise for the Royal Air Force's victory over the German Luftwaffe. However, he, like Dowding, was removed from command shortly after the battle was concluded. To his death in 1975, Park was very bitter about his removal, feeling it was unjust. His next assignment entailed training potential fighter pilots. Later, he was Air Officer Commanding on Malta during its aerial siege. His excellent abilities were put to good use during the defensive air campaign. In 1944, he commanded RAF units in the Middle East, then became Allied Air Commander for Southeast Asia. He retired in 1946 and returned to his native New Zealand. Vincent Orange's biography is recommended for reading.

Bibliography

Orange, Vincent. *A Biography of Air Chief Marshal Sir Keith Park, G.C.G., K.B.E., M.C., D.F.C., D.C.L.* London: Methuen, 1984.

Lieutenant General Arthur Percival
British Army
1887-1966

Percival began his military career as a private and advanced through the ranks. He served in France with the British Expeditionary Force and was evacuated at Dunkirk. In July 1941, he was transferred to Malaya to command all British troops stationed there. The cornerstone of the British presence in the Far East was the island of Singapore. The defences relied mainly on air and sea power, but there were few suitable aircraft and after HMS *Prince of Wales* and HMS *Repulse* were sunk on 10 December 1941 by Japanese naval planes, the remaining sea forces were negligible. When Japanese forces under the command of Lieutenant General Tomoyuki Yamashita attacked south through the jungle, the British could not stop them. By late January 1942, all British units not yet captured had retreated to Singapore. On 8 February, Japanese troops attacked from the rear. After a week of fighting, Percival felt he could not hold out any longer due to lack of supplies and water. He surrendered his command to Yamashita on 15 February 1942. The loss of Singapore was considered one of the worst defeats in British military history. Percival was sent to a prison camp in Manchuria where he remained until the conclusion of the war. He was released in time to be present at the signing of the Japanese surrender on the USS *Missouri* in Tokyo Bay on 2 September 1945. Though Percival has been blamed for the loss of Singapore, British pre-war strategy has to be held at least partially responsible. Soldiers had not been trained to fight in the jungle, provisions were inadequate, and all major artillery emplacements were pointed out to sea to repel a seaborne invasion that never came. Recommended for reading are General Percival's memoir, *The War in Malaya*, and John Smyth's *Percival and the Tragedy of Singapore*.

Bibliography

Percival, Arthur Ernest. *The War in Malaya*. London: Eyre & Spottiswoode, 1949.
Smyth, John George. *Percival and the Tragedy of Singapore*. London: Macdonald & Co., 1971.

**Admiral Sir Bertram Home Ramsay
Royal Navy
1883-1945**

Ramsay was one of the Royal Navy's finest commanders during the Second World War. Due to his position as Flag Officer Dover, he was in command of the evacuation of the British Expeditionary Force from Dunkirk in May/June 1940. Over 330 000 British, French and Belgian troops were rescued. For his actions, Ramsay was knighted by King George VI. Ramsay planned most of the naval operations for Operation Torch, the invasion of North Africa, and was deputy commander during the operation. He then planned the naval portion of Operation Husky, the invasion of Sicily, and commanded Eastern Task Force during the landings. He was instrumental in planning Operation Neptune, the naval portion of Operation Overlord, the invasion of France in June 1944. His responsibilities included landing five combat divisions onto a hostile coastline and keeping them resupplied and reinforced. The operation was a tremendous success and a credit to his planning and execution. After Paris was liberated in late August 1944, he moved his headquarters there to be closer to the front lines. Unfortunately, Ramsay did not live to see the end of the war. He was killed in a plane crash in January 1945 while on his way to a staff meeting of the 21st Army Group. Recommended for reading are William Chalmers' *Full Cycle* and David Woodward's *Ramsay at War*.

Bibliography

Chalmers, William Scott. *Full Cycle: The Biography of Admiral Sir B. H. Ramsay, K.C.B., K.B.E., M.V.O.* London: Hodder & Stoughton, 1959.
Woodward, David. *Ramsay at War: The Fighting of Admiral Sir Bertram Ramsay, K.C.B., K.B.E., M.V.O.* London: W. Kimber, 1957.

Marshal of the Royal Air Force Sir John Cotesworth Slessor
Royal Air Force
1897-1979

Slessor was Director of Plans from 1937 to 1939. In 1941, he attended the Anglo-American conference in Washington, DC at which the American and British commanders established the Germany-first policy, meaning the majority of the Allied war effort would be directed toward Germany. Japan would be held at bay as best possible, then defeated once Germany was vanquished. After the conference, Slessor commanded No. 5 Bomber Group, then was given the post of Air Officer Commander-in-Chief Coastal Command. His air units played a vital role during the Battle of the Atlantic. The Allies soon discovered that German U-boats were reluctant to attack convoys that were provided with air cover. In January 1944, Slessor assumed the post of Commander-in-Chief Royal Air Force in the Mediterranean Theatre of Operations and the dual post of Deputy Commander-in-Chief Allied Air Forces. In August 1944, his air units participated in the Operation Anvil-Dragoon landings in southern France. After the war, Slessor became Chief of the Air Staff, serving from 1950 to 1952, and retired with the rank of Marshal of the Royal Air Force. His autobiography, *The Central Blue*, is recommended for reading about his career in the RAF.

Bibliography

Slessor, John Cotesworth. *The Central Blue: Autobiography*. New York: Praeger, 1957.

______. *These Remain: A Personal Anthology: Memories of Flying, Fighting and Field Sports*. London: Joseph, 1969.

Viscount Slim of Burma
Field Marshal Lord Slim
(William Slim)
British Army
1891-1970

Slim was one of the outstanding commanders of the Second World War. He was a division commander in the Sudan when the war began. His troops performed impressively and defeated their Italian counterparts in numerous engagements. In 1942, Slim headed the operation that secured Iran and its vital oil deposits for the Allies. For this achievement, he was promoted to corps commander and sent to Burma. When he arrived, all Allied forces were in full retreat and he had to rebuild his command in India rather than in Burma. In late 1943, he launched an operation that ultimately became the largest Allied victory against Japanese forces during the war. Burma was recaptured and the overland Burma Road to China was re-opened. Late in the war, he was promoted to Commander-in-Chief of Allied Land Forces in Southeast Asia. Recommended for reading are Geoffrey Evans' *Slim as Military Commander*, Ronald Lewin's *Slim, the Standardbearer* and Field Marshal Slim's *Unofficial History*.

Bibliography

Abhyankar, M. G. *The War in Burma, 1943-45*. 5th ed. Dehra Dunn, India: Natraj Publishers, 1977. (A biography of General Sir William Joseph Slim is included, pp. 173-204.)

Brinkley, Phillip L. *The Operational Commander's Will: An Intangible Element in Victory*. Fort Leavenworth, KS: School of Advanced Military Studies, U.S. Army Command and General Staff College, 1987.

Brown, Mary L. Field Marshal William J. *Slim: Evolution of A General*. Quantico, VA: Marine Corps Command and Staff College, 1986.

Calvert, Michael. *Slim*. New York: Ballantine Books, 1973.

Dulat, J. S. *Partners in Victory: Mountbatten, Slim and the Campaign in Burma, 1942-1945*. New Delhi: ABC Publishing, 1983.

Evans, Geoffrey. *Slim as Military Commander*. Princeton, NJ: Van Nostrand, 1969.

Lewin, Ronald. *Slim, the Standardbearer: A Biography of Field-Marshal the Viscount Slim, K.G., G.C.B., G.C.M.G., G.C.V.O., G.B.E., D.S.O., M.C.* Hamden, CT: Archon Books, 1976.

Slim, William. *Defeat Into Victory*. New York: David McKay, 1961.

______. *Unofficial History*. New York: David McKay, 1959.

Marshal of the Royal Air Force Lord Tedder, 1st Baron
(Arthur Tedder)
Royal Air Force
1890-1967

Tedder, as Commander-in-Chief of the Middle East Air Force, perfected the method of pattern or carpet bombing. He believed that air superiority was the key to ground combat success and was known for his ability to work in close cooperation with ground commanders to maximize the use of his bombers and fighter planes. In 1942, he became deputy commander in charge of air operations in Tunisia and continued the role in 1943 in Sicily and Italy. In 1944, he was named deputy air commander for Operation Overlord, the invasion of France. His forces were given the task of isolating the battlefield to deny the Germans the opportunity to reinforce their coastal units. By the end of the war, he was in command of all Allied air forces operating in Northwest Europe. Tedder worked closely with General Dwight Eisenhower in fostering a good working relationship between American and British officers in the Allied high command. Lord Tedder's memoir, *With Prejudice*, and *Air Power in War* are recommended for reading.

Bibliography

Owen, Roderic. *Tedder*. London: Collins, 1952.

Tedder, Arthur William. *Air Power in War*. London: Hodder & Stoughton, 1948.

______. *With Prejudice: The War Memoirs of Marshal of the Royal Air Force, Lord Tedder*. Boston: Little, Brown, 1966.

Admiral of the Fleet Sir Philip Vian
Royal Navy
1894-1968

Vian was a destroyer captain at the start of the Second World War. He was in command of the destroyer flotilla that captured the German supply ship *Altmark* in a Norwegian fiord. Nearly 300 British sailors were rescued who had been captured earlier as a result of the raiding exploits of the German pocket battleship *Admiral Graf Spee*. The Nazi government protested that Vian had violated the neutrality of Norway when he ordered his sailors to board the *Altmark*. Despite the protests, the sailors remained free. Vian was in command of the 4th destroyer flotilla during the successful hunt and sinking of the German battleship *Bismarck*. Following promotion to rear admiral, Vian's next assignment was command of a cruiser squadron in the Mediterranean Sea. His cruisers successfully fought off attacks by Italian naval vessels while escorting a much-needed supply convoy to the island of Malta. For his actions during the battle, Vian was knighted. In September 1943, Vian commanded an aircraft carrier force during the Salerno, Italy landings. During the invasion of France in June 1944, he commanded the naval force that screened the landing armada. In 1945, Vian was transferred to the Pacific Theatre of Operations to command a British carrier force that participated in the Okinawa campaign. After the war, he commanded the Home Fleet and was Admiral of the Fleet. Vian's memoir, *Action This Day*, is recommended for reading.

Bibliography

Vian, Philip. *Action This Day: A War Memoir*. London: F. Muller, 1960.

Field Marshal Earl Wavell
(Archibald Percival Wavell)
British Army
1883-1950

Wavell was responsible for victories over the Italians in North Africa during the first year of the war. However, his inability to defeat the Afrika Korps once it landed in North Africa and the defeat of British troops he sent to Greece, caused Prime Minister Winston Churchill to lose faith in his ability. He was transferred to the Far East just prior to the Japanese invasion of Malaya. His troops were quickly defeated and most were captured when Lieutenant General Arthur Percival surrendered at Singapore. After this defeat, Wavell was placed in charge of military operations in India until 1943 when he was given the post of Viceroy of India, a mostly political position. Recommended for reading are John Connell's two-volume set *Wavell* and Ronald Lewin's *The Chief*.

Bibliography

Arthur, George Compton Archibald. *From Wellington to Wavell*. London: Hutchinson & Co. Ltd., 1942.

Burbidge, William Frank. *The Military Viceroy*. London: J. Crowther, 1943.

Carver, Michael. *Wavell and the War in the Middle East, 1940-1941*. College of Liberal Arts, Harry Ransom Humanities Research Center, The University of Texas at Austin, 1993.

Collins, Robert J. *Lord Wavell, 1883-1941: A Military Biography*. London: Hodder & Stoughton, 1948.

Connell, John. *Wavell: Scholar and Soldier. To June 1941*. London: Collins, 1964.

_____. *Wavell: Supreme Commander, 1941-1943*. Edited and completed by Michael Roberts. London: Collins, 1969.

Cowie, Donald. *The Campaigns of Wavell*. London: Chapman & Hall Ltd., 1942.

DeWeerd, H. A. "Wavell's Middle East Command." *Infantry Journal* 49 (September 1941): 2-13.

Fergusson, Bernard. *Wavell: Portrait of A Soldier*. London: Collins, 1961.

Jinnah, Mahomed Ali. *Jinnah-Wavell Correspondence, 1943-1947*. Edited by Sher Muhammad Gerewal. Lahore: Research Society of Pakistan, University of the Punjab, 1986.

Kiernan, Reginald Hugh. *Wavell*. London: G. G. Harrap, 1946.

Lewin, Ronald. *The Chief: Field Marshal Lord Wavell, Commander-in-Chief and Viceroy, 1939-1947*. New York: Farrar, Straus, Giroux, 1980.

Quantrill, John R. *Churchill and Wavell: A Study in Political/Military Relationships*. Carlisle Barracks, PA: U.S. Army War College, 1990.

Raugh, Harold Ernest, Jr. *"Wavell in the Middle East, 1939-1941: A Study in Generalship."* Ph.D. diss., University of California at Los Angeles, 1991. (DAI, 52:3, 1046A, UMI Order # DA9122719)

______. *Wavell in the Middle East, 1939-1941. A Study in Generalship.* London: Brassey's, 1993.

Rowan-Robinson, Henry. *Wavell in the Middle East.* London: Hutchinson & Co., 1942.

Wavell, Archibald Percival. *Generals and Generalship. The Lees Knowles Lectures Delivered at Trinity College, Cambridge, in 1939.* New York: Macmillan, 1941.

______. *The Good Soldier.* London: Macmillan, 1948.

______. *Soldiers and Soldiering.* London: Cape, 1953.

______. *Speaking Generally: Broadcasts, Orders and Addresses in Time of War (1939-1943).* London: Macmillan, 1946.

______. *Speeches by Earl Wavell. From 26th October 1943 to 21st March 1947.* New Delhi: Superintendent Government-General's Press, 1948.

______. *Wavell: The Viceroy's Journal.* Edited by Penderel Moon. London: Oxford University Press, 1973.

Woollcombe, Robert. *The Campaigns of Wavell, 1939-1943.* London: Cassell, 1959.

**Field Marshal Lord Wilson, 1st Baron
(Henry Maitland Wilson)
British Army
1881-1964**

Wilson never experienced spectacular success on the battlefield, but performed his duties in a competent manner throughout the Second World War. When the war began, he was General Officer Commander-in-Chief Egypt. In 1941, he was in charge of the abortive mission to rescue Greece from the German invasion. Wilson handled the evacuation of British forces from Greece in commendable fashion. After holding various posts in the Middle East, he was appointed Commander-in-Chief Middle East in 1943. Wilson then succeeded Field Marshal Sir Harold Alexander in 1944 as Supreme Allied Commander, Mediterranean Theatre and was promoted to field marshal. In 1945, after the death of Field Marshal Sir John Dill, Wilson went to Washington, DC to head the British Joint Staff Mission and remained until 1947. His memoir, *Eight Years Overseas, 1939-1947*, is recommended for reading about his military career.

Bibliography

Wilson, Henry Maitland. *Eight Years Overseas, 1939-1947*. New York: Hutchinson, 1948.

_____. *Report by the Supreme Allied Commander, Mediterranean, to the Combined Chiefs of Staff on the Operations in Southern France, August 1944*. Washington: U.S. Government Printing Office, 1946.

Major General Orde Wingate
British Army
1903-1944

Wingate was the British Army's most controversial and unorthodox combat commander during the Second World War. In 1940, he formed the Gideon Force which he used to outfox, bluff, and ultimately defeat the Italians in Ethiopia. After this victorious campaign, he contracted malaria, and, while suffering serious bouts of depression, attempted suicide. After recovering and passing a medical examination, Wingate was sent to Burma. Once there, he created a long range penetration group designed to operate independently behind Japanese lines. His unit was popularly known as the Chindits. In February 1943, he launched a campaign deep into Burma. The invasion achieved only limited success, but impressed Prime Minister Winston Churchill. Wingate attended the Quebec Conference in August 1943 and received permission to try a larger assault into Burma. The operation was launched in February 1944. A few weeks later, Wingate was killed in a plane crash. The operation continued and was successful in stopping a Japanese attack on Imphal, India, but nearly all 9 000 Chindits were either killed, wounded, or became medical casualties by the end of the operation. Wingate's entire military career was devoted to irregular operations of one kind or another. Recommended for reading are Leonard Mosley's *Gideon Goes to War* and Christopher Sykes' *Orde Wingate*.

Bibliography

Bidwell, Shelford. *The Chindit War: Stilwell, Wingate and the Campaign in Burma, 1944*. New York: Macmillan, 1979.

Burchett, Wilfred G. *Wingate Adventure*. Melbourne: F. W. Cheshire Pty Ltd., 1944.

______. *Wingate's Phantom Army*. Bombay: Thacker, 1944.

Fergusson, Bernard. *Beyond the Chindwin*. London: A. Mott, 1945.

Hay, Alice Ivy. *There Was A Man of Genius. Letters to My Grandson, Orde Jonathan Wingate*. (A biography of the author's son-in-law, Orde Charles Wingate.) London: Neville Spearman, 1963.

Hertz, Joseph H. *Orde Charles Wingate*. London: Jewish Agency for Palestine, 1944.

Jeffrey, William Frederick. *Sunbeams Like Swords*. London: Hodder & Stoughton, 1950.

Mead, Peter. *Orde Wingate and the Historians*. Braunton, Devon: Merlin Books, 1987.

Mosley, Leonard. *Gideon Goes to War*. New York: Scribner, 1956.

Nath, Prithvi. *Wingate: His Relevance to Contemporary Warfare*. New Delhi: Sterling, 1990.

Palsokar, R. D. *Wingate: The Clive of Burma*. Pune: R. D. Palsokar, 1974.

Rolo, Charles James. *Wingate's Raiders*. New York: Viking Press, 1944.

Rossetto, Luigi. *Major-General Orde Wingate and the Development of Long-Range Penetration*. Manhattan, KS: MA/AH Publishers, 1982.

Sykes, Christopher. *Orde Wingate: A Biography*. Cleveland, OH: World Publishing Co., 1959.

Thomas, Lowell. *Back to Mandalay*. New York: Greystone Press, 1951.

Tulloch, Derek. *Wingate in War and Peace*. Edited by Arthur Swinson. London: Macdonald, 1972.

Verma, Virendra. *Wingate and His Chindits*. Pune: Youth Education Publications, 1974.

14 French Commanders

During the 1920s and 1930s, the French high command devised a military doctrine based on a strategy of static defence and limited offensive capability.   To enforce this doctrine, the defensive Maginot Line was built to protect France's border with Germany.   The fortifications proved to be virtually worthless against the mobile armour warfare the Germans employed when they invaded France via Belgium and Holland. France's military forces were shattered in a matter of days and the government surrendered after six weeks of combat. Only a few military commanders emerged from the humiliating defeat with any honour or reputation. The most notable was General Charles De Gaulle whose bibliography appears in Chapter 6 because he spent most of the war as head of the Free France government. This chapter lists the works about and by the other French commanders who distinguished themselves during the war. The commanders profiled are listed in alphabetical order by their last name.

Admiral Jean Francois Darlan
French Navy
1881-1942

Darlan was commander-in-chief of the French Navy when the war began in September 1939. After the defeat of France in June 1940, Marshal Philippe Petain formed a new French government at Vichy. Darlan accepted the position of Minister of the Navy and moved the fleet to North Africa. The British government then asked for the surrender of the fleet, but Darlan refused. He assured the British that his ships would not fight against Great Britain, but would defend themselves if attacked. However, the British Navy saw the French fleet as a potential threat in the Mediterranean Sea and attacked the ships anchored at Oran and

Mers-el-Kabir, Algeria. Many ships were sunk or damaged and the French suffered many casualties. In February 1942, Darlan was appointed vice-premier to Marshal Petain, but lost this position when Pierre Laval assumed control of the government in April 1942. In compensation, Darlan was named head of all French forces in North Africa. When the Allies invaded North Africa in November 1942, Darlan was in a position to negotiate the surrender of the French forces and began to do so. He announced on 17 December 1942 that all French ships in North African ports would fight for the Allies. Before he could cooperate further with the Allies, he was assassinated by a French monarchist on 24 December 1942. Admiral Darlan was placed in a difficult situation from June 1940 until his death in late 1942. He tried to walk a tightrope between the Allies and the Germans while trying to preserve some autonomy over the forces he commanded. Recommended for reading are Peter Tompkins' *The Murder of Admiral Darlan* and Anthony Verrier's *Assassination in Algiers*.

Bibliography

De Montmorency, Alec. *The Enigma of Admiral Darlan*. New York: E. P. Dutton & Co., 1943.

Melton, George Edward. "*Admiral Darlan and the Diplomacy of Vichy, 1940-1942*." Ph.D. diss., University of North Carolina at Chapel Hill, 1966. (DAI, 27:8, 2482A, UMI Order # 671033)

Mikes, George. *Darlan, A Study*. London: Constable & Co., 1943.

Tompkins, Peter. *The Murder of Admiral Darlan: A Study in Conspiracy*. New York: Simon & Schuster, 1965.

Verrier, Anthony. *Assassination in Algiers: Churchill, Roosevelt, DeGaulle, and the Murder of Admiral Darlan*. New York: W. W. Norton, 1990.

General Maurice Gustave Gamelin
French Army
1872-1958

Gamelin was commander of France's land forces when the war began. His primary duty was to coordinate defensive strategy between the French Army and the British Expeditionary Force. He was unable to respond to the rapid advance of the German Army panzers during the

German invasion of France and was removed from command on 19 May 1940. He was replaced by General Maxime Weygand. A month later France surrendered to Germany. Martin Alexander's *The Republic in Danger* is recommended for reading.

Bibliography

Alexander, Martin S. *The Republic in Danger: General Maurice Gamelin and the Politics of French Defence, 1933-1940*. New York: Cambridge University Press, 1992.

DeWeerd, H. A. "Academic Soldier: Gamelin and the Fall of France." *Infantry Journal* 49 (November 1941): 10-19.

Gamelin, Maurice Gustave. *Correspondence of General Gamelin*. London: Public Record Office, 1985. (microfiche)

Geraud, Andre. *The Gravediggers of France: Gamelin, Daladier, Reynaud, Petain, and Lavel: Military Defeat, Armistice, Counter-revolution*. Garden City, NY: Doubleday, Doran, 1944.

General Henri Giraud
French Army
1879-1949

Giraud was commander of the French Seventh Army when German forces invaded France in May 1940. His units were routed and he was captured on 19 May and imprisoned at Konigstein, Germany. On 21 April 1942, he escaped to Switzerland and then returned to Vichy France. He was smuggled out of France to Gibraltar by the Allies in hope that he could persuade French forces in North Africa not to resist the Allied landings during Operation Torch. However, he had no real political or military power and was ineffective. After Admiral Jean Darlan was murdered in December 1942, Giraud was named High Commissioner of French North and West Africa. General Charles De Gaulle saw him as a political rival and the western Allies played the two men off one another, naming them joint Presidents of the Committee of National Liberation. De Gaulle proved to be much more politically adept and constantly out-maneuvered Giraud. Giraud finally resigned in April 1944, leaving De Gaulle as the political heir apparent of post-war France. Only one book was found concerning the career of General Giraud. It is listed in the following bibliography.

Bibliography

Price, G. (George) Ward. *Giraud and the African Scene*. New York: Macmillan, 1944.

Marshal Alphonse Pierre Juin
French Army
1888-1967

Juin was in command of the French Army's 15th Motorized Infantry Division when German armed forces invaded France on 10 May 1940. His division fought very well before being surrounded and forced to surrender at Lilly, France. Juin spent the next year as a prisoner of war before being released at the request of Marshal Philippe Petain, head of the Vichy government. Petain then placed Juin in command of Vichy French land forces in North Africa. When the Allies invaded North Africa in November 1942, Juin immediately joined the Allied cause and fought against the Germans in North Africa until they were defeated in May 1943. Juin then commanded a French corps in Italy. He was promoted to chief of staff of the French National Defence in 1944 and held this position until 1947. From 1951 to 1956, he was Commander-in-Chief, NATO Land Forces, Central Europe. He was promoted to Marshal of France in 1952. Anthony Clayton's *Three Marshals of France* is recommended for reading.

Bibliography

Clayton, Anthony. *Three Marshals of France: Leadership After Trauma*. London: Brassey's, 1992.

Marshal Jean Marie De Lattre De Tassigny
French Army
1889-1952

De Lattre de Tassigny was a combat veteran of the First World War, during which he was wounded four times. He was an aide to General Maxime Weygand in the 1930s until Weygand's retirement in 1935. De

Lattre then transferred to the staff of General Alphonse Georges, who was chief assistant to General Maurice Gamelin, the new commander-in-chief of the French Army. When German forces invaded France in May 1940, de Lattre was given command of the French 14th Infantry Division. His troops fought well against the Germans but had to retreat south as the campaign progressed. His units were still intact when the armistice was signed on 22 June 1940. The new Vichy government gave de Lattre a position in the small French Army that was formed after the surrender. He was arrested in late 1942 when he tried to resist the takeover of the interior of France by the German Army. He soon escaped and made his way to Algiers. Upon his arrival, he was given command of the French First Army. In Operation Anvil-Dragoon, his troops, in conjunction with the U.S. Seventh Army, invaded southern France in August 1944. Once on shore, his units quickly advanced into the Alsace region and to the German border. A large German counter-attack was defeated in the winter and by spring 1945, de Lattre's troops were across the Rhine River and moving into southern Germany. After the war, he held several major positions in the French Army and NATO. He died in 1952 and was posthumously promoted to Marshal of France. Recommended for reading are Marshal de Lattre's *The History of the First French Army*, Anthony Clayton's *Three Marshals of France*, and Guy Salisbury-Jones' *So Full A Glory: A Life of Marshal de Lattre de Tassigny*.

Bibliography

Clayton, Anthony. *Three Marshals of France: Leadership After Trauma*. London: Brassey's, 1992.

Lattre de Tassigny, Jean de. *The History of the First French Army*. Translated by Malcolm Barnes. London: Allen & Unwin, 1952.

Salisbury-Jones, Guy. *So Full A Glory: A Life of Marshal de Lattre de Tassigny*. London: Weidenfeld, 1954.

Marshal Philippe LeClerc De Harteclocque
French Army
1902-1947

Leclerc had many adventures during the German invasion of France in 1940. He was captured, escaped and rejoined the French Army, was captured a second time, escaped a second time, and finally made his way to England to join Charles De Gaulle's Free France forces. At this time he assumed the name Leclerc to avoid any potential reprisals against his family by the occupying German forces. De Gaulle sent Leclerc to French Chad to be military governor and to command the French Equatorial African Forces. In late 1942, his troops crossed the Sahara Desert, destroying Italian forces along the way, and linked up with the British Eighth Army at Tripoli. During the invasion and liberation of France, Leclerc commanded the French 2nd Armoured Division. His troops fought well, restoring some of the national honour that had been lost during the 1940 defeat. Leclerc was given the honour of leading French troops into Paris and accepted the German surrender of the city. After the war, Leclerc was commander of French forces in Indochina during 1945 and 1946. In 1947, while conducting his duties as Inspector of Land Forces, French North Africa, he was killed in an airplane crash in Algeria. Leclerc was posthumously promoted to Marshal of France in 1952. Recommended for reading are Anthony Clayton's *Three Marshals of France* and Henry Maule's *Out of the Sand*.

Bibliography

Clayton, Anthony. *Three Marshals of France: Leadership After Trauma.* London: Brassey's, 1992.
Maule, Henry. *Out of the Sand: The Epic Story of General LeClerc and the Fighting Free French.* London: Oldhams, 1966.

General Maxine Weygand
French Army
1867-1965

Weygand was one of France's best generals in both the First and Second World Wars. During the First World War, he was Marshal Ferdinand Foch's chief of staff. Retired at the beginning of the Second World War, he was re-activated and given command of French troops in Syria and Lebanon. When General Maurice Gamelin proved unable to stop the German invasion of France, Weygand was promoted to Supreme Allied Commander on 19 May 1940. He immediately established the Weygand Line south of the Somme River, but the British Expeditionary Force and the French First Army were already cut off. When the Germans attacked his line in early June, the units did not hold and Weygand recommended that Marshal Philippe Petain ask for an armistice to avoid further bloodshed. France surrendered on 21 June 1940 and signed an armistice the next day. Weygand was then placed in command of French land forces in North Africa by the Vichy government, but was relieved of duty in November 1941 because of his anti-German views. He was arrested and imprisoned by the Germans in 1942. Released from prison in May 1945, Weygand was returned to France to stand trial for treason against the French state. He was acquitted and freed after the trial. Weygand was a competent general, but had very little time and very few resources to repel the German Army that invaded and ultimately conquered France in six short weeks. General Weygand's memoir, *Recalled to Service*, is recommended for reading.

Bibliography

Bankwitz, Philip C. *Maxime Weygand and Civil Military Relations in Modern France*. Cambridge, MA: Harvard University Press, 1967.
Weygand, Maxime. *Recalled to Service: The Memoirs of General Maxime Weygand*. Translated by E. W. Dickes. Garden City, NY: Doubleday, 1952.
_____. *The Role of General Weygand: Conversations with His Son, Commandant J. Weygand, Jr*. Translated by J. H. F. McEwen. London: Eyre & Spottiswoode, 1948.

15 Soviet Commanders

Colossal battles were fought on the Eastern Front involving millions of soldiers and thousands of tanks and airplanes, but few people know exactly what occurred during the war between Nazi Germany and the Soviet Union. The language barrier and Soviet government secrecy have caused many problems in the publication of books about the war. Primary sources were rarely available for use by western historians. Hopefully, with the recent dissolution of the Soviet empire, more primary material will be made available. Despite these restrictions, there have been a few excellent works published in the English language about or by the top Soviet military commanders. The most notable were written by Marshal Gerogi Zhukov and Marshal Vasili Chuikov. This chapter lists works about and by the top Soviet commanders who helped guide their country's armed forces to victory over Nazi Germany during four years of the most brutal warfare in the history of mankind. The commanders profiled are listed in alphabetical order by their last name.

Marshal Vasili Ivanovich Chuikov
Red Army
1900-1982

Chuikov was one of the Red Army's top commanders during the war. He is best known for his defence of Stalingrad during the winter of 1942. Ultimately, the German Sixth Army was trapped and over 300 000 troops were killed or captured. The fighting in Stalingrad was intense. Nearly every building in the city was completely destroyed. Chuikov's command, the 62nd Army, was renamed the 8th Guards Army in honour of its defence. The 8th Guards Army participated in the western march to Germany and was involved in the capture of Berlin in April 1945. Both of Marshal Chuikov's works are recommended for reading.

Bibliography

Chuikov, Vasili Ivanovich. *The Battle for Stalingrad*. Translated from the Russian by Harold Silver. New York: Holt, Rinehart & Winston, 1964.

______. *The Fall of Berlin*. Translated from the Russian by Ruth Kirsch. New York: Ballantine Books, 1969.

Zhukov, Georgi, and others. *Battles Hitler Lost; And the Soviet Marshals Who Won Them: Marshals Zhukov, Konev, Malinovsky, Rotmistrov, Chuikov, and Other Commanders*. New York: Richardson & Steirman, 1986.

Admiral Arseni Grigorevich Golovko
Red Navy
1906-1962

Golovko was Commander-in-Chief of the Northern Fleet during the Second World War. The Northern Fleet was responsible for convoy protection in the northern regions of the Soviet Union, the most vital area of Red Navy operations. *With the Red Fleet* is an English translation of the diaries Admiral Golovko kept during the war. Because there are very few English translations of Soviet commanders' writings, this book is an important addition to Second World War literature even though it is at times historically inaccurate and tends to praise all Soviet efforts and downgrade the abilities and accomplishments of the Western Allies.

Bibliography

Golovko, Arseni Grigorevich. *With the Red Fleet: The War Memoirs of the Late Admiral Arseni G. Golovko*. Translated from the Russian by Peter Bloomfield. London: Putnam, 1965.

Marshal Ivan Stepanovich Konev
Red Army
1897-1973

Konev was one of the Red Army's most outstanding generals. He was in command of the Kalinin Front where his forces stopped the Germans from capturing Moscow in 1941 and again in 1942. His units fought at Kursk in July 1943. During the battle, which involved the largest tank assault of the war, the German advance was stopped. His units then counterattacked and captured Orel. Victories continued in 1944 with the capture of Kirovgrad and Lvov. Late in the war, his forces advanced from the Vistula River to the Oder River and then to Berlin. At the conclusion of the war, units of his armies linked up with American troops at Torgau. His final actions as a field commander came when his armies swept south and captured Prague, Czechoslovakia in May 1945. *Years of Victory* relate Marshal Konev's experiences during the Second World War. He was involved in strategic and tactical command decisions during four years of hard fighting where neither side yielded ground without a bloody struggle.

Bibliography

Konev, Ivan Stepanovich. *Marshal Konev's Reminiscences of 1945: USSR*. Washington, DC: U.S. Department of Commerce, Clearing-house for Federal Scientific and Technical Information Joint Research Service, 1965.

______. *Years of Victory*. Translated from the Russian by David Mishne. Moscow: Progress Publishers, 1969.

Zhukov, Georgi, and others. *Battles Hitler Lost; And the Soviet Marshals Who Won Them: Marshals Zhukov, Konev, Malinovsky, Rotmistrov, Chuikov, and Other Commanders*. New York: Richardson & Steirman, 1986.

Marshal Konstantin Rokossovsky
Red Army
1896-1968

Rokossovsky gained his pre-war military experience in the Far East. He survived Premier Josef Stalin's purge in 1938 to become one of the Red

Army's ablest commanders. He was in charge of a Siberian army during the defence of Moscow in the winter of 1941. In 1942, he was in command of the Don Front in the Stalingrad area of operations. His armies broke the Rumanian and Italian divisions that guarded the flanks of the German Sixth Army. As a result, the Sixth Army was trapped and forced to surrender in February 1943. Later in 1943, Rokossovsky commanded the Central Front. During the battle of Kursk, his troops held until the Germans spent themselves, then counterattacked and moved forward to the Dnieper River. In June 1944, two panzer corps were encircled and captured by his troops on the 1st Belorussian Front. By July 1944, his units were near Warsaw, Poland, but when the Polish uprising began, he waited, on orders from the Soviet high command, until the Germans had crushed the resistance. Rokossovsky's offensive resumed in January 1945 and Warsaw was captured. Danzig fell by the end of March and in May, his troops contacted British troops at Wittenberg, Germany. Marshal Rokossovsky's memoir, *A Soldier's Duty*, should be of interest to readers who want to learn more about the tremendous battles that took place on the Eastern Front during the Second World War.

Bibliography

Rokossovsky, Konstantin. *A Soldier's Duty*. Translated from the Russian by Vladimir Talmy. Edited by Robert Daglish. Moscow: Progress Publishers, 1970.

General of the Army Sergei Matveevich Shtemenko
Red Army
1907-1976

Shtemenko, because of his operational planning expertise, was a member of the Red Army's General Staff during most of the Second World War. He also did service at the front during the Polish campaign in the fall of 1939 and during the Russo-Finnish War of 1939-40. He was named Deputy Chief of Operations in April 1943 and Chief of Operations in May 1943. By the end of the war, he was Deputy Chief of the General Staff and had been promoted to General of the Army. Both of his books are recommended for reading.

Bibliography

Shtemenko, S. M. (Sergei Matveevich). *The Last Six Months: Russia's Final Battles with Hitler's Armies in World War II*. Garden City, NY: Doubleday, 1977.

______. *The Soviet General Staff at War, 1941-1945*. Translated by Robert Daglish. Moscow: Progress Publishers, 1975.

Marshal Semyon Timoshenko
Red Army
1895-1970

Timoshenko survived Premier Josef Stalin's purge of the Red Army in the mid-1930s, due in part to his friendship with the Soviet dictator. Timoshenko participated in the occupation of eastern Poland in 1939 and commanded the Red Army units that finally emerged victorious over Finland during the Russo-Finnish War of 1939-40. In May 1940, he was promoted to marshal, named Defence Minister, and was given the task of reorganizing and retraining the Red Army. When German armed forces invaded the Soviet Union on 22 June 1941, Timoshenko was placed in command of the Western Front and ordered to stop the German onslaught. During the early weeks of the invasion, his forces were badly beaten and huge amounts of territory and men were lost. Other generals established defences in front of Moscow which delayed the Germans long enough for winter to arrive. The bitter cold stopped the offensive and gave the Red Army time to prepare a counterattack. In September 1941, Timoshenko was sent to command the South Western Front. His task was to stop the German invasion of the Crimea, but he failed. Sevastopol fell and the Crimea was lost, not to be regained until mid-1944. Timoshenko was then given the Kharkov sector and launched an offensive that was stopped by German units which inflicted heavy casualties on the attacking Red Army units. After this failure, Stalin finally lost faith in Timoshenko, transferring him to the quiet North Western Front. Timoshenko also acted as a roving coordinator for the Soviet High Command, visiting various fronts as the war progressed. He never regained the high positions he had held during the early part of the war. Only two sources were located concerning the career of Marshal Timoshenko.

Bibliography

DeWeerd, H. A. "Timoshenko and the Defensive Phase of the War."
   Infantry Journal 53 (December 1943): 30-38.
Mehring, Walter. *Timoshenko, Marshal of the Red Army.* New York:
   A. Unger, 1942.

Marshal Mikhail Tukhachevsky
Red Army
1893-1937

Tukhachevsky was the Russian creator of the "deep battle" concept of warfare which involved the close coordination of airborne, infantry, armour, and air forces. He was also responsible for the mechanization of the Red Army in the pre-war period. However, he ran afoul of Josef Stalin and was placed on trial for treason in 1937. Tukhachevsky was found guilty and executed by firing squad on 12 June 1937. He is included in this chapter because many of his innovations were implemented during the Second World War by Red Army commanders. Recommended for reading are Thomas Butson's *The Tsar's Lieutenant, The Soviet Marshal* and Richard Simpkin's and John Erickson's *Deep Battle*.

Bibliography

Alexandrov, Victor. *The Tukhachevsky Affair.* Translated by John
   Hewish. London: Macdonald, 1963.
Butson, Thomas G. *The Tsar's Lieutenant, The Soviet Marshal.* New
   York: Praeger, 1984.
Simpkin, Richard and John Erickson. *Deep Battle: The Brainchild of
   Marshal Tukhachevskii.* London: Brassey's Defence, 1987.

Marshal Georgi Konstantinovich Zhukov
Red Army
1896-1974

By the end of the Second World War, Zhukov was the second most powerful figure in the Soviet Union. His official title was Deputy Supreme Commander-in-Chief of the Red Army. He was responsible for grand strategy as well as battlefield command. He first came to prominence in 1939 when he commanded the Far Eastern Soviet forces that decisively defeated units of the Japanese Kwangtung Army in Manchuria. Though the battle was not generally known by most people, Premier Josef Stalin realized Zhukov's potential and promoted him to Red Army Chief of Staff in 1940. When war erupted between Germany and the Soviet Union, Zhukov was placed in charge of the Leningrad defence. Though under siege for nearly 1 000 days, his early defensive efforts secured the city from capture and defeat. In December 1941, he was ordered by Stalin to assume the defence of Moscow which, at this time, was in serious danger of being captured. Zhukov brought in reinforcements from Siberia and counterattacked in the dead of winter, stunning the Germans. Eventually the attack faltered, but Moscow was saved. When the Germans attacked Stalingrad in the fall of 1942, he was placed in command of the sector and organized the counterattacks that by February 1943 had cut off the German Sixth Army and forced the surrender of 300 000 men. He also planned the defensive strategy at Kursk in the summer of 1943 in which the Germans were defeated in the largest tank battle of the war. That fall, his forces regained the Ukraine. In June 1944, he launched an all-out assault that destroyed the German armies in the central sector of the Eastern Front and his units began advancing into Prussia and Poland. Warsaw was captured in January 1945. He personally directed the battle of Berlin as Soviet shock troops captured the Nazi capital, laying waste to much of it. Recommended for reading is Otto Chaney's *Zhukov*. Despite being denied permission to interview Marshal Zhukov or have access to his personal papers, Chaney has written a solid, historically-researched biography of the Soviet marshal. Also recommended are William Spahr's *Zhukov*, and Marshal Zhukov's *Memoirs*.

Bibliography

Chaney, Otto Preston. *"The Contribution of Georgi Konstantinovich Zhukov to the Soviet Scene, 1918-1968: An Appraisal."* Ph.D. diss., The American University, 1968. (DAI, 30:5, 1951A, UMI Order # 6917738)

______. *Zhukov*. Norman, OK: Oklahoma University Press, 1971.

______. *Zhukov, Marshal of the Soviet Union*. New York: Ballantine Books, 1974.

Peterson, Charles L. *Field Marshal Georgi K. Zhukov: A Study of Soviet Operational Command in World War II*. Quantico, VA: Marine Corps Command and Staff College, 1986.

Sethi, A. L. *Marshal Zhukov, The Master Strategist*. Dehra Dun: Natraj Publishers, 1988.

Spahr, William J. *Zhukov: The Rise and Fall of A Great Captain*. Novato, CA: Presidio Press, 1993.

Zhukov, Georgi, and others. *Battles Hitler Lost; And the Soviet Marshals Who Won Them: Marshals Zhukov, Konev, Malinovsky, Rotmistrov, Chuikov, and Other Commanders*. New York: Richardson & Steirman, 1986.

______. *Marshal Zhukov's Greatest Battles*. Translated from the Russian by Theodore Shabad. New York: Harper & Row, 1969.

______. *The Memoirs of Marshal Zhukov*. Translated from the Russian. New York: Delacorte Press, 1971.

16 Yugoslavian Commanders

Marshal Josip Broz Tito is included in the category of Allied military commanders because his Communist partisans engaged many German Army divisions during the Second World War.   After the war, Tito established an independent Communist government much to the displeasure of Soviet Premier Josef Stalin.   A short biographical profile and a bibliography of works about the life of Tito follows.

Marshal Josip Broz Tito
Communist Partisans
1892-1980

Tito was leader of the Communist partisans in Yugoslavia during the Second World War. By 1943, he had gained the support of the Allies in his fight against Germany. Tito excelled as a guerilla leader, only striking the enemy when he had the advantage and retreating whenever he was outnumbered.   His partisans occupied the attention of many German divisions that could have been used on other fronts.   Tito emerged as the postwar leader of Yugoslavia and established a Communist dictatorship independent of the Stalinist government in Moscow. Vladimir Dedijer's *Tito* is recommended for reading. Dedijer was a close friend of Tito and admitted that his biography might appear biased because of their relationship, but he felt he could best relate the life of Yugoslavia's greatest leader. The chapters covering the partisan war against Nazi Germany are of special merit in that Dedijer was an officer in Tito's command and wrote of the events with first-hand knowledge. The biography ends in 1953 with Tito having made a clean break with Stalin and Russian Communism.   Also recommended are Milovan Djilas' *Tito* and Fitroy Maclean's *Tito, A Pictorial Biography*.

Bibliography

Adamic, Louis. *The Eagle and the Roots*. Garden City, NY: Doubleday, 1952.

Aiyer, H. R. *Marshal Tito: (The Story of His Life)*. Malad, Bombay Krishna Raja Publications, 1954.

Archer, Jules. *Red Rebel: Tito of Yugoslavia*. New York: J. Messner, 1968.

Armstrong, Hamilton Fish. *Tito and Goliath: Marshal Tito's Relationship with Soviet Russia*. New York: Macmillan, 1951.

Auty, Phyllis. *Tito*. New York: Ballantine Books, 1970.

______. *Tito: A Biography*. Rev. ed. Harmondsworth: Penguin, 1974.

Banac, Ivo. *With Stalin Against Tito: Conformist Splits in Yugoslav Communism*. Ithaca, NY: Cornell University Press, 1988.

Beloff, Nora. *Tito's Flawed Legacy: Yugoslavia and the West Since 1939*. Boulder, CO: Westview Press, 1985.

Bilainkin, George. *Tito*. New York: Philosophical Library, 1950.

Carter, April. *Marshal Tito: A Bibliography*. Westport: Meckler, 1990.

Clissold, Stephen. *Whirlwind: An Account of Marshal Tito's Rise to Power*. New York: Philosophical Library, 1949.

Dedijer, Vladimir. *Tito*. New York: Simon & Schuster, 1953.

Djilas, Milovan. *Tito: The Story from Inside*. New York: Harcourt, Brace, Jovanovich, 1980.

Franchere, Ruth. *Tito of Yugoslavia*. New York: Macmillan, 1970. (juvenile)

Gibson, Michael. *Tito*. Hove: Wayland, 1981.

Halperin, Ernst. *The Triumphant Heretic: Tito's Struggle Against Stalin*. Translated from the German by Ilsa Barea. London: Heinemann, 1958.

Hout, Louis. *Guns for Tito*. New York: L. B. Fischer, 1945.

Kapetanovic, Nikola. *Tito and His Partisans: What Really Happened in Yugoslavia from 1941 to 1945*. Belgrade: Jugoslovenska Krjiga, 1950.

Lees, Michael. *The Rape of Serbia: The British Role in Tito's Grab for Power, 1943-1944*. San Diego: Harcourt, Brace, Jovanovich, 1990.

Maclean, Fitzroy. *Heretic, the Life and Times of Josep Broz-Tito*. New York: Harper, 1957.

______. *Tito, a Pictorial Biography*. New York: McGraw-Hill, 1980.

Maodus, Stevo, ed. *Tito's Military Accomplishment*. Belgrade: Narodna Armija, 1977.

Markham, Reuben Henry. *Tito's Imperial Communism*. Chapel Hill: University of North Carolina Press, 1947.

Martin, David. *Ally Betrayed: The Uncensored Story of Tito and Mihailovich*. New York: Prentice-Hall, 1946.

Padev, Michael. *Marshal Tito*. London: F. Muller, 1944.

Pavlowitch, Stevan K. *Tito: Yugoslavia's Great Dictator. A Reassessment*. Columbus: Ohio State University Press, 1992.

Roberts, Walter R. *Tito, Mihailovic, and the Allies, 1941-1945*. New Brunswick, NJ: Rutgers University Press, 1973.

Roucek, Joseph S. *Tito: Modern Leader of Yugoslavia*. Charlotteville, NY: SamHar Press, 1973.

Schiffman, Ruth. *Josip Broz Tito*. New York: Chelsea House, 1987. (juvenile)

Stanojevic, Tihomir and Dragan Markovic. *Tito, His Life and Work*. Translated by Ivo Vidan. New York: Vanous, 1964.

Tito, Josip Broz. *The Essential Tito*. Edited by Henry M. Christman. Newton Abbot: David & Charles, 1971.

______. *Selected Military Works*. Translated from the Serbo-Croatian by Kordija Kveder. Belgrade: Vojnoizdavacki Zavod, 1966.

______. *Selected Speeches and Articles, 1941-1961*. Translated by Dorian Cooke, et al. New York: Vanous, 1964.

______. *Tito's Historical Decisions, 1941-45*. Translated from the Serbo-Croat. Belgrade: Narodna Armija, 1980.

______. *The Yugoslav Peoples Fight to Live*. New York: The United Committee of South-Slavic Americans, 1944.

Vucinich, Wayne S., ed. *At the Brink of War and Peace: The Tito-Stalin Split in A Historic Perspective*. New York: East European Quarterly, 1982.

West, Richard. *Tito and the Rise and Fall of Yugoslavia*. London: Sinclair-Stevenson, 1994.

White, Leigh. *Balkan Caesar: Tito Versus Stalin*. New York: Scribner, 1951.

Yindrich, Jan Holman. *Tito vs Stalin: The Battle of the Marshals*. London: Benn, 1950.

Zilliacus, Konni. *Tito of Yugoslavia*. London: M. Joseph, 1952.

PART IV

AXIS MILITARY COMMANDERS

17 German Commanders

Germany's defeat in 1918 forced the post-war German military commanders to re-evaluate the way in which they would conduct warfare in the future. Unlike the Allies, especially the French, who continued to over-emphasize defensive weapons and tactics, the Germans developed the concept of blitzkrieg warfare. Blitzkrieg, or lightning war, was based upon the principles of rapid movement of armoured units combined with mobile artillery and close air support. German military strategists borrowed many of these concepts from the writings of two British Army officers, B. H. Liddel Hart and J. F. C. Fuller. Victories won by Germany early in the war, notably in Poland, Norway, the Low Countries, France, and Greece, were attributed more to the skilful planning of the German high command rather than to superiority of weapons. After initial success against the Soviet Union in 1941 and 1942, war conditions turned against Germany due to Allied superiority in technology and manpower. Adolf Hitler's belief that German strength and fortitude would eventually overwhelm and defeat the opposition was incorrect. Only the German commanders' abilities as tacticians kept the war going for as long as it did, but once the Allies grasped the finer points of modern mobile warfare, combined with strategic and tactical air support, Germany was defeated. This chapter contains brief biographical profiles and bibliographies of the top German military commanders. Officers are listed in alphabetical order by their last name.

Colonel General Ludwig Beck
German Army
1880-1944

Beck was the German Army's chief of staff during the early years of Adolf Hitler's Third Reich. He resigned his position in 1938 because he believed that Hitler's foreign policy would involve Germany in a war it could not win. During the war, Beck joined a group of officers that opposed Hitler and was a member of the "bomb plot" group that attempted to kill the fuehrer on 20 July 1944. When the attempt failed, Beck was arrested and given the option of suicide. When he failed to kill himself by his own hand, he was shot. While Beck was not directly involved in the war against the Allies, he was chief of staff during the crucial period of the 1930s when Hitler rearmed Germany and he was a conspirator in the attempt to kill Hitler in 1944. For these reasons, he is included in this bibliography. Nicholas Reynolds has written, to this compiler's knowledge, the only English-language biography of General Beck. Reynolds made use of many German documents in his research and analysis of Beck's military career. The biography should be of interest to those readers who desire to learn about Germany's pre-war military structure and those who wish to know more about the plot to assassinate Hitler in 1944.

Bibliography

Reynolds, Nicholas. *Treason was No Crime: Ludwig Beck, Chief of German General Staff*. London: Kimber, 1976.

Field Marshal Fedor von Bock
German Army
1880-1945

Von Bock was one of three field marshals who commanded army groups at the outset of the Second World War. During the Polish campaign of 1939, he commanded Army Group North. During the invasion of France in 1940, he commanded Army Group B and was responsible for the conquest of the Low Countries and the piercing of the French line along the Seine River. His career came to a halt during the invasion of the Soviet Union. In command of Army Group Centre, his troops made tremendous gains early on, but failed to capture Moscow before winter set in. When the Red Army counterattacked in the dead of winter, he was relieved of command. A few weeks later, he was recalled to duty as commander of Army Group South, but disagreements with Adolf Hitler led to permanent retirement in the summer of 1942. Von Bock was killed during the last days of the war when an airplane strafed his car as he attempted to drive to the city of Kiel to meet Admiral Karl Doenitz, the new leader of Germany. Alfred Turney has made excellent use of primary sources to analyze the first six months of Operation Barbarossa as it pertained to Army Group Centre's attack on Moscow. Turney interviewed many German officers after the war and used many captured German documents to support his contention that von Bock's failure to capture Moscow by October 1941 was the turning point of the war. *Disaster at Moscow* is recommended for reading.

Bibliography

Turney, Alfred W. *Disaster at Moscow: Von Bock's Campaigns, 1941-1942*. Albuquerque, NM: University of New Mexico Press, 1970.
______. *"Field Marshal Fedor von Bock and the German Campaigns in Russia: 1941-1942."* Ph.D. diss., University of New Mexico, 1969. (DAI, 30:4, 1513A, UMI Order # 6917736)

Field Marshal Walter von Brauchitsch
German Army
1881-1948

Von Brauchitsch was promoted to the position of Commander-in-Chief of the German Army in February 1938. He and his staff planned the Polish and French campaigns that resulted in brilliant victories for the Third Reich. However, von Brauchitsch's military career came to an abrupt halt in late 1941 when he informed Adolf Hitler that German forces could not capture Moscow and recommended a retreat to more defensible positions. Hitler fired him immediately and von Brauchitsch did not serve for the remainder of the war. The only source found on the career of Field Marshal von Brauchitsch is a master's thesis written by James Carstairs.

Bibliography

Carstairs, James Joseph. *"General Von Brauchitsch: Aspects of His Career as Commander-in-Chief of Hitler's Army, 1938-1941."* M.A. thesis, University of Washington, 1966.

Admiral Wilhelm Canaris
Abwehr, Intelligence Department, German Armed Forces
1887-1945

Canaris was head of the Abwehr, the intelligence branch of the German Armed Forces, from 1935 to 1944. During the Second World War, he walked a tightrope, dispatching spies and saboteurs to aid the German war effort, while, at the same time, aiding a small, but dedicated anti-Hitler group that passed information to the Allies. As head of the Abwehr, Canaris was always at odds with Heinrich Himmler, head of the SS and Gestapo. Their paths crossed many times concerning intelligence matters. Himmler finally got the upper hand when Canaris was forced to retire in February 1944 after another intelligence failure. Though not directly involved in the 20 July 1944 bombing attempt on Adolf Hitler's life, Canaris was arrested on 23 July by the SS. He was able to prolong his execution by feeding his captors bits of information, but was finally killed at Flossenburg concentration camp on 9 April 1945. Recommended for reading are Andre Brissaud's *Canaris*, Heinz Hohne's *Canaris*, and Roger Manvell's and Heinrich Fraenkel's *The Canaris Conspiracy*.

Bibliography

Abshagen, Karl Heinz. *Canaris*. London: Hutchinson, 1956.

Bartz, Karl. *The Downfall of the German Secret Service*. London: W. Kimber, 1956.

Brissaud, Andre. *Canaris: The Biography of Admiral Canaris, Chief of German Military Intelligence in the Second World War*. Translated from the French and edited by Ian Colvin. New York: Grosset & Dunlap, 1974.

______. *The Nazi Secret Service*. Translated from the French by Milton Waldman. New York: Norton, 1974.

Colvin, Ian Goodhope. *Master Spy: The Incredible Story of Admiral Wilhelm Canaris, Who, While Hitler's Chief of Intelligence, Was A Secret Ally of the British*. New York: McGraw-Hill Book Co., 1951.

Hohne, Heinz. *Canaris*. Translated from the German by J. Maxwell Brownjohn. New York: Doubleday & Co., 1979.

Leverkuehn, Paul. *German Military Intelligence*. Translated from the German by R. H. Stevens and Constantine FitzGibbon. New York: Praeger, 1954.

Manvell, Roger and Heinrich Fraenkel. *The Canaris Conspiracy: The Secret Resistance to Hitler in the German Army*. New York: McKay, 1969.

Paine, Lauran. *German Military Intelligence in World War II: The Abwehr*. New York: Stein & Day, 1984.

Time-Life Book Eds. *The Shadow War*. Alexandria, VA: Time-Life Books, 1991.

Whiting, Charles. *Canaris*. New York: Ballantine Books, 1973.

SS Colonel General Josep "Sepp" Dietrich
Waffen-SS
1892-1966

Dietrich was an ardent Nazi and a member of Adolf Hitler's elite bodyguard during the early years of the Nazi party. He participated in the Blood Purge of 30 June 1934 when Hitler had many of his enemies murdered or interned in prison. When German forces invaded the Soviet Union in June 1941, Dietrich commanded units of the Waffen-SS, the military arm of the SS. He served on the Eastern Front for three years until he was transferred to the Western Front where he commanded the Sixth Panzer Army during the Battle of the Bulge (December 1944-January 1945). During the battle, his troops committed atrocities at Malmedy. After the war, he was tried at Nuremberg and sentenced to 25 years in prison, but was paroled in 1955. In 1957, he was tried for his part in the Blood Purge and was sentenced to eighteen months in prison. After serving six months, he was released due to health reasons. Dietrich's sole function as a military commander was to serve Adolf Hitler and do his bidding. Though not displaying any military genius as a strategic planner, Dietrich was an able ground commander. Charles Messenger's *Hitler's Gladiator* is recommended for reading.

Bibliography

Dietrich, Sepp and Joachim Peiper. *War Experiences of General Sepp Dietrich and Colonel Joachim Peiper*. (Written by Dietrich and Peiper as they awaited trial for the Malmedy massacre.) n.p., n.d.

Messenger, Charles. *Hitler's Gladiator: Oberstgruppenfuehrer und Panzergeneral-Oberst der Waffen-SS Sepp Dietrich*. London: Brassey's Defence Publishers, 1988.

Taylor, Blaine. *Guarding the Fuehrer: Sepp Dietrich, Johann Rattenbuber and the Protection of Adolf Hitler*. Missoula, MT: Pictorial Histories Publishing Co., 1993.

Grand Admiral Karl Doenitz
German Navy
1891-1980

Doenitz was commander of all U-boat operations during the first three years of the war. His submarines nearly won the Battle of the Atlantic, sinking Allied shipping vessels at an alarming rate. Only after the Allies employed proper air and sea coverage and improved their sonar detection systems did the tide of battle turn against Germany's submarine forces. In January 1943, Doenitz was promoted to commander-in-chief of the German Navy, replacing Grand Admiral Erich Raeder. In April 1945, Adolf Hitler still had enough confidence in Doenitz, despite the setbacks the navy suffered in 1943 and 1944, to name Doenitz his successor as head of the German government. Doenitz assumed the position on 30 April 1945 and negotiated the surrender of all German armed forces. He was tried at Nuremberg for war crimes and sentenced to ten years in prison. Doenitz' memoirs, either the abridged or complete edition, are recommended for reading. He describes the strategy he devised for U-boat operations against Allied shipping, the wolf-pack method of attack. Doenitz was a skilful commander whose strategy nearly defeated Great Britain during the early years of the conflict. He was one of Germany's highest ranking military commanders and the last leader of the Third Reich, making his memoir an important edition to the literature of the Second World War. Also recommended are Peter Padfield's *Doenitz, The Last Fuhrer: Portrait of A Nazi War Leader* and Marlis Steinert's *23 Days: The Final Collapse of Nazi Germany*.

Bibliography

Doenitz, Karl. *Memoirs: A Documentary of the Nazi Twilight*. Abridgement of *Memoirs: Ten Years and Twenty Days*. Translated from the German by R. H. Stevens and David Woodward. New York: Belmont Books, 1961.

______. *Memoirs: Ten Years and Twenty Days*. Translated by R. H. Stevens in collaboration with David Woodward. Cleveland, OH: World Publishing Co., 1959.

Hoyt, Edwin P. *The Death of the U-Boats*. New York: McGraw-Hill, 1988.

Padfield, Peter. *Doenitz, The Last Fuehrer: Portrait of a Nazi War Leader*. New York: Harper & Row, 1984.

Steinert, Marlis G. *23 Days: The Final Collapse of Nazi Germany*. Translated from the German by Richard Barry. New York: Walker, 1969.

Thompson, Harold Keith and Henry Strutz. *Doenitz at Nuremberg, a Reappraisal: War Crimes and the Military Professional*. New York: Amber Pub. Corp., 1976.

Zabecki, David T. *Karl Doenitz, a Defense*. Bennington, VT: Weapons and Warfare Publications, 1984.

Lieutenant General Adolf Galland
German Air Force
1912-

Galland was one of Germany's top fighter aces during the Second World War with seventy downed planes to his credit. In November 1941, he was named commander of the Fighter Arm and was responsible for the air defence of occupied Europe. During the war, he had numerous disagreements with Adolf Hitler concerning the role of Germany's revolutionary jet fighter, the Me 262. Galland believed that the jet should be used as a fighter, but Hitler saw it more as a bomber. Finally, Galland was relieved of his duties in January 1945 and given command of a Me 262 squadron. The jets were far superior to any plane the Allies had in operation, but were too few in number to alter the air war's outcome. Galland was shot down in an Me 262 on 26 April 1945, only a few days before the war ended. Recommended for reading is Galland's *The First and the Last*. The chapters detailing the production and combat use of the Me 262 are especially interesting.

Bibliography

Galland, Adolf. *The First and the Last: The Rise and Fall of the German Fighter Forces in World War II, 1938-1945*. Translated by Mevyn Savill. New York: Holt, 1954.

______. *The Luftwaffe at War, 1939-1945*. Translated by David Mondey. Chicago: Regnery, 1972.

Held, Werner. *Adolf Galland: A Pilot's Life in War and Peace*. Mesa, AZ: Champlin Museum Press, 1986.

Toliver, Raymond F. and Trevor J. Constable. *Fighter General: The Life of Adolf Galland*. Zephyr Cove, NV: Ampress Pub., 1990.

Reichsmarshal Hermann Goering
German Air Force
1896-1946

Goering falls in the area between a true military commander and a political figure. As the number two Nazi in Adolf Hitler's Third Reich, he held a variety of posts and positions. He created the Gestapo, was Minister of the Interior of Prussia, and was head of the German Air Force (the Luftwaffe). In 1939, Hitler officially named Goering his successor and gave him the title of reichsmarshal. Goering was a legitimate member of the German aristocracy, one of the few Nazis who could claim that distinction. During the First World War, he was a fighter pilot and shot down 22 planes. He commanded the famed Richthofen fighter squadron after Baron von Richthofen was killed in action. As commander of the Luftwaffe during the Second World War, he made many mistakes. His most serious was not developing sufficient numbers of long-range bombers. Tactically, his forces failed to defeat the Royal Air Force during the Battle of Britain in the fall of 1940, causing Hitler to cancel the invasion of Great Britain. Also, during the siege of Stalingrad in the winter of 1942, he pledged that the Luftwaffe would supply the trapped German Sixth Army, but his planes and men were overwhelmed by the brutal Russian winter. Ultimately, the Sixth Army was defeated and over 300 000 German soldiers were captured. Goering was a complex man of many strengths and weaknesses. When the war started to go badly for Germany, he stopped trying to find solutions for reversing the tide and gave in to his indulgences which included plundering occupied Europe of much of its art treasures. After his capture by the Allies at the conclusion of the war, he returned to his former, forceful self and conducted a spirited defence at the Nuremberg trials. He was one of the few Nazis who accepted full responsibility for his actions. For his finale, he cheated the hangman by committing suicide at the conclusion of the trial, swallowing a cyanide capsule that he had hidden in a jar of cold cream. Recommended for reading are Roger Manvell's and Heinrich Fraenkel's *Goering*, Leonard Mosley's *The Reich Marshal*, and R. J. Overy's *Goering, The "Iron Man"*.

Bibliography

Bender, Roger J. and George A. Peterson. *Hermann Goering: From Regiment to Fallschirmpanzerkorps*. Rev. ed. Atglen, PA: Schiffer Publishing, Ltd., n.p. (Reprint of 1975 edition.)

Bewley, Charles Henry. *Hermann Goering and the Third Reich: A Biography Based on Family and Official Records*. New York: Devin-Adair Co., 1962.

Blood-Ryan, H. W. *Goering: The Iron Man of Germany*. London: John Long, 1938.

Butler, Ewan and Gordon Young. *Marshal Without Glory: A Biography of Hermann Goering*. London: Hodder & Stoughton, 1951.

Frischaver, Willi. *The Rise and Fall of Hermann Goering*. Boston: Houghton Mifflin, 1951.

Goering, Emmy. *My Life with Goering*. London: David Bruce & Watson, 1972.

Goering, Hermann. *Germany Reborn*. London: E. Mathews & Marrot, Ltd., 1934.

______. *Hermann Goering*. Report of an interrogation of Hermann Goering. Headquarters, Air P/W Interrogation Detachment, Military Intelligence Service, 1945.

______. *Highlights from the Direct and Cross-Examination of Hermann Goering in the Nuremberg Trials*. Minnetonka, MN: Professional Education Group, 1988.

______. *The Political Testament of Hermann Goering. A Selection of Important Speeches and Articles*. Arranged and translated by H. W. Blood-Ryan. London: John Long, 1939.

Gregory, Frank H. *Goering*. London: Wayland, 1974.

Gritzbach, Erich. *Hermann Goering, The Man and His Work: The Only Authorized Biography*. Translated from the German by Gerald Griffin. London: Hurst & Blackett, 1939.

Hoyt, Edwin P. *Angels of Death: Goering's Luftwaffe*. New York: Forge, 1994.

_____. *Goering's War*. London: Hale, 1990.

Irving, David. *Goering: A Biography*. New York: William Morrow, 1989.

Lee, Asher. *Goering: Air Leader*. New York: Hippocrene Books, 1972.

Manvell, Roger. *Goering*. New York: Ballantine Books, 1972.

_____ and Heinrich Fraenkel. *Goering*. New York: Simon & Schuster, 1962.

Mosley, Leonard. *The Reich Marshal: A Biography of Hermann Goering*. Garden City, NY: Doubleday, 1974.

Overy, R. J. *Goering, the "Iron Man"*. Boston: Routledge & Kegan Paul, 1984.

Singer, Kurt D. *Goering: Germany's Most Dangerous Man*. London: Hutchinson & Co., Ltd., 1940.

Skipper, G. C. *Goering and the Luftwaffe*. Chicago: Children's Press, 1980. (juvenile)

Swearingen, Ben E. *The Mystery of Hermann Goering's Suicide*. San Diego: Harcourt, Brace, Jovanovich, 1985.

Colonel General Heinz Guderian
German Army
1888-1954

Guderian was Germany's leading armour expert at the beginning of the Second World War. In 1937, he wrote a training manual, *Actung! Panzer!*, extolling the virtues of armour in combat. His theories stressed mobility on the battlefield. His corps performed very well during the invasion and conquest of Poland, but he won everlasting fame during the invasion of France. His units broke through the French line at Sedan and crossed the Meuse River in a few days. This manoeuvre cut off the British Expeditionary Force from the main body of French forces. The British retreated to Dunkirk and immediately evacuated the continent. The French Army surrendered a few weeks later. When German armed forces invaded the Soviet Union in June 1941, Guderian commanded the 2nd Panzer Army. His units encircled and captured several Soviet armies at Kiev and Uman, but, like other German armies, failed to capture Moscow before winter began. Guderian was dismissed by Adolf Hitler after disagreement concerning withdrawal and redeployment of his troops and armour. In February 1943, he was recalled to duty and given the title Inspector of the Armoured Troops. After the 20 July 1944 bombing attempt failed to kill Hitler, Guderian was named Chief of the

General Staff as a reward for his loyalty, but Hitler did not accept his advice concerning strategic withdrawals to better protect Germany's borders. Guderian was dismissed for the final time in March 1945. Recommended for reading are Guderian's memoir, *Panzer Leader*, and *Actung! Panzer!*, John Keegan's *Guderian*, and Kenneth Macksey's *Guderian, Panzer General*.

Bibliography

Guderian, Heinz. *Actung-Panzer! The Development of Armoured Forces, Their Tactics and Operational Potential*. Translated by Christopher Duffy. London: Arms & Armour, 1992. (First published in 1937.)
_____. *Panzer Leader*. Translated from the German by Constantine Fitzgibbon. New York: Ballantine Books, 1965.
Higgins, George A. *"The Operational Tenets of Generals Heinz Guderian and George S. Patton, Jr."* M.M.A.S. thesis, U.S. Army Command and General Staff, 1986.
Keegan, John. *Guderian*. New York: Ballantine Books, 1973.
Landry, Vincent J. *Blitzkrieg Masters: Guderian and Patton*. Maxwell Air Force Base, AL: Air Command and Staff College, Air University, 1985.
Macksey, Kenneth. *Guderian, Panzer General*. London: Greenhill Books, 1992.
McLaughlin, James M. *Guderian: A Study in Military Innovation*. Quantico, VA: Marine Corps Command and Staff College, 1986.
Rothbrust, Florian K. *Guderian's XIXth Panzer Corps and the Battle of France: Breakthrough in the Ardennes, May 1940*. New York: Praeger, 1990.

Colonel General Franz Halder
German Army
1884-1972

Halder became Chief of the Army General Staff in 1938. He was involved in the planning of the Polish campaign of 1939, the French campaign of 1940, and the Russian campaign of 1941. The Polish and French campaigns were complete successes while the early stages of the Russian campaign went exceptionally well. However, Halder was never included in Adolf Hitler's inner circle and their continual disagreements over strategic matters eventually led to his removal and forced retirement in September 1942. When the assassination attempt against Hitler failed in July 1944, Halder was arrested. He was interned at Dachau while the Gestapo tried to prove he was an active conspirator. He was released when the camp was liberated in the spring of 1945 and gave valuable testimony at the Nuremberg trials. General Halder's diary is recommended for reading. It is an important primary source concerning the German high command's strategy for the first three years of the war.

Bibliography

Addington, Larry Holbrook. "*General Franz Halder and the German Army and General Staff, 1938-1941.*" Ph.D. diss., Duke University, 1962. (DAI, 23:12, 4663, UMI Order # 633577)

Halder, Franz. *The Halder Diaries: The Private War Journals of Colonel General Franz Halder, Chief of the General Staff, Supreme Command of the German Army (OKH), 14 August 1939-24 September 1942.* 2 volumes. Boulder, CO: Westview Press, 1976.

Reichsfuehrer-SS Heinrich Himmler
SS
1900-1945

Himmler remains one of the most complex figures of the Third Reich long after his death by suicide at the conclusion of the war. He was ultimately responsible for the extermination of the majority of Europe's Jewish citizens, yet he has been described as shy and retiring. Estimates are that his troops and concentration guards murdered more than fifteen million people. At the beginning of the war, Himmler was the second-most powerful person in Nazi Germany. He was head of the Gestapo, the SS, and the Waffen-SS. He later assumed the duties of Minister of the Interior and Commandant of the Replacement Army, and, finally, commanded Army Group Vistula on the Eastern Front. Himmler's expertise lay in his administrative abilities rather than his military abilities, which were mediocre at best. Recommended for reading are Richard Breitman's *The Architect of Genocide*, Roger Manvell's and Heinrich Fraenkel's *Himmler*, Peter Padfield's *Himmler* and Albert Speer's *The Slave State*.

Bibliography

Aronson, Shlomo. *Beginnings of the Gestapo System: The Bavarian Model in 1933*. Jerusalem: Israel Universities Press, 1969.

Breitman, Richard. *The Architect of Genocide: Himmler and the Final Solution*. New York: Knopf, 1991. Distributed by Random House.

______. *Himmler and the Origins of the "Final Solution"*. Washington, DC: Woodrow Wilson Center, Smithsonian Institution, 1989.

Browder, George C. *Foundations of the Nazi Police State: The Formation of Sipo and SD*. Lexington, KY: University of Kentucky Press, 1990.

Combs, George Hamilton. *Himmler - Nazi Spider Man*. Philadelphia: David McKay Co., 1942.

Frischaver, Willi. *Himmler: The Evil Genius of the Third Reich*. Boston: Beacon Press, 1953.

Himmler, Heinrich. *Once in 2000 Years: Secret Speech Delivered by Heinrich Himmler, Chief of the German Secret State Police (Gestapo), to the German Army General Staff*. New York: American Committee for Anti-Nazi Literature, 1938.

Kersten, Felix. *The Kersten Memoirs, 1940-1945*. Translated from the German by Constantine Fitzgibbon and James Oliver. New York: H. Fertig, 1993.

Lee, Robert J. *Fascinating Relics of the Third Reich*. Franklin, TN: R. J. Lee, 1985.

Manvell, Roger and Heinrich Fraenkel. *Himmler*. New York: Putnam, 1965.

Padfield, Peter. *Himmler: Reichsfuehrer-SS*. New York: Holt, 1991.

Smith, Bradley F. *Heinrich Himmler: A Nazi in the Making, 1900-1926*. Stanford, CA: Hoover Institution Press, 1971.

Snodgrass, W. D. *Heinrich Himmler: Platoons and Files*. San Francisco: Pterodactyl Press, 1982.

Speer, Albert. *The Slave State: Heinrich Himmler's Masterplan for SS Supremacy*. London: Weidenfeld & Nicolson, 1981.

United States War Department. *Strategic Services Unit. The Career of Heinrich Himmler*. Washington, DC: The War Department, 1940.

Wulff, Wilhelm. *Zodiac and Swastika: How Astrology Guided Hitler's Germany*. New York: Coward, McCann & Geoghegan, 1973.

Wykes, Alan. *Himmler*. New York: Ballantine Books, 1972.

Field Marshal Wilhelm Keitel
German Army
1882-1946

Keitel was promoted to the position of military advisor to Adolf Hitler in 1938. He retained this position throughout the war. By most observers, he was considered to lack any outstanding military qualities and generally was seen as a yes man for Hitler's ideas and strategy. After the war ended, he was tried as a war criminal at Nuremberg and hanged on 16 October 1946. Keitel wrote his memoirs after the war as he awaited trial. Though he did not command an army, Keitel's role as military advisor to Adolf Hitler makes him an important figure of the Second World War. Keitel's memoir relates what transpired during the conferences Hitler held and the military decisions the fuehrer made.

Bibliography

Keitel, Wilhelm. *The Memoirs of Field Marshal Keitel*. Edited by Walter Gorlitz. Translated by David Irving. New York: Stein & Day, 1965.

Mueller, Gene Albert. *The Forgotten Field Marshal, Wilhelm Keitel*. Durham, NC: Moore Pub. Co., 1979.

______. *"Wilhelm Keitel: Chief of the Oberkommando der Wehrmacht, 1938-1945."* Ph.D diss., University of Idaho, 1972. (DAI, 34:3, 1217A, UMI Order # 7321752)

Schmeller, Helmut J. *Hitler and Keitel: An Investigation of the Influence of Party Ideology on the High Command of the Armed Forces of Germany Between 1938 and 1945*. Hays, KS: Fort Hays State College, 1970.

Field Marshal Albert Kesselring
German Air Force
1884-1960

Kesselring is acknowledged as one of the outstanding military commanders of the Second World War. In 1933, the first year of the Nazi regime, he transferred to the Luftwaffe. When the war began, he was in command of an air fleet and his planes and pilots performed very well during the Polish and French campaigns. During the Battle of Britain, his air forces had nearly defeated the British Royal Air Force when Adolf Hitler, on the advice of Reichsmarshal Hermann Goering, ordered Kesselring to attack the English cities and discontinue direct engagement with the RAF and its airfields and radar stations. This respite allowed the RAF to regroup and the bombing of civilian targets stiffened the will of the English people. By October 1940, the Luftwaffe had lost too many planes and crews to support a seaborne invasion of Great Britain. In 1941, Kesselring was transferred to Italy to take command of all southern European and African Axis forces. He worked with General (later Field Marshal) Erwin Rommel during the North African campaign and tried his best to supply Rommel with enough equipment and men. However, the Eastern Front was a constant drain on Germany's limited manpower and very little was left for other vital areas. North Africa was lost in May 1943 and Sicily was invaded in July. The Sicilian campaign, followed by the Italian campaign, marked Kesselring as one of the true defensive geniuses in modern warfare. Under his direction, German units took every possible advantage of the mountainous terrain, first in Sicily, then in Italy. He gave ground grudgingly, but never allowed large numbers of his troops to be trapped and captured. At the Nuremberg trials, Kesselring was sentenced to death for war crimes, but his sentence was changed to life in prison upon reconsideration by the presiding tribunal. He was released in 1952 for health reasons. Kesselring wrote his memoir after his release from prison. It is an accurate account of his service to his country and to Adolf Hitler. Kesselring was one of Germany's top commanders and occupied the rare dual role of commanding both air and ground units. His memoir is well worth reading. Kenneth Macksey's *Kesselring* is also recommended.

Bibliography

Bitner, Teddy D. *Kesselring: An Analysis of the German Commander at Anzio*. Fort Leavenworth, KS: U.S. Army Command and General Staff College, 1983.

Kesselring, Albert. *The Memoirs of Field-Marshal Kesselring*. Novato, CA: Presidio Press, 1989.

Macksey, Kenneth. *Kesselring: The Making of the Luftwaffe*. New York: David McKay, 1978.

Field Marshal Paul Ludwig von Kleist
German Army
1881-1954

Von Kleist commanded panzer units in four major campaigns in Poland, France, Yugoslavia, and Russia. His panzers won a spectacular victory at Sedan in France, opening the way for the drive to the English Channel. In the spring of 1941, he commanded the German First Panzer Group in Yugoslavia, capturing Belgrade in April 1941. During the opening phases of Operation Barbarossa, the invasion of the Soviet Union, his armoured units advanced into the Ukraine, capturing nearly 700 000 prisoners. In 1942, von Kleist was ordered to capture the oil fields in Baku, but his attempt failed. He was in command of Army Group A during the retreat from the Ukraine in 1944 and was captured by the British in 1945. He was extradited to Yugoslavia where he was convicted of war crimes. In 1949, he was transferred to the Soviet Union and died in a prison camp in 1954. Despite von Kleist's high rank of field marshal, only one biography of his life could be located. Clyde R. Davis has written a short summary of von Kleist's career, consisting of ten pages of text and ninety pages of photographs. The photos are excellent with many depicting the warfare on the Eastern Front from 1941 to 1944.

Bibliography

Davis, Clyde R. *Von Kleist: From Hussar to Panzer Marshal*. Houston, TX: Lancer Militaria, 1979.

Field Marshal Wilhelm Ritter von Leeb
German Army
1876-1956

Von Leeb retired from the German Army in 1938. He was recalled to duty in 1939 and commanded Army Group C during the Polish campaign. In 1940, Army Group C attacked the Maginot Line. This action held large numbers of French units in place and allowed other German panzer units to attack France through Belgium. Von Leeb commanded Army Group North during the invasion of the Soviet Union in 1941. His objective was Leningrad. The city was besieged, but never taken. Adolf Hitler removed von Leeb from command in April 1942 for failure to capture Leningrad. As far as can be determined, a biography of Field Marshal von Leeb has not been written or translated in English. However, von Leeb published a book before the war entitled *Defense*, which was devoted to the art of defensive warfare.

Bibliography

Leeb, Wilhelm Ritter von. *Defense*. Translated by Stefan T. Possony and Daniel Vilfroy. Harrisburg, PA: Military Service Pub. Co., 1943.

Field Marshal Erich von Manstein
German Army
1887-1973

Von Manstein is considered by many historians to be Germany's best ground commander during the Second World War. He developed the alternative plan for the invasion of France in 1940 which called for armoured units to attack through the Ardennes Forest. Military planners on both sides had previously thought that the Ardennes was unsuited for armour traffic because of its dense forest and narrow roads and bridges. Manstein's plan was first rejected by the army high command, due in part to his antagonistic personality, but Adolf Hitler heard about it and called Manstein to Berlin for a conference. Hitler approved the plan and as a result, British and French forces were split apart and the French coast was reached in ten days. The British evacuated the continent at Dunkirk, Belgium, and France surrendered a few weeks later. When German armed forces invaded the Soviet Union, Manstein enjoyed tremendous success. His units captured the Crimea in 1942, nearly relieved the trapped Sixth Army at Stalingrad in the dead of winter, and recaptured Kharkov in 1943 in a brilliant offensive manoeuvre. However, like many other German generals, Manstein fell into disfavour with Hitler when he asked permission to reposition his armies to allow the Red Army to overextend its lines and open itself to counterattack. Hitler was adamant about not retreating one yard on the Eastern Front and saw Manstein's plan as a formula for defeat. Consequently, Manstein was relieved of command in March 1944 and retired to his home for the duration of the war. Manstein wrote his memoir, *Lost Victories*, after the war. Considering the role he played during the war, his memoir contains a wealth of information concerning strategic planning and tactical execution of military operations. Also recommended for reading are Reginald Paget's *Manstein* and Dana Sadarananda's *Beyond Stalingrad*.

Bibliography

Blakemore, Porter R. "*Manstein in the Crimea: The Eleventh Army Campaign, 1941-1942.*" Ph.D. diss., University of Georgia, 1979. (DAI, 39:12, 7475A, UMI Order # 7914015)

Lusey, Rodney S. "*Operational Principles: A Study of General Omar Bradley and Field Marshal Eric von Manstein in World War II.*" M.M.A.S. thesis, U.S. Army Command and Staff College, 1985.

Manstein, Erich von. *Lost Victories*. Edited and translated by Anthony G. Powell. Chicago: H. Regnery Co., 1958.

Paget, Reginald T. *Manstein: His Campaigns and His Trial*. London: Collins, 1951.

Palsokar, R. D. *Manstein: The Master General*. Poona: Colonel R. D. Palsokar, 1970.

Sadarananda, Dana V. *Beyond Stalingrad: Manstein and the Operations of Army Group Don*. New York: Praeger, 1990.

______. "*The Genius of Manstein: Field Marshal Erich von Manstein and the Operations of Army Group Don, November 1942-March 1943.*" Ph.D. diss., Temple University, 1989. (DAI, 49:1, 134A, UMI Order # DA8803841)

Wood, Walter J. *Manstein's Campaigns More Than Tactics*. Carlisle Barracks, PA: U.S. Army War College, 1988.

General of Panzer Troops Hasso von Manteuffel
German Army
1896-1978

Von Manteuffel's combat career began as a battalion commander on the Eastern Front in 1941. By 1945, he was commander of the Third Panzer Army. Promotions came at a rapid rate for von Manteuffel because of his success on the battlefield. Armoured units of his Fifth Panzer Army made the deepest penetrations during the Battle of the Bulge (December 1944-January 1945) on the Western Front. The war ended for von Manteuffel when he surrendered his command to units of the Second British Army. Donald Brownlow has written a short biography of the career of General Hasso von Manteuffel. One of the more interesting portions of this work is von Manteuffel's own recollections of the gradual degeneration of Adolf Hitler's physical appearance and mental stability during the course of their infrequent meetings.

Bibliography

Brownlow, Donald Grey. *Panzer Baron: The Military Exploits of General Hasso Von Manteuffel*. North Quincy, MA: Christopher Publishing House, 1975.

Yale, Wesley W., I. D. White, and Hasso E. von Manteuffel. *Alternative to Armageddon: The Peace Potential of Lightning War*. New Brunswick, NJ: Rutgers University Press, 1970.

Field Marshal Erhard Milch
German Air Force
1892-1972

Milch was a fighter squadron leader during the First World War. After the war, he was involved in commercial aviation and in 1926 was named chairman of the Lufthausa, Germany's civilian airline. Milch used the airline as a secret training centre for pilots and mechanics who would later serve in the Luftwaffe. Milch proved to be an exceptionally able administrator and supervised the production of war planes for the Luftwaffe during the Second World War. He had many disagreements with Reichsmarshal Hermann Goering concerning matters of production and air strategy. By 1944, Milch had lost some of his status and was forced to work with Albert Speer, the armaments minister, on production issues. Milch was tried at Nuremberg as a war criminal and served a prison term until 1955. Field Marshal Milch was a pioneer in the use of jet powered planes as offensive weapons. It was the Allies' good fortune that Adolf Hitler and Hermann Goering were not so far sighted. David Irving's *The Rise and Fall of the Luftwaffe* is recommended for reading.

Bibliography

Irving, David. *The Rise and Fall of the Luftwaffe: The Life of Field Marshal Erhard Milch*. Boston: Little, Brown, 1973.

Field Marshal Friedrich Paulus
German Army
1890-1957

Paulus was a general staff officer when the war began in 1939. As Deputy Chief of Staff to General Franz Halder, he was a principal planner of Operation Barbarossa, the invasion of the Soviet Union. In January 1942, he was given command of the German Sixth Army. In the summer, the Sixth Army struck out for Stalingrad and the city was occupied by November. However, the Red Army counterattacked and eventually Stalingrad became a giant trap for the Sixth Army as winter descended. The Luftwaffe failed to supply Paulus' men adequately and Paulus was forced to surrender on 1 February 1943, one day after Adolf Hitler promoted him to the rank of field marshal. Hitler had counted on the fact that no German field marshal had ever surrendered and was enraged when he learned what Paulus had done. When the war ended, Paulus gave testimony for the Soviets at the Nuremberg trials. Walter Gorlitz has written a short biography of Paulus' career and published a selected portion of Paulus' private papers pertaining to Operation Barbarossa and Stalingrad complete in one volume. The papers were recovered after the war by Ernst Paulus, the field marshal's son. Portions of the papers were written before Paulus' captivity and others afterwards. Paulus had been considered a rising star during the early days of the war. The tenacity of the Red Army at Stalingrad, however, ended his career.

Bibliography

Gorlitz, Walter. *Paulus and Stalingrad: A Life of Field-Marshal Friedrich Paulus with Notes, Correspondence, and Documents from His Papers*. Translated by R. H. Stevens. New York: Citadel Press, 1963.

Grand Admiral Erich Raeder
German Navy
1876-1960

Raeder was commander-in-chief of the German Navy for the first three years of the war. During the 1930s, he developed the concept of "pocket" battleships, ships with heavy guns and fast speed, and supervised the construction of the U-boat fleet. As commander-in-chief, he planned the strategy for the naval portion of the Norwegian campaign of 1940. During the early years of the war, Raeder's relationship with Adolf Hitler was stormy at best. They constantly argued over strategic use of the surface fleet. Raeder resigned in January 1943 after Hitler ordered the scrapping of the High Seas fleet after its poor performance during the Battle of the Barents Sea in late December 1942. Grand Admiral Karl Doenitz, head of the U-boat fleet, replaced him. After the war, Raeder was tried for war crimes at Nuremberg and sentenced to ten years in prison. Raeder's memoir, *My Life*, is of importance because of the high position he held in Germany's military command. His strategy before and during the war dictated the German Navy's actions in combat. His memoir should be read by persons interested in German naval strategy.

Bibliography

Buchanan, Robert Harold. "*The Era of Erich Raeder, 1894-1943: Dreams of World Empire: A Study in Historical Continuity*." Ph.D. diss., University of Colorado, 1980. (DAI, 41:8, 3685A, UMI Order # 8103077)

Raeder, Erich. *My Life*. Translated from the German by Henry W. Drexel. Annapolis, MD: United States Naval Institute, 1960.

Field Marshal Erwin Rommel
German Army
1891-1944

Rommel was one of Germany's best generals and probably the most well known because of his command of German forces in North Africa. During the First World War, Rommel helped perfect infantry assault tactics on the Italian Front that allowed the Germans to make sizeable gains on the battlefield. After the war, he wrote a book, *Infantry Attacks*, that was widely read by many military officers, both German and foreign. At the start of the Second World War, he commanded the 7th Panzer Division. His troops performed very well during the Battle of France in part due to Rommel stationing his command post at the front to have first-hand information concerning the ebb and flow of the advance. In February 1941, he was placed in command of the Afrika Korps, consisting of several German and Italian divisions. Rommel's main objectives were to wrest control of North Africa from the British and drive into Egypt and capture the Suez Canal. These objectives were never totally achieved due to inadequate military supplies and the spirited opposition of the British Eighth Army. The desert war flowed back and forth for over two years before Allied supremacy in equipment and personnel forced the surrender of all German forces in Africa in May 1943. Rommel was not in Tunisia when his troops surrendered, having returned to Germany to recuperate from an illness. Once sufficiently recovered, he was placed in charge of fortifying Adolf Hitler's famed Atlantic Wall in the Normandy sector of France. The Allies landed there in June 1944 and Rommel's defensive tactics caused the Allied troops many serious problems before the fortifications were breached. During the early days of the invasion, Rommel was at odds with Field Marshal Gerd von Rundstedt on the deployment of German armoured units. Rommel wanted to deploy them on the shoreline to drive the Allies immediately back into the sea, but was overruled by von Rundstedt. In mid-July 1944, Rommel's staff car was strafed by a British fighter plane and he was seriously wounded. While recovering from his wounds, he was implicated in the July bomb plot against Adolf Hitler. Though not directly involved in the attempt on the fuehrer's life, Rommel knew of the conspiracy and was sympathetic with its goal. After his arrest, he was given the choice of committing suicide or facing a show trial in which he would be found guilty and executed. Rommel chose suicide to spare any reprisals against his family.   Upon his death, the Nazi government released information that he had died of his wounds and he was given a state funeral with full military honours. Recommended for reading are David Fraser's *Knight's Cross*, Ronald Lewin's *Rommel as Military Commander* and Desmond Young's *Rommel: The Desert Fox*. Also recommended are Field Marshal Rommel's *Infantry Attacks* and *The Rommel Papers*, edited by B. H. Liddell Hart and others.

Bibliography

Barker, A. J. *Afrika Korps*. London: Bison Books, 1978.

Behrendt, Hans-Otto. *Rommel's Intelligence in the Desert Campaign, 1941-1943*. London: W. Kimber, 1985.

Bergot, Erwan. *The Afrika Korps*. Translated from the French by Richard Barry. London: Wingate, 1976.

Blanco, Richard L. *Rommel, the Desert Warrior*. New York: Messner, 1982.

Carell, Paul. *The Foxes of the Desert*. Translated from the German by Mervyn Savill. New York: Dutton, 1961.

Chandler, David G. *Rommel: Battles and Campaigns*. New York: Mayflower Books, 1979.

Cordier, Sherwood Stanley. "*Erwin Rommel as Commander: The Decisive Years, 1940-1942*." Ph.D. diss., University of Minnesota, 1963. (DAI, 24:5, 1993, UMI Order # 637919)

DeWeerd, Harvey A. "The Rommel Legend." *Infantry Journal* 53 (July 1943): 16-23.

Douglas-Home, Charles. *Rommel*. New York: Saturday Review Press, 1973.

Forty, George. *Afrika Korps at War*. London: I. Allan, 1978.

Fraser, David. *Knight's Cross. The Life of Field Marshal Erwin Rommel*. New York: HarperCollins, 1993.

Green, Jack and Alessandro Massignani. *Rommel's North Africa Campaign: September 1940-November 1942*. Conshohocken, PA: Combined Books, 1994. Distributed in North America by Stackpole Books.

Gregory, Frank H. *Rommel*. London: Wayland, 1974.

Heckmann, Wolf. *Rommel's War in Africa*. Translated from the German by Stephen Seago. Garden City, NY: Doubleday, 1981.

Holtzendorff, Hans Henning. *Reasons for Rommel's Successes (1941-1942)*. Washington, DC: Office of the Chief of Military History, Department of the Army, 1947.

Hoyt, Edwin P. *North African Struggle*. New York: Avon Books, 1993.

Irving, David. *The Trail of the Fox*. New York: Dutton, 1977.

Kuhn, Volkamr. *Rommel in the Desert: Victories and Defeat of the Afrika Korps, 1941-1943*. Translated from the German. West Chester, PA: Schiffer Publishing Ltd., 1991.

Law, Richard D. and Craig W. H. Luther. *Rommel: A Narrative and Pictorial History*. San Jose, CA: R. James Bender Publishers, 1980.

Lewin, Ronald. *The Life and Death of the Afrika Korps: A Biography*. London: B.T. Batsford, 1977.

______. *Rommel as Military Commander*. Princeton, NJ: Van Norstrand, 1968.

Macksey, Kenneth. *Afrika Korps*. New York: Ballantine Books, 1968.

______. *Rommel: Battles and Campaigns*. London: Arms & Armour Press, 1979.

Marshall, Charles F. *Discovering the Rommel Murder: The Life and Death of the Desert Fox*. Mechanicsburg, PA: Stackpole Books, 1994.

McGuirk, Dal. *Rommel's Army in Africa*. London: Stanley Paul, 1987.

McMahon, Timothy L. *Operational Principles: The Operational Art of Erwin Rommel and Bernard Montgomery*. Fort Leavenworth, KS: U.S. Army Command and General Staff College, 1985.

Mitcham, Samuel W., Jr. *Rommel's Desert War: The Life and Death of the Afrika Korps*. New York: Stein & Day, 1982.

______. *Rommel's Last Battle: The Desert Fox and the Normandy Campaign*. New York: Stein & Day, 1983.

______. *Triumphant Fox: Erwin Rommel and the Rise of the Afrika Korps*. New York: Stein & Day, 1984.

Piekalkiewicz, Janusz. *Rommel and the Secret War in North Africa, 1941-1943: Secret Intelligence in the North African Campaign*. Atglen, PA: Schiffer Publishing Ltd., 1992.

Rommel, Erwin. *Infantry Attacks*. With a new introduction by Manfred Rommel. Novato, CA: Presidio Press, 1990.

______. *Rommel: In His Own Words*. London: Greenhill Books, 1994.

______. *The Rommel Papers*. Edited by B. H. Liddell Hart, and others. Translated by Paul Findlay. New York: Harcourt, Brace, 1953.

Ruge, Friedrich. *Rommel and the Atlantic Wall, (Dec. 1943-Jul. 1944)*. Historical Division EUCOM, 1946.

______. *Rommel in Normandy: Reminiscences*. Translated by Ursula R. Moessner. San Rafael, CA: Presidio Press, 1979.

Rutherford, Ward. *The Biography of Field Marshal Erwin Rommel*. London: Hamlyn, 1981.

Schmidt, Heinz Werner. *With Rommel in the Desert*. New York: Ballantine Books, 1951.

Sibley, Roger and Michael Fry. *Rommel*. New York: Ballantine Books, 1974.

Skipper, G. C. *The Fall of the Fox, Rommel*. Chicago: Children's Press, 1980. (juvenile)

Speidel, Hans. *Invasion 1944: Rommel and the Normandy Campaign*. Chicago: H. Regnery, 1950.

Young, Desmond. *Rommel: The Desert Fox*. New York: Harper, 1950.

Field Marshal Gerd von Rundstadt
German Army
1875-1953

Von Rundstedt was one of Germany's highest ranking officers during the Second World War. He commanded Army Group A when German armed forces invaded Poland in 1939 and when France was invaded in May 1940. During the early part of Operation Barbarossa, the invasion of the Soviet Union, he commanded Army Group South until relieved of his duties by Adolf Hitler. He was reinstated in 1942 as Commander-in-Chief West. His responsibilities included defence of the Atlantic Wall, a series of fortifications built to stop any invasion attempt by the western Allies. He was relieved of command again in July 1944 after the invasion of Normandy, France was successful, but was reinstated a few months later and commanded military operations during the Battle of the Bulge. Von Rundstedt and Hitler had many disagreements during the course of the war, but Hitler usually came back to him in times of crises because of his expertise. Recommended for reading are Guenther Blummentritt's *Von Rundstedt*, John Keegan's *Rundstedt*, and Charles Messenger's *The Last Prussian*.

Bibliography

Blummentritt, Guenther. *Von Rundstedt, the Soldier and the Man*. Translated by Cuthbert Reavely. London: Odhams Press, 1952.
Keegan, John. *Rundstedt*. New York: Ballantine Books, 1974.
Messenger, Charles. *The Last Prussian: A Biography of Field Marshal Gerd von Rundstedt, 1875-1953*. London: Brassey's, 1991.

Colonel General Kurt Student
German Air Force
1890-1978

Student began his military career as a fighter pilot in the First World War. He joined the Luftwaffe in 1934 and was given command of all airborne and glider borne combat troop training. Soon his soldiers were known for their fighting spirit. They performed very well during the invasion of the Low Counties and France in 1940, especially during the glider attack on Fort Eban Emael in Belgium. Adolf Hitler used Student's airborne troops to capture Crete from the British in 1941, but casualties were so high, Hitler forbid their use as airborne assault troops for the remainder of the war. They continued to serve as ground troops in numerous engagements in the Soviet Union, Holland, and France. A small unit also rescued Benito Mussolini from his mountain-top detention in 1943. One unit of less than one thousand men was airdropped during the Battle of the Bulge in December 1944. The mission failed because the troops were scattered during the drop, did not have communication capabilities with the main German forces, and did not have sufficient ammunition to engage the American units that opposed them. After the war, Student was tried for war crimes, but was found not guilty. Anthony Farrar-Hockley has written a short biography of Germany's top-ranking airborne general. The work will be of interest to readers who want to know about the battles fought by Germany's paratroopers.

Bibliography

Farrar-Hockley, Anthony H. *Student*. New York: Ballantine Books, 1973.

General Walther Warlimont
German Army
1894-1976

Warlimont was deputy chief of staff of OKW operations from September 1939 to September 1944. He went on sick leave in September as a result of wounds suffered during the 20 July 1944 bombing attempt on Adolf Hitler's life. He was only a short distance from Hitler when the bomb exploded. Though not a combat soldier, Warlimont is an important contributor to Second World War military literature. His position as deputy chief of staff in Hitler's headquarters gave him close contact with the fuehrer. General Warlimont's *Inside Hitler's Headquarters* is a valuable first-hand account of Hitler's involvement in German military operations during the Second World War.

Bibliography

Warlimont, Walther. *Inside Hitler's Headquarters, 1939-1945*. Translated from the German by R. H. Barry. New York: Praeger, 1964.

SS General Karl Wolff
Waffen-SS
1900-1984

Wolff was an early member of the Nazi Party. In 1933, he joined Heinrich Himmler's staff as adjutant chief of staff. He soon became a close friend of Himmler. In 1942, Wolff was promoted to the rank of Obergruppenfuhrer (Lieutenant General) and General der Waffen SS. He was sent to northern Italy in 1943 to serve as military governor and to command all SS units stationed there. By 1945, he realized the war was lost and entered into secret negotiations with Allen Dulles of the United States Office of Strategic Services. Wolff surrendered all German forces operating in northern Italy on 2 May 1945, six days before the surrender in Germany. After the war, he was a witness at the Nuremberg trials and was detained for four years. Because of his position in the SS hierarchy, he was a valuable witness for the prosecution. In 1962, he was arrested and tried by a German court for crimes involving genocide. He was convicted of the murders of three hundred thousand Jews at the Treblinka extermination camp and was sentenced to fifteen years in prison. The only source found concerning the career of Karl Wolff was a Ph.D. dissertation by Charles Wayne Smith.

Bibliography

Smith, Charles Wayne. *"S.S. General Karl Wolff and the Surrender of the German Troops in Italy, 1945."* Ph.D. diss., University of Southern Mississippi, 1970. (DAI, 31:8, 4101A, UMI Order # 715400)

18 Finnish Commanders

The history of the Russo-Finnish War of 1939-40 and the fact that the Finns fought with Germany against the Soviet Union from 1941 to 1944 is not well known by western readers. The Finns and Russians had been enemies ever since the Communist Revolution of 1917. Finnish nationalists defeated Soviet-backed Communist forces in a civil war in 1918. In late 1939, the Red Army invaded Finland to secure more territory against the threat of a possible German invasion. Early on, the Finns were victorious, but the Red Army's overwhelming numbers won out by March 1940 and Finland was forced to cede one-tenth of her territory to the Soviet Union. When German military forces invaded the Soviet Union in June 1941, Finland, once again, went to war to regain her lost territories. Initially, Finland won back her ceded lands, but was eventually defeated by 1944. Surrender terms were not extremely harsh, though territory was lost, reparations were made, and Finland was forced to lease naval bases to the Soviet Union. Finland's national hero during these two wars was Marshal Carl Gustav Mannerheim. A brief biographical profile of Mannerheim and a bibliography of works follows.

Marshal Carl Gustav Mannerheim, Baron
Finnish Army
1867-1951

Mannerheim is a national hero in Finland. Though not as well known as other military commanders of the Second World War, his leadership ability was excellent. At the turn of the century, he was a career army officer in the Russian Army. He fought during the Russo-Japanese War and the First World War. In 1918, he led White Army units that defeated Communist Red Army units that were trying to gain control of the Finnish government. In 1939, he was recalled to duty when the Red

Army again invaded. Mannerheim's skilled ability at defence, coupled with limited offensive tactics, destroyed the first invading forces in the dead of winter. Soviet Premier Josef Stalin then renewed the attack with massive numbers of troops and armour. Mannerheim was forced to capitulate in March 1940, but obtained favourable surrender terms. When Adolf Hitler's German forces invaded the Soviet Union in June 1941, Finland, once again, went to war. Finland's alliance with Nazi Germany was one of national necessity rather than of ideological agreement. Early on, victories were won, but by 1944, defeat was inevitable. Mannerheim, then head of state as well as military commander, secured surrender terms that were not devastating to the Finnish population. Only a few works have been published in English about the life of Marshal Mannerheim. Stig Jagerskiold has written the definitive biography of Mannerheim's life. The work, published in Finnish, totals eight volumes. The English version is a one-volume abridgement. Jagerskiold spent many years researching and writing the biography. He had access to all of Mannerheim's surviving papers in the possession of relatives or the Finnish national archives, though, unfortunately, many other papers were destroyed during several political crises during Mannerheim's career. Marshal Mannerheim's *Memoirs* is also recommended for reading.

Bibliography

Jagerskiold, Stig Axel Fridolf. *Mannerheim, Marshal of Finland*. Minneapolis: University of Minnesota Press, 1986.

Lappalainen, Matti. C.G.E. *Mannerheim, The Marshal of Finland*. Klaukkala: Recalimed, 1989.

Mannerheim, Carl Gustav. *Memoirs*. Translated by Count Eric Lewenhaupt. New York: Dutton, 1954.

Rintala, Marvin. *Four Finns: Political Profiles*. Berkeley: University of California Press, 1969. (One section is devoted to Marshal Mannerheim.)

Screen, J. E. O. *Mannerheim: The Years of Preparation*. London: Hurst, 1970.

Warner, Oliver. *Marshal Mannerheim and the Finns*. London: Weidenfeld & Nicolson, 1967.

19 Italian Commanders

Italy's leader, Benito Mussolini, had illusions of building a second Roman empire in the Mediterranean basin. However, his military forces were hopelessly inadequate for the task once they engaged in combat during the Second World War. The air force was subpar and the infantry and armour units were poorly led and equipped, resulting in disasters in North Africa, Greece, and the Eastern Front. The navy, the one area in which Italy had a credible force, failed to seriously challenge the British Royal Navy in the Mediterranean Sea after British carrier planes sunk or damaged several ships lying at anchor in Taranto harbour in November 1940. In summary, Italian military forces did not distinguish themselves to any great degree during the years of warfare. The subject search revealed only two books written in English about or by Italian commanders. Both were written by Field Marshal Pietro Badoglio. Badoglio was named head of the Italian government after Mussolini was arrested and removed from power. Badoglio negotiated surrender terms with the Allies in the fall of 1943. A brief biographical profile of Badoglio and a bibliography of works follows.

Field Marshal Pietro Badoglio
Italian Army
1871-1956

Badoglio was Italy's top-ranking military commander in the 1930s and during the early part of the Second World War. He commanded the Italian forces that invaded Ethiopia in 1935. However, he was opposed to Italy's entry into the Second World War, believing that Italy's military forces were not prepared to fight. When the invasion of Greece ended in failure, he resigned. He remained in retirement until July 1943 when the Fascist Grand Council ousted Mussolini. He was then asked to lead the new government.   After accepting, he started negotiations that resulted in the unconditional surrender of all Italian armed forces to the Allies. In October 1943, the new Italian government declared war on Germany. When Rome was liberated in June 1944, Badoglio resigned as head of the government and retired to his family estate. Badoglio's memoir relates his experiences during the Second World War. He was instrumental in the transfer of Italy from an Axis power to the side of the Allies.

Bibliography

Badoglio, Pietro. *Italy in the Second World War: Memories and Documents*. Translated by Muriel Currey. New York: Oxford University Press, 1948.
_____. *The War in Abyssinia*. London: Methuen, 1937.

20 Japanese Commanders

The Japanese military gradually gained control of its government's foreign policy during the 1930s. The general staff saw territorial expansion as the answer to Japan's critical problems of over-population and lack of raw materials such as oil and rubber. Their expansionist policy involved them in a war with China that started in 1931 and turned into full scale conflict in 1937. By 1941, the war effort was at a standstill. Rather than admit defeat, the decision was made to expand the war to include all of Southeast Asia and the Pacific basin. The attack on the American naval base at Pearl Harbor, Hawaii marked the beginning of Japan's military downfall which culminated in the destruction of Hiroshima and Nagasaki by atomic bombs in August 1945. Only works about or by six Japanese military commanders were located during the search of bibliographic indexes. This result does not seem too unusual in that very few western historians can read or translate Japanese writing and many of the top commanders were either killed in combat, committed suicide, or were executed at the conclusion of the war. Brief biographical profiles and bibliographies follow.

Lieutenant General Masaharu Homma
Imperial Army
1887-1946

Homma, despite his lack of combat experience, commanded Japanese land forces that invaded the Philippines in January 1942. Previously, he had been involved in military intelligence. His major tactical blunder was immediately capturing Manila, giving General Douglas MacArthur time to establish a defensive perimeter on the Bataan peninsula. Repeated frontal assaults failed to defeat the American and Filipino forces, but the defenders were gradually reduced in effectiveness due to disease and the lack of equipment and supplies. The Bataan defenders resisted until April 1942 when they finally surrendered. Thousands died during the Bataan Death March that followed the surrender. The defenders on the island of Corrigedor surrendered in May. Despite achieving victory, Homma was removed from field command. Even the Japanese high command felt that the price of victory was too costly. At the conclusion of the war, Homma was arrested and put on trial for his involvement in the Bataan Death March. He was found guilty of failure to control his troops and for not providing proper treatment of prisoners of war. He was executed in February 1946. Recommended for reading are Arthur Swinson's *Four Samurai*, (one chapter concerns the career of General Homma) and Lawrence Taylor's *A Trial of Generals*.

Bibliography

Hanson, John Frederick. *"The Trial of Lieutenant General Masaharu Homma."* Ph.D. diss., Mississippi State University, 1986. (DAI, 38:7, 4326A, UMI Order # 7728548)

Kenworthy, Aubrey Saint. *Tiger of Malaya: The Story of General Tomoyuki Yamashita and "Death March" General Masaharu Homma.* New York: Exposition Press, 1953.

Swinson, Arthur. *Four Samurai. A Quartet of Japanese Army Commanders in the Second World War: Masaharu Homma, Tomoyuki Yamashita, Renya Mutaguchi, and Masaki Honda.* London: Hutchinson, 1968.

Taylor, Lawrence. *A Trial of Generals: Homma, Yamashita, MacArthur.* South Bend, IN: Icarus, 1981.

Lieutenant General Masaki Honda
Imperial Army
1889-1964

Honda was one of the Japanese Imperial Army's better combat commanders. In 1938, he served as second-in-command of the Infantry School and from 1941 to 1943, served as Chief of the Armoured Warfare Department. In 1943, he commanded the Twentieth Army in Manchukuo. He was given command of the Thirty-Third Army in Burma in April 1944. In November 1944, General (later Field Marshal) William Slim launched Operation Extended Capital. The objective of the

Allied Fourteenth Army was to regain northern Burma and reopen the Burma Road to China. Though outnumbered and possessing inadequate artillery and armour, Honda manoeuvred his troops very well, giving ground grudgingly. It was not until late January 1945 that the Burma Road was reopened at considerable cost to the Allies. During July 1945, Honda organized one last attempt to break out of an encirclement constructed by Allied forces. Although limited success was achieved at first, the Thirty-Third Army was ultimately destroyed, along with the Fifteenth and Twenty-Seventh Armies. Honda surrendered on 25 August 1945 to General Sir Montagu Stopford, commander of the Allied Twelfth Army. Honda was interned, but was not tried as a war criminal and returned to Japan in 1947. The only source found on the military career of General Honda was Arthur Swinson's *Four Samurai*. One chapter is devoted to Honda's command of the Thirty-Third Army in Burma. It is recommended for reading.

Bibliography

Swinson, Arthur. *Four Samurai. A Quartet of Japanese Army Commanders in the Second World War: Masaharu Homma, Tomoyuki Yamashita, Renya Mutaguchi, and Masaki Honda*. London: Hutchinson, 1968.

Lieutenant General Renya Mutaguchi
Imperial Army
1888-1966

Mutaguchi commanded the Japanese troops that instigated the Marco Polo Bridge incident on 7 July 1937 which ultimately led to war with China. A favourite of Hideki Tojo, Mutaguchi rose quickly in rank, becoming a major general in March 1938 and a lieutenant general in August 1940. He commanded the 18th Division during the successful Malaysia campaign of 1942. In March 1943, he was given command of the Fifteenth Army in Burma. He planned the unsuccessful Imphal/Kohima, India campaign that was launched in March 1944. The objectives were to capture airfields, work shops, food, and ammunition stored in and around Imphal and the important rail centre at Kohima. It was also hoped that the attack would cause the Indian populace to rise up against the British and secure India for the Japanese empire. The attack failed with Mataguchi's troops being defeated by mostly Indian troops. By July 1944, the Fifteenth Army had suffered over 53 000 casualties from an original force of 85 000. Orders were finally received to retreat across the Chindwin River in northern Burma. Mataguchi was relieved of command in December 1944. After the war, he was questioned about his role during the Marco Polo Bridge incident in 1937, but was not tried as a war criminal. The only source found on the career of General Mataguchi was Arthur Swinson's *Four Samurai*. One chapter concerns Mataguchi's command of the Fifteenth Army during the Imphal/Kohima campaign of 1944. It is recommended for reading.

Bibliography

Swinson, Arthur. *Four Samurai. A Quartet of Japanese Army Commanders in the Second World War: Masaharu Homma, Tomoyuki Yamashita, Renya Mutaguchi, and Masaki Honda*. London: Hutchinson, 1968.

Rear Admiral Matome Ugaki
Imperial Navy
1890-1945

Ugaki was Admiral Isoroku Yamamoto's chief of staff. He was actively involved in the planning of the Pearl Harbor attack and campaigned vigorously for its acceptance and eventual execution despite opposition from other Japanese naval commanders. On 18 April 1943, Yamamoto and Ugaki flew from Rabaul to the Solomons to inspect naval installations. Unknown to them, American code breakers had intercepted and decoded radio messages announcing their flight plan. P-38 Lightning fighter planes attacked the two Japanese bombers carrying the admirals as they neared Bougainville. Yamamoto's plane was shot down and crashed in the jungle. There were no survivors. Ugaki's plane was hit, but the pilot managed to ditch the craft in the ocean near shore. Ugaki survived. Later, Ugaki was placed in command of all naval kamikaze units. Even after Emperor Hirohito's radio message effectively ended all organized Japanese resistance on 15 August 1945, Ugaki vowed to continue the fight. He led ten other kamikaze pilots on a suicide mission to attack American ships near Okinawa. Four planes turned back, but seven continued on. The seven planes disappeared and Ugaki's body was never found. Admiral Ugaki's position as Yamamoto's chief of staff during the early years of the war placed him in close contact with Japan's greatest admiral. His diary is recommended for reading. Edwin Hoyt's *The Last Kamikaze* is also recommended.

Bibliography

Hoyt, Edwin P. *The Last Kamikaze: The Story of Admiral Matome Ugaki*. New York: Praeger, 1993.

Ugaki, Matome. *Fading Victory: The Diary of Admiral Matome Ugaki, 1941-1945*. Translated by Masataka Chihaya-san. Edited by Donald E. Goldstein and Catherine V. Dillon. Pittsburgh: University of Pittsburgh Press, 1991.

Admiral Isoroku Yamamoto
Imperial Navy
1884-1943

Yamamoto was commander-in-chief of the Imperial Fleet at the beginning of the war and was primarily responsible for the buildup of the fleet and the use of aircraft as offensive weapons. Personally, he opposed war with the United States, feeling that Japan would eventually lose because of America's technological and industrial might. However, he felt that if Japan were to fight, the United States Pacific Fleet, stationed at Pearl Harbor, Hawaii, would have to be neutralized. The destruction of the fleet would allow Japanese land and sea forces to capture Indochina, Southeast Asia, and the Philippines and establish a defensive perimeter that would hopefully deter the United States from attempting to retake the area. His plan, the air attack on Pearl Harbor, was only partially successful because the American aircraft carriers were at sea during the attack and because fuel depots were not destroyed. Following the tactical draw at the Battle of the Coral Sea in May 1942, Yamamoto devised a complicated, multi-phased plan to lure the remainder of the US Pacific Fleet to battle and destroy it. However, US code breakers had deciphered Japanese naval transmissions and the bulk of the American naval forces were waiting near Midway Island. The Americans attacked first and their aircraft sank four Japanese carriers under the command of Admiral Chuichi Nagumo. Nearly all the air crews were lost as well. The Americans lost only one carrier. The tide of war turned against Japan in one day. Yamamoto remained in command of Japanese naval forces until April 1943. For the last time, he was thwarted by American code breakers. They had deciphered transmissions announcing his forthcoming visit to the western Solomons for an inspection tour. He was killed when his plane was shot down by American P-38 Lightning fighter planes. Recommended for reading are Hirouki Agawa's *The Reluctant Admiral,* Carroll Glines' *Attack on Yamamoto*, and Edwin Hoyt's *Yamamoto*.

Bibliography

Agawa, Hiroyuki. *The Reluctant Admiral: Yamamoto and the Imperial Navy*. Translated by John Bester. New York: Kodansha International, 1979.

Davis, Burke. *Get Yamamoto*. New York: Random House, 1969.

Glines, Carroll V. *Attack on Yamamoto*. New York: Orion Books, 1990.

Hoyt, Edwin P. *Three Military Leaders: Heihachiro Togo, Isoroku Yamamoto, Tomoyuki Yamashita*. New York: Kodansha International, 1994.

______. *Yamamoto: The Man Who Planned Pearl Harbor*. New York: McGraw-Hill, 1990.

Isaman, Robert J. *Pearl Harbor: Strategy and Principles of War*. Maxwell Air Force Base, AL: Air Command and Staff College, Air University, 1985.

Potter, John D. *Yamamoto: The Man Who Menaced America*. New York: Viking Press, 1965.

Smithsonian History of Aviation Series. *Lightning over Bougainville: The Yamamoto Mission Reconsidered*. Washington, DC: Smithsonian Institution Press, 1991.

Wible, John T. *The Yamamoto Mission: Sunday, April 18, 1943*. Fredericksburg, TX: The Admiral Nimitz Foundation, 1988.

Lieutenant General Tomoyuki Yamashita
Imperial Army
1885-1946

Yamashita was commander of the Twentieth-fifth Army which invaded Malaya shortly after Pearl Harbor was attacked. By February 1942, as a result of speed and surprise, the entire country as well as Singapore was captured. The defeat was one of Great Britain's worst in its long military history. In July 1942, Yamashita was sent to Manchuria to command the 1st Area Army. He remained there until the fall of 1944 when he was given command of the defence of the Philippines. Before he could organize his defences, US forces under the command of General Douglas MacArthur invaded. When American troops approached Manila, Yamashita ordered his troops to withdraw, but Imperial Navy sailors fighting as land troops failed to obey and ran amok, raping and murdering civilians and burning much of the city. After the war, Yamashita surrendered and was placed on trial for war crimes. He was found guilty and hanged in February 1946. Recommended for reading are Richard Lael's *The Yamashita Precedent*, John Potter's *Life and Death of a Japanese General*, A. Frank Reel's *The Case of General Yamashita*, and Lawrence Taylor's *A Trial of Generals*.

Bibliography

Barker, A. J. *Yamashita*. New York: Ballantine Books, 1973.

Bein, Peter J. *General MacArthur and the Yamashita Decision, September 1944-February 1946*. Carlisle Barracks, PA: U.S. Army War College, 1989.

Hoyt, Edwin P. *Three Military Leaders: Heihachiro Togo, Isoroku Yamamoto, Tomoyuki Yamashita*. New York: Kodansha International, 1994.

Kenworthy, Aubrey Saint. *Tiger of Malaya: The Story of General Tomoyuki Yamashita and "Death March" General Masaharu Homma*. New York: Exposition Press, 1953.

Lael, Richard L. *The Yamashita Precedent: War Crimes and Command Responsibility*. Wilmington, DE: Scholarly Resources, 1982.

Potter, John D. *The Life and Death of a Japanese General*. New York: New American Library, 1962.

Reel, A. (Adolf) Frank. *The Case of General Yamashita*. Chicago: University of Chicago Press, 1949.

Swinson, Arthur. *Four Samurai. A Quartet of Japanese Army Commanders in the Second World War: Masaharu Homma, Tomoyuki Yamashita, Renya Mutaguchi, and Masaki Honda*. London: Hutchinson, 1968.

Taylor, Lawrence. *A Trial of Generals: Homma, Yamashita, MacArthur*. South Bend, IN: Icarus, 1981.

Whitney, Courtney. *The Case of General Yamashita: A Memorandum*. n.p., 1949.

Yamashita, Tomoyuki. *Before the Military Commission Convened by the Commanding General, United States Army Forces, Western Pacific, United States of America vs. Tomoyuki Yamashita. Proceedings.* Manila: n.d. (Microfilm held by the New York Public Library, New York City, NY.)

PART V

OTHER NOTABLE FIGURES AND MISCELLANEOUS ENTRIES

21 Other Allied Figures

The figures listed in this chapter played significant roles during the Second World War. Several had distinguished political careers in the post-war period. Selection of the figures was arbitrary on the part of the compiler.

Clement Attlee, 1st Earl
British Prime Minister
1883-1967

Attlee replaced Winston Churchill as prime minister after the Conservative Party suffered a strong defeat in elections held in July 1945. He was the leader of the Labour Party, first being elected to Parliament in 1922. In May 1940, Churchill named Attlee Lord Privy Seal and Deputy Leader of the House of Commons in his coalition cabinet. In 1945, Attlee was a member of the British delegation that attended the formation of the United Nations. After the Labour Party won the July 1945 elections, Attlee replaced Churchill at the Potsdam Conference. He agreed with the major decisions that had been made previously, those being that Germany would be partitioned into four zones of occupation, top Nazi leaders would be tried as war criminals, and that Japan would have to surrender unconditionally. He remained in office until February 1950. Recommended for reading are Attlee's memoir, *As It Happened*, Kenneth Harris' *Attlee*, and Kevin Jeffrey's *The Attlee Government, 1945-1951*.

Bibliography

Attlee, Clement. *As It Happened*. New York: Viking Press, 1954.

_____. *Empire into Commonwealth*. London: Oxford University Press, 1961.

_____. *War Comes to Britain: Speeches of the Rt. Hon. C. R. Attlee, M.P.* London: V. Gollancz, 1940.

Brome, Vincent. *Clement Attlee*. London: Lincolns-Prager, 1949.

Burridge, T. D. (Trevor D.) *Clement Attlee: A Political Biography*. London: J. Cape, 1985.

Clemens, Cyril. *The Man from Limehouse: Clement Richard Attlee*. Webster Grove, MO: International Mark Twain Society. J. P. Didier, distributors, New York, 1946.

Haney, John. *Clement Attlee*. New York: Chelsea House, 1988. (juvenile)

Harris, Kenneth. *Attlee*. New York: Norton, 1982.

Jeffreys, Kevin. *The Attlee Governments, 1945-1951*. London: Longman, 1992.

Jenkins, Roy. *Mr. Attlee, an Interim Biography*. London: Heinemann, 1948.

Johman, Lewis and Nick Tiratsoo, eds. *The Attlee Government, 1945-1951*. New York: St. Martin's Press, 1992.

Morgan, Kenneth O. *Labour in Power, 1945-1951*. Oxford: Oxford University Press, 1984.

Pearce, Robert. *Attlee's Labour Governments, 1945-1951*. London: Routledge, 1994.

Saville, John. *The Politics of Continuity: British Foreign Policy and the Labour Government, 1945-46*. London: Verso, 1993.

Tiratsoo, Nick, ed. *The Attlee Years*. New York: Pinter Publishers, 1991.

Williams, Francis. *A Prime Minister Remembers: The War and Post-War Memoirs of the Rt. Hon. Earl Attlee. Based on His Private Papers and A Series of Recorded Conversations*. London: Heinemann, 1961.

Neville Chamberlain
British Prime Minister
1869-1940

Chamberlain was prime minister of Great Britain from 1937 to 1940. He is most remembered for the policy of appeasement his government adopted during the Czech crisis of 1938 which resulted in the Munich Agreement. He and French Premier Edouard Daladier agreed to Adolf Hitler's demand that the Sudetenland of Czechoslovakia be ceded to

Germany. The Czech government was not invited to the conference. Though Chamberlain believed that he had successfully avoided a potential military confrontation, in reality, he only handed Hitler another bloodless conquest. One year later Chamberlain was leading Great Britain into war after German military forces invaded Poland on 1 September 1939. He resigned as prime minister on 10 May 1940, the very same day German forces invaded France and the Low Countries. Chamberlain was a decent man who was out of step with the changes that were sweeping across Europe in the late 1930s. Of all the decisions Chamberlain made as prime minister, the decision he made to resign, allowing Winston Churchill to form a new government, ultimately aided his country the most as it faced the most difficult period in its long history. Recommended for reading are John Charmley's *Chamberlain and the Lost Peace*, Keith Feiling's *The Life of Neville Chamberlain*, Larry Fuchser's *Neville Chamberlain and Appeasement*, Iain Macleod's *Neville Chamberlain*, and William Rock's *Chamberlain and Roosevelt*.

Bibliography

Brooks, Collin. *Can Chamberlain Save Britain?* London: Eyre & Spottiswoode, 1938.

Chamberlain, Neville. *In Search of Peace, by the Rt. Hon. Neville Chamberlain, M.P., Prime Minister of Great Britain.* New York: G. P. Putnam's Sons, 1939.

Charmley, John. *Chamberlain and the Lost Peace.* London: Hodder & Stoughton, 1989.

Cockett, Richard. *Twilight of Truth: Chamberlain, Appeasement, and the Manipulation of the Press.* London: Weidenfeld & Nicolson, 1989.

Colvin, Ian. *The Chamberlain Cabinet: How the Meetings in 10 Downing Street, 1937-1939, Led to the Second World War-Told for the First Time from the Cabinet Papers.* New York: Taplinger Pub. Co., 1971.

Cullen, Emma Lucille. "*Chamberlain and Hitler: Failure of Appeasement.*" Ph.D. diss., St. John's University, 1943. (Not available from UMI)

Dilks, David. *Neville Chamberlain. Volume 1: Pioneering and Reform.* New York: Cambridge University Press, 1984.

Feiling, Keith. *The Life of Neville Chamberlain.* London: Macmillan & Co., 1970.

Fuchser, Larry William. *Neville Chamberlain and Appeasement: A Study in the Politics of History.* New York: Norton, 1982.

Gilbert, Martin and Richard Gott. *The Appeasers*. Boston: Houghton Mifflin, 1963.

Hodgson, Stuart. *The Man Who Made Peace: Neville Chamberlain, a Study*. New York: E. P. Dutton, 1938.

Hutt, Allen. *"Peace for Our Time": Mr. Chamberlain and Munich. The Truth About A Policy*. London: The Labour Research Dept., 1938.

Hyde, H. Montgomery. *Neville Chamberlain*. London: Weidenfeld & Nicolson, 1976.

Kelly, Thomas Lauren. *"Appeasement: The Ploy that Failed; Henderson, Chamberlain, The Foreign Office and Anglo-German Relations, 1937-1939."* Ph.D. diss., The University of Alabama, 1979. (DAI, 41:1, 360A, UMI Order # 8015577)

Leslie, Van Michael. *"Neville Chamberlain as Wartime Prime Minister, 1939-1940."* Ph.D. diss., University of Kentucky, 1987. (DAI, 48:4, 1001A, UMI Order # DA8715933)

Macleod, Iain. *Neville Chamberlain*. New York: Atheneum, 1962.

Maisky, I. *The Munich Drama*. Translated from the Russian. Moscow: Novosti Press Agency, 1972.

Neville, Peter. *Neville Chamberlain: A Study in Failure?* London: Hodder & Stoughton, 1992.

Parker, R. A. C. (Robert Alexander Clarke). *Chamberlain and Appeasement: British Policy and the Coming of the Second World War*. New York: St. Martin's, 1993.

Petrie, Charles Alexander. *The Chamberlain Tradition*. New York: Frederick A. Stokes Company, 1938.

Rock, William R. *British Appeasement in the 1930s*. New York: Norton, 1977.

_______. *Chamberlain and Roosevelt: British Foreign Policy and the United States, 1937-1940*. Columbus: Ohio State University Press, 1988.

_______. *Neville Chamberlain*. New York: Twayne Publishers, 1969.

Shaw, Duncan Keith. *Prime Minister Neville Chamberlain*. London: W. Gardner, Darton & Co., Ltd., 1939.

Shepherd, Robert. *A Class Divided: Appeasement and the Road to Munich, 1938*. London: Macmillan, 1988.

Walker-Smith, Derek. *Neville Chamberlain, Man of Peace*. London: R. Hale, 1940.

Watt, Donald Cameron. *Personalities and Appeasement*. Austin: University of Texas at Austin, Harry Ransom Humanities Research Center, 1991.

Edouard Daladier
French Premier
1884-1970

Daladier, a member of the French Radical Socialist Party, was Premier of France on three occasions in 1933, 1934, and 1938-40. He was also Minister of War from 1936 to 1940 and was responsible for military preparedness with French Army Commander-in-Chief, General Maurice Gamelin. Daladier was a veteran of the First World War and a survivor of Verdun. He was a strong proponent of defensive fortifications to protect France's border with Germany, but was hesitant to consider offensive concepts. The government of France declared war on Germany in September 1939 after the invasion of Poland as was mandated in the French and British treaties with Poland. During the next few months, Daladier was blamed for failing to aid Finland when it was invaded by the Soviet Union and for failing to stop shipments of iron ore from Scandinavia to Germany. He resigned as Premier on 20 March 1940, but remained as Minister of War. Paul Reynaud succeeded him as Premier. On 10 May 1940, France was invaded by German armed forces. Daladier was removed as Minister of War after German panzer units broke through French defensive positions at Sedan on 13 May and raced across northern France toward the coast. In September 1940, he was placed on trial by the new Vichy government for contributing to France's defeat. In 1941, he was turned over to the Germans and remained a prisoner until being released in 1945. Only four sources were found concerning the political career of Edouard Daladier. They are listed in the bibliography that follows.

Bibliography

Daladier, Edouard. *In Defense of France*. New York: Doubleday, Doran & Company Inc., 1939.

Gay, Albert Carl. "*The Daladier Administration, 1938-1940*." Ph.D. diss., University of North Carolina at Chapel Hill, 1970. (DAI, 31:8, 4085A, UMI Order # 713556)

Geraud, Andre. *The Gravediggers of France: Gamelin, Daladier, Reynaud, Petain, and Laval: Military Defeat, Armistice, Counterrevolution*. Garden City, NY: Doubleday, Doran, 1944.

Leeds, Stanton B. *These Rule France. The Story of Edouard Daladier and the Men Around Daladier*. New York: Bobbs-Merrill Company, 1940.

Earl of Avon
Sir Anthony Eden
British Foreign Secretary
1897-1977

Eden was Prime Minister Winston Churchill's Foreign Secretary during the Second World War. Eden had been prominent in international affairs for many years prior to the start of the war. As Minister of the League of Nations Affairs, he lobbied for sanctions against Italy after Benito Mussolini's military forces invaded Ethiopia. Sanctions were imposed, but not enforced. Eden was Foreign Secretary from 1935 to 1938 under Prime Minister Neville Chamberlain. He resigned in 1938 because he felt Chamberlain's policy of appeasement only encouraged the Fascist regimes of Germany and Italy to be more aggressive politically and militarily. When Churchill became Prime Minister in May 1940, he named Eden his Foreign Secretary. All during the war, Eden worked tirelessly, making numerous trips aboard and attending all the major conferences. Churchill had complete confidence in his abilities and named Eden his successor should he die. After the war, Eden worked to make the United Nations a strong organization. In 1951, when Churchill was again elected Prime Minister, Eden assumed his old position as Foreign Minister, holding it until 1955 when he was chosen as prime minister upon Churchill's final retirement. Recommended for reading are Sidney Aster's *Anthony Eden*, Lewis Broad's *Anthony Eden, The Chronicle of A Career*, Robert Rhodes James' *Anthony Eden*, and Sir Anthony Eden's memoir, *The Reckoning*.

Bibliography

Aster, Sidney. *Anthony Eden*. London: Weidenfeld & Nicolson, 1976.

Bardens, Dennis. *Portrait of a Statesman: [The Personal Life Story of Sir Anthony Eden]*. New York: Philosophical Library, 1956.

Barker, Elisabeth. *Churchill and Eden at War*. New York: St. Martin's Press, 1978.

Broad, Lewis. *Anthony Eden, The Chronicle of A Career*. New York: Thomas Y. Crowell, 1955.

Campbell-Johnson, Alan. *Anthony Eden: A Biography*. London: R. Hale, 1955.

Carlton, David. *Anthony Eden, A Biography*. London: A. Lane, 1981.

Churchill, Randolph S. *The Rise and Fall of Sir Anthony Eden*. New York: Putnam, 1959.

Eden, Anthony. *Facing the Dictators: The Memoirs of Anthony Eden, Earl of Avon*. Boston: Houghton Mifflin, 1962.

______. *Foreign Affairs*. New York: Harcourt, Brace, 1939.

______. *Freedom and Order: Selected Speeches, 1939-1946*. Boston: Houghton Mifflin, 1948.

______. *Full Circle: The Memoirs of Anthony Eden, Earl of Avon*. Boston: Houghton Mifflin, 1960.

______. *The Reckoning: The Memoirs of Anthony Eden, Earl of Avon*. Boston: Houghton Mifflin, 1965.

James, Robert Rhodes. *Anthony Eden*. New York: McGraw-Hill, 1987.

Peters, A. R. (Anthony R.) *Anthony Eden at the Foreign Office, 1931-1938*. New York: St. Martin's Press, 1986.

Rees-Mogg, William. *Sir Anthony Eden*. London: Rockliff, 1956.

Rothwell, Victor. *Anthony Eden: A Political Biography, 1931-1957*. Manchester: Manchester University Press, 1992.

Smith, Gene. *The Ends of Greatness: Haig, Petain, Rathenau, and Eden. Victims of History*. New York: Crown Publishers Inc., 1990.

Trukhanovsky, V. G. (Vladimir Grigorevich). *Anthony Eden*. Translated from the Russian by Ruth English. Moscow: Progress Publishers, 1984.

Harry L. Hopkins
Advisor to President Franklin D. Roosevelt
1890-1946

Hopkins was President Franklin D. Roosevelt's top advisor and close confidante during the Second World War. Before the war, Hopkins was a government administrator, running such departments as the Federal Emergency Relief Administration and the Works Progress Administration. Once the Lend-Lease program was passed by Congress, he controlled it. After German armed forces invaded the Soviet Union, Hopkins went to Moscow in July 1941 to meet with Premier Josef Stalin. His mission was to arrange for loans and supplies to be sent to the Soviets. Hopkins' last major accomplishment came during the final weeks of the war. President Harry S. Truman sent him to Moscow to discuss several problems with Stalin. The Polish question was addressed and the veto impasse at the United Nations meetings was resolved. Also, Stalin agreed to a major conference in July 1945. The conference was held at Potsdam, a suburb of Berlin, and plans were finalized for the partition of Germany and Japan was called upon to surrender unconditionally. By July 1945, Hopkins was at his end physically. He resigned to rest and regain his health, but only lived another six months, dying in January 1946. Hopkins was one of the war's behind-the-scenes heroes. Recommended for reading are Henry Adams' *Harry Hopkins*, George T. McJimsey's *Harry Hopkins*, Robert Sherwood's *Roosevelt and Hopkins* (winner of the 1949 Pulitzer prize for biography), and Dwight Tuttle's *Harry L. Hopkins and Anglo-American-Soviet Relations, 1941-1945*.

Bibliography

Adams, Henry H. *Harry Hopkins, A Biography*. New York: Putnam, 1977.

McJimsey, George T. *Harry Hopkins: Ally of the Poor and Defender of Democracy*. Cambridge: Harvard University Press, 1987.

Rader, Frank John. "*Harry L. Hopkins: The Works Progress Administration and National Defense, 1935-1940.*" Ph.D. diss., University of Delaware, 1973. (DAI, 34:10, 6573A, UMI Order # 748742)

Sherwood, Robert E. *Roosevelt and Hopkins: An Intimate History*. New York: Harper, 1950.

______. *White House Papers of Harry L. Hopkins: An Intimate History*. 2 volumes. London: Eyre & Spottiswoode, 1948-1949.

Tuttle, Dwight William. *Harry L. Hopkins and Anglo-American-Soviet Relations, 1941-1945*. New York: Garland Pub., 1983.

______. "*Harry L. Hopkins and Anglo-American-Soviet Relations, 1941-1945.*" Ph.D. diss., Washington State University, 1980. (DAI, 41:6, 2741A, UMI Order # 8025966)

Cordell Hull
United States Secretary of State
1871-1955

Hull was one of the leading statesmen of his era. He served as President Franklin D. Roosevelt's Secretary of State from 1933 to 1944. Previously, he had served in Congress and was chairman of the Democratic National Committee, helping Roosevelt gain the presidential nomination in 1932. Hull strongly supported the League of Nations and was disappointed when America failed to join. As Secretary of State, he engineered the Good Neighbour Policy with Latin American countries and pushed for low import tariffs. Hull is probably most well known for his diplomatic negotiations with Japanese ambassadors Kichisburo Nomura and Saburo Kurusu prior to the attack on Pearl Harbor on 7 December 1941. Hull denounced the duplicity of the Japanese government after the attack. Despite America's failure to join the League of Nations, Hull was strongly in favour of an international organization to help nations settle their disputes peacefully. He has been credited with creating the concept of the United Nations and worked tirelessly for its formation. Hull was forced to retire from office in 1944 due to ill health. He was awarded the Nobel Peace prize in 1945 for his diplomatic efforts. Recommended for reading are the *Memoirs of Cordell Hull* and Jonathan Utley's *Going to War with Japan, 1937-1941*.

Bibliography

Beck, Robert Thomas. "*Cordell Hull and Latin America, 1933-1939*." Ph.D. diss., Temple University, 1977. (DAI, 38:4, 2296A, UMI Order # 7721796)

Burns, Richard Dean. "*Cordell Hull: A Study in Diplomacy, 1933-1941*." Ph.D. diss., University of Illinois, 1960. (DAI, 21:9, 2685, UMI Order # 6194)

Grollman, Catherine Anne. "*Cordell Hull and His Concept of A World Organization*." Ph.D. diss., University of North Carolina at Chapel Hill, 1965. (DAI, 26:7, 3901, UMI Order # 6514344)

Hinton, Harold B. *Cordell Hull, a Biography*. Garden City, NY: Doubleday, Doran, 1942.

Hull, Cordell. *Foreign Policy of the United States of America*. Washington, DC: U.S. Government Printing Office, 1944.

_____. *The Memoirs of Cordell Hull*. 2 volumes. New York: Macmillan Co., 1948.

_____. *The Moscow Conference*. Washington, DC: U.S. Government Printing Office, 1943.

_____. *Our Foreign Policy in the Framework of Our National Interests*. Washington, DC: U.S. Government Printing Office, 1943.

_____. *The War and Human Freedom*. Washington, DC: U.S. Government Printing Office, 1942.

Jablon, Howard. "*Cordell Hull, The State Department, and the Foreign Policy of the First Roosevelt Administration, 1933-1936*." Ph.D. diss., Rutgers, The State University of New Jersey, 1967. (DAI, 28:2, 595A, UMI Order # 679250)

Library of Congress. Manuscript Division. *Cordell Hull: A Register of His Papers in the Library of Congress.* Washington, DC: The Library, 1975.

Milner, Cooper. "*The Public Life of Cordell Hull, 1907-1924.*" Ph.D. diss., Vanderbilt University, 1960. (DAI, 22:1, 239, UMI Order # 602731)

Pratt, Julius W. *Cordell Hull, 1933-44.* 2 volumes. (The American Secretaries of State and their Diplomacy, Volumes 12 and 13.) New York: Cooper Publishers, 1964.

Utley, Jonathan G. *Going to War with Japan, 1937-1941.* Knoxville: University of Tennessee Press, 1985.

Frank Knox
United States Secretary of the Navy
1874-1944

Knox was Secretary of the Navy from 1940 until his death in 1944. President Franklin D. Roosevelt named Knox, along with fellow Republican Henry Stimson as Secretary of War, to his cabinet in an effort to broaden public support for his foreign policy. Knox served in the First World War as an artilleryman. He was the publisher of the Chicago Daily News from 1931 to 1940. Knox totally supported Roosevelt's foreign policy and directed the largest expansion of the U.S. Navy in its history. He was completely dedicated to the war effort and eventual Allied victory. The only biography found about the life of Frank Knox was written in 1936, four years before he became Secretary of the Navy. Two dissertations have been written about his life and career.

Bibliography

Beasley, Norman. *Frank Knox, American: A Short Biography.* Garden City, NY: Doubleday, Doran & Company, 1936.

Cash, Kevin Richard. *Who the Hell is William Loeb?* Hooksett, NH: Amoskeag Press, 1975.

Knox, Franklin. *The Meaning of Munich.* n.p., Priv. printing, 1938.

______. *The United States Navy in National Defense.* Washington, DC: American Council on Public Affairs, 1941.

Lobdell, George Henry, Jr. "*A Biography of Frank Knox*." Ph.D. diss., University of Illinois, 1954. (DAI, 14:11, 2049, UMI Order # 9101)
Mark, Steven MacDonald. "*An American Interventionist: Frank Knox and United States Foreign Relations*." Ph.D. diss., University of Maryland, 1977. (DAI, 38:8, 5007A, UMI Order # 7730543)

Harold Macmillan
Political Advisor to Winston Churchill
1894-1986

Macmillan was a valuable member of Prime Minister Winston Churchill's Conservative government. In the late 1930s, Macmillan was an opponent of Prime Minister Neville Chamberlain's policy of appeasement. From 1942 to 1943, he served as a political advisor at General Dwight Eisenhower's headquarters in Northwest Africa. He participated in the negotiations of Italy's surrender in the fall of 1943 and remained active on the political end of Mediterranean affairs for the remainder of the war. Prime Minister Anthony Eden selected him to be Foreign Secretary in 1955 and Macmillan became prime minister upon Eden's resignation in 1957. Macmillan was prime minister until 1963 when he was forced to retire due to illness. Recommended for reading are Harold Macmillan's *War Diaries* and *The Blast of War, 1939-1945*, Nigel Fisher's *Harold Macmillan*, Alistair Horne's *Harold Macmillan, Volume I, 1894-1956*, and John Turner's *Harold Macmillan*.

Bibliography

Edwards, Ruth Dudley. *Harold Macmillan: A Life in Pictures*. London: Macmillan, 1983.
Fisher, Nigel. *Harold Macmillan, A Biography*. London: Weidenfeld & Nicolson, 1982.
Horne, Alistair. *Harold Macmillan, Volume I, 1894-1956*. New York: Viking, 1989.
_____. *Harold Macmillan, Volume II, 1957-1986*. New York: Viking, 1989.
Hughes, Emrys. *Macmillan: Portrait of a Politician*. London: G. Allen & Unwin, 1962.
Hutchinson, George. *The Last Edwardian at No. 10: An Impression of Harold Macmillan*. London: Quartet Books, 1980.

Macmillan, Harold. *At the End of the Day, 1961-1963*. New York: Harper & Row, 1973.

______. *The Blast of War, 1939-1945*. New York: Harper & Row, 1968.

______. *Economic Aspects of Defence*. London: Macmillan, 1939.

______. *The Middle Way: A Study of the Problem of Economic and Social Progress in A Free and Democratic Society*. London: Macmillan, 1938.

______. *Past Masters: Politics and Politicians, 1906-1939*. New York: Harper & Row, 1975.

______. *Pointing the Way, 1959-1961*. London: Macmillan, 1972.

______. *Riding the Storm, 1956-1959*. New York: Harper & Row, 1971.

______. *Tides of Fortune, 1945-1955*. New York: Harper & Row, 1969.

______. *War Diaries: Politics and War in the Mediterranean, January 1943-May 1945*. New York: St. Martin's Press, 1984.

______. *Winds of Change, 1914-1939*. New York: Harper & Row, 1966.

Sampson, Anthony. *Macmillan, a Study in Ambiguity*. New York: Simon & Schuster, 1967.

Tolstoy, Nikolai. *The Minister and the Massacres*. London: Century Hutchinson, 1986.

Turner, John. *Harold Macmillan*. New York: Longman, 1993.

Paul Reynaud
French Premier
1878-1966

Reynaud was the leading political figure of the French Conservative Party during the 1930s. He was a strong proponent of offensive military responses to counter Germany's growing military power, but was unsuccessful in having his plans implemented. In November 1938, he was named Minister of Finance and on 21 March 1940, succeeded Edouard Daladier as Premier. On 28 March 1940, Reynaud signed a pact with Great Britain stating the two countries would not negotiate a separate treaty with Germany. After German armed forces invaded France on 10 May 1940 and broke through the French defensive positions at Sedan on 13 May, Reynaud dismissed Edouard Daladier as Minister of War and removed General Maurice Gamelin as Army commander-in-chief. Reynaud took over the duties of Minister of War and appointed General Maxime Weygand as commander-in-chief. He also named Marshal Philippe Petain to his cabinet. However, these changes did very little to change the way the war was going for the

French. By mid-June, Reynaud and his cabinet knew the war was lost. Reynaud resigned on 16 June. He was succeeded by Petain, who negotiated the surrender with Germany. Reynaud was arrested by the Vichy government and interned until 1942 when he was deported to Germany. He remained in custody in Germany until the conclusion of the war in 1945. He was active in French politics after the war. Paul Reynaud's *In The Thick of the Fight, 1930-1945* is recommended for reading.

Bibliography

Brandstadter, Michael. "*Paul Reynaud and the Third French Republic, 1919-1939: French Political Conservatism in the Interwar Years.*" Ph.D. diss., Duke University, 1971. (DAI, 32:10, 5702A, UMI Order # 7211070)

Connors, Joseph David. "*Paul Reynaud and French National Defense, 1933-1939.*" Ph.D. diss., Loyola University of Chicago, 1977. (DAI, 37:12, 7908A, UMI Order # 7713411)

Geraud, Andre. *The Gravediggers of France: Gamelin, Daladier, Reynaud, Petain, and Lavel: Military Defeat, Armistice, Counterrevolution*. Garden City, NY: Doubleday, Doran, 1944.

Reynaud, Paul. *In the Thick of the Fight, 1930-1945*. Translated by James D. Lambert. New York: Simon & Schuster, 1955.

Silvestri, Gino Dominic. "*Paul Reynaud and the Fall of France.*" Ph.D. diss., Syracuse University, 1969. (DAI, 30:12, 5396A, UMI Order # 7010397)

Henry L. Stimson
United States Secretary of War
1867-1950

Stimson was Secretary of War in President Franklin D. Roosevelt's cabinet from 1940 to 1945. Stimson was a New York Republican with much government experience prior to the Second World War. He was President William Taft's Secretary of War from 1911 to 1913, Governor of the Philippines from 1927 to 1929, and President Calvin Coolidge's Secretary of State from 1929 to 1933. When war began in Europe in 1939, Stimson was a strong supporter of aid to Great Britain and wanted America to begin preparations for war. He was an early advocate of the atomic bomb project, lobbying for its development as a military weapon. When President Harry S. Truman debated using the atomic bomb against Japan, Stimson advised him to use it to shorten the war and save American and Allied lives. Recommended for reading are Godfrey Hodgson's *The Colonel*, Elting Morison's *Turmoil and Tradition*, and Stimson's memoir, *On Active Service in War and Peace*.

Bibliography

Current, Richard Nelson. *Secretary Stimson, a Study in Statecraft*. New Brunswick: Rutgers University Press, 1954.

Ferrell, Robert H. *Frank B. Kellogg. Henry L. Stimson*. New York: Cooper Square, 1963.

Gerber, Larry George. *"The Limits of Liberalism: A Study of the Careers and Ideological Development of Josephus Daniels, Henry Stimson, Bernard Baruch, Donald Richberg, and Felix Frankfurter."* Ph.D. diss., University of California at Berkeley, 1979. (DAI, 40:7, 4192A, UMI Order # 8000353)

Hodgson, Godfrey. *The Colonel: The Life and Wars of Henry Stimson, 1867-1950*. New York: Knopf, 1990. Distributed by Random House.

Kaplan, Diane Ellen. *Guide to a Microfilm Edition of the Papers of Henry Lewis Stimson (Not Including the Diaries) in the Yale University Library*. New Haven, CT: Yale University Library Manuscripts and Archives, 1973.

Morison, Elting E. *Turmoil and Tradition: A Study of the Life and Times of Henry L. Stimson*. Boston: Houghton Mifflin, 1960.

Rappaport, Armin. *Henry L. Stimson and Japan, 1931-33*. Chicago: University of Chicago Press, 1963.

Stimson, Henry L. *Democracy and Nationalism in Europe*. Princeton: Princeton University Press, 1934.

______. *The Far Eastern Crisis: Recollections and Observations*. New York: Published for the Council on Foreign Relations by Harper & Brothers, 1936.

______. *Microfilm Edition of the Papers of Henry Lewis Stimson*. New Haven: Yale University Library, Manuscripts and Archives, 1973.

______ and McGeorge Bundy. *On Active Service in Peace and War*. New York: Octagon Books, 1971.

______. *Prelude to Invasion, An Account Based Upon Official Reports by Henry L. Stimson, Secretary of War*. Washington: Public Affairs Press, 1944.

22 Other Axis and Vichy Figures

The figures listed in this chapter played significant roles during the Second World War. Many did not survive the war and those that did were eventually tried in courts of law, convicted, and sentenced to death or imprisonment with the exception of Dr. Josef Mengele who escaped to South America after Germany's defeat. Selection of the figures was arbitrary on the part of the compiler.

Klaus Barbie
SS
1913-1991

Barbie was an officer in Heinrich Himmler's SS. He earned the nickname "Butcher of Lyon" because he deported French Jews to the Nazi death camps. Barbie escaped to South America after the war where he lived until his arrest by Bolivian government authorities in 1983. He was returned to Lyon, France to stand trial. Twice before, he had been tried in absentia by French courts and found guilty. When the trial began in 1987, he refused to participate, stating that he had been kidnapped and returned to France illegally. After presentation of testimony and evidence, Barbie was convicted of crimes against humanity and sentenced to life in prison. Ironically, he could not be sentenced to death because France does not have a death penalty. Barbie died of leukemia in September 1991. Recommended for reading are Tom Bower's *Klaus Barbie*, Alan Finkielkraut's *Remembering in Vain*, Magnus Linklater's *The Nazi Legacy*, and Ted Morgan's *An Uncertain Hour*.

Bibliography

Beattie, John. *The Life and Career of Klaus Barbie: An Eyewitness Record*. London: Methuen, 1984.

Bower, Tom. *Klaus Barbie: The Butcher of Lyon*. New York: Pantheon Books, 1984.

Dabringhaus, Erhard. *Klaus Barbie, the Shocking Story of How the U.S. Used This Nazi War Criminal as an Intelligence Agent*. Washington, DC: Acropolis Books, 1984.

Finkielkraut, Alan. *Remembering in Vain: The Klaus Barbie Trial and Crimes Against Humanity*. Translated by Roxanne Lapidus with Sima Godfrey. New York: Columbia University Press, 1992.

Hoyos, Ladislas de. *Klaus Barbie: The Untold Story*. Translated from the French by Nicholas Courtin. London: W. H. Allen, 1985.

Kahn, Annette. *Why My Father Died: A Daughter Confronts Her Family's Past at the Trial of Klaus Barbie*. New York: Summit Books, 1991.

Klarsfeld, Serge. *The Children of Izieu: A Human Tragedy*. Translated by Kenneth Jacobson. New York: H. Abrams, 1985.

Linklater, Magnus, and others. *The Nazi Legacy: Klaus Barbie and the International Fascist Connection*. New York: Holt, Rinehart & Winston, 1985.

Morgan, Ted. *An Uncertain Hour: The French, The Germans, The Jews, The Klaus Barbie Trial, and the City of Lyon, 1940-1945*. New York: Arbor House/William Morrow, 1990.

Murphy, Brendan. *The Butcher of Lyon: The Story of Infamous Nazi Klaus Barbie*. New York: Empire Books, 1983.

Paris, Erna. *Unhealed Wounds: France and the Klaus Barbie Affair*. New York: Grove Press, 1986.

Ryan, Allan A. *Klaus Barbie and the United States Government: The Report, with Documentary Appendix, to the Attorney General of the United States*. Frederick, MD: University Publications of America, 1984.

Wilson, Robert. *The Confessions of Klaus Barbie, the Butcher of Lyon*. Edited by James Osborne. Vancouver, B.C., Canada: Arsenal Editions, 1984.

Martin Bormann
Nazi Party Secretary
1900-1945

Bormann was an early member of the Nazi Party. In 1933, he became Rudolf Hess' deputy and by 1941 was a powerful figure in the Nazi Party. He was particularly adept at handling the day-to-day management of the party's affairs. When Hess flew a German fighter plane to Scotland in May 1941, Adolf Hitler promoted Bormann to Hess' position and gave him the rank of minister. During the war, especially after the conflict began to turn against Germany, Bormann wielded immense power. He controlled Hitler's schedule and all fuhrer appointments had to be made through him, causing much resentment by other high-ranking Nazi officials. Bormann stayed with Hitler to the end, witnessing the marriage of Hitler to his long-time mistress, Eva Braun, on 29 April 1945. After Hitler committed suicide on 30 April, Bormann tried to escape from Berlin. Though there is disagreement as to the actual fate of Martin Bormann, it appears he was killed in the escape attempt and did not reach South America as some historians have speculated. In 1973, the West German government announced that his skeleton had been recovered in the ruins of a Berlin building and pronounced him dead. Earlier, during the Nuremberg trials, Bormann was tried in absentia, found guilty, and was given a death sentence. Recommended for reading are *The Bormann Letters* and Jochen von Lang's *The Secretary: Martin Bormann.*

Bibliography

Bezymensky, L. *Tracing Martin Bormann.* Translated from the Russian by David Skvirsky and Igor Sokolov. Moscow: Progress Publishers, 1966.

Bormann, Martin. *The Bormann Letters: The Private Correspondence Between Martin Bormann and His Wife from January 1943 to April 1945.* Translated by R. H. Stevens. Edited with an introduction by H. R. Trevor-Roper. London: Weidenfeld & Nicolson, 1954.

Farago, Ladislas. *Aftermath: Martin Bormann and the Fourth Reich.* New York: Simon & Schuster, 1974.

Gray, Ronald D. *I Killed Martin Bormann!* New York: Lancer, 1972.

Lang, Jochen von. *The Secretary: Martin Bormann. The Man Who Manipulated Hitler.* Translated from the German by Christa Armstrong and Peter White. New York: Random House, 1979.

Manning, Paul. *Martin Bormann, Nazi in Exile*. Secaucus, NJ: Stuart, 1981.

McGovern, James. *Martin Bormann*. New York: Morrow, 1968.

Melchior, Ib and Frank Brandenburg. *Quest: Searching for Germany's Nazi Past: A Young Man's Story*. Novato, CA: Presidio, 1990.

Schmier, Louis Eugene. "*Martin Bormann and the Nazi Party, 1941-1945*." Ph.D. diss., University of North Carolina at Chapel Hill, 1969. (DAI, 30:8, 3410A, UMI Order # 703309)

Sognnaes, Reider F. *Dental Evidence in the Postmortem Identification of Adolf Hitler, Eva Braun, and Martin Bormann*. New York: Appleton-Century-Croft, 1977.

Stevenson, William. *The Bormann Brotherhood*. New York: Harcourt, Brace, Jovanovich, 1973.

Whiting, Charles. *The Hunt for Martin Bormann*. New York: Ballantine Books, 1973.

Count Galeazzo Cinao
Italian Minister for Foreign Affairs
1903-1944

Count Ciano was an early member of the Italian Fascist Party. He cemented his relationship with Benito Mussolini by marrying Il Duce's daughter, Edda, in 1930. Ciano rose quickly in the government ranks and in 1936 was named Minister for Foreign Affairs. He negotiated the Pact of Steel with the German Nazi government which linked the two nations militarily, but was suspicious of Germany's intentions in Europe. His fears were well-founded when Germany invaded Poland on 1 September 1939 without informing the Italian government beforehand. Ciano wanted to pull out of the alliance, but the quick fall of France in June 1940 prohibited any opportunity. As the war escalated in 1942 and the Soviet Union's Red Army began massive counteroffensives, destroying German and Italian divisions, Ciano urged Mussolini to negotiate a separate peace with the Allies. Mussolini refused and saw this request as a sign of disloyalty. Ciano was removed as Foreign Minister and was given the ambassadorship to the Vatican in February 1943. Ciano remained a member of the Italian Grand Council and led the movement that ousted Mussolini from power and placed the dictator under arrest. The new Italian government soon turned on Ciano and charged him with corruption. He fled to northern Italy where he was captured by Italians loyal to Mussolini. Ciano was shot by firing squad on 11 January 1944. *The Ciano Diaries, 1939-1943* are recommended for reading.

Bibliography

Ciano, Edda Mussolini. *My Truth.* As told to Albert Zarca. Translated from the French by Eileen Finletter. New York: Morrow, 1977.

Ciano, Galeazzo. *The Ciano Diaries, 1939-1943: The Complete, Unabridged Diaries of Count Galeazzo Ciano, Italian Minister for Foreign Affairs, 1936-1943.* Edited by Hugh Gibson. New York: H. Fertig, 1973.

______. *Ciano's Diplomatic Papers, Being A Record of Nearly 200 Conversations Held During the Years 1936-42 with Hitler, Mussolini, Franco, Goering, Ribbentrop, Chamberlain, Eden, Sumner Welles, Schuschnigg, Lord Perth, Francois-Poncet, and Many Other World Diplomatic and Political Figures, Together with Important Memoranda, Letters, Telegrams, Etc.* Edited by Malcolm Muggeridge. Translated by Stuart Hood. London: Odhams Press, 1948.

______. *Ciano's Hidden Diary, 1937-1938.* Translation and notes by Andreas Mayor. New York: E. P. Dutton, 1953.

Lavine, Marcia Fishel. "*Count Ciano: Foreign Affairs and Policy Determination in Fascist Italy, January 1939-June 1940.*" Ph.D. diss., Vanderbilt University, 1977. (DAI, 38:3, 1586A, UMI Order # 7719383)

Smyth, Howard McGaw. *Secrets of the Fascist Era: How Uncle Sam Obtained Some of the Top-Level Documents of Mussolini's Period.* Carbondale, IL: Southern Illinois University Press, 1975.

Obersturmbannfuehrer (Lieutenant Colonel) Adolf Eichmann
SS
1906-1962

Eichmann was a high-ranking member of Heinrich Himmler's SS. He worked directly with Obergruppenfuhrer (Lieutenant General) Reinhard Heydrich until Heydrich's death in 1942. During the war, Eichmann was responsible for transporting Jews from occupied Europe to the extermination camps in Poland. This was the Third Reich's "Final Solution" to the perceived Jewish problem. In April 1945, he changed his identity and managed to escape from Germany to Argentina where he remained until 1960. After Israeli intelligence agents located him, a commando team captured and transported him to Israel to stand trial. During his pre-trial interrogation, Eichmann revealed much about the Holocaust and his testimony covered some 3 500 pages. What made Eichmann so chilling was his insistence that he was just following orders and that his task of transporting Jews to the extermination camps was only his job. Eichmann was found guilty and hanged on 31 May 1962. Recommended for reading are Hannah Arendt's *Eichmann in Jerusalem*, Isser Harel's *The House on Garibaldi Street*, Jochem von Lang's *Eichmann Interrogated*, and Peter Z. Malkin's and Harry Stein's *Eichmann in My Hands*.

Bibliography

American Jewish Committee. *The Eichmann Case in the American Press*. New York: Institute of Human Relations Press, American Jewish Committee, 1962.

Arendt, Hannah. *Eichmann in Jerusalem: A Report on the Banality of Evil*. Rev. and enl. ed. New York: Penguin Books, 1977.

Braham, Randolph L. *Eichmann and the Destruction of Hungarian Jewry*. New York: World Federation of Hungarian Jews. Distributed by Twayne Publishers, 1961.

_____. *The Eichmann Case: A Source Book*. New York: World Federation of Hungarian Jews, 1969.

Clarke, Comer. *Eichmann: The Man and His Crimes*. New York: Ballantine, 1960.

Deutsch, Akiva W. *The Eichmann Trial in the Eyes of Israeli Youngsters: Opinions, Attitudes and Impact*. Jerusalem: Bar-Ilan University, 1974.

Donovan, John. *Eichmann, Man of Slaughter*. New York: Avon Book Division, Hearst Corporation, 1960.

Eichmann, Adolf. *Transcript of the Trial in the Case of the Attorney-General of the Government of Israel v. Adolf, the Son of Adolf Karl Eichmann, in the District Court of Jerusalem. Criminal Case No. 40161*. Washington, DC: Microcard Editions, 1962.

_____. *The Trial of Adolf Eichmann. Record of the Proceedings*. 5 volumes. Translated from the Hebrew. Hewlett, NY: Gefen Books, 1993.

Francq, H. G. *A Study of Guilt: The Eichmann Story*. London: Third Eye, 1991.

Friedman, Towiah. *The Blind Man Who Discovered Adolf Eichmann in Argentina*. Haifa, Israel: Institute of Documentation in Israel for the Investigation of Nazi War Crimes, 1987.

Glock, Charles Y., and others. *The Apathetic Majority: A Study Based on Public Responses to the Eichmann Trial*. New York: Harper & Row, 1966.

Gollancz, Victor. *The Case of Adolf Eichmann*. London, 1961.

Harel, Isser. *The House on Garibaldi Street: The First Full Account of the Capture of Adolf Eichmann*. New York: Viking Press, 1975.

Hausner, Gideon. *Justice in Jerusalem*. New York: Harper & Row, 1966.

______. *6,000,000 Accusers: Israel's Case Against Eichmann: The Opening Speech and Legal Argument of Mr. Gideon Hausner, Attorney-General*. Translated from the Hebrew and edited by Shabtai Rosenne. Jerusalem: Jerusalem Post, 1961.

Herzberg, Abel J. *Eichmann in Jerusalem*. Den Haag: B. Bakker, 1962.

Hull, William Lovell. *The Struggle for a Soul*. Garden City, NY: Doubleday, 1963.

Lang, Jochen von, in collaboration with Claus Sibyll. *Eichmann Interrogated*. Translated from the German by Ralph Manheim. New York: Farrar, Straus & Giroux, 1983.

Levai, Jeno, ed. *Eichmann in Hungary: Documents*. New York: H. Fertig, 1987.

Linze, Dewey W. *The Trial of Adolf Eichmann*. Los Angeles: Holloway House Pub. Co., 1961.

Malkin, Peter Z. and Harry Stein. *Eichmann in My Hands*. New York: Warner Books, 1990.

Murray, Michael Patrick. *"A Study in Public International Law: Comparing the Trial of Adolf Eichmann in Jerusalem with the Trial of the Major German War Criminals of Nuremberg."* Thesis, J.S.D., George Washington University, 1973. (DAI, 34:6, 3442A, UMI Order # 7328750)

Musmanno, Michael Angelo. *The Death Sentence in the Case of Adolf Eichmann: A Letter to His Excellency Itzhak Ben-Zvi, President of the State of Israel*. Pittsburgh, n.p., 1962.

Paneth, Philip. *Eichmann: Technician of Death*. New York: R. Speller, 1960.

Papadatos, Pierre. *The Eichmann Trial*. New York: F. A. Praeger, 1964.

Pearlman, Moshe. *The Capture and Trial of Adolf Eichmann*. New York: Simon & Schuster, 1963.

Rassinier, Paul. *The Real Eichmann Trial: or, The Incorrigible Victors*. Translated from the original French. Chapel Ascote: Historical Review Press, 1979.

Reynolds, Quentin, and others. *Minister of Death: The Adolf Eichmann Story*. New York: Viking Press, 1960.

Robinson, Jacob. *And the Crooked Shall Be Made Straight: The Eichmann Trial, the Jewish Catastrophe, and Hannah Arendt's Narrative*. Philadelphia: Jewish Publication Society of America, 1965.

Rogat, Yosal. *The Eichmann Trial and the Rule of Law*. Santa Barbara, CA: Center for the Study of Democratic Institutions, 1961.

Russell, Edward Frederick Langley. *The Record: The Trial of Adolf Eichmann for His Crimes Against the Jewish People and Against Humanity*. New York: Knopf, 1963.

Woetzel, Robert K. *The Nuremberg Trials in International Law. With A Postlude on the Eichmann Case*. New York: Praeger, 1962.

Zeiger, Henry A., ed. *The Case Against Adolf Eichmann*. New York: New American Library, 1960.

Hans Frank
Governor General of Poland
1900-1946

Frank was Adolf Hitler's legal advisor prior to the establishment of the Third Reich. From 1933 to 1939, Frank held several positions in the Nazi government, including Reich Commissioner of Justice and Minister without Portfolio, and was president of the Law Academy. After Poland was conquered in 1939, Frank was named governor general of central Poland, the section of the country that was not annexed outright by either Germany or the Soviet Union. As governor general, he instituted programs that used the Polish population as slave labourers and forced the Jewish populace into ghettos. Later, most of the Jews were shipped to exterminations camps at Auschwitz and Treblinka. Frank resigned his position when the Warsaw Ghetto Uprising started in August 1944. By that time, Red Army units were near Warsaw, but waited until January 1945 to capture the city. By waiting, time was given to the Germans to crush the only organized Polish resistance that might have contested the post-war occupation of Poland by the Soviet Union. Frank was captured at the conclusion of the war and placed on trial at Nuremberg. He admitted his guilt and was hanged on 16 October 1946. Niklas Frank's *In the Shadow of the Reich* is recommended for reading.

Bibliography

Frank, Niklas. *In the Shadow of the Reich*. Translated by Arthur S. Wensinger with Carole Clew-Hoey. New York: Knopf. Distributed by Random House, 1991.

Pitrowski, Stanislaw, ed. *Hans Frank's Diary*. Warszawa, Panstwowe Wydawn: Naukowe, 1961.

Dr. Josef Goebbels
Minister for Propaganda and Public Enlightenment
Nazi Party
1897-1945

Goebbels wielded immense power, greatly influencing the opinions of the German people by his control of radio broadcasts and newspaper publication. He was an early member of the Nazi party, joining in 1924. When Adolf Hitler was named chancellor in 1933, Goebbels became propaganda minister and remained loyal to the end. He and his family lived in the Chancellory bunker with Hitler and Eva Braun during the final weeks of the war. After Hitler and Braun killed themselves on 30 April 1945, Goebbels poisoned his six children, then shot his wife and himself. During the late stages of the war, Goebbels continually exhorted the German populace to make sacrifices for the good of the reich and to resist until miracle weapons were ready which would reverse the tide. The Allies took his messages seriously. Fortunately for the Allies, the miracle weapons, mainly the V1 and V2 rockets and jet fighter planes, though deadly, were not enough to alter the outcome. Also of concern was Goebbels' announcement of a "national redoubt" in the mountains of Bavaria where the remaining elements of the army would fight to the last man. However, the "national redoubt" proved to be a myth and was merely a propaganda ploy. Recommended for reading are *The Goebbels Diaries, 1939-1941*, *The Goebbels Diaries, 1942-43*, and *Final Entries, 1945*. Also recommended are Helmet Heiber's *Goebbels* and Victor Reiman's *Goebbels*.

Bibliography

Bramsted, Ernest K. *Goebbels and National Socialist Propaganda, 1925-1945*. East Lansing, MI: Michigan State University Press, 1965.

Ebermayer, Erich and Hans Otto Meissner. *Evil Genius*. Translated and adapted from the German by Louis Hagen. London: Tandem, 1973.

Goebbels, Josef. *The Early Goebbels Diaries, 1925-1926*. Edited by Helmut Heiber. Translated from the German by Oliver Watson. New York: Praeger, 1963.

______. *Final Entries, 1945: The Diaries of Joseph Goebbels*. Edited, introduced and annotated by Hugh Trevor-Roper. Translated from the German by Richard Barry. New York: Putnam, 1978.

______. *The Goebbels Diaries, 1939-1941*. Translated and edited by Fred Taylor. New York: Putnam, 1983.

______. *The Goebbels Diaries, 1942-1943*. Edited and translated with an introduction by Louis P. Lochner. Garden City, NY: Doubleday, 1948.

______. *Kampf um Berlin*. New York: H. Fertig, 1980.

______. *Michael: A German Destiny in the Pages of a Diary* (fiction). Translated, with an introduction by Donald L. Niewyk. Baton Rouge, LA: Louisiana State University Press, 1985.

______. *My Part in Germany's Fight*. Translated by Kurt Fiedler. New York: H. Fertig, 1979. (Reprint of the 1940 edition published by Hurst & Blackett.)

______. *Nazi-Sozi. Questions and Answers for National Socialists*. Translated from the German. Valley Forge, PA: The Landpost Press, n.d. (Originally published in 1931.)

______. *The Secret Conferences of Dr. Goebbels: The Nazi Propaganda War, 1939-1943*. Selected and edited by Willi A. Boelcke. Translated from the German by Ewald Osers. New York: E. P. Dutton, 1970.

Hardy, Alexander G. *Hitler's Secret Weapon: The "Managed" Press and Propaganda Machine of Nazi Germany*. New York: Vantage Press, 1967.

Heiber, Helmut. *Goebbels*. Translated by John K. Dickinson. New York: Hawthorn Books, 1972.

Lemmons, Russel William. *"Joseph Goebbels, Berlin, and 'Der Angriff': The Blood Years, 1927-1933."* Ph.D. diss., Miami University, 1991. (DAI, 2681A, UMI Order # DA9200973)

Manvell, Roger and Heinrich Fraenkel. *Doctor Goebbels*. 2nd rev. ed. London: New English Library, 1968.

McKenzie, Vernon. *Here Lies Goebbels!* London: M. Joseph Ltd., 1940.

Meissner, Hans Otto. *Magda Goebbels: A Biography*. London: Sidgwick & Jackson, 1980.

Pick, Frederick Walter. *The Art of Dr. Goebbels*. London: R. Hale Limited, 1942.

Reichenau, Joachim. *This Man Goebbels*. London: Pallas Publishing Company Limited, 1940.

Reimann, Viktor. *Goebbels*. Translated from the German by Stephen Wendt. Garden City, NY: Doubleday, 1976.

Reuth, Ralf Georg. *Goebbels*. Translated from the German by Krishna Winston. New York: Harcourt Brace, 1993.

Riess, Curt. *Joseph Goebbels*. Garden City, NY: Doubleday, 1948.

Rutherford, Ward. *Hitler's Propaganda Machine*. New York: Grosset & Dunlap, 1978.

Semmler, Rudolf. *Goebbels, The Man Next to Hitler*. New York: AMS Press, 1981. (Originally published in 1947 by Westhouse.)

Wykes, Alan. *Goebbels*. New York: Ballantine Books, 1973.

Rudolf Hess
Deputy Fuehrer of the Nazi Party
1894-1987

Hess is one of the Second World War's more intriguing figures. He was Adolf Hitler's personal aide and deputy leader of the Nazi Party until the night of 10 May 1941 when he flew a German fighter plane to Great Britain. Hess maintained that the purpose of his flight was to secure peace with the British because the common enemy of both Germany and Great Britain was the Soviet Union. Hitler was enraged by Hess' actions, denounced him as a madman, and had his name purged from all party records. The British treated Hess as a prisoner of war and held him for the remainder of the conflict. He was convicted of crimes against peace at the Nuremberg trials. The Russians asked for the death penalty, but other Allied representatives opted for life imprisonment. Hess died in 1987, still a prisoner of the victorious Allies. Recommended for reading are James Douglas-Hamilton's *Motive for A Mission*, Roger Manvell's and Heinrich Fraenkel's *Hess*, and Peter Padfield's *Hess*.

Bibliography

Allen, Peter. *The Windsor Secret: New Revelations of the Nazi Connection*. New York: Stein & Day, 1984.

Bird, Eugene K. *Prisoner # 7, Rudolf Hess: The Thirty Years in Jail of Hitler's Deputy Fuehrer*. New York: Viking Press, 1974.

Costello, John. *Ten Days to Destiny: The Secret Story of the Hess Peace Initiative and British Efforts to Strike a Deal with Hitler*. New York: Morrow, 1991.

Douglas-Hamilton, James. *Motive for a Mission: The Story Behind Hess's Flight to Britain*. New York: St. Martin's Press, 1971.

Hess, Ilse. *Prisoner of Peace*. Translated from the German by Meyrick Booth. Edited by George Pile. Torrance, CA: Institute for Historical Review, 1954.

Hess, Rudolf. *Germany and Peace: A Soldier's Message*. Berlin: M. Muller, n.d. (Translation of a speech delivered July 8, 1934.)

______. *Selected Speeches*. United States: Hammer, 1990.

Hess, Wolf Rudiger. *My Father, Rudolf Hess*. Translated by Frederick Crowley. London: W. H. Allen, 1986.

Hutton, J. Bernard. *Hess: The Man and His Mission*. New York: Macmillan, 1971.

Irving, David. *Hess: The Missing Years, 1941-1945*. London: Macmillan, 1987.

Kilzer, Louis. *Churchill's Deception: The Dark Secret That Destroyed Nazi Germany*. New York: Simon & Schuster, 1994.

Leasor, James. *The Uninvited Envoy*. New York: McGraw-Hill, 1962.

Manvell, Roger and Heinrich Fraenkel. *Hess, a Biography*. London: MacGibbon & Kee, 1971.

Moriarty, David M. *Rudolf Hess, Deputy Fuehrer: A Psychological Study*. St. Louis: Warren H. Green Inc., n.d.

Padfield, Peter. *Hess: Flight for the Fuehrer*. London: Weidenfeld & Nicolson, 1991.

Rees, John R. *The Case of Rudolf Hess: A Problem in Diagnosis and Forensic Psychiatry, by the Following Physicians in the Services Who Have Been Concerned with Him from 1941 to 1946*. London: W. Heinemann, 1947.

Schwarzwaller, Wulf. *Rudolf Hess, the Last Nazi*. Bethesda, MD: National Press, 1988.

Thomas, Hugh. *Hess: A Tale of Two Murders*. Rev. ed. London: Hodder & Stoughton, 1988.

Obergruppenfuehrer (Lieutenant General) Reinhard Heydrich
SS
1904-1942

Heydrich was second in command in the SS at the time of his death in 1942. If he had lived, he would have been a possible successor to Adolf Hitler as leader of Germany. Heydrich arranged the border incident that allowed Hitler to invade Poland in 1939. He was in command of the extermination squads that followed the German Army as it swept across Russia in 1941. Tens of thousands of Russians and Jews were killed by his men. He was author of the "Final Solution" which called for the total extermination of all Jewish citizens in occupied Europe. The plan was presented at the Wannsee conference in January 1942. A few months earlier, Heydrich was named Reich Protector of Czechoslovakia. The Czech government-in-exile, in an attempt to rekindle the underground movement that Heydrich was effectively stamping out with his mostly nonviolent policies, decided to assassinate him. On 29 May 1942, Heydrich was ambushed and severely injured. He died on 4 June. In reprisal, the village of Lidice was razed to the ground. All women and children were sent to concentration camps and all males over the age of fifteen were shot. Heydrich was the one man that the Nazis themselves feared the most because of the cold and methodical way he carried out his orders and of his determination for advancement in the hierarchy of the Third Reich. Recommended for reading are Edouard Calic's *Reinhard Heydrich*, Callum MacDonald's *The Killing of SS Obergruppenfuhrer Reinhard Heydrich*, and Alan Wyke's *Heydrich*.

Bibliography

Burgess, Alan. *Seven Men at Daybreak*. New York: Dutton, 1960.

Calic, Edouard. *Reinhard Heydrich: The Chilling Story of the Man Who Masterminded the Nazi Death Camps*. Translated by Lowell Bair. New York: Morrow, 1985.

Czechoslovak Republic. *Memorandum of the Czechoslovak Government on the Reign of Terror in Bohemia and Moravia Under the Regime of Reinhard Heydrich*. London: Czechoslovak Ministry of Foreign Affaires, Dept. of Information, 1942.

Deschner, Gunther. *Reinhard Heydrich: A Biography*. New York: Stein & Day, 1981.

Erdely, Eugene V. *Prague Braves the Hangman*. London: "The Czechoslovak" Independent Weekly, 1942.

Graber, G. S. *The Life and Times of Reinhard Heydrich*. New York: McKay, 1980.

Hutak, J. B. *With Blood and With Iron*. London: Hamilton, 1958.

Ivanov, Miroslav. *Target: Heydrich*. Translated from the French by Patrick O'Brian. New York: Macmillan, 1973.

MacDonald, Callum. *The Killing of SS Obergruppenfuhrer Reinhard Heydrich*. New York: The Free Press, 1989.

Wiener, Jan G. *The Assassination of Heydrich*. New York: Grossman Publishers, 1969.

Wighton, Charles. *Heydrich: Hitler's Most Evil Henchman*. Philadelphia: Chilton Co., 1962.

Wykes, Alan. *Heydrich*. New York: Ballantine Books, 1973.

X, a former Gestapo officer. *Heydrich the Murderer*. Rendered into English by Richard Baxter. London: Quality Press Ltd., 1942.

Rudolf Hoess
SS
1900-1947

Hoess was an early and ardent member of the Nazi party. In 1923, he was convicted of participating in the murder of a political opponent and sentenced to ten years in prison, but served only five. He joined the SS in 1933 and in 1934 was appointed to the Dachau concentration camp staff. His managerial ability was noted by Heinrich Himmler, head of the SS, and from 1940 to 1943, Hoess was commandant of the infamous extermination camp at Auschwitz. At the Nuremberg trials, Hoess was unrepentant and showed little feeling about what he had done. Following his conviction, he was transferred to Poland to stand trial for crimes committed against the Polish nation. He was found guilty and taken to Auschwitz where he was hanged. Hoess' memoir, *Death Dealer*, is recommended for reading. The memoir was originally published in the United States in 1960 under the title *Commandant of Auschwitz*.

Bibliography

Hoess, Rudolf. *Death Dealer: The Memoirs of the SS Kommandant at Auschwitz*. Edited by Steven Paskuly. Translated by Andrew Pollinger. Buffalo, NY: Prometheus Books, 1992.

Pierre Laval
French Premier
1883-1945

Laval was one of France's leading politicians during the 1930s. He was premier in 1931, foreign minister in 1934, and premier again in 1936. After a government reorganization in 1936, he did not hold a political position until 1940 when he helped establish the Vichy government after France was defeated by Nazi Germany. Marshal Philippe Petain was chosen as head of state and Laval was named Vice-President of the Council of Ministers. Laval was fired in December 1940, but was reinstated in 1942. He is most known for his collaboration with Nazi Germany. On his orders, French citizens were forcibly sent to Germany to work in war production factories. When the Allies invaded and liberated France, Laval went to Germany, then to Austria, and finally to Spain to avoid arrest. After the war, he agreed to voluntarily return to France to stand trial for treason. By most accounts, he did not receive a fair hearing. Convicted of treason, he was executed by firing squad on 15 October 1945. Recommended for reading are Rene de Chambrun's *Pierre Laval* and Geoffrey Warner's *Pierre Laval and the Eclipse of France*.

Bibliography

Abrahamsen, David. *Men, Mind, and Power*. New York: Columbia University Press, 1945.

Anonymous. *Petain-Laval, the Conspiracy*. Translated by Michael Sadleir. London: Constable & Co. Ltd., 1945.

Chambrun, Rene de. *Pierre Laval: Traitor or Patriot?* New York: Scribner, 1984.

Cole, Hubert. *Laval, a Biography*. New York: Putnam, 1963.

Geraud, Andre. *The Gravediggers of France: Gamelin, Daladier, Reynaud, Petain, and Laval: Military Defeat, Armistice, Counterrevolution*. Garden City, NY: Doubleday, Doran, 1944.

Laval, Pierre. *The Diary of Pierre Laval*. New York: C. Scribner's Sons, 1948.

Thomson, David. *Two Frenchman: Pierre Laval and Charles de Gaulle*. London: Cresset Press, 1951.

Tissier, Pierre. *I Worked with Laval*. London: G. G. Harrap & Co. Ltd., 1942.

Torres, Henry. *Pierre Laval*. Translated by Norbert Guterman. New York: Oxford University Press, 1941.

Warner, Geoffrey. *Pierre Laval and the Eclipse of France*. New York: Macmillan, 1969.

Dr. Josef Mengele
SS
1911-1979

Mengele was a medical doctor in Heinrich Himmler's SS. In 1940, he participated in Adolf Hitler's euthanasia program in which thousands of mentally disabled Germans were murdered. Later, at Auschwitz, the most notorious of all the Nazi concentration camps, he conducted medical experiments on prisoners, especially dwarfs and twins. Actually, his experiments were nothing more than torture sessions inflicted upon innocent victims. Another of his duties consisted of deciding which prisoners would live or die as they disembarked from the trains. Mengele has been described as arrogant, cruel, vain, and lacking any compassion whatsoever. At the end of the war, he managed to escape to South America. He apparently drowned off the coast of Brazil in 1979. Recommended for reading are Gerald Astor's *The Last Nazi* and Gerald Posner's and John Ware's *Mengele*.

Bibliography

Astor, Gerald. *The Last Nazi: The Life and Times of Dr. Joseph Mengele*. New York: Donald I. Fine, 1985.

Erdstein, Erich with Barbara Bean. *Inside the Fourth Reich*. New York: St. Martin's Press, 1977.

Lagnado, Lucette M. and Sheila Cohn Dekel. *Children of the Flames: The Untold Story of the Twins of Auschwitz*. New York: Morrow, 1991.

Moskovitz, Elizabeth. *By the Grace of Satan: The Story of the Dwarves Family in Aushvitz and Dr. Mengele's Experiments*. Rewriting and editing by Judith Rotem. Translation by Karen Adler. Ramat-Gan: Rotem Publication, 1987.

Nyiszli, Miklos. *Auschwitz: A Doctor's Eyewitness Account*. Translated by Tibere Kremer and Richard Seaver. New York: F. Fell, 1960.

Posner, Gerald L. and John Ware. *Mengele: The Complete Story*. New York: McGraw-Hill, 1986.

United States Congress. Senate Committee on the Judiciary. Subcommittee on Juvenile Justice. *Searching for Dr. Josef Mengele: Hearings Before the Subcommittee on Juvenile Justice of the Committee on the Judiciary, United States Senate, Ninety-ninth Congress, First Session, To Inquire into Dr. Mengele's Whereabouts and on the Role of the U.S. Army, If He Was in Custody of the U.S. Government, February 19; March 19; and August 2, 1985*. Washington, DC: U.S. Government Printing Office, 1986.

Waymire, Ray V. *The Mengele Hoax*. Nashville: Winston-Derek Publishers Inc., 1990. (juvenile)

Lieutenant General Hiroshi Oshima
Japanese Ambassador to Nazi Germany
1886-1975

Oshima spent most of his career in diplomacy. In the 1930s, he was the military attache at the Japanese embassy in Berlin. During this time, he established many valuable contacts in the Nazi government. He helped negotiate the Anti-Comintern Pact which was signed by representatives of the Japanese and German governments on 25 November 1936. Both countries pledged to fight the international expansion of Communism. Oshima was promoted to lieutenant general in 1940 and named ambassador to Germany. He played a major role in negotiating the Tripartite Pact signed on 27 September 1940 by Japan, Germany, and Italy. He remained in Berlin during the war. After the war, he was arrested and tried as a war criminal. He was sentenced to life in prison, but was paroled in 1955. Recommended for reading are Carl Boyd's *The Extraordinary Envoy* and *Hitler's Japanese Confidant*.

Bibliography

Boyd, Carl. *The Extraordinary Envoy: General Hiroshi Oshima and Diplomacy in the Third Reich, 1934-1939*. Washington, DC: University Press of America, 1980.

_____. *Hitler's Japanese Confidant: General Hiroshi Oshima and MAGIC Intelligence, 1941-1945*. Lawrence, KS: University Press of Kansas, 1993.

Joachim von Ribbentrop
German Foreign Minister
1893-1946

Von Ribbentrop was Adolf Hitler's top diplomat from 1938 to 1945. Previously, he had served as ambassador to Great Britain from 1936 to 1938. Von Ribbentrop was named Foreign Minister in charge of diplomatic affairs in 1938. During the next few years, he scored many diplomatic victories. Most notable were the Munich Agreement, signed in September 1938, the occupation of the remainder of Czechoslovakia in March 1939, and the Nazi-Soviet Non-aggression Pact, signed in August 1939. The Non-aggression Pact divided Poland between Germany and the Soviet Union and gave control of the Baltic states of Latvia, Lithuania, and Estonia to the Soviet Union. In June 1940, Von Ribbentrop persuaded Benito Mussolini to enter the war against France and Great Britain. As the war continued, von Ribbentrop gradually lost favour with Hitler, then was completely discredited when a few members of the Foreign Office were implicated in the 20 July 1944 bombing attempt against the fuehrer. After the war, von Ribbentrop tried to escape, but was captured by the Allies and placed on trial at Nuremberg. He was found guilty of crimes against humanity, sentenced to death, and hanged on 16 October 1946. Recommended for reading are Michael Bloch's *Ribbentrop* and John Weitz's *Hitler's Diplomat*.

Bibliography

Bloch, Michael. *Ribbentrop*. New York: Crown Publishers, 1993.

Craig, Andrew W. "*The Limits of Success: Joachim Von Ribbentrop and German Relations with Great Britain, 1934-1939*." Ph.D. diss., Bowling Green State University, 1982. (DAI, 43:10, 3394A, UMI Order # DA8306233)

Glen, Douglas. *Von Ribbentrop is Still Dangerous*. London: Rich & Cowan, 1941.

Gunther, Gerhard von. *Von Ribbentrop*. London: Pallas Pub. Co., 1939.

Ribbentrop, Joachim von. *The Ribbentrop Memoirs*. Translated by Oliver Watson. London: Weidenfeld & Nicolson, 1953.

Schwarz, Paul. *This Man Ribbentrop: His Life and Times*. New York: J. Messner Inc., 1943.

Vizulis, I. Joseph. *The Molotov-Ribbentrop Pact of 1939: The Baltic Case*. New York: Praeger, 1990.

Waddington, Geoffrey T. "*The Career and Political Views of Joachim von Ribbentrop, 1932-1938, with Special Reference to Anglo-German Relations.*" Ph.D. diss., University of Leeds, 1987. (DAI, 49:5, 1251A, UMI Order # BRD81031)

Weitz, John. *Hitler's Diplomat: The Life and Times of Joachim von Ribbentrop*. New York: Ticknor & Fields, 1992.

Albert Speer
German Minister for Armaments and Munitions
1905-1981

Speer was the Nazi Party's chief architect. He was chosen to create a new Berlin for Adolf Hitler that would be an architectural wonder. However, only the Reich Chancellory was completed before the Second World War began. Speer's excellent administrative abilities were soon recognized and in 1942, after Fritz Todt was killed in an airplane crash, Speer was named Minister for Armaments and Munitions. Speer increased war materiel production despite the heavy Allied air bombardment campaign directed at German factories and oil refineries. One of the principle ways he increased production was by the use of slave labour. After the war, Speer was tried at Nuremberg for crimes against humanity and sentenced to 20 years in prison at Spandau. He was released in 1966. Speer's memoir gives an excellent insight to the inner workings of the Third Reich and the role he played as do the other works he has written.

Bibliography

Becker, Peter Wolfgang. "*The Basis of the German War Economy Under Albert Speer, 1942-1944.*" Ph.D. diss., Stanford University, 1971. (DAI, 32:10, 5700A, UMI Order # 7211508)

Hamsher, William. *Albert Speer-Victim of Nuremberg?* London: Leslie Frewin Publishers Ltd., 1970.

Helmer, Stephen D. *Hitler's Berlin: The Speer Plans for Reshaping the Central City*. Ann Arbor, MI: UMI Research Press, 1985.

Schmidt, Matthias. *Speer: The End of A Myth*. Translated by Joachim Neugroschel. New York: St. Martin's Press, 1984.

Sereny, Gitta. *Albert Speer: His Battle with Truth*. New York: Alfred A. Knopf, 1995.

Speer, Albert. *Infiltration*. Translated by Joachim Neugroschel. New York: Macmillan, 1981.

______. *Inside the Third Reich: Memoirs*. Translated from the German by Richard and Clara Winston. New York: Macmillan, 1970.

______. *The Slave State: Heinrich Himmler's Masterplan for SS Supremacy*. London: Weidenfeld & Nicolson, 1981.

______. *Spandau: The Secret Diaries*. Translated from the German by Richard and Clara Winston. New York: Macmillan, 1976.

United States. Office of Strategic Services. Research and Analysis Branch. *Speer's Appointment As Dictator of the German Economy*. Washington, DC: n.p., 1943.

White Morris, Judith J. "*Albert Speer: The Hitler Years. Views of A Reich Minister*." Ph.D. diss., Ball State University, 1987. (DAI, 48:5, 1295A, UMI Order # DA8713553)

Zilbert, Edward R. *Albert Speer and the Nazi Ministry of Arms: Economic Institutions and Industrial Production in the German War Economy*. Rutherford, NJ: Fairleigh Dickenson University Press, 1981.

Julius Streicher
Nazi Party
1885-1946

Streicher was an early member of the Nazi Party. He merged his smaller anti-Semitic party with Adolf Hitler's National Socialist German Workers Party in 1921. Streicher played a major role in the abortive Munich putsch of 1923. He founded the virulent, anti-Semitic journal, *Der Strumer*, in 1922 and was its editor until 1933. By then, circulation had reached 500,000. Streicher was party gauleiter of Franconia from 1925 to 1940. He was forced to retire from active party operations in 1940 because of improper personal conduct involving the misappropriation of confiscated Jewish property. He was tried at Nuremberg after the war on the basis that his writings and speeches incited mass hatred and murder of the Jewish population. He was hanged on 15 October 1946. Recommended for reading are Randall Bytwerk's *Julius Streicher* and William Varga's *The Number One Jew Baiter*.

Bibliography

Bondy, Louis W. *Racketeers of Hatred, Julius Streicher and the Jew-Baiters' International*. London and Leicester: N. Wolsey Limited, 1946.

Bytwerk, Randall L. *Julius Streicher*. New York: Stein & Day, 1983.

Showalter, Dennis E. *Little Man, What Now? Der Strumer in the Weimer Republic*. Hamden, CT: Archon Books, 1982.

Varga, William Paul, Sr. "*Julius Streicher: A Political Biography, 1885-1933*." Ph.D. diss., The Ohio State University, 1974. (DAI, 35:5, 2921A, UMI Order # 7424419)

______. *The Number One Jew Baiter: A Political Biography of Julius Streicher*. New York: Carlton Press, 1981.

23 Miscellaneous Entries

The bibliographic entries in this chapter are listed here because their subject content does not allow them to be placed in any of the other chapters. However, they should be of interest to the military or political historian or the general reader. To determine what works are in this chapter, scan the entries under the subject headings. Please note that the entries in this chapter should not be considered exhaustive, but only a fair representation of what is available on the subject.

Bibliography

Allied/Axis Military Commanders

Dupuy, Treavor Nevitt. *Combat Leaders of World War II*. New York: Watts, 1965. (juvenile)

Howarth, Stephen. *Men of War: Great Naval Leaders of World War II*. New York: St. Martin's Press, 1989.

Livesey, Anthony. *Great Commanders and Their Battles*. New York: Macmillan, 1987.

Ryan, Cornelius. *Papers*. Athens, OH: Ohio University Library, Department of Archives and Special Collections, n.d. (Includes interviews with various Allied and Axis military commanders.)

Smyth, John George. *Leadership in War, 1939-1945: The Generals in Victory and Defeat*. New York: St. Martin's Press, 1974.

Wilt, Alan F. *War from the Top: German and British Military Decision Making During World War II*. Bloomington, IN: Indiana University Press, 1990.

Allied/Axis Political Leaders

Clark, Philip. *Tyrants of the Twentieth Century*. Morristown, NJ: Silver Burdett, 1981. (juvenile)

Lee, Stephen J. *The European Dictatorships, 1918-1945*. New York: Methuen, 1987.

Roberts, Geoffrey. *The Unholy Alliance: Stalin's Pact with Hitler*. Bloomington: Indiana University Press, 1989.

Taylor, A. J. P. (Alan John Percvale). *The War Lords*. New York: Atheneum, 1977.

Wiskemann, Elizabeth. *Europe of the Dictators, 1919-1945*. New York: Harper & Row, 1966.

Wolman, Benjamin B., ed. *The Psychoanalytic Interpretation of History*. New York: Basic Books, 1971.

Allied Military Commanders

Anders, Curtis. *Fighting Generals*. (U.S Army). New York: Putnam, 1965.

Andrews, Allen. *The Air Marshals: The Air War in Western Europe*. New York: Morrow, 1970.

Barclay, C. N. (Cyril Nelson). *On Their Shoulders: British Generalship in the Lean Years, 1939-1942*. London: Faber & Faber, 1964.

Barnett, Correlli. *The Desert Generals*. 2nd ed. Bloomington, IN: Indiana University Press, 1982.

Bell, William Gardner. *Commanding Generals and Chiefs of Staff, 1775-1991. Portraits and Biographical Sketches of the United States Army's Senior Officers*. Washington, DC: Center of Military History, U.S. Army, 1992.

Bialer, Seweryn, comp. *Stalin and His Generals: Soviet Military Memoirs of World War II*. New York: Pegasus, 1969.

Binkley, John Charles. "*The Role of the Joint Chiefs of Staff in National Security Policy Making: Professionalism and Self-Perspectives, 1942-1961*." Ph.D. diss., Loyola University of Chicago, 1985. (DAI, 46:7, 2050A, UMI Order # DA8517356)

Blaxland, Gregory. *Alexander's Generals: The Italian Campaign, 1944-45*. London: Kimber, 1979.

Carver, Michael. *The War Lords*. London: Weidenfeld, 1976.

Chamberlain, Thomas H. *The Generals and Admirals: Some Leaders of United States Forces in World War II*. Freeport, NY: Books for Libraries Press, 1945.

Copp, Dewitt S. *A Few Great Captains: The Men and Events That Shaped the Development of U.S. Air Power*. Garden City, NY: Doubleday, 1980.

Craf, John R. *Invasion Leaders: American Military Leaders, 1942-1944*. Philadelphia: McKinley Publishing Company, 1944.

Creswell, John. *Generals and Admirals: The Story of Amphibious Command*. New York: Longmans, Green, 1952.

Dykes, Vivian. *Establishing the Anglo-American Alliance*. London: Brassey's, 1990.

Erickson, John. *The Soviet High Command: A Military-Political History, 1918-1941*. New York: St. Martin's Press, 1962.

Frissell, Toni. *World War II American Generals Serving in the European Theater*. n.p., 1945. (192 Photoprints).

Grimley, Edmund. *The Big Six: Montgomery, Eisenhower, Tedder, Ramsay, Leigh-Mallory, Bradley*. London: Alliance Press Limited, 1944.

Hayes, Grace Person. *The History of the Joint Chiefs of Staff in World War II: The War Against Japan*. Annapolis, MD: Naval Institute Press, 1982.

Horner, D. M. (David Murray). *Crisis of Command: Australian Generalship and the Japanese Threat, 1941-1943*. Canberra: Australian National University Press, 1978.

Hoyt, Edwin P. *How They Won the War in the Pacific: Nimitz and His Admirals*. New York: Weybright & Tally, 1970.

Irving, David. *The War Between the Generals*. New York: Congdon & Lattes. Distributed by St. Martin's Press of New York, 1981.

Jackson, W. G. F. *Chiefs: The Story of the United Kingdom Chiefs of Staff*. Oxford: Brassey's Defence Publishers, 1992.

James, D. Clayton. *A Time for Giants: Politics of the American High Command in World War II*. New York: Franklin Watts, 1987.

Keegan, John, ed. *Churchill's Generals*. New York: Grove Weidenfeld, 1991.

Kohn, Richard H. and Joseph P. Harahan, eds. *Air Superiority in World War II and Korea: An Interview with Gen. James Ferguson, Gen. Robert M. Lee, Gen. William W. Momyer and Lt. Gen. Elwood R. Quesada*. Washington, DC: Office of Air Force History, United States Air Force, 1983.

______. *Strategic Air Warfare: An Interview with Generals Curtis E. LeMay, Leon W. Johnson, David A. Burchinal, and Jack J. Catton.* Washington, DC: Office of Air Force History, U.S. Air Force. U.S. Government Printing Office, 1988.

Larrabee, Eric. *Commander-in-Chief: Franklin Delano Roosevelt, His Lieutenants, and Their War.* New York: Simon & Schuster, 1987.

Leary, William M. *We Shall Return! MacArthur's Commanders and the Defeat of Japan, 1942-1945.* Lexington, KY: University of Kentucky Press, 1988.

Love, Robert W., Jr., ed. *The Chiefs of Naval Operations.* Annapolis, MD: Naval Institute Press, 1980.

Marrinan, Patrick. *Churchill and the Irish Generals.* Northern Ireland: Pretani Press, 1986.

Millis, Walter, forward by. *These Are the Generals.* New York: A. Knopf, 1943.

Murfett, Malcolm H., ed. *The First Sea Lords: From Fisher to Mountbatten.* Westport, CT: Praeger, 1995.

Murphy, Edward F. *Heroes of World War II.* Novato, CA: Presidio Press, 1990.

Murray, G. E. Patrick. *"Eisenhower and Montgomery: Broad Front Versus Single Thrust, The Historiography of the Debate Over Strategy and Command, August 1944-April 1945."* Ph.D. diss., Temple University, 1991. (DAI, 52:10, 3704A, UMI Order # DA9207885)

Perret, Geoffrey. *There's a War to Be Won. The United States Army in World War II.* New York: Random House, 1991.

Pfannes, Charles E. and Victor A. Salamone. *The Great Admirals of World War II: The Americans.* New York: Kensington Publications Corporation, 1983.

Pitt, Barrie. *Churchill and the Generals.* New York: Bantam Books, 1981.

Pratt, Fletcher. *Eleven Generals: Studies in American Command.* New York: William Sloan Associates, 1949.

Probert, Henry. *High Commanders of the Royal Air Force.* London: HMSO, 1991.

Puryear, Edgar F., Jr. *19 Stars: A Study in Military Character and Leadership.* Washington, DC: Coiner Publications, 1971.

Reynolds, Clark G. *Famous American Admirals.* New York: Van Nostrand Reinhold, 1978.

Roskill, Stephen Wentworth. *Churchill and the Admirals.* New York: Morrow, 1978.

Shtemenko, S. M. (Sergei Matveevich). *The Soviet General Staff at War, 1941-1945*. Translated from the Russian by Robert Daglish. Moscow: Progress, 1970.

Shukman, Harold, ed. *Stalin's Generals*. New York: Grove Press, 1993.

Sixsmith, E. K. G. (Eric Kerr Gilborne). *British Generalship in the 20th Century*. London: Arms & Armour Press, 1970.

Spiller, Roger J., ed., and others. *American Military Leaders*. New York: Praeger, 1989.

Stephen, Martin. *The Fighting Admirals: British Admirals of the Second World War*. Annapolis, MD: Naval Institute Press, 1991.

Sweeney, James B. *Army Leaders of World War II*. New York: Watts, 1984. (juvenile)

United States Department of the Army. Office of Military History. *Command Decisions*. Washington, DC: Government Printing Office, 1960.

Walters, Vernon A. *Silent Missions*. Garden City, NY: Doubleday, 1978.

Webb, Willard J. and Ronald H. Cole. *The Chairmen of the Joint Chiefs of Staff*. Washington, DC: Historical Division, Joint Chiefs of Staff, 1989.

Weigley, Russell Frank. *Eisenhower's Lieutenants: The Campaign of France and Germany, 1944-1945*. Bloomington, IN: Indiana University Press, 1981.

Zhukov, Georgi, and others. *Battles Hitler Lost; And the Soviet Marshals Who Won Them: Marshals Zhukov, Konev, Malinovsky, Rotmistrov, Chuikov, and Other Commanders*. New York: Richardson & Steirman, 1986.

Allied Political Leaders

Astley, Joan Bright. *The Inner Circle: A View of War at the Top*. Boston: Little, Brown and Co., 1971.

O'Connor, Raymond G. *Force and Diplomacy: Essays Military and Diplomatic*. Coral Gables, FL: University of Miami Press, 1972.

Reynolds, David. *Creation of the Anglo-American Alliance, 1937-1941: A Study in Competitive Cooperation*. Chapel Hill: University of North Carolina Press, 1981.

Axis Military Commanders

Addington, Larry H. *The Blitzkrieg Era and the German General Staff, 1865-1941*. New Brunswick, NJ: Rutgers University Press, 1971.

Barnett, Correlli, ed. *Hitler's Generals*. New York: Grove Weidenfeld, 1989.

Bartov, Omer. *Hitler's Army: Soldiers, Nazis, and War in the Third Reich*. New York: Oxford University Press, 1991.

Bayerlein, Fritz. *A Crack German Panzer Division and What Allied Air Power Did to It Between D-Day and V-Day*. U.S. Army, Air P/W Interrogation Detachment, Military Intelligence, 1945.

Blummentritt, Guenther. *Evaluation of the Armies of 1914-18 and 1939-45*. Originally prepared for Headquarters, European Command, Office of Chief Historian, 1946.

Brett-Smith, Richard. *Hitler's Generals*. London: Osprey Publishing, 1976.

Cooper, Matthew. *The German Army, 1933-1945: Its Political and Military Failure*. New York: Stein & Day, 1978.

Deist, Wilhelm, ed. *The German Military in the Age of Total War*. Dover, NH: Berg Publishers Limited, 1985.

DePuy, William. *Generals Balck and von Mellenthin on Tactics: Implications for NATO Military Doctrine*. McLean, VA: BDM Corporation, 1980.

Deutsch, Harold C. *Hitler and His Generals: The Hidden Crisis, January-June 1938*. Minneapolis: University of Minnesota Press, 1974.

Downing, David. *The Devil's Virtuosos: The German Generals at War, 1940-1945*. New York: St. Martin's Press, 1977.

Freidin, Seymour and William Richardson, eds. *The Fatal Decisions: Kreipe, Blummentritt, Bayerlein, Zeitzler, Zimmerman, and Manteuffel*. Translated from the German by Constantine Fitzgibbon. New York: William Sloan Associates, 1956.

Fujiwara, Iwaichi. *Japanese Army Intelligence Operations in Southeast Asia During World War II*. Translated by Akoshi Yoji. Hong Kong: Heinemann Asia, 1983.

Gorlitz, Walter. *History of the German General Staff, 1657-1945*. Translated by Brian Battershaw. New York: Praeger, 1953.

Hart, W. E., pseud. *Hitler's Generals*. New York: Doubleday & Doran, 1944.

Hogg, I. V., intro. *German Order of Battle: 1944. The Directory*. London: Greenhill Books, 1994.

Humble, Richard. *Hitler's Generals*. Garden City, NY: Doubleday, 1974.

Kramer, Fritz. *Questions To Be Answered by Kramer and Beyerlein Concerning 12th SS Panzer Division and Panzer Lehr Division.* Landsberg, Germany, n.p., 1948.

Leach, Barry A. *German General Staff.* New York: Ballantine Books, 1973.

Liddell Hart, Basil. *The German Generals Talk.* New York: William Morrow, 1948.

Martienssen, Anthony K. *Hitler and His Admirals.* New York: E. P. Dutton, 1949.

Mellenthin, F. W. (Friedrich Wilhelm) von. *German Generals of World War II: As I Saw Them.* Norman, OK: University of Oklahoma Press, 1977.

Mitcham, Samuel W., Jr. and Gene Mueller. *Hitler's Commanders.* Chelsea, MI: Scarborough House, 1991.

______. *Hitler's Field Marshals and Their Battles.* New York: Stein & Day, 1988.

______. *Hitler's Legions: The German Army Order of Battle, World War II.* New York: Stein & Day, 1985.

______. *Men of the Luftwaffe.* Novato, CA: Presidio Press, 1988.

Muller, Klaus-Jurgen. *The Army, Politics, and Society in Germany, 1933-1945: Studies in the Army's Relation to Nazism.* Translated from the German. New York: St. Martin's Press, 1987.

O'Neill, Robert J. *The German Army and the Nazi Party, 1933-1939.* London: Cassell, 1966.

Pfannes, Charles E. and Victor A. Salamone. *The Great Admirals of World War II: The Germans.* New York: Zebra Books, 1980.

______. *The Great Commanders of World War II: The Germans.* New York: Zebra Books, 1980.

______. *The Great Commanders of World War II: The Japanese.* New York: Zebra Books, 1982.

Riess, Curt. *The Self Betrayed: Glory and Doom of the German Generals.* New York: C. P. Putnam's Sons, 1942.

Rosinski, Herbert. *The German Army.* London: Pall Mall, 1966.

Taylor, Telford. *Sword and Swastika: Generals and Nazis in the Third Reich.* New York: Simon & Schuster, 1952.

Tsouras, Peter G., ed. *The Anvil of War: German Generalship in Defense on the Eastern Front.* London: Greenhill Books, 1994.

Westphal, Siegfried. *The German Army in the West.* London: Cassell, 1951.

Wheeler-Bennett, John W. *The Nemesis of Power: The German Army in Politics, 1918-1945.* 2nd ed. New York: St. Martin's Press, 1964.

Axis Political Leaders

Capelle, Heck van and Peter van de Bovenkamp. *Hitler's Henchmen*. New York: Gallery Books, 1990.

Dutch, Oswald, pseud. *Hitler's Apostles*. London: Edward Arnold, 1939.

Fest, Joachim C. *Faces of the Third Reich: Portraits of Nazi Leadership*. Translated from the German by Michael Bullock. London: Weidenfeld & Nicolson, 1970.

Hamilton, Charles. *Leaders and Personalities of the Third Reich: Their Biographies, Portraits, and Autographs*. San Jose, CA: R. J. Bender Publishers, 1984.

Herzstein, Robert Edwin and others. *The Nazis*. Alexandria, VA: Time-Life Books, 1980.

Kater, Michael H. *The Nazi Party: A Social Profile of Members and Leaders, 1919-1945*. Cambridge, MA: Harvard University Press, 1983.

Lewinson, Thea Stein. *The Evil of the Mind in Graphic Expression: Handwriting Assessments of 11 Leading Nazis*. Published by the author, 1980.

Price, G. (George) Ward. *I Know These Dictators*. London: Harrap, 1937.

Quinnett, Robert Lee. "*Hitler's Political Officers: The National Socialists Leadership Officers*." Ph.D. diss., University of Oklahoma, 1973. (DAI, 34:12, 7688A, UMI Order # 7412320)

Snyder, Louis L. *Hitler's Elite: Biographical Sketches of Nazis Who Shaped the Third Reich*. New York: Hippocrene Books, 1989.

Time-Life Book Eds. *The Center of the Web*. Alexandria, VA: Time-Life Books, 1990.

Official Histories

Australia. *Australia in the War of 1939-1945*. 21 volumes. Canberra: Australian War Memorial, 1952-1968.

Butler, James Ramsay Montagu. *Grand Strategy*. 6 volumes. London: Her Majesty's Stationery Office, 1956-1976.

Kirby, S. Woodburn with C. T. Addis and others. *The War Against Japan*. 5 volumes. London: Her Majesty's Stationery Office, 1957-1969.

Macmillan, Norman. *The Royal Air Force in the World War*. 4 volumes. London: Harrap, 1942-1950.

Morison, Samuel Eliot. *History of the United States Naval Operations in World War II*. 15 volumes. Boston: Little, Brown and Co., 1947-60.

Nicholson, Gerald W. L. *The Canadians in Italy, 1943-1945. Official History of the Canadian Army in the Second World War. Volume II*. Ottawa: Queen's Printer, 1957.

Playfair, I. S. O. (Ian Stanley Ord). *The Mediterranean and Middle East*. 6 volumes. London: Her Majesty's Stationery Office, 1954-1988.

Richards, D. (Denis) and H. St. G. Saunders. *The Royal Air Force, 1939-1945*. 3 volumes. London: Her Majesty's Stationery Office, 1953-1954.

Roskill, Stephen Wentworth. *The War at Sea, 1939-1945*. 3 volumes. London: Her Majesty's Stationery Office, 1954-1961.

Shaw, Henry I., Jr. and others. *History of U.S. Marine Corps Operations in World War II*. 5 volumes. Washington, DC: Historical Branch, G-3, U.S. Marine Corps. Washington, DC: Government Printing Office, 1958-1968.

Stacey, C. P. (Charles Perry). *The Canadian Army, 1939-1945*. Ottawa: Edmond Cloutier, King's Printer, 1948.

_____. *Six Years of War: The Army in Canada, Britain, and the Pacific. Official History of the Canadian Army in the Second World War. Volume I*. Ottawa: Queen's Printer, 1957.

_____. *The Victory Campaign: The Operations in North-west Europe, 1944-45. Official History of the Canadian Army in the Second World War. Volume III*. Ottawa: Queen's Printer, 1960.

United States Air Force, USAF Historical Division. *The Army Air Forces in World War II*. Edited by Wesley F. Craven and James L. Cate. 7 volumes. Chicago: University of Chicago Press, 1948-1958.

United States. Department of the Army. Office of Military History. *United States Army in World War II*. Kent Roberts Greenfield, general editor. (Over 80 volumes to date.) Washington, DC: Government Printing Office, 1947-1993.

Webster, Charles and Noble Frankland. *The Strategic Air Offensive Against Germany*. 4 volumes. London: Her Majesty's Stationery Office, 1961.

Reference

Baudot, Marcel, ed., and others. *The Historical Encyclopedia of World War II*. Translated by Jesse Dilson. New York: Greenwich House, 1984. Distributed by Crown Publishers of New York.

Bauer, Eddy. *Illustrated World War II Encyclopedia*. 24 volumes. Westport, CT: H. S. Stuttman Inc., 1978.

Brown, David. *Warship Losses of World War II*. London: Arms & Armour, 1990.

Chant, Christopher. *The Encyclopedia of Codenames of World War II*. London: Routledge & Kegan Paul, 1986.

Coger, William B. *Dictionary of Admirals of the U.S. Navy*. Annapolis, MD: Naval Institute Press, 1989.

Dear, I. C. B., ed. *Oxford Companion to World War II*. New York: Oxford University Press, 1995.

Dupuy, Trevor Nevitt. *Chronological Military History of World War II*. New York: F. Watts, 1967.

Edelheit, Hershel and Abraham J. Edelheit. *A World in Turmoil: An Integrated Chronology of the Holocaust and World War II*. New York: Greenwood Press, 1991.

Goralski, Robert. *World War II Almanac, 1931-1945: A Political and Military Record*. New York: Putnam, 1981.

Husted, H. H. *Thumb-Nail History of World War II*. Boston: Humphries, 1948.

Keegan, John, ed., and others. *The Rand McNally Encyclopedia of World War II*. Chicago: Rand McNally & Company, 1977.

_______. *Who Was Who in World War II*. New York: Crowell, 1978.

Legrand, Jacques and Derrik Mercer, ed. *Chronicle of the Second World War*. London: Chronicle Communications, 1990.

McCombs, Don and Fred L. Worth. *World War II Super Facts*. New York: Warner, 1983.

McHenry, Robert, ed. *Webster's American Military Biographies*. Springfield, MA: G. & C. Merriam Co., 1978.

Messenger, Charles. *The Chronological Atlas of World War II*. New York: Macmillan, 1989.

Parrish, Thomas, ed. *The Simon and Schuster Encyclopedia of World War II*. New York: Simon & Schuster, 1978.

Perrett, Bryan and Ian Hogg. *Encyclopedia of the Second World War*. Novato, CA: Presidio, 1989.

Polmar, Norman and Thomas B. Allen. *World War II: America At War, 1941-1945*. New York: Random House, 1991.

Reid, Alan Scott. *A Concise Encyclopedia of the Second World War*. Reading: Osprey Publishing, 1974.

Richard, Dorothy Elizabeth. *The U.S. Navy in World War II: A Chronology*. Washington, DC: n.p., 1949.

Royal Institute of International Affairs. *Chronology of the Second World War*. London and New York: n.p., 1947.

Salmaggi, Cesare and Alfredo Pallavisini, comp. *2194 Days of War: An Illustrated Chronology of the Second World War with 620 Illustrations and 84 Maps*. Translated from the Italian by Hugh Young. English language edition edited by Malcolm Falkus. New York: Windward, 1979.

Snyder, Louis L. *Encyclopedia of the Third Reich*. New York: McGraw-Hill, 1976.

______. *Louis L. Snyder's Historical Guide to World War II*. Westport, CT: Greenwood Press, 1982.

Spiller, Roger J., ed., et al. *American Military Leaders*. New York: Praeger, 1989.

______. *Dictionary of American Military Biography*. 3 volumes. Westport, CT: Greenwood Press, 1984.

Stanton, Shelby L. *Order of Battle, U.S. Army, World War II*. Novato, CA: Presidio, 1984.

Sulzberger, C. L. (Cyrus Leo). *American Heritage Picture History of World War II*. New York: American Heritage Publishing Co. Inc., 1966.

Tourtellot, Arthur B., ed. *Life Picture History of World War II*. New York: Time Incorporated, 1950.

Tunney, Christopher. *Biographical Dictionary of World War II*. New York: St. Martin's Press, 1972.

United States. Naval History Division. *United States Naval Chronology, World War II*. Washington: U.S. Government Printing Office, 1955.

United States. War Dept. *Prelude to Invasion: An Account Based Upon Official Reports*. Westport, CT: Greenwood Press, 1974.

Viet, Fritz. *Presidential Libraries and Collections*. New York: Greenwood Press, 1987.

Wheal, Elizabeth-Anne and others. *A Dictionary of the Second World War*. New York: P. Bedrick Books, 1990.

Williams, Mary H., comp. *Chronology, 1941-1945*. Washington, DC: Office of Military History, Dept. of the Army, 1960.

Wistrich, Robert. *Who's Who in Nazi Germany*. New York: Macmillan, 1982.

Young, Peter, ed. *Atlas of the Second World War*. Cartography by Richard Natkiel. New York: Berkley Publishing Corp., 1974.

______. *The World Almanac Book of World War II: The Complete and Comprehensive Documentary of World War II*. 1st rev. ed. New York: World Almanac, 1986.

Zentner, Christian and Friedemann Bedurftig. *The Encyclopedia of the Third Reich*. 2 volumes. Translated from the German by Amy Hackett. New York: Macmillan, 1991.

Strategy

Allen, Thomas B. and Norman Polmar. *Code-Name Downfall: The Secret Plan to Invade Japan - And Why Truman Dropped the Bomb.* New York: Simon & Schuster, 1995.

Beitzell, Robert Enger. "*Major Strategic Conferences of the Allies, 1941-1943: Quadrant, Moscow, Sextant, and Eureka.*" Ph.D. diss., University of North Carolina at Chapel Hill, 1967. (DAI, 28:9, 3594A, UMI Order # 682153)

Bengtson, John Robert. "*Nazi War Aims: Plans for the Thousand Year Reich.*" Ph.D. diss., State University of Iowa, 1953. (DAI, 14:3, 518, UMI Order # 17209)

Breuer, William B. *Hoodwinking Hitler: The Normandy Deception.* Westport, CT: Praeger, 1993.

Brower, Charles F., IV. "*The Joint Chiefs of Staff and National Policy: American Strategy and the War with Japan, 1943-1945.*" Ph.D. diss., University of Pennsylvania, 1987. (DAI, 49:2, 328A, UMI Order # DA8804885)

Burdick, Charles Burton. "*German Military Planning for the War in the West, 1939-1940.*" Ph.D. diss., Stanford University, 1955. (DAI, 15:3, 398, UMI Order # 11168)

Cochran, Alexander Smith. "*Spectre of Defeat: Anglo-American Planning for the Invasion of Italy in 1943.*" Ph.D. diss., University of Kansas, 1985. (DAI, 46:10, 3132A, UMI Order # DA8529075)

Ellis, John. *Brute Force: Allied Strategy and Tactics in the Second World War.* New York: Viking, 1990.

Fugate, Bryan I. *Operation Barbarossa, Strategy and Tactics on the Eastern Front, 1941.* Novato, CA: Presidio Press, 1984.

Glantz, David M. *Soviet Military Intelligence in War.* London: Frank Cass, 1990.

Greenfield, Kent Roberts. *American Strategy in World War II: A Reconsideration.* Baltimore: Johns Hopkins Press, 1963.

Grier, Howard Davis. "*Hitler's Baltic Strategy, 1944-1945.*" Ph.D. diss., The University of North Carolina at Chapel Hill, 1991. (DAI, 53:1, 265A, UMI Order # DA9216721)

Handel, Michael I., ed. *Strategic and Operational Deception in the Second World War.* Totowa, NJ: F. Cass, 1985.

Harvey, Donald Joseph. "*French Concepts of Military Strategy, (1919-1939).*" Ph.D. diss., Columbia University, 1953. (DAI, 14:9, 1374, UMI Order # 8681)

Hickok, James Neil, II. *"Anglo-French Military Cooperation, 1935-1940."* Ph.D. diss., University of Wisconsin-Madison, 1991. (DAI, 52:5, 1866A, UMI Order # DA9124669)

Higgins, Trumbull. *"The Problem of a Second Front: An Interpretation of Coalition Strategy Before and During the Turning Point of the Second World War."* Ph.D. diss., Princeton University, 1951. (DAI, 13:3, 378, UMI Order # 5144)

Horner, D. M. (David Murray). *High Command: Australia and Allied Strategy, 1939-1945.* Boston: Allen & Unwin, 1982.

Johnsen, William Thomas. *"Forging the Foundations of the Grand Alliance: Anglo-American Military Collaboration, 1938-1941."* Ph.D. diss., Duke University, 1986. (DAI, 47:8, 3158A, UMI Order # DA8626986)

Kublin, Michael Baru. *"The Role of China in American Military Strategy from Pearl Harbor to the Fall of 1944."* Ph.D. diss., New York University, 1981. (DAI, 42:7, 3274A, UMI Order # 8127927))

Leach, Barry Arthur. *"German Strategic Planning for the Campaign in the East, 1939-1941."* Ph.D. diss., University of British Columbia, 1968. (Not available from UMI)

______. *German Strategy Against Russia, 1939-1941.* Oxford: Clarendon Press, 1973.

Leighton, Richard H. and Robert W. Coakley. *Global Logistics and Strategy.* 2 volumes. Washington, DC: U.S. Government Printing Office, 1955, 1968.

Levine, Alan Julius. *"British, American and Soviet Political Aims and Military Strategies 1941-1945: A Study in the Beginnings of the "Cold War"."* Ph.D. diss., New York University, 1977. (DAI, 38:12, 7489A, UMI Order # 7808541)

Matloff, Maurice and Edward M. Snell. *Strategic Planning for Coalition Warfare, 1941-42 and 1943-44.* 2 volumes. Washington, DC: U.S. Government Printing Office, 1953, 1959.

McIlvenna, Don Edward. *"Prelude to D-Day: American Strategy and the Second Front Issue."* Ph.D. diss., Stanford University, 1966. (DAI, 27:10, 3402A, UMI Order # 674401)

Mings, Stephen Daniel. *"Strategies in Conflict: Britain and the Anglo-American Alliance, 1941-1943."* Ph.D. diss., University of Texas at Austin, 1975. (DAI, 36:10, 6866A, UMI Order # 768079)

Morison, Samuel Eliot. *Strategy and Compromise.* Boston: Little, Brown, 1958.

Parker, Sally Lister. *"Attendant Lords: A Study of the British Joint Staff Mission in Washington, 1941-1945."* Ph.D., diss., University of Maryland, 1984. (DAI, 46:2, 500A, UMI Order # DA8508512)

Renn, Walter Frederik. "*Hitler's West Wall: Strategy in Concrete and Steel, 1938-1945.*" Ph.D. diss., The Florida State University, 1970. (DAI, 35:2, 1026A, UMI Order # 7418021)

Robertson, John and John McCarthy. *Australian War Strategy, 1939-1945: A Documentary History*. St. Lucia: University of Queensland Press, 1985.

Rolak, Bruno John. "*European Military Thought in the 1930's.*" Ph.D. diss., Indiana University, 1968. (DAI, 29:7, 2195A, UMI Order # 6815460)

Sherry, Michael Stephen. "*Preparing for the Next War: American Plans for Postwar Defense, 1941-1945.*" Ph.D. diss., Yale University, 1975. (DAI, 38:7, 4332A, UMI Order # 7727829)

Steele, Richard W. *The First Offensive, 1942: Roosevelt, Marshall and the Making of American Strategy*. Bloomington, IN: Indiana University Press, 1973.

Strange, Joseph Lot. "*Cross-Channel Attack, 1942: The British Rejection of Operation Sledgehammer and the Cherbourg Alternative.*" Ph.D. diss., University of Maryland, 1984. (DAI, 46:2, 500A, UMI Order # DA8508543)

Van Crefeld, Martin. *Hitler's Strategy 1940-1941, the Balkan Clue*. Cambridge: Cambridge University Press, 1973.

Westwood, John. *Strategy and Tactics of the Great Commanders of World War II and Their Battles*. New York: Gallery, 1990.

Wilt, Alan Freese. "*The Atlantic Wall: German Defenses in the West, 1941-1944.*" Ph.D. diss., University of Michigan, 1969. (DAI, 31:2, 722A, UMI Order # 7014683)

______. *War from the Top: German and British Military Decision Making During World War II*. London: Tauris, 1990.

War Crimes

Aarons, Mark. *Sanctuary: Nazi Fugitives in Australia*. Port Melbourne: Heinemann Australia, 1989.

Abzug, Robert H. *Inside the Vicious Heart: Americans and the Liberation of Nazi Concentration Camps*. New York: Oxford University Press, 1985.

Allen, Charles R., Jr. *Nazi War Criminals in America: Facts-Action. The Basic Handbook*. New York: Highgate House, 1985.

Andrus, Burton C. *I Was the Nuremberg Jailer*. New York: Coward-McCann, 1969.

Ashman, Charles and Robert J. Wagman. *The Nazi Hunters*. New York: Warner, 1990.

Auge, Thomas Edward. "*Justice and Injustice: The French Collaboration Trials, 1944-1949.*" Ph.D. diss., State University of Iowa, 1957. (DAI, 17:12, 2986, UMI Order # 23713)

Bar-Zohar, Michael. *The Avengers*. Translated from the French by Len Ortzen. New York: Hawthorne Books, 1969.

Beals, Walter B. *The First German War Crimes Trial: Chief Judge Walter B. Beals' Desk Notebook of the Doctors' Trial, Held in Nuremberg, Germany, December, 1945 to August, 1947.* New ed. Edited and revised by W. Paul Burman. Chapel Hill, NC: Documentary Pub., 1985.

Benton, Wilbourne E., ed. *Nuremberg: German Views of the War Trials*. Dallas: Southern Methodist University Press, 1961.

Best, Geoffrey. *Nuremberg and After: The Continuing History of War Crimes and Crimes Against Humanity*. Reading: University of Reading, 1984.

Biddiss, Michael D. *The Nuremberg Trial and the Third Reich*. Harlow: Longman, 1992.

Blue Series. *Trials of War Criminals Before the Nuremberg Military Tribunals Under Control Council Law No. 10, Nuremberg, October 1946-April 1949*. 42 Volumes. Washington, DC: U.S. G.P.O., 1949.

Blum, Howard. *Wanted: The Search for Nazis in America*. New York: Simon & Schuster, 1989.

Bosch, William J. *Judgement on Nuremberg: American Attitudes Toward the Major German War-Crime Trials*. Chapel Hill, University of North Carolina Press, 1970.

Bower, Tom. *The Paperclip Conspiracy: The Hunt for the Nazi Scientists*. Boston: Little, Brown, 1987.

Brackman, Arnold C. *The Other Nuremberg: The Untold Story of the Tokyo War Crimes Trial*. London: Fontana, 1987.

Browning, Christopher R. *Ordinary Men: Reserve Police Battalion 101 and the Final Solution in Poland*. New York: HarperCollins, 1992.

Buscher, Frank M. *The U.S. War Crimes Trial Program in Germany, 1946-1955*. New York: Greenwood Press, 1989.

______. "*The United States, Germany, and the Problem of Convicted War Criminals, 1946-1955.*" Ph.D. diss., Marquette University, 1988. (DAI, 49:12, 3843A, UMI Order # DA8904265)

Calvocoressi, Peter. *Nuremberg: The Facts, the Law and the Consequences*. London: Chatto & Windus, 1947.

Cesarani, David. *Justice Delayed*. London: William Heinemann, 1992.

Conot, Robert E. *Justice at Nuremberg*. New York: Harper & Row, 1983.

Crankshaw, Edward. *Gestapo*. New York: Pyramid Books, 1961.

Creel, George. *War Criminals and Punishment*. New York: R. M. McBride & Company, 1944.

De Zayas, Alfred M. with the collaboration of Walter Rabus. *The Wehrmacht War Crimes Bureau, 1939-1945*. Lincoln: University of Nebraska Press, 1989.

Dicks, Henry Victor. *Licensed Mass Murder: A Socio-Psychological Study of Some SS Killers*. London: Chatto, Heinmann for Sussex University Press, 1972.

Dull, Paul S. and Michael Takaaki Umemura. *The Tokyo Trials: A Functional Index to the Proceedings of the International Military Tribunal for the Far East*. Ann Arbor: University of Michigan Press, 1957.

Edwards, Bernard. *Blood and Bushido: Japanese Atrocities at Sea, 1941-1945*. Upton-upon-Severn: Self Publishing Association, 1991.

Fishman, Jack. *Long Knives and Short Memories: The Spandau Prison Story*. New York: Richardson & Steirman, 1987.

______. *The Seven Men of Spandau*. New York: Rinehart, 1964.

Friedmann, Tuvyah. *The Hunter*. Edited and translated by David C. Gross. Garden City, NY: Doubleday, 1961.

Gaskin, Hilary. *Eyewitness at Nuremberg*. London: Arms & Armour, 1990.

Ginn, John L. *Sugamo Prison, Tokyo. An Account of the Trial and Sentencing of Japanese War Criminals in 1948, by a U.S. Participant*. Jefferson, NC: McFarland & Company Inc., 1992.

Ginsburgs, George and V. N. Kudriavtsev, eds. *The Nuremberg Trial and International Law*. London: Martinus Nijhoff, Dordrecht, 1990.

Glueck, Sheldon. *The Nuremberg Trial and Aggressive War*. New York: A. A. Knopf, 1946.

Great Britain. Attorney-General. *International Military Tribunal. The Trial of German Major War Criminals by the International Military Tribunal Sitting at Nuremberg, Germany 1945-1946: Speeches of the Prosecutors... at the Close of the Case Against the Indicted Organisations*. London: His Majesty's Stationery Office, 1946.

Green Series. *Trials of War Criminals Before the Nuremberg Military Tribunals Under Control Council Law No. 10, Nuremberg, October 1946-April 1949*. 15 volumes. Washington, DC: U.S. Government Printing Office, 1949-1953.

Grossmith, F. T. *The Cross and the Swastika*. Boise, ID: Pacific Press, 1984.

Halow, Joseph. *Innocent at Dachau*. Long Beach, CA: Institute for Historical Review, 1993.

Harris, Whitney R. *Tyranny on Trial: The Evidence at Nuremberg*. Dallas: Southern Methodist University Press, 1970.

Harwood, Richard E. *Nuremberg and Other War Crime Trials: A New Look*. Southam, England: Historical Review Press, 1978.

Hetherington, Thomas and William Chalmers. *War Crimes: Report of the War Crimes Inquiry*. London: H.M.S.O., 1989.

Heydecker, Joe Julius and Johannes Leeb. *The Nuremberg Trials*. Translated by E. A. Downie. London: Heinemann, 1962.

Hoedeman, Paul. *Hitler or Hippocrates: Medical Experiments and Euthanasia in the Third Reich*. Translated from the Dutch by Ralph de Rijke. Lewes: Book Guild, 1991.

Hunt, Linda. *Secret Agenda: The United States Government, Nazi Scientists, and Project Paperclip, 1945 to 1990*. New York: St. Martin's Press, 1991.

International Auschwitz Committee. *Nazi Medicine: Doctors, Victims, and Medicine in Auschwitz*. New York: Howard Fertig, 1986. (Originally published in 1971 in Warsaw, Poland.)

Jackson, Robert H. *The Case Against the Nazi War Criminals: Opening Statement for the United States of America*. New York: A. A. Knopf, 1946.

Jacobs, Steven L., ed. *Raphael Lemkin's Thoughts on Nazi Genocide: Guilty?* Lewiston, NY: Mellen, 1992.

Jaworski, Leon. *After Fifteen Years*. Houston: Gulf Pub. Co., 1961.

Kater, Michael H. *Doctors Under Hitler*. Chapel Hill: University of North Carolina Press, 1989.

Katz, Stephen T. *The Holocaust in Historical Context*. New York: Oxford University Press, 1994.

Kemp, Anthony. *The Secret Hunters*. London: O'Mara, 1986.

Klee, Ernst, and others. *"The Good Old Days": The Holocaust as Seen by Its Perpetrators and Bystanders*. Translated by Deborah Burnstone. New York: Free Press, 1991.

Knieriem, August von. *The Nuremberg Trials*. Chicago: H. Regnery Co., 1959.

Kolcjanov, Rudolf. *In the Labyrinths of Revenge-Seekers: The 40th Anniversary of the Trials of the Major Nazi War Criminals in Nuremberg*. Moscow: Novosti Press Agency Pub. House, 1986.

Lankevich, George J. *United Nations Archives, New York: United Nations War Crimes Commission*. New York: Garland Pub., 1990.

Levie, Howard S. *Terrorism in War: The Law of War Crimes*. Dobbs Ferry, NY: Oceana Publications, 1993.

Levy, Alan. *The Wiesenthal File*. London: Constable, 1993.

Lewis, John R., comp. *Uncertain Judgement: A Bibliography of War Crimes Trials*. Santa Barbara, CA: ABC-Clio, 1979.

Library of Congress. General Reference and Bibliography Division. *The Nazi State, War Crimes and War Criminals*. Compiled by Helen F. Conover for the U.S. Chief of Counsel for the Persecution of Axis Criminality. Washington, DC: n.p., 1945.

Lifton, Robert Jay. *The Nazi Doctors: Medical Killing and the Psychology of Genocide*. New York: Basic Books, 1986.

Loftus, John. *The Belarus Secret*. Edited by Nathan Miller. New York: Knopf. Distributed by Random House, 1982.

Lukas, Richard C. *The Forgotten Holocaust: The Poles Under German Occupation, 1939-1944*. Lexington: University Press of Kentucky, 1986.

Lyttle, Richard B. *Nazi Hunting*. New York: F. Watts, 1982. (juvenile)

Maser, Werner. *Nuremberg: A Nation on Trial*. Translated from the German by Richard Barry. London: Allen Lane, 1979.

Matas, David with Susan Charendoff. *Justice Delayed: Nazi War Criminals in Canada*. Toronto: Summerhill Press, 1987.

Maugham, Frederick Herbert Maugham. *U.N.O. and War Crimes*. Westport, CT: Greenwood Press, 1975.

McHugh, Michael Caldwell. *"With Malice Toward None: The Punishment and Pardon of German War Criminals, 1945-1958."* Ph.D. diss., Miami University, 1991. (DAI, 52:7, 2676A, UMI Order # DA9200975)

McMillan, James. *Five Men at Nuremberg*. London: Harrap, 1985.

Miale, Florence R. and Michael Selzer. *The Nuremberg Mind: The Psychology of the Nazi Leaders*. New York: Quadrangle/The New York Times Book Co., 1975.

Mitscherlich, Alexander and Fred Mielke. *Doctors of Infamy, The Story of the Nazi Medical Crimes*. Translated by Heinz Norden. New York: H. Schuman, 1949.

Moczarski, Kazimierz. *Conversations with an Executioner*. (Based on conversations with SS-General Jurgen Stroop.) Englewood Cliffs, NJ: Prentice-Hall, 1981.

Molchanov, V. K. (Vladimir Kirillovich). *There Shall Be Retribution: Nazi War Criminals and Their Protectors*. Translated from the Russian by Dora Cox and Tatyana Gorshunoval. Moscow: Progress Publishers, 1984.

Muller-Hill, Benno. *Murderous Science: Elimination by Scientific Selection of Jews, Gypsies, and Others, Germany, 1933-1945*. Translated by George Fraser. New York: Oxford University Press, 1988.

Murray, Michael Patrick. "*A Study in Public International Law: Comparing the Trial of Adolf Eichmann in Jerusalem with the Trial of Major Nazi German War Criminals at Nuremberg.*" Thesis, J.S.D., George Washington University, 1973. (DAI, 34:6, 3442A, UMI Order # 7328750)

Musmanno, Michael Angelo. *The Eichmann Kommandos*. Philadelphia: Macrae Smith, 1961.

Neave, Airey. *Nuremberg: A Personal Record of the Trial of the Major Nazi War Criminals, 1945-1946*. London: Grafton, 1978.

Neumann, Inge S., comp. *European War Crimes Trials: A Bibliography*. Edited by Robert A. Rosenbaum. New York: Carnegie Endowment for International Peace, 1951.

Nikitin, M. N. and P. I. Vagin. *The Crimes of the German Fascists in the Leningrad Region: Materials and Documents*. New York: Hutchinson, 1946.

Office of United States Chief Counsel for Prosecution of Axis Criminality. *Nazi Conspiracy and Aggression*. 8 volumes. Washington, DC: United States Government Printing Office, 1946.

Persico, Joseph E. *Nuremberg: Infamy on Trial*. New York: Viking, 1994.

Piccigallo, Philip Rocco. "*In the Shadow of Nuremberg: Trials of Japanese in the East, 1945-1951.*" Ph.D. diss., City University of New York, 1977. (DAI, 38:1, 441A, UMI Order # 7713667)

______. *The Japanese on Trial: Allied War Crimes Operations in the East, 1945-1951*. Austin: University of Texas Press, 1979.

Pilichowski, Czesaw. *No Time Limit for These Crimes*. Translated by Jan Sek. Warsaw: Interpress Publishers, 1980.

Prichard, R. John. *Overview of the Historical Importance of the Tokyo War Crimes Trials*. Oxford: Nissan Institute of Japanese Studies, 1987.

______ and Sonia Magbanua Zaide, comp. and ed. *The Tokyo War Crimes Trial: Index and Guide*. 4 volumes. New York: Garland, 1981-1987.

Proctor, Robert N. *Racial Hygiene: Medicine Under the Nazis*. Cambridge: Harvard University Press, 1988.

Reitlinger, Gerald. *The Final Solution: The Attempt to Exterminate the Jews of Europe, 1939-1945*. New York: A. S. Barnes, 1961.

Rosenbaum, Alan S. *Prosecuting Nazi War Criminals*. Boulder: Westview Press, 1993.

Ruckerl, Adalbert. *The Investigation of Nazi Crimes, 1945-1978: A Documentation*. Translated by Derek Rutter. Hamden, CT: Archon Books, 1980.

Russell, Edward Frederick Langley. *The Knights of Bushido*. New York: Dutton, 1958.

Ryan, Allan A., Jr. *Quiet Neighbors: Prosecuting Nazi War Criminals in America*. San Diego: Harcourt Brace Jovanovich, 1984.

Saidel, Rochelle G. *The Outraged Conscience: Seekers of Justice for Nazi War Criminals in America*. Albany: State University of New York Press, 1984.

Schwarberg, Gunther. *The Murders at Bullenhuser Damm: The SS Doctor and the Children*. Translated by Erna Rosenfeld with Alvin H. Rosenfeld. Bloomington: Indiana University Press, 1984.

Segev, Tom. *"The Commanders of Nazi Concentration Camps."* Ph.D. diss., Boston University Graduate School, 1977. (DAI, 38:4, 2293A, UMI Order # 7721618)

Shkapskaia, Mariia. *It Actually Happened, a Book of Facts*. Moscow: Foreign Languages Publishing House, 1942.

Silvergate, Jesse Joseph. *"The Role of the Conspiracy Doctrine in the Nuremberg War Crimes Trials."* Ph.D. diss., University of Wisconsin, 1969. (DAI, 30:5, 1969A, UMI Order # 6912418)

Simpson, Christopher. *Blowback: America's Recruitment of Nazis and Its Effect on the Cold War*. New York: Weidenfeld & Nicolson, 1988.

Singer, Donald Lewis. *"German Diplomats at Nuremberg: A Study of the Foreign Office Defendants of the Ministries Case."* Ph.D. diss., The American University, 1980. (DAI, 41:12, 5216A, UMI Order # 8111204)

Smith, Bradley F. *The Road to Nuremberg*. New York: Basic Books, 1981.

Sosnowski, Kiry. *The Tragedy of the Children Under Nazi Rule*. New York: Howard Fertig, 1983.

Stipp, John L., ed. *Devil's Diary: The Record of Nazi Conspiracy and Aggression*. Yellow Springs, OH: Antioch Press, 1955.

Stroop, Jurgen. *The Stroop Report: The Jewish Quarter of the Warsaw Ghetto Is No More*. New York: Pantheon Books, 1979.

Syjuco, Ma. Felisa A. *The Kempei Tai in the Philippines, 1941-1945*. Quezon City: New Day Publishers, 1988.

Taylor, Lawrence. *A Trial of Generals: Homma, Yamashita, MacArthur*. South Bend, IN: Icarus, 1981.

Taylor, Telford. *The Anatomy of the Nuremberg Trials: A Personal Memoir*. New York: Knopf, 1992.

Tusa, Ann and John Tusa. *The Nuremberg Trial*. London: Macmillan, 1983.

Tutorow, Norman E., comp. with the special assistance of Karen Winnovich. *War Crimes, War Criminals, and War Crimes Trials: An Annotated Bibliography and Source Book*. New York: Greenwood Press, 1986.

United Nations War Crimes Commission. *Law Reports of Trials of War Criminals*. 15 volumes. London: His Majesty's Stationery Office, 1947-1949.

United States Army. *United States Army Investigation and Trial Records of War Criminals: United States v. Kurt Andrae et al. (and Related Cases), April 27, 1945-June 11, 1958*. 16 microfilm reels. Washington, DC: National Archives Microfilm Publications, 1979.

Watts, Tim J. *Nazi War Criminals in the United States: A Bibliography*. Monticello, IL: Vance Bibliographies, 1989.

Weingartner, James J. *Crossroads of Death: The Story of the Malmedy Massacre and Trial*. Berkeley: University of California Press, 1979.

Weir, Patricia Ann Lyons. "*The German War-Crimes Trials, 1949 to Present: Repercussions of American Involvement*." Ph.D. diss., Ball State University, 1973. (DAI, 34:8, 5086A, UMI Order # 743466)

Wiesenthal, Simon. *Justice Not Vengeance*. Translated from the German by Ewald Osers. New York: Grove Weidenfeld, 1989.

______. *The Murderers Among Us*. New York: McGraw-Hill, 1967.

Williams, Peter and David Wallace. *Unit 731: Japan's Secret Biological Warfare in World War II*. New York: Free Press, 1989.

Woetzel, Robert K. *The Nuremberg Trials in International Law*. New York: Praeger, 1960.

Zuroff, Efraim. *Occupation Nazi Hunter*. Southampton: Ashford, 1988.

PART VI

AUTHOR INDEX

Author Index

Baur, Brian C., *Franklin D. Roosevelt and the Stamps of the United States, 1933-1945*, 41

Baur, Hans, *Hitler at My Side*, 91

Bayerlein, Fritz, *A Crack German Panzer Division and What Allied Air Power Did to It Between D-Day and V-Day*, 348

Bayles, William D., *Caesars in Goose Step*, 91

Bayne-Jardine, Colin C., *Mussolini and Italy*, 115

Baynes, H. G., *Germany Possessed*, 91

Baynes, John, *The Forgotten Victor*, 232

Bazhanov, Boris, *Bazhanov and the Damnation of Stalin*, 28

Beals, Walter B., *The First German War Crimes Trial*, 357

Beard, Charles A., *President Roosevelt and the Coming of the War, 1941*, 41

Beasley, Norman, *Frank Knox, American*, 316

Beattie, John, *The Life and Career of Klaus Barbie*, 322

Beck, John J., *MacArthur and Wainwright*, 175, 206

Beck, Robert T., "Cordell Hull and Latin America, 1933-1939," 315

Becker, Peter W., "The Basis of the German War Economy Under Albert Speer, 1942-1944," 339

Beckhard, Arthur J., *The Story of Dwight D. Eisenhower*, 151

Behr, Edward, *Hirohito*, 130

Behrendt, Hans-Otto, *Rommel's Intelligence in the Desert Campaign, 1941-1943*, 286

Bein, Peter J., *General MacArthur and the Yamashita Decision, September 1944-February 1946*, 175, 303

Beitzell, Robert E., "Major Strategic Conferences of the Allies, 1941-1943," 354

Belden, Jack, *Retreat with Stilwell*, 200

Bell, William G., *Commanding Generals and Chiefs of Staff, 1775-1991*, 344

Bellah, James W., "Stilwell's Chinese Offensive," 201

Bellamy, Frank, *High Command*, 6, 226

Bellush, Bernard, "Apprenticeship for the Presidency," 41

Beloff, Nora, *Tito's Flawed Legacy*, 260

Ben-Moshe, Tuvia, *Churchill, Strategy and History*, 6

Ben-Zvi, Abraham, *The Illusion of Deterrence*, 41

Bender, Mark C., *Watershed at Leavenworth*, 151

Bender, Roger J. and Peterson, George A., *Hermann Goering*, 273
______. *The Hitler Albums*, 91

Bendersky, Joseph W., *A History of Nazi Germany*, 91

Benedict, Blaine D., "Roosevelt and Poland, 1943-1945," 41

Bengston, John R., "Nazi War Aims," 354